Subjects and Sovereign

Subjects and Sovereign

Bonds of Belonging in the Eighteenth-Century British Empire

HANNAH WEISS MULLER

OXFORD
UNIVERSITY PRESS

OXFORD
UNIVERSITY PRESS

Oxford University Press is a department of the University of Oxford. It furthers the University's objective of excellence in research, scholarship, and education by publishing worldwide. Oxford is a registered trade mark of Oxford University Press in the UK and certain other countries.

Published in the United States of America by Oxford University Press
198 Madison Avenue, New York, NY 10016, United States of America.

Library of Congress Cataloging-in-Publication Data
Names: Muller, Hannah Weiss, 1978– author.
Title: Subjects and sovereign : bonds of belonging in the eighteenth-century British empire / Hannah Weiss Muller.
Description: New York, NY : Oxford University Press, 2017. |
Includes bibliographical references and index.
Identifiers: LCCN 2016059696 (print) | LCCN 2017011154 (ebook) |
ISBN 9780190465810 (hardcover) | ISBN 9780190465827 (Updf) |
ISBN 9780190465834 (Epub)
Subjects: LCSH: Citizenship—Great Britain—History—18th century. |
Law—Great Britain—Colonies—History—18th century. |
Allegiance—Great Britain—History—18th century. |
Monarchy—Great Britain—History—18th century. |
Great Britain—Politics and government—18th century.
Classification: LCC KD4050 .M85 2015 (print) |
LCC KD4050 (ebook) | DDC 323.60941/09033—dc23
LC record available at https://lccn.loc.gov/2016059696

For Marcus

Contents

Acknowledgments

WRITING IS OFTEN described as a solitary task, but in preparing these acknowledgments, I am reminded of how profoundly books grow from communities and conversations. In my particular case, some of those communities are the warmly anonymous ones of cafés around the world, in which I readily admit to having drafted a rather large part of this book. The most vital, however, remain those communities of family, friends, and colleagues who have sustained me with questions and curiosity and to whom I have incurred innumerable debts.

This project would not have developed as it has without the dedication and guidance of mentors in the Princeton University Department of History who have continued to be insightful readers in the intervening years. Since my first tea with her, Linda Colley has always encouraged me to think globally and comparatively, to consider the larger stakes; she has led by example and urged me to find confidence in my own voice. Dan Rodgers has warmly continued to ask questions that inevitably get right to the heart of the matter, whether those concern writing, teaching, or the more profound choices that are also made along the way. Dirk Hartog has generously accepted me into the world of legal historians and offered his unflagging wisdom and necessary critiques. At universities beyond Princeton, David Armitage, who initially served as my outside reader, has helped me to navigate the world of publishing with great kindness and reassurance. In more recent years, Paul Halliday has patiently read manuscripts several times, offering unwavering mentorship and invaluable suggestions that have made this a far stronger book. I only hope that each of these distinguished scholars knows how deeply valued such guidance has been.

During the years this project has evolved from dissertation to book, I have been privileged to be part of a number of university communities, including as a Golieb Fellow at the New York University School of Law, as a Lecturer in the Harvard Committee on Degrees in History and Literature, as an Assistant Professor in the Department of History at Denison University, and, most recently, as an Assistant Professor in the Department of History at Brandeis University. My colleagues in each of these settings have offered encouragement, critique, and camaraderie, as well as warm welcomes. The itinerancy of academic life has served, in my case, to provide me with an array of perspectives and to strengthen those of this book. I have also benefited from opportunities to present portions of this manuscript at job talks and works-in-progress seminars over the years, as well as to engaged participants at the British Legal History Conference, the Imperial History Seminar (IHR), the North American Conference on British Studies, the North Eastern Conference on British Studies, the Omohundro Institute of Early American Culture and History, the Princeton University Eighteenth-Century Seminar, the 1763 and All That Conference, and the 1759 Revisited Conference.

I remain indebted to the scholars and archivists who have graciously assisted with my research over the years. During my many travels researching this book, I have benefited from the support of librarians and archivists at the British Library (London), the National Archives (Kew), Houghton Library (Cambridge, MA), the Arxiú Historic de Mao (Minorca), the Government of Gibraltar Archives (Gibraltar), the High Court (Calcutta), the Victoria Memorial Library (Calcutta), and the National Library (Calcutta). Anthony Seymour and Tito Benady, in particular, selflessly gave of their time and proved instrumental in helping me navigate the archives in Minorca and Gibraltar. At Brandeis University, Laura Hibbler went out of her way to assist in locating images for this book.

Across its different stages, a wonderfully engaged group of friends and colleagues has provided the intellectual and moral support through which this project has come to fruition. I would like to thank Carolyn Biltoft, Christopher Brown, Jonathan Bush, David Cannadine, Arianne Chernock, Greg Childs, Nancy Christie, Adam Davis, Cathy Dollard, Biliana Draganova, David Engerman, Jeanne Follansbee, François Furstenberg, John-Paul Ghobrial, Rachel Gillett, Travis Glasson, Molly Greene, John Haldon, Mark Hulliung, Daniel Hulsebosch, Maya Jasanoff, Jennifer Johnson, Aditi Khana, Kris Manjapra, Peter Marshall, Phil Misevich, Michel Morin, William Nelson, Abi Ocobock, Paul Ocobock, Nilay Özok-Gündoğan, Sandy Polu, Emma Rothschild, Rachel Sanders, Elena

Schneider, Mitra Sharafi, Jason Sharples, Caroline Shaw, Penny Sinanoglou, Naghmeh Sohrabi, Karen Spierling, Philip Stern, Karyn Thomas, Robert Travers, Teresa Villa-Ignacio, Vlasta Vranjes, Patricia Ward, Amanda Irwin Wilkins, Kathleen Wilson, Nurfadzilah Yahaya, and David Zaret. But it is Susan Ferber who believed in this project from the very beginning and who, in her indefatigable way, has helped bring it to completion.

My thanks to Taylor & Francis (http://www.tandfonline.com) for permission to use portions of my article, "The Garrison Revisited: Gibraltar in the Eighteenth Century," *The Journal of Imperial and Commonwealth History* 41, no. 3 (2013): 353–376, in Chapter 3, and to Cambridge University Press for permission to use portions of my article, "Bonds of Belonging: Subjecthood and the British Empire," *The Journal of British Studies* 53, no. 1 (2014): 29–58, in Chapter 4 and the Conclusion of *Subjects and Sovereigns*. I am also grateful to the British Library; the British Museum; the David Rumsey Map Collection; the Houghton Library, Harvard University; the National Archives, Kew; the National Portrait Gallery; the New York Public Library; ProQuest; the Victorian Picture Library; and the Yale Center for British Art for assistance with finding images in their collections and with securing permission to publish them. The Theodore and Jane Norman Fund at Brandeis University, in particular, made possible the publication of these images. Research support from New York University School of Law, Harvard University, Denison University, and Brandeis University has also been greatly appreciated.

My last and deepest thanks must be to family. Although I am saddened that my four grandparents have passed away in the years since I have been writing, I am grateful to have had so many years with each of them and to have benefited from their diverse perspectives. My parents, Thomas Weiss and Priscilla Read, and my sister, Rebeccah Weiss Filsoof, have encouraged my historical interests since childhood, and their conviction that life is about doing what is meaningful has provided me with incredible freedom. My extended family, particularly Liz Read and Tad Read, have never hesitated in their support and ready questions about this project. I am deeply mindful of how much Penny and Gari Muller, whose unerring faith in my ability to complete this project, combined with limitless supplies of biscotti and entertainment for grandchildren, have provided the loving reassurance upon which we have all depended. My children, whose births, first words and steps, and now first school years, are documented in Word files saved alongside emerging chapters, must be credited with furnishing a rather entertaining historical record of their own. Amara's prescient prodding ("Mommy, why don't you just sit down and finish your book after I am asleep?") and Kieran's affectionate reassurances

("Mommy, I will still like your book even if it doesn't have trucks") have provided untold sustenance. But it is to Marcus, my person, my most loyal critic, and my greatest supporter, that I dedicate this book. For without him, this journey would not have been possible, and without him, I would have been without my most joyful of communities.

Subjects and Sovereign

Introduction

OF SUBJECTS AND SOVEREIGNS

WHEN INHABITANTS OF the thirteen North American colonies challenged British authority, many did so initially as loyal subjects. The year before he signed the Declaration of Independence and renounced the king, John Hancock joined other well-known figures in submitting the Olive Branch Petition. Even as he and other petitioners excoriated royal ministers, they also made a final attempt to declare themselves faithful subjects and to profess their hopes for reconciliation. If in July 1776, John Adams and Thomas Jefferson accused George III of "repeated injuries and usurpations, all having in direct object the establishment of an absolute Tyranny over these states,"[1] in July 1775, they, too, had proclaimed their attachment "to your Majesty's person, family, and Government" and beseeched him to intervene on their behalf.[2] Ironic as it may seem, numerous colonists insisted on their humble subjection to George III well into the revolutionary period.[3] Others continued to rely upon their inherited rights as British subjects to defend themselves against incursions of crown and parliamentary power. That they ultimately broke with the crown must not obscure the fact that even radical Americans had once seen subject status as a means to claim and secure certain time-honored rights.[4]

These early protestations of loyalty notwithstanding, the struggles in America have generally been held to signal an era of extensive political reform, the beginning of what Thomas Paine called the "age of revolution."[5] The late eighteenth century is itself considered a period of transformational events and tremendous change, a turning point in world history when monarchies became republics and subjects morphed into citizens.[6] The narratives of the ubiquitous "Age of Revolution" remain quite familiar: after years of a destructive civil war that polarized individuals in both the realm and the thirteen colonies, George III was forced to accept the loss of his subjects in America. A French sovereign witnessed the disintegration of an existing social and political system, and he was eventually swept aside by political upheavals and consigned to the guillotine. The spirit of revolution was also evident in Saint-Domingue, where free people of color claimed their rights to political representation, opening paths for enslaved peoples to fight for freedom and citizenship in a struggle that became known as the Haitian Revolution. And this revolutionary momentum continued to spread throughout other parts of the Americas and the world. Revolutionary sentiments, which historian Eric Hobsbawm once argued linked Europe in a single "current of subversion," are said to have been endemic among the generation that reached maturity in the early nineteenth century.[7] The fractures of empires and the frailties of monarchy, cataclysms that together birthed new citizens, remain familiar tropes in historical and political accounts of the modern world.

And yet the invocation of their subject status by prominent revolutionary figures like Adams, Hancock, and Jefferson offers an important reminder of another, arguably more prominent, worldview also in existence during this same period.[8] As colonial Americans ultimately renounced their subject status and French radicals escorted their royals to the execution block, an even larger number of individuals continued to acknowledge their hereditary leaders and to recognize royal authority. Elsewhere, this period was one of enduring continuities that saw the familiar structures of sovereign and state widely affirmed. Monarchy persisted as the predominant form of government, as it would for more than another century. Loyal subjects remained invaluable to monarchs who relied on their labor and bodies to fuel the engines of global war and to mark the boundaries of overseas empires. Examined from these vantage points, the age of citizens and revolutions was still largely an era of subjects and sovereigns.

In recent decades, scholars have shown themselves increasingly willing to acknowledge the importance of monarchy in the eighteenth century, noting, among other things, that sovereigns consistently served as crucial focal points for subjects as they dispersed across the expanding European empires.[9] In these overseas empires, and in polities across the world, individuals who otherwise might have had little interaction with states and empires continued to swear allegiance to monarchical figures whom they believed would protect them once informed of their grievances. Loyalty to a distant but personalized ruler often provided one of the only shared experiences between inhabitants with little or no other connection to one another. Even as the state became central to eighteenth-century political discourse, the individual qualities of monarchs continued to be crucial to uniting these polities. A personal vision of kingship thus endured that was "fundamentally at odds with the objective concept of the state."[10] Louis XIV's famous quip—*l'état c'est moi*—was as much a reflection of the continued relevance of monarchy as it was a commentary on absolutism. Moreover, when George III recovered from his "madness" in 1788, he received more addresses congratulating him on his recovery than the number of addresses generated by the seven most controversial issues of the previous generations.[11] Such numbers are a reminder that concern for the royal house routinely proved more important than individuals' partisan interests.

In the colonies, as in much of Europe, the rhythms of life were often punctuated by events that instilled in inhabitants a sense of connection to the monarchy. The arrivals of governors or viceroys, the monarchs' personal representatives, and the reading of royal commissions, were public ceremonies treated with great solemnity. Celebrations of royal births, deaths, and coronations were events in the lives of inhabitants just as they were for royal families. The swearing of oaths of allegiance reminded old and new subjects alike of their promises to reigning monarchs.[12] Justice was often administered in the king's name, serving as an ongoing reminder of the sovereign's significance in subjects' daily lives. Most important, monarchs were widely understood as being bound to all of their subjects by a "tacit compact" or "covenant" in which they promised protection in exchange for allegiance.[13]

But if the role of monarchy and monarchical culture as unifying forces in the overseas empires has been examined, the nature of the relationship between subjects and sovereigns has remained largely neglected. Subject status has usually been viewed as a matter for those interested in specific shifts in statute or case law; the everyday opportunity provided by that status, as well as its global significance, has generally been overlooked.[14] Moreover, the subject has typically been taken to mean a subjected person, a passive forerunner to the assertive and rights-bearing modern citizen.[15] This overarching propensity to view subjects and citizens as an "ideological antithesis" has largely prevented any extensive analysis of subject status in its own right.[16]

Indeed, the argument that subjects evolve into citizens has proved remarkably resilient. Influenced by the examples of France, where the French *citoyens* were *sujets* under the monarchy before 1789, as well as by the Roman Empire, which possessed both *civites Romani* and *subjecti imperio Romano*, historians and political scientists have often regarded subjecthood as a kind of precursor to citizenship.[17] Subjects are seen as an inferior group, whereas citizens "engage in politics and thereby legitimate as well as influence government,"[18] and their perceived differences are aptly summarized by Rodney Baker: "whilst all citizens are subjects, not all subjects are citizens . . . as a mere subject she is not participant in the activity of governing, the activity whereby she is subjected. Citizenship contributes another dimension. The citizen engages in politics and by so doing authorizes and influences government."[19] The teleological argument that the individual evolves from subject to citizen, from someone who obediently accepts law and membership to a person who actively manages and chooses his relationship to the state, however, creates a false distinction.[20]

Viewing the subject as a kind of disenfranchised citizen overlooks the possibilities embedded in the relationship between subject and monarch. Subjects persistently laid claim to economic, political, and legal concessions, and they powerfully expressed both deference and demands. Accurately assessing the significance of subject status in the eighteenth century therefore requires recovering an understanding of how contemporaries themselves viewed that status and its inherent opportunities. Here, historical evidence suggests that few living in the early modern world would have considered the "subject" to be antithetical to the "citizen." The terms were frequently used interchangeably to describe the relationships of human beings to the political systems in which they lived, even as "subject" may have prevailed in contexts where the monarchical state became more important than the princely or city-state.[21]

Well into the eighteenth century, the terms were still employed virtually synonymously in many situations, although contemporaries acknowledged that confusion and inaccuracies often resulted from this elision.[22] The *Encyclopédie*, for example, published by Denis Diderot and Jean le Rond d'Alembert between 1751 and 1772, contained separate entries for both *citoyen* and *sujet*, but described each with reference to the other.[23] An initial paragraph noted that "subjects of a state are sometimes called citizens; some make no distinction between these two terms, but it is better to distinguish them."[24] But even as entries sought to better define the two terms, authors still visibly struggled to differentiate them.[25] In many passages, *sujet* and *citoyen* were simply substituted one for the other. Despite the multiple definitions and ideas evidently present in its entries, the *Encyclopédie* confirmed that, in the eighteenth century, *sujet* nonetheless remained a term widely applied to describe those individuals who derived certain advantages from having recognized a sovereign authority.

English-language publications, however, pointed out that "subject" was the term most appropriate for describing members of a monarchical body politic. Citing historic quotations about the subject's duty to his king, Samuel Johnson's *Dictionary of the English Language* (1755) defined "subject" as "one who lives under the dominion of another." By contrast, a "citizen" was defined as "a freeman of the city," referring to men of an English city who were neither slaves nor serfs, and clearly tied to the ancient concept of a city-state.[26] Subsequent mid-nineteenth-century editions of the *Dictionary* continued to define "citizen" as "one inhabiting a city, a freeman," suggesting that "citizen" did not always evoke the ideas of more developed rights and participation popularized by the French Revolution. Indeed, inhabitants of the British Isles routinely used "subject" to describe their relationship to their monarch and to one another at this time. For eighteenth- and nineteenth-century Britons, subject status was not inferior to, or defined in opposition to, citizen status. If anything, citizen status evoked a local and specific identity focused on a city like London, whereas subject status was a more encompassing identity available to all those who lived under the dominion of the monarch.[27]

The work of sixteenth- and seventeenth-century political theorists arguably provides the most relevant reminder about how many contemporaries actually viewed the subject: not as an immature version of the citizen, but as an individual who actively consented to his position. For sixteenth-century theorist Jean Bodin: "it is therefore the submission and obedience of a free subject to his prince, and the tuition, protection, and jurisdiction exercised by the prince over his subject that makes the citizen." The citizen was identified as a free subject who remained "dependent on the authority of another."[28] In addition to eliding *sujet* and *citoyen*, the idea emerged that submission to the sovereign, the linchpin of the monarchical order, required the active participation of the subject. In the relationship with the monarch, characterized by obligation and dependence, also lay the seed of the subject's autonomy. During the seventeenth century, John Locke offered an analogous interpretation of subjecthood. Even if his political goals were radically different from those of Bodin, Locke also believed in the subject's volitional submission. For Locke, it was the "consent of freemen, born under government, which only makes them members of it . . . a child is born a subject of no country or government." Man was, according to Locke, "naturally free," and the only act that might "put him into subjection to any earthly power" was his own consent.[29] Both these early political theorists defined subject status as an active one, and their interpretations offer a crucial framework for gauging more general attitudes to the subject and citizen.

Perhaps most important, the bond between subjects and sovereign was not merely one of passive subjection because active subservience to a monarch created powerful access to rights. The king was often viewed as a "bulwark against particularistic oppression," and numerous writers who argued for consolidation of royal power, even absolutism, "were not unconcerned with the securities and liberties of subjects" but believed they would be best preserved by the monarchical order.[30] The seventeenth-century historian Robert Brady, among others, believed that all liberties and privileges derived from the crown.[31] The coronation oath, interpreted by many parliamentarian historians as a "mutual and conditional covenant between king and people," a moment at which subjects renewed their allegiance, was also widely believed to confirm the fundamental rights of Britons.[32] In the seventeenth and eighteenth centuries, loyal submission to a monarch seemed to guarantee liberties and freedoms.

Without glorifying royalist or absolutist positions, this book aims to breathe new life into these earlier understandings of subjecthood, arguing that the traditionally dependent relationship between subject and sovereign nonetheless remained a powerful and relevant site for claims-making well into the era of revolution. Although "subjecthood" was not a mainstay of eighteenth-century vernacular, it is a term that effectively evokes the personal bond between subject and sovereign in monarchical societies, while simultaneously calling to mind the status, practices, and qualities associated with being a subject of the monarch. Like the word "citizenship," it implies that there is a larger community of belonging: with subjecthood, however, the community is one composed of subjects rather than of citizens. While "citizenship" and "nationality" are now arguably more familiar terms, neither is really appropriate for the eighteenth-century British Empire, as each relies on the relationship between a person and a state, rather than the relationship between a subject and a monarch, in defining belonging.[33]

If "subjecthood" is slightly anachronistic, the term "British subject" was widely used in the eighteenth century. It was a ubiquitous figure of speech in parliamentary papers, treaties, pamphlets, newspapers, sermons, and official correspondence, as well as in petitions addressed to the monarch and his representatives. Subject status was evoked by members of all social classes and by peoples dispersed across the globe. At times, "British subject" was intended simply to describe someone as the monarch's subject who was of British origin. At other times, it was used to denote a specific legal status distinct from that of an alien, referring to all those who were subjects of the British sovereign, regardless of whether they were of British origin. However, "British subject" had yet another provocative and potentially very expansive use. It could be wielded to evoke an inherent set of rights and privileges, not unlike those liberties often associated with the "free-born Englishman."[34]

It is this last understanding of "British subject" that this book aims to recover. While individuals across the globe routinely identified as dutiful and humble subjects of reigning monarchs, most "British subjects" also considered themselves peculiarly blessed, with innumerable rights, liberties, and privileges. Debates over the meanings and possibilities of subject status occurred throughout the realm and colonies, a testament to the continued relevance of sovereigns, as well as to subjects' capacities to shape their own destinies. The reciprocal bond between subject and sovereign—in which subjects owed allegiance and obedience and monarchs offered protections and privileges—will therefore receive sustained attention. Indeed, many looked to their relationship with the monarch as the means to attain rights, using the language of loyal subjecthood to simultaneously profess an unwavering loyalty and to lay claim to an array of privileges. Leveraging subject status to secure rights was, in fact, a broadly understood social and legal practice both before and after the eighteenth century, just as subject status itself was understood to represent a powerful opportunity.

While struggles over subjects' rights and liberties were arguably endemic to most monarchies, there were places and times in which questions regarding these privileges became more pressing. This book focuses on key discussions that emerged in the British Empire during the three decades following the Seven Years' War (1756–1763). The massive transfers of territories occasioned by the Treaty of Paris (1763) and the accelerating expansion of the East India Company in Bengal after the acquisition of the *diwani,* or revenue administration (1765), brought a range of new peoples into the British Empire whose rights and statuses were far from clear. This empire, conceived of as Protestant, commercial, maritime, and free in the early eighteenth century,[35] incorporated "subject populations of Native Americans, French Canadians, and Indians, none of whom were Protestant, British, or free, according to 'British notions of freedom.' "[36] With the Treaty of Paris, George III pledged to protect freedom of worship for "his new Roman Catholic subjects," acknowledging that French and Spanish Catholic inhabitants of the conquered and ceded territories became his subjects.[37] Moreover, as parliamentary papers from the early 1760s attested, George III recognized the role that "gallant subjects" had played in winning the Seven Years' War, just as members of Parliament recognized the array of "faithful subjects in North America" and "fellow subjects in the islands" who had joined the empire.[38]

In seeking to integrate these increasingly varied communities and to consolidate imperial control during peacetime, administrators necessarily confronted and renegotiated the boundaries of British subjecthood. But so, too, did inhabitants. Individuals throughout the British Empire quickly embraced their British subject status. The numerous expressions of loyalty from natural-born and adopted British subjects that reached the king throughout 1763 and 1764 reflected a shared language of humility, supplication, and subjecthood. And as many of these inhabitants began to make demands for privileges they associated with their subject status, they often raised pressing legal and administrative questions regarding the status of multireligious, multinational, and multiracial peoples and triggered wide-ranging debates over the contours of British subjecthood. Colonial inhabitants repeatedly revealed that they were more than capable of engaging their governments and sovereign without overthrowing them.

Tracing the debates that arose between the 1760s and 1780s reveals not only the meanings and possibilities inherent to subject status, but also provides an alternative view of the period. The financial and military exhaustion wrought by the Seven Years' War and the administrative and fiscal reforms enacted in its aftermath have traditionally been seen as pivotal precursors to both the American and French revolutions.[39] But while administrators worried about strengthening the army and navy and about extracting revenues from the colonies, they were also preoccupied with how best to govern conquered peoples. This period witnessed the adoption of reforms that alienated many in the thirteen North American colonies and elsewhere, just as it was marked by flexible and expansive attitudes toward subjecthood and toward the rights of subjects. The 1760s and 1770s were not merely a prelude to democratic revolution, imperial dissolution, and subsequent upheaval. The postwar era was also a period of remarkable adaptation as administrators and inhabitants negotiated the terms of belonging and participation across an expanding empire.

If anything, as administrators wrestled with how to govern and control vast territories added to the British Empire after 1763, they often became increasingly dependent on the labor and resources of new populations and found that they needed to accommodate these "new subjects" with an array of privileges. Reliance on non-British immigrants or on indigenous populations was hardly a new phenomenon; recognizing that a small domestic population would be unable to supply the settlers and military power for a burgeoning empire,[40] the British government had already welcomed many converts by the 1750s.[41] The Treaty of Paris, however, suddenly transferred numerous new peoples into the British Empire who seemed to promise a way to increase Britain's demographic and economic power and whose allegiance was critical to securing and settling the new colonies. And the crisis resulting from the American colonists' declaration of independence and subsequent establishment of a new republic only accentuated the British Empire's reliance on its remaining subjects. In order to combat "rebellious subjects" to the south, administrators demonstrated greater sensitivity to the importance of maintaining and rewarding French Canadian loyalties. British dependence on Gibraltarian assistance and willingness to supply the garrison during the siege of Gibraltar between 1779 and 1783 was pronounced. And everywhere, the example of American disobedience provided other subjects with fodder to make demands of their own.[42] Although the American Revolution marked the estrangement of some British subjects from the monarch to whom they had once sworn allegiance, it also signaled a rapprochement between the empire and its other subjects.

In many respects, then, subjecthood and loyalty to the monarch bound together the resurgent British Empire of the 1760s. As examples drawn from across the empire demonstrate, "British subject" remained a remarkably expansive and inclusive term claimed by a wide variety of inhabitants. Identifying as a British subject was a shared practice, a shared language, a shared opportunity well before 1763, and it was a practice that would proliferate and diversify in the aftermath of a global war. It was, however, the flexibility and fluidity of British subjecthood that ultimately rendered it so significant for inhabitants and administrators alike. At its core, subjecthood was defined as a legal and intensely personal relationship between the subject and the monarch—one characterized by obedience and protection and its accessibility to diverse peoples. By claiming allegiance, subjects of the empire might all identify as British subjects regardless of religion, place of origin, or race.[43] But where subjecthood was inclusive, it was also imprecise, porous, and ill-defined, which made it an opportunity and tool in the hands of those who proposed new interpretations of allegiance and protection.

Understanding how subject status became an organizing principle of the eighteenth century requires analyzing legal and popular conceptions of the bond between subject and sovereign before surveying some of the new contexts in which inhabitants and administrators chose to leverage that bond. Chapter 1 therefore begins by exploring the myriad legal understandings of subject status that coexisted in the seventeenth and eighteenth centuries. It revisits the landmark case of *Calvin v. Smith*, among others, in order to examine notions of allegiance, obedience, and protection that cast a long shadow over subsequent interpretations of subject status. Many of the questions left unanswered by this case, particularly those relating to the specific nature of allegiance and protection, led to further definitions and legal quandaries. The treaties, opinions, and correspondence in which subjecthood was also discussed illuminate the importance of local factors and agents in shaping the multivalent legal ideas available to contemporaries.

Chapter 2 contends that subjecthood attracted considerable attention from subjects themselves. Indeed, both official and unofficial declarations of rights from the seventeenth and eighteenth centuries popularized British subject status and lent it an almost-mythical allure. Declaring and debating rights had a long history in the British world, and the notion that British subjects had inherited and ancient privileges was widely held. Many of these declarations drew on popular understandings of allegiance and of the relationship between subjects and sovereign that echoed legal ones. But their numerous differences suggest that the rights, liberties, and privileges associated with subject status remained at once limitless and ill-defined. By analyzing a range of declarations, Chapter 2 demonstrates that subjects of diverse backgrounds had consistently and actively used their relationship to the monarch to make demands and that subject status, at least in the everyday understanding, had been conceived of as a vibrant category of identity well before 1763.

Invoking allegiance to the monarch also mattered in countless practical ways. Chapters 3–5 focus on the five specific territories of Gibraltar, Minorca, Grenada, Quebec, and Calcutta to excavate some of the day-to-day usages, struggles, and repercussions of subjecthood in the postwar period. Each chapter explores what subject status actually meant in terms of rights, access, and duties between the 1760s and 1780s—and what opportunities subjecthood presented. Each illustrates what individuals in the colonies gained or lost by claiming subject status and why colonial administrators had vested interests in according subjecthood to their "new subjects," sometimes to the point of antagonizing long-time subjects. Struggles over the meanings of subjecthood were intimately connected with the histories, demographies, and local exigencies of the territories that joined or remained part of the empire after the Seven Years' War.

Chapter 3 begins with the geopolitically strategic Mediterranean colonies of Gibraltar and Minorca. After its capture by France seven years earlier, Minorca reverted to being a British colony in 1763. Both Minorca and Gibraltar continually raised crucial issues about which of its diverse inhabitants could be counted as British subjects. A need for labor meant that most administrators wished to extend the protections of subjecthood to numerous individuals. In turn, a range of inhabitants began to employ the language of subjecthood to assert claims to various protections. Protective passes and redemption from captivity gradually became the assumed and particular privileges of those who could prove themselves to be British subjects. As economic protections were gradually associated with British subject status in the Mediterranean territories, administrators played a crucial role in shaping the boundaries of subjecthood.

Chapter 4 turns to the Atlantic world, where Grenada and Quebec were officially ceded by France under the Treaty of Paris. Although economic protections were certainly of interest to settlers in these territories, it was debates over the political and legal rights of the white French Catholic inhabitants that dominated political life in both colonies throughout the 1760s and 1770s. These struggles demonstrate that the privileges associated with British subject status in the Atlantic often differed dramatically from those in the British Isles and were shaped by demographic, economic, and political imperatives. Chapter 4 emphasizes the struggles of individuals who actively negotiated their political and legal rights, particularly the ways in which "new subjects," who were predominantly French Catholic, and "old subjects," who identified as British-born and Protestant, used petitions.

Chapter 5 moves to the Indian Ocean and to the vibrant trading community of Calcutta. The East India Company's assumption of the *diwani* for Bengal in 1765 and its accelerating territorial expansion in the Indian subcontinent provoked concerns about subject status and jurisdiction over those residing in Company territories. These concerns were never fully resolved by the 1773 Regulating Act and were intimately connected to struggles over authority between the British government and the East India Company. This chapter identifies the range of individuals actually subject to the Supreme Court of Judicature, founded in 1774, at the same time as it focuses on the political and jurisdictional repercussions of subject status. It underlines why the judiciary became a central site for negotiations over subjecthood and how subject status became a malleable tool in the hands of judges. Although its acquisition, governance, and patterns of settlement differed dramatically from those of Grenada or Quebec, Calcutta's inclusion in the British Empire also triggered questions about the status of those living there vis-à-vis subjects in the imperial metropolis.

Drawing parallels between the British Atlantic, British Mediterranean, and British Asia, these chapters not only call attention to the variety of plantation and farming colonies, strategic and garrison colonies, and trading colonies of the eighteenth-century empire, but also highlight how the needs of each particular territory shaped the contours of subjecthood and the privileges that might be accorded to subjects in each. Factors such as the number of British settlers, the availability of labor, the type of territorial administration, a colony's perceived importance within the empire, and the onset of war, among others, might have an impact on the relative inclusiveness or exclusiveness of subjecthood at a given moment or in a given colony and on subjects' success in securing political, legal, or economic privileges. The different nature of struggles in each colony simultaneously suggests that the parameters of subjecthood continued to be defined and negotiated by subjects in the colonies rather than emanating from London.

Each of the case studies draws attention to the various written documents in which subjecthood was invoked. The forms used—including correspondence, petitions, and court records—reveal how subjects wrote themselves into this monarchical empire and how administrators responded to them. Indeed, analyzing subjects' written claims and common language illustrates how subjects drew on understandings of allegiance and protection that had long been in circulation but then actively redefined the nature of those protections and the rights associated with subjecthood. They did not have to sit in representative assemblies or storm the Bastille to make themselves heard. Neither did they have to shape imperial policy in London to effect the rights they were granted in the colonies. Instead, as they carefully testified to their loyalties, participated in a centuries-old written tradition of claiming rights, and launched wide-ranging debates about the boundaries of subjecthood, inhabitants of the empire gradually proposed, and often secured, new economic, political, and legal rights.

Had subject status been advantageous only to inhabitants, struggles over subject status would not have received the attention they did from colonial administrators. Subjecthood was appealing to inhabitants who perceived its utility in securing privileges and protections, but it was just as instrumental for administrators who needed a certain flexibility as they sought to integrate conquered populations. British colonial administrators readily understood that by accepting numerous inhabitants as subjects, they might secure valuable soldiers and mariners for future wars with their European rivals. Allowing inhabitants to express grievances as members of the empire promoted better governance, permitting administrators to gauge problems or frustrations among their constituents, often before they erupted into violent conflict. Official responses to subjects' demands underline the various reasons administrators countenanced the claims of subjects and illustrate how an expansive and flexible subjecthood worked to bind the empire more generally.

Subjecthood was, of course, many things to many people, and one of the implications inherent in each case study is that it was a potentially inclusive and highly protean concept that could be used in seemingly infinite ways. *Subjects and Sovereign* can only begin to explore the myriad individuals who used the language of subjecthood, the diverse territories in which subject status was debated, and the political, social, economic, and cultural repercussions of the relationship between subject and sovereign. As a whole, it argues that acceptance as a British subject was perceived to ensure protection and uphold vaguely defined liberties, and that it was subjects themselves who forged new understandings of their economic, political, and legal rights. Subjecthood, here, is viewed as both a legal and everyday opportunity, one that was constantly shifting both in response to, and to accommodate, the vagaries of imperial rule.

This book does not attempt a political or intellectual history of subjecthood, focusing instead on intersections between legal understandings of subjecthood and popular traditions of declaring rights in order to demonstrate why subjects believed they were entitled to make a multitude of claims of their monarch. It also does not document a coherent change over time, except within some of the individual case studies themselves, instead offering an overarching argument about the profound historical relevance of subjecthood during the three decades after the Seven Years' War. These studies rely on a largely official archive to underscore that subject status remained contested among both colonial inhabitants and administrators and relevant at the highest levels of officialdom.

Moreover, although *Subjects and Sovereign* touches on questions relating to the status of nonwhite peoples, it focuses primarily on debates over the status of Catholic and continental European men, of those formerly French and Spanish subjects who became "His Britannick Majesty's subjects" by treaty or by convention and who actively sought to leverage that new status. This approach is based on a number of considerations. First, although colonies like Grenada possessed large enslaved populations and a province like Quebec a significant indigenous population, the struggles that consumed official attention after the Seven Years' War centered on the rights of the white French Catholic population on whom administrators believed they depended. Second, questions relating to the status of women, enslaved peoples, and indigenous inhabitants were certainly raised during this period, but the nuances of these questions would be impossible to address within the purview of this study, particularly given that other scholars are themselves already doing so.[44] Finally, and most important, the decision to focus on debates relating to largely white and continental European subjects reflects a broader argument—that subjecthood was not just articulated by settlers in opposition to nonwhite peoples or by loyalists in response to American patriots. The rights associated with subject status were also articulated in a range of lesser-known contexts, including military garrisons in the Mediterranean and the territories of a trading company in the East Indies.

It would, of course, be a mistake to assume that the utility and the possibilities of subjecthood were suddenly recognized in the 1760s, just as it would be wrong to ignore subjecthood's continued importance after 1790. The Seven Years' War brought questions relating to subject status to the fore, but the opportunities and challenges of subjecthood had a far longer history. When the British were struggling to defeat the Spanish during the War of Jenkins' Ear (1739–1748), for example, Lord Cathcart planned to lead the main expedition to the West Indies and to distribute a proclamation to the inhabitants of the Spanish colonies intended to woo them away from the hostilities and into His Britannic Majesty's protection. The promise to be held out was that "in all cases and in all respects they shall be attended to, assisted, favoured, and treated as the natural born subjects of Great Britain." It was enough, thought many writers at the time, to offer foreign inhabitants the privileges of British subjects.[45] Such an enticement was thought to be useful in advancing British wartime and imperial goals well before the 1760s.

Nonetheless, the range of territories and peoples added to the empire after the Treaty of Paris meant that questions about the status, duties, and rights of "new subjects" were asked with increasing intensity and became progressively multifaceted. The three decades after the Seven Years' War provide an important opportunity to explore the everyday practices of subjecthood and the extent to which subject status worked to connect otherwise disparate and distinct colonies. On the one hand, individuals living in different territories confidently laid claim to a wide range of protections due subjects as they swore loyalty to George III. On the other hand, since the rights associated with subjecthood remained largely uncodified, these inhabitants often secured rights that conflicted with those of subjects in other colonies or the British Isles, resulting in divisions and inequalities across the later-eighteenth-century British Empire. Though such stories are not peculiar to the postwar era, the examples of "old" and "new" subjects who negotiated an array of privileges with colonial administrators, Parliament, and their king during these crucial decades nonetheless recast historical understandings of the period more generally. The age of revolution, which witnessed rejections of monarchy and radical declarations of universal rights, was also an era when the bonds between sovereign and subject remained remarkably relevant and resilient. They would, in fact, prove themselves to be integral to the unity of the British Empire.

I

The Laws of Subjecthood

IN 1781, NATHANIEL DAVISON, consul in Algiers, wrote to the governor of Gibraltar for advice, noting his hesitation about whether he could redeem two captives as "British subjects." Lorenzo Canippa and Vincenzo Fiallo, Genoese inhabitants of Gibraltar, had been captured by Barbary corsairs while carrying important official dispatches from the governor to the British consul stationed at Tangier. Although these men were loyal servants of the empire, Davison remained unclear about both their subject status and the privileges to which they were entitled. He was not alone in his confusion. Throughout the British Empire, administrators struggled with similar questions. British governors and secretaries of state were unsure what rights to grant the French Catholic freeholders who chose to remain in the ceded colonies of Grenada and Quebec. Judges in the Calcutta Supreme Court of Judicature deliberated over whether European, Hindu, and Muslim inhabitants were British subjects in the eyes of the law. Everywhere, uncertainties about the legal identity of these individuals abounded, and everywhere, administrators such as Davison drew their own conclusions about how British subjects were to be defined.

In the eighteenth century, as in earlier and subsequent periods, subjecthood was often a matter of and for the law.[1] But when Davison inquired about the status and rights of individuals in the Mediterranean, he was not only seeking legal clarification; he was also raising fundamental questions about the relationship between subject and sovereign. Indeed, in the era before territorial definitions of nation and state became dominant,[2] subjecthood was at once a personal bond between subjects and their sovereign and also a legal tie between individuals and their monarch in his or her political capacity.[3] As William Blackstone argued in his widely circulated *Commentaries on the Laws of England* (1765), an "original contract" existed between monarch and subject, "in all states impliedly, in ours most expressly." It was the duty of allegiance "which binds the subject to the king, in return for that protection which the king affords the subject."[4] For Blackstone and other legal experts, the subject was described by reference to the alien, who was born outside the king's allegiance, and subjecthood was often addressed in chapters or sections entitled "the law of subject and alien."[5] Perhaps more significant, Blackstone evoked an enduring link between allegiance and protection, drawing on a legal tradition that had been articulated in the early seventeenth century and that connected monarchy, subject status, and allegiance. At that time, Sir Edward Coke, then Chief Justice of the Common Pleas, had famously argued that "ligeance" was the mutual bond that "joins together the sovereign and all his subjects."[6] Not too many years later, Sir Matthew Hale, Lord Chief Justice of the King's Bench, had stressed the mutual *liga*, or obligation, that existed between the king and his people and was at the heart of subject status.[7] It was in the relationship between subject and sovereign that answers to Davison's questions were therefore to be found.

As Davison and other colonial administrators consulted with their superiors, they documented the diverse legal understandings on which they actually relied in determining subject status. The correspondence between inhabitants, governors, and representative bodies in the colonies, and individuals or entities in London such as secretaries of state, the Board of Trade, and the Privy Council, contains rich evidence that both judicial and extrajudicial interpretations of subjecthood remained influential in the later eighteenth century. Although these officials consulted law as recorded in statutes and court decisions, they also looked to the contributions of people who were not officially part of the legal hierarchy.[8] In the documents used, cited, and written by colonial inhabitants and administrators are reflected the everyday practices of subjecthood in the British Empire and the meanings of law in individuals' lives.[9] This chapter therefore begins with an analysis of subjecthood as defined by case law and then considers both the other sources to which colonial administrators turned for legal guidance as well as the numerous legal ideas that shaped debates over subject status in the colonies between the 1760s and 1780s.

Calvin v. Smith, a landmark case tried in 1608, is traditionally regarded as the starting point for any legal discussion of subject status. It has alternatively represented the "most important event in the long history of English or British nationality law," the articulation of a "theoretical basis for territorial birthright citizenship," and a case that began to make possible an imperial conception of subjecthood.[10] But Calvin's Case, as it became known, was instrumental for two additional reasons. First, the judges' discussion of the expansive nature of allegiance, combined with their characterization of the relationship between subject and sovereign as one of obedience and protection, exerted a lasting influence over subsequent conceptions of subjecthood in the British Empire and over the opportunities associated with subject status. Second, the questions left unanswered by Calvin's Case and later case law shaped the extrajudicial legal world after the Seven Years' War, encouraging the emergence of varied understandings of subjecthood across the British Empire.

However, the presence of myriad new peoples after 1763, many of whom made confident claims about their allegiance to the monarch and their rights as subjects, frequently brought to light the possibilities and limitations of existing case law and prompted colonial officials to look beyond the central judiciary for legal clarification. As administrators in the far-flung colonies grappled with demands made by their constituents, they often consulted the treaties or instructions they had in their possession, sought guidance from law officers of the crown who communicated with the Board of Trade, or relied on their own sense of judgment and equity.[11] Tracing the legal discussions of subject status in these extrajudicial sources uncovers more practical approaches to subjecthood that operated alongside the theoretical formulations of the common law courts. It simultaneously demonstrates that both judicial and extrajudicial actors evoked enduring and common understandings of allegiance and protection, even if subtle divergences were manifest in how they each conceived of subject status.

Integrating and accommodating the populations added to the British Empire after the Seven Years' War was facilitated in part by the range of legal opinions available to inhabitants and administrators at the time. Exploring these many laws of subjecthood reveals that, particularly in the colonies, subjecthood was a compilation of often-conflicting ideas and a set of practices wielded by inhabitants and administrators to negotiate complex questions. It was a perpetually shifting concept of belonging rather than a coherent body of law. It was as much justice "on the spot" as it was a body of decisions preserved in case law. Ultimately, because subjecthood left considerable room for disagreement over the contours of allegiance and protection, it remained at once a desirable legal status and also a powerful opportunity.

Revisiting Territory, Allegiance, and Protection in Calvin's Case

Where case law was concerned, the judiciary had attempted to define subject status and to clarify the rights of subjects since the ruling in *Calvin v. Smith* provided a legal basis for distinguishing between subjects and aliens. Despite this chapter's broader contention that critical legal discussions emerged outside the realm of case law, this case remains essential to understanding how and why the relationship between subject and sovereign continued to figure so prominently in negotiations over subjecthood well after 1608. Like many court rulings, *Calvin v. Smith* formalized categories of persons that had been emerging over the centuries. Terms such as "natural-born" and "naturalized" subjects, "aliens," and "denizens" regularly appeared in both printed works and legal practice in the decades preceding Calvin's Case, but they gained significant traction only in 1608. By the early sixteenth century, for example, the alien status of foreign merchants was recognized and aliens' inability to inherit lands in England had been repeatedly confirmed.[12] Within a century, John Cowell's 1607 law dictionary defined an alien as "one born in a strange country." A subject, by contrast, was "a man born out of the land, so it be within the limits of the king's obedience, beyond the seas, or of English parents, out of the king's obedience (so the parents at the time of the birth, be of the king's allegiance) is no alien in account, but a subject to the king."[13]

The notion that subjects and aliens were differentiated both by birthplace and allegiance and defined by reference to one another, was becoming more familiar to educated audiences in the years before *Calvin v. Smith*. When Sir Edward Coke (figure 1.1) noted in 1608 that "denizens" were those who had acquired allegiance and been granted privileges by the king, he referenced an already well-established procedure for denization and naturalization and acknowledged the several statuses available to those who owed allegiance to the monarch of England.[14] It was *Calvin v. Smith*, however, that would make allegiance the defining factor in distinguishing between subjects and aliens.

Furthermore, by the early seventeenth century, the judiciary had available several interpretations of how subjecthood was acquired. Just as the geographical boundaries of the English king's territories had changed throughout the wars of the medieval period, so too had the populations subject to the king and the legislation regarding them. By 1351, a statute known as *De Natis Ultra Mare* recognized that English subjects might find themselves abroad in an increasingly mobile world and extended subjecthood to their offspring, a decision that on the surface appeared to confer subjecthood by *jus sanguinis* ("right of blood"). Seventeen years later, another statute stipulated that persons born in any of the king's territories were actually subjects in England, a decision that suggested that *jus soli* ("right of soil") had begun to coexist with *jus sanguinis*. Indeed, an earlier medieval judicial tradition of recognizing the subject status of all those born in the king's

FIGURE 1.1 Frontispiece with portrait of Sir Edward Coke, *The Second Part of the Institutes of the Lawes of England*, 1642. © The British Library Board (508.f.9.1).

diverse dominions would be referred to in the various published reports of *Calvin v. Smith*, alongside examples of subjecthood conferred on individuals born overseas of parents who were subjects. Coke's report, in particular, noted that "the Laws of England" regarding the subject's relationship to the king were "copious," and he was keen to establish continuity with earlier statutes.[15] However, if Coke and others cited the diverse precedents for subjecthood, their most important observations in 1608 concerned allegiance and the ways in which the bond between subject and sovereign, in fact, served to define the boundaries of subjecthood.

Calvin v. Smith was intimately connected to lingering political and legal questions that remained unanswered in the aftermath of the Union of Crowns (1603). When Elizabeth I died without heirs, her cousin, James VI of Scotland, ascended the English throne as James I. Two kingdoms composed of separate legislatures, court systems, and established churches came to share one monarch. In the years immediately following that union, several separate committees grappled with the legal status of James's Scottish subjects, but ultimately failed to reach a resolution.[16] Many in Parliament remained bitterly divided over whether James's Scottish subjects needed to be naturalized and whether legislative action for naturalization was even desirable. Several accounts suggest that the suits initiated in 1607 were contrived by the crown to remove the question of naturalization from Parliament and to place it in the hands of the judiciary, where a number of leading figures had already shown themselves to be sympathetic to naturalizing James's Scottish subjects.[17]

Regardless, in 1607, John and William Parkinson initiated civil suits in both the Court of King's Bench and Court of Chancery for two separate estates in England. They claimed that their charge, Robert Calvin, an infant born in Scotland after the union of the crowns, had been unjustly dispossessed of lands in England. The defendants responded that Calvin's plea was inadmissible because he was an alien and, as such, could not own freeholds in England. The defendants' plea resuscitated a fundamental legal and political question that had been contested for several years: were the *postnati*, or those born in Scotland after the English throne had descended to James, aliens or subjects? The answer to this question would then determine whether they were eligible to bring real or personal actions before the royal courts for lands within the realm of England.

As published reports of the case indicated (figure 1.2), the matter was recognized as one of "great import and consequence," and both suits were adjourned to the Exchequer Chamber, where the Lord Chancellor and

THE SPEECH OF THE LORD CHANCELLOR OF England, in the Eſchequer Chamber, touching the *Poſt-nati.*

LONDON,
Printed for the Societie of
Stationers. An. 1609.

FIGURE 1.2 Title page, *The Speech of the Lord Chancellor of England, in the Eschequer Chamber, touching the Post-nati*, 1609. Image published with the permission of ProQuest as part of *Early English Books Online*. Further reproduction is prohibited without permission.

fourteen judges from the common-law courts of King's Bench, Common Pleas, and Exchequer might together consider them "according to the ancient and ordinary course of the law."[18] All but two of the fourteen justices assembled eventually concluded that the *postnati* were natural-born subjects of the king of England, meaning that they were entitled to hold property in England, a right denied to aliens.

Although Sir Edward Coke's report of the case was the most widely accessible to subsequent generations and emerged as the definitive statement of the applicable law, each of the several reports published confirmed that the judges considered fundamental questions relating to the nature and extent of allegiance.[19] They responded to a series of three interconnected arguments made by the defendants who claimed that Calvin was an alien. First, the defendants insisted that there were two "ligeances," or allegiances, one of "King James of his kingdom of England" and one of "King James of his kingdom of Scotland." Individuals born within the ligeance of the kingdom of Scotland were born out of the ligeance of England and therefore remained aliens to the kingdom of England. Next, they argued that allegiance was due to the king's political capacity. King James had several political capacities—one for each of his several kingdoms—and because Calvin was born owing allegiance to James in his political capacity as king of Scotland rather than in his political capacity as king of England, Calvin remained an alien in England. Finally, the defendants asserted that because Calvin was not "at the time and in the place of his birth inheritable to the laws of England," he could not enjoy the privileges of those laws. He could benefit only from the laws of Scotland under which he was born.[20]

In challenging these arguments, the justices outlined a contrasting vision of allegiance and of the relationship between subject and sovereign. Their definition not only embraced as subjects Robert Calvin and the *postnati* more generally, but would also work in subsequent generations to accommodate the new peoples of an expanding empire. Allegiance, described most simply, was the "true and faithful obedience of the subject due to his sovereign." It was also referred to as an immutable birthright of the subject, one that could not be taken from him: it was an "incident inseparable to every subject; for as soon as he is born he oweth by birthright ligeance and obedience."[21] Moreover, the judges recognized the spiritual nature of ligeance, with Coke describing it as a "quality of the mind" and Lord Chancellor Ellesmere calling it a bond that "bindeth soul and conscience."[22]

It was by relying on ideas of allegiance and obedience that the judges distinguished between subjects and aliens. The subject was someone born under the "obedience, power, faith, ligealty, or ligeance of the king," just as an alien was defined as one "born out of the king's dominions, under the obedience of another king."[23] There was, in such definitions, an intertwined emphasis on both territory and allegiance. Legal historians have often observed that a territorially expansive view of subjecthood was present in the decision, offering a means to bring all those born within any one of the king's dominions into the fold of subjecthood, regardless of religion, race, or ancestry, and facilitating the idea of subjects spread across an expanding empire. Focusing on passages in which Coke, Ellesmere, and Sir Francis Bacon referred to the natural-born subject as someone born within any one of the king's dominions has led Polly Price to argue that the case "established a territorial rule for the acquisition of subject status at birth," just as it has encouraged others to see 1608 as foundational to emerging understandings of *jus soli*.[24] A close re-reading of the reports, however, reveals that territory did not alone make the subject. It was allegiance, even more than birth within the king's dominions, that played the crucial role.

In Coke's words, it was "neither the climate nor the soil, but ligeantia and obedientia that make the subject born." Coke certainly confirmed the paths to subjecthood familiar from the medieval tradition: a subject was someone who was either born within the king's dominions (what is sometimes referred to as *jus soli*) or born outside those dominions of parents under the obedience of the king (what is sometimes referred to as *jus sanguinis*). But *jus soli* and *jus sanguinis* were concepts imposed by subsequent generations of legal scholars. What Coke, in fact, emphasized was that it was the "time of birth" that mattered, since allegiance had to be present at that moment. Coke demonstrated this most clearly by using the example of an enemy born in the king's dominions. That person could never be a subject because he was not born within the king's ligeance:

> But if enemies should come into any of the king's dominions and surprise any castle or fort, and possess the same by hostility, and have issue there, that issue is no subject to the king, though he be born within his dominions, for that he was not born under the king's ligeance or obedience. But the time of his birth is of the essence of a subject born; for he cannot be a subject to the king of England, unless at the time of his birth he was under the ligeance and obedience of the king.[25]

Where a territorially expansive understanding of subjecthood was well suited to accommodating Robert Calvin, a definition of subjecthood that relied on a spiritual allegiance to the king was arguably even more so. It was this relationship of allegiance between subject and sovereign—one grounded in "faith and truth"—that could transcend the limits of territory, providing vast possibilities for an expanding empire.[26]

If the judges viewed allegiance as the delimiter of subject status, they also wrote of a personal relationship between subject and sovereign that characterized that allegiance. While the defendants had claimed that allegiance was owed to the king in his political capacity, Coke instead argued that it was due to the natural person of the king:

> And it was resolved, that it [ligeance] was due to the natural Person of the King (which is ever accompanied with the Politick Capacity, and the Politick Capacity as it were appropriated to the natural Capacity) and it is not due to the Politick Capacity only . . . every subject (as it hath been affirmed by those that argued against the Plaintiff) is presumed by Law to be sworn to the King, which is to his natural person, and likewise the King is sworn to his subjects . . . which Oath he taketh in his natural Person.[27]

By focusing on the oath taken by the king as a "natural person" and the corresponding allegiance due to his natural body, Coke and several of the other judges traced a direct connection between the natural bodies of subjects and their sovereign.[28] Such a personal understanding of allegiance strengthened the argument that neither allegiance nor subjecthood was territorially bounded or restricted to those who inhabited a specific kingdom. Rather, subjects were those who had a personal relationship of allegiance with their sovereign, a spiritual connection that could extend well beyond the territories of the realm. Once again, published reports reveal that the judges formulated an expansive and inclusive definition of subjecthood.

The decision went even further, however, stating that this personal allegiance was simultaneously a natural, almost primordial, allegiance, "due unto the King by law of Nature." Because natural law predated "any judicial or municipal law" and was immutable, natural allegiance could not be changed or sundered by later legal innovations.[29] And because the bond between subject and sovereign predated the enactment of local laws, subjects might be unified in their allegiance to a sovereign (a "union of ligeance") without necessarily sharing the same laws (a "union of laws").[30] Subjects did not have to be born within the ambit of the English common law, as the defendants had claimed, and individuals who lived under a wide variety of laws might therefore still be subjects to one monarch. Here, too, was a definition of allegiance and subjecthood that could encompass a wide variety of legal systems.

The bond of allegiance between subject and sovereign was poetically described by Coke as a "dual and reciprocal tie," and it was this "tie" that held immeasurable promise for future generations.[31] Just as the subject was bound to the king by obedience, so was the king bound to the protection of the subject; Coke wrote that "for as the subject oweth to the king his true and faithful ligeance and obedience, so the sovereign is to govern and protect his subjects."[32] The reciprocity of this bond is fundamental to what Philip Hamburger has called the "principle of protection": those who owed allegiance were owed protection, just as those who were without allegiance were without protection.[33] Paul Halliday has likewise emphasized the potential inherent to this bond: "from allegiance, actual or implied, came liberties."[34]

According to this reading of the relationship between subject and monarch, individuals who could assert and prove their allegiance and subject status gained access to certain rights, liberties, and privileges.[35] The idea that allegiance brought with it certain privileges, was one voiced by proponents and opponents of naturalization alike between 1606 and 1608 in both the parliamentary debates regarding naturalization and the reports of *Calvin v. Smith*. Sir Edwin Sandys, who was opposed to the naturalization of the *postnati* in 1606, perhaps was so precisely because he believed that subject status would provide Scots with access to "the full rights of Englishmen born among us."[36] In his speech as counsel for Calvin, Bacon furthermore noted that "by the law of England, the subject, that is natural born, hath a capacity or ability to all benefits whatsoever."[37] Even the Lord Chancellor claimed that the subject was "to have all the freedoms, privileges, and benefits pertaining to his birthright."[38] Although very few rights were ever formally associated with subjecthood and codified by case law or statute, the understanding that in the relationship between subject and sovereign lay access to protection was a powerful one.

Coke and others present in the Exchequer Chamber, however, arguably outlined their most expansive vision of subjecthood—a vision that had profound consequences for an emerging empire—in their exposition of the various types of allegiance. Coke's, the most detailed of the reports, documented four kinds of allegiance, which he called natural, acquired, local, and legal.[39] Natural allegiance, which was largely the focus in Calvin's Case, was defined quite expansively in 1608. Due by nature and birthright, it was permanent and immutable. The second form of allegiance, acquired allegiance, resulted from denization or naturalization, and it meant that additional subjects might be brought into the fold by letters patent, by act of Parliament, or, as he hinted vaguely, by conquest.

It was Coke's very brief discussion of the third form of allegiance, or local allegiance, that suggested where subjecthood might, in fact, be broadened further than the specific case of Robert Calvin. Coke explained that an alien in amity who lived in England, even if he had been born outside the king's ligeance, nonetheless lived under the king's protection and therefore owed the king a local allegiance. This made him a temporary subject while he remained in England, whether or not he was ever endenizened or naturalized. Although Coke specified that local allegiance related only to alien friends residing in England, not to alien enemies, it was unclear whether there were other circumstances in which local allegiance might also be present. Did alien friends residing in the empire also owe local allegiance? Did those brought into the empire because they resided in conquered territories owe a local allegiance or an acquired allegiance? Coke's references to a local allegiance stemming from a local protection were cited in the colonies after 1763, particularly among judges of the Supreme Court of Judicature in Calcutta who sought to extend it overseas. Notwithstanding its brevity, Coke's discussion of local allegiance and the related notion of temporary protection became increasingly important as the territorial possessions of the British monarch expanded and as local actors were called upon to determine the subject status of local peoples.

The fourth kind of allegiance addressed was legal obedience, characterized by an oath of allegiance to the king. Coke argued that this oath was prescribed by ordinance of man, originally instituted by King Arthur, and that the ligeance intended was natural allegiance. Coke said little, however, about who was eligible to take such oaths or about whether these oaths themselves might ever naturalize the subject. Was anyone who subscribed to an oath of allegiance considered a subject? Despite the evident uncertainties in Coke's report, petitioners on the island of Grenada would actively leverage the notion that oaths conferred subject status and its associated protections. Although natural allegiance was what preoccupied the judiciary in 1608, the multiple understandings of allegiance discussed by Coke would be employed by future generations as they faced novel circumstances.

Speaking for Calvin in 1608, Bacon reflected on the significance of the personal and natural allegiance elaborated: "allegiance is of a greater extent and dimension than laws or kingdom . . . because it began before laws, it continueth after laws, and it is in vigour where laws are suspended, and have not their force."[40] As Bacon hinted, the personal and reciprocal bond of allegiance, which rested on a direct, spiritual connection between subject and sovereign, laid the groundwork for a subjecthood that transcended and embraced multiple kingdoms and diverse systems of law. The territorially expansive understanding of British subjecthood evident in 1608 was certainly important to the empire. But the even more inclusive argument about birth within the monarch's allegiance arguably did as much, if not more, to free subjecthood from territorial, political, and legal limits and to ensure that the "mutual bond and obligation between the King and his subjects" remained at the heart of negotiations over subject status.[41] Whether or not it was the intention of the justices in 1608, they had provided the legal and intellectual foundations for an empire in which all peoples born within the king's allegiance—regardless of religion, race, or place of origin—might claim subject status and its associated protections.

Pursuing Territory, Allegiance, and Protection across the Seas

In the years following 1608, *Calvin v. Smith* became the *sine qua non* for decisions on subject status, whether these were juridical rulings or extrajudicial considerations of subjecthood. Given the growth of the British Empire in the seventeenth and eighteenth centuries, questions of subject status quickly came to involve individuals living outside England or Scotland. Cases tried before the Courts of King's Bench, Exchequer, and Common Pleas, or resolved by appeals to the House of Lords and Privy Council, revealed that subject status in the overseas territories repeatedly surfaced as a topic of concern. The expansive notions of subjecthood voiced in 1608 continued to cast a long shadow over the central judiciary as judges considered the limits of naturalization, the protections of subjecthood, and specific questions relating to whether British subjects carried English laws with them.

Indeed, cases initiated by individuals, many of whom resided in the more recently added colonies, reinforced the expansive notions of allegiance and protection at the heart of Calvin's Case, just as they confirmed the opportunities available to those who positioned themselves as subjects of the British sovereign. In *Craw v. Ramsey* (1681), for example, the Court of King's Bench was asked to consider an action of trespass and ejectment. Though, on its surface, *Craw v. Ramsey* addressed issues of inheritance within the Ramsey family, the fact that one of the Ramsey sons had been naturalized in Ireland meant that the judges considered another fundamental question as they weighed the evidence: did naturalization in Ireland also naturalize a person in England? Thus, much of the report for the case corroborated the several ways men "born out of England may inherit in England." These included birth in one of the king's dominions, naturalization by act of Parliament, birth in the territories of a prince who held those territories as a liegeman to the monarch of England, and birth in territories controlled by the king's armies. The report noted that the "natural born subjects of Ireland, Guernsey, Jersey, Berwick, and all the English plantations inherit . . . they are born liege-men to the same king." The emphasis on birth as "liege-men to the same king" throughout an expanding empire was complemented by passages that spoke of birth within the king's "protection."[42] By affirming the points made in *Calvin v. Smith*, *Craw v. Ramsey* revealed that understandings of birth within the territory, allegiance, and protection of the monarch remained central to any decision regarding subject status, just as the case demonstrated that individuals who were deemed to be subjects might inherit lands in England.

Another case, *Fabrigas v. Mostyn*, tried nearly a century later, extended these understandings of subjecthood to the British Mediterranean. In 1773, Anthony Fabrigas, a native of Minorca, brought an action against Lieutenant-General John Mostyn in the Court of Common Pleas for having arrested, imprisoned, and deported him to Spain without proper trial. Mostyn maintained that he was justified in his actions against the seditious Fabrigas by the "ancient laws of Minorca," which had been granted to the Minorcans in 1713 despite the British conquest. The plaintiff, however, argued that he was entitled to the protection of the laws of England given that he was a "free-born subject of England." In its ruling, the Court of Common Pleas repeatedly stated that inhabitants of Minorca, "being born in Minorca since its subjection to the crown of England," were natural-born subjects. The court affirmed the principle, initially elaborated in *Calvin v. Smith*, that subject status was conferred by birth in any of the king's dominions, but it also emphasized the inseparable ideas of subjection, allegiance, and protection, referencing and drawing directly on Coke: "Mr. Fabrigas is under the king's protection, because he owes him allegiance, therefore he may be aided by the king's laws." The judges determined that even if British subjects lived under laws different from those in force in England—in this case "the usages and customs of Spain"—they were still allowed to sue for damages inflicted by colonial administrators in English courts and still due the broader protections of English law because of their allegiance.[43]

Still other cases in the seventeenth and eighteenth centuries began to explore whether British subjects carried English laws with them as they moved across territories.[44] In *Dutton v. Howell* (1693), for example, the judiciary argued that when British subjects settled in the "uninhabited country" of Barbados, they carried with them the common law of England.[45] By contrast, in the cases of *Blankard v. Galdy* (1694) and *Smith v. Brown and Cooper* (1702), the courts ruled that in the "conquered territories" of both Jamaica and Virginia, the English statutes and law did not apply. British subjects who inhabited those colonies might live under laws that were not necessarily English.[46] Still other cases, like *Anonymous* (1722) and *Rex v. Cowle* (1759), which examined the differences between "conquered" and "settled" colonies, also considered the issue of English law, with the 1722 decision stating that law was the "birthright of every subject."[47] It was the case of *Christian v. Corren* (1716), however, that helped to clarify the parameters of this argument, noting that subjects had "an inherent right, inseparable from them as subjects, to apply to the Crown for justice . . . the King as the fountain of justice had an inherent right, inseparable from the Crown, to distribute justice among his subjects."[48] The short reports remaining from these cases suggest that the subject's allegiance and corresponding sense of being owed protection from the monarch shaped the various opinions offered. Even if judges were not necessarily concerned to establish individuals' subject status in these cases, they did routinely link questions about subjects' access to law to concepts of allegiance and protection. These cases reveal that the principle of protection continued to shape legal decisions, with subjects' rights and access to justice repeatedly considered as part of subjects' relationship with the sovereign.

Cases like *Craw v. Ramsey* and *Fabrigas v. Mostyn* worked to extend and perpetuate some of the expansive notions of subjecthood articulated in Calvin's Case—first, that subject status was conferred by birth within the dominions and allegiance of the monarch and was not limited to birth within the kingdom of England; second, that allegiance was a mutual and personal bond of obedience and protection, which meant that the subject gained access to certain protections and rights; and third, that subjects owed allegiance and were joined in common to the sovereign regardless of the particular territories or legal systems under which they lived. These ideas about subjecthood theoretically permitted multiple local identities to coexist within a unified community of allegiance. They meant that inhabitants who did not necessarily share common blood or common culture might still share a powerful and common bond with the monarch. Just as these notions continued to shape the deliberations of the central judiciary, they also remained influential in the legal and everyday world of the eighteenth century and proved critical to accommodating the growing number of imperial subjects.

Silences and Opportunities

Despite its influence in subsequent decades and centuries, *Calvin v. Smith* had left several important questions unanswered—questions that weighed increasingly upon those negotiating the progressively more complex problems of subject status after the mid-eighteenth century. This was in part because Calvin's Case focused on answering certain questions relating to the status and allegiance of those born in Scotland after the Union of the Crowns and about their rights to hold land within the kingdom of England. The case was largely uninterested in issues of subjecthood outside of England, not least because the overseas empire was still in its infancy in the early seventeenth century, and the judges did not anticipate the dilemmas that might arise as additional territories became part of the British Empire.[49] It is, in fact, somewhat ironic that Calvin's Case made possible an expansive, even imperial, definition of subjecthood, since the case was relatively silent where the empire was concerned. At least three of these silences, however, when combined with notions of allegiance, became increasingly relevant to the British Empire after the 1760s.

To begin, Calvin's Case addressed the status of the *postnati*, but it provided no definitive direction about the status of the *antenati*, or those Scots born before 1603. In other words, despite insisting that those born in territories that were part of the king's dominions and who owed allegiance were British subjects, *Calvin v. Smith* said little about the status of individuals born in territories before they had become part of the king's dominions and before they had come within the king's allegiance.[50] Did such individuals have to be formally naturalized or might naturalization occur with the cession or conquest of territory? Might this happen by treaty? Did such individuals owe "local allegiance," or another kind of allegiance, and did that then render them British subjects? Because Calvin's Case and subsequent cases were concerned with the particular matter of the *postnati*, the guidance they could provide would ultimately prove somewhat limited, particularly with regards to peoples added to the empire in 1763.

Second, because the judges determined that allegiance was due by "the law of nature" in 1608, they also argued that allegiance and subjecthood were indissoluble and permanent. The tie between subject and king could not be "severed" if a territory fell into enemy hands, since that bond was personal, due to the "natural body" of the king upon birth in one of his territories. Coke noted that "naturalization due and vested by Birth-right, cannot by any Separation of the Crown afterward be taken away: nor he that was by

Judgement of Law a natural Subject at the Time of his Birth, become an Alien by such a Matter *ex post facto*."[51] If Coke's argument in *Calvin v. Smith* was applied universally to other monarchies and empires, then subjects of one king could never become subjects of another. The reality in the eighteenth century, as in other eras, was that territories and subjects were regularly traded between the European empires. French or Spanish subjects became British, as happened at the cession of Grenada or Florida to Britain in 1763. Nominally British subjects suddenly become French or Spanish, as was the case in 1763 when Guadeloupe and Cuba, both briefly British territories, were returned to France and Spain, respectively. There was thus a fundamental difference between case law and international diplomatic practice. As soon became evident, administrators needed legal guidance attuned to the realities of the postwar empire, which they often sought outside the common law courts.

Third, neither Calvin's Case nor the cases that followed substantially addressed the question of the "protections" due "liege-men," or British subjects. Most of the court decisions considered dealt with specific issues raised by individual cases, and, though the justices often opined on allegiance and protection, they resisted establishing any extensive set of rights or privileges for British subjects. *Calvin v. Smith* and subsequent cases did affirm the subject's right to own freeholds in England and to sue before the courts in England, but these were rights centered on England that were at best marginally relevant to many inhabitants of the empire.[52] Only *Christian v. Corren* (1716), which originated as an appeal from a decree in the Isle of Man, addressed the issue of any additional rights for subjects residing outside England. In that case, the court confirmed that it was the "right of subjects to appeal to the sovereign to redress a wrong done to them in any court of justice," just as it was a "right, inseparable from the Crown, to distribute justice among his subjects," allowing them to petition even if they resided across the seas.[53] Although this was a right already confirmed by statute on several occasions, the case relied on the relationship between subject and sovereign, and the connections between allegiance and protection, to establish the right to petition.[54]

Nonetheless, case law had hardly established any extensive set of rights, nor, by the 1760s, had court decisions significantly clarified what protections were owed to loyal subjects, particularly those who lived overseas. Were they owed any economic protections? Were they entitled to redemption from captivity? Were they required to live under a Protestant ascendancy and to subscribe to the Test, or declaration against transubstantiation, before standing for election? Were subjects entitled to English common law and to English courts when residing overseas? Despite their significance, neither *Calvin v. Smith* nor subsequent cases had anticipated these increasingly pressing questions. Ultimately, lack of clarity in case law provided individuals with an opportunity to redefine the rights of loyal subjects in their everyday lives.

While the central judiciary regularly upheld an expansive definition of subjecthood, subsequent administrators and judges who tried to rely solely on case law would find it surprisingly difficult to identify subjects' unalienable rights. Requests for clarification surfaced throughout the colonies and became increasingly frequent as large swaths of territory were added to the British Empire after the Seven Years' War. The definition of subjecthood first enunciated in 1608 would continue to provide an essential foundation, particularly because the idea that in the relationship between subject and sovereign lay access to rights remained powerful. Nonetheless, because case law could not provide certain specific guidance when territories and peoples were dramatically reconfigured, competing legal understandings would also flourish. Only by considering the range of additional interpretations that emerged to fill the judiciary's silences is it possible to fully analyze the multivalent legal understandings of subjecthood that coexisted after the Seven Years' War.

The Layers of Legal Opinion

Some cases, like *Fabrigas v. Mostyn*, revealed that case law could prove to be an appropriate forum for handling questions particular to the colonies. Judges were sometimes well positioned to consider the local circumstances of an outpost like Minorca. More often than not, however, colonial secretaries of state and governors could not wait for the decisions of the courts and sought more immediate and specific resolutions to the everyday problems arising in their variegated territories. Perhaps there was not necessarily a plaintiff willing to bring suit in the English courts. Perhaps the legal forum provided by the common law courts seemed too removed from the realities of day-to-day colonial life for administrators who were thousands of miles away. Regardless, eighteenth-century officials often looked beyond case law for answers, and accepted that they had significant room to interpret legal matters themselves. They turned for advice to the Board of Trade or to secretaries of state, who in turn might rely on treaties or the opinions of law officers of the crown for guidance. In these other layers of legal opinion, which drew on understandings of allegiance and protection already articulated in case law, additional and at times more expansive perspectives on subject status emerged and were communicated to colonial governors and consuls.

The first such layer comprised international treaty articles and official instructions sent to colonial administrators from London. Such documents, which often provided governors and consuls with their only quasi-legal understandings of the various peoples under their purview, were instrumental in influencing ideas and decisions about subject status. Copies of the Treaty of Paris, for example, were sent to administrators throughout the empire and frequently cited when demonstrating royal concern for "new subjects."[55] As Secretary of State Lord Egremont wrote to Governor James Murray of Quebec, "you will have seen by the Definitive Treaty, which has been already transmitted to you from my office, the particular care the King has taken of the interests of His Canadian Subjects."[56] Excerpts from the treaty were recopied and enclosed along with routine correspondence,[57] and governors were commanded to apprise inhabitants living in certain colonies of the contents of treaty articles.[58] Royal instructions to governors themselves referenced the Treaty of Paris and reiterated its specific articles, indicating the central role the document played in governing the postwar territories and in guiding administrative practice.[59]

Administrators were not alone in relying on this treaty when contemplating the possibilities of subjecthood. Inhabitants themselves evoked it as they made claims of their monarch. The French Catholics of Grenada, for example, believed that they were entitled to "the enjoyment of every privilege and indulgence stipulated by Capitulation and by Treaty." Several of the British Protestants on the island concurred with this statement, arguing that "by Capitulation and by Treaty," the French Catholics were entitled to "the name and to the immunities of British subjects."[60] Even letters sent to colonial governors reflected the notion that those who remained in the conquered and ceded territories had done so with the expectation of certain rights being forthcoming. In Grenada, Governor Robert Melvill was instructed that it was only "justice and sound policy" that a limited number of French Catholic subjects should be allowed to sit in the assembly and council, given that they had chosen to remain in Grenada "under the faith of the Treaty of Paris, and professing the religion of the Church of Rome, the free Exercise of which is allowed by the said Treaty."[61] Because the treaty and later instructions were central to framing discussions about subject status and subjects' rights in the new territories, they represented a key source in the development of legal understandings of subjecthood.

The guidance offered by the Treaty of Paris, however, differed subtly from that evident in case law. Articles that conveyed the French king's territories and subjects to George III simultaneously contained clauses in which the English monarch pledged that "his new Roman Catholic subjects may profess the worship of their religion according to the rites of the Romish church, as far as the laws of Great Britain permit." By such simple phrases, French inhabitants "who had been subjects of the Most Christian King" were permitted either to sell their estates and depart, retaining their French subjecthood, or to remain in the territories, becoming "new Roman Catholic subjects" of George III.[62] Allegiance to the monarch shaped each aspect of these exchanges, but this allegiance was transferable rather than immutable. It signaled a subjecthood that was acquired not by letters patent or act of Parliament, as Coke had once described, but by international treaty. It indicated that subjecthood was no longer merely a result of birth within the monarch's allegiance, but that it might result from an individual's decision to remain within the king's allegiance and protection.

Similarly, correspondence between British colonial administrators in the Mediterranean reveals that many of them relied on royal commissions, official instructions, and treaty agreements in order to make decisions about the status of inhabitants in these outposts. When consuls and governors explained their decisions regarding the subject status of individuals who came before them in the Mediterranean, they regularly cited particular treaty articles, among other documents. When Governor Eliott of Gibraltar provided the secretary of state with his perspective on whether foreign inhabitants might be viewed as British subjects for the purposes of trade, he enclosed copies of treaties concluded in 1716, 1751, and 1760 that he believed to be relevant.[63] Royal instructions and treaty articles were thus more than administrative and diplomatic records; in the colonies, they came to provide essential guidance to those making legal determinations about subject status.[64]

These documents suggest that inhabitants of the colonies found alternative paths to subjecthood than those imagined by the courts. The earliest instructions regarding the conquered island of Minorca, issued in 1713, stated that the "People and Inhabitants of Our Island of Minorca are now to be looked upon as Our Natural born Subjects . . . and to enjoy all the benefits thereof as well as the rest of Our Subjects in Our other Dominions."[65] This particular clause would be reprinted and recycled throughout the century. Echoing these instructions, the second article of the treaty concluded between Britain and Algiers in October 1716 confirmed that the inhabitants of both Minorca and Gibraltar were to be "looked upon as His Majesty's subjects in the same manner as if they had been born in any other part of Great Britain."[66] In each of these documents, another subtle shift had occurred in how subject status might be acquired. Inhabitants of these strategic outposts were no longer required to have been born within the monarch's allegiance to attain subjecthood; they were to be regarded as natural-born subjects, "as if they had been born" in the monarch's dominions, by stipulation of the treaty. None of this aligned with Cokeian notions of allegiance, of course; according to Coke, individuals could be treated as "natural-born" only if they had been born within the king's allegiance or naturalized into it by letters patent or act of Parliament. In both Minorca and Gibraltar, however, individuals who acquired allegiance outside the avenues outlined by case law were nonetheless still regarded as subjects and were entitled to enjoy the "benefits," or "protections," of being subjects.

A second source of legal opinions in the eighteenth century was the reports of law officers of the crown. When colonial governors sought guidance from the Board of Trade on legal matters, their questions were typically forwarded to law officers of the crown rather than to legal personnel affiliated with the common law courts. This was in part because appeals from foreign dominions lay to the king in his council rather than to the king in his bench, and partly because the Board of Trade had been empowered to call for the advice and aid of these law officers by a special clause in its initial commission. Answers to these queries usually came in the form of reports from advocates, attorneys, and solicitors general, which in turn led to the emergence of a body of legal opinions whose exact relationship to case law was unclear but whose purpose was to represent and protect the rights of the monarch as well as the rights of the public.[67] Unlike the more famous *English Law Reports*, the responses of law officers were rarely published, though an editor who compiled them in 1814 noted that these opinions could be deemed of "little less authority than decided law," especially when they were presented to the king or his council.[68]

In an important incident at the end of the Seven Years' War, the Lords Commissioners for Trade and Plantations sought the attorney general's advice on precisely how the inhabitants of the ceded territories were to be viewed and treated. Noting that they had been born out of the allegiance of the king, this board wondered whether the French and Spanish inhabitants of Canada, Florida, and Grenada were to be considered as aliens and strangers. In 1764, the attorney general determined that these new inhabitants, "having intituled themselves to the Benefits thereof by taking the Oaths, etc., are not to be considered in the light of Aliens," and that they were entitled to the rights promised them under the Treaty of Paris.[69] Both the query and report weighed familiar matters of birth outside the king's allegiance and its associated protections. But the 1764 report suggested that birth within the dominions and allegiance of the king, so important to case law, was not the only criterion for determining subject status. According to the attorney general, choosing to remain in conquered territories and swearing oaths of allegiance might provide other paths to subjecthood.[70] Ascertaining what shaped his reasoning is difficult. Did he consider that these "new subjects" had acquired a "local allegiance"? Was he drawing on popular understandings that the Treaty of Paris had conveyed subjecthood? Nor is it evident how and whether the Lords Commissioners ever acted directly upon this opinion. It is clear, however, that crown counsel had offered an opinion that significantly expanded the understanding of allegiance and protection accepted in case law and that quite possibly helped to bring new members of the British Empire into the fold of subjecthood.

Law officers were likely better positioned to weigh local peculiarities than were the common law courts, particularly since they were typically responding to specific issues raised by colonial administrations rather than to court cases that might pose several entangled questions and that necessarily became part of established precedent. For example, on several occasions, law officers of the crown were consulted on the position of Roman Catholics in the territories added to the empire. In 1765, the attorney general and solicitor general jointly opined that the "Roman Catholick Subjects, residing in the Countries, ceded to his Majesty, in America, by the Definitive Treaty of Peace, are not Subject, in those Colonies, to the incapacities, disabilities, and penalties to which Roman Catholics in the Kingdom, are Subject by the Laws thereof."[71] Inhabitants of the ceded colonies were classified as subjects—but as Roman Catholic subjects whose rights differed from those of Roman Catholics in England or Ireland.

A second report submitted by the king's advocate, attorney general, and solicitor general to the Privy Council in 1768 confirmed this earlier report, noting that "the several Acts of Parliament which impose disabilities and penalties upon the publick exercise of the Roman Catholicks do not extend to Canada."[72] Both these reports conceded that the Test, required for occupants of public offices in England and theoretically rendering practicing Catholics ineligible for public office, was not to be extended to the colonies added in 1763. These were conclusions that the common law courts in England would not, in all likelihood, have been able to draw, given the continued importance of the penal laws for regulating Catholic subjects within the realm. Law officers of the crown thus proposed differing and increasingly flexible interpretations of subjects' rights from those found in case law, even suggesting that new subjects in Grenada and Quebec had a set of rights that varied from those of subjects within the British Isles.

The flurry of reports from law officers in response to queries from colonial administrators and the Board of Trade suggests that foundational cases like *Calvin v. Smith* were unable to provide satisfactory answers. On occasion, the legal opinions generated in London also began to weigh the repercussions of an expansive subjecthood, addressing what an inclusive allegiance and protection might actually mean for colonial administrators. For example, in 1766, James Marriott, the advocate general, was approached to determine whether the king, consistent with the treaty signed with Spain in 1763, might establish any kind of civil government or jurisdiction over the British subjects residing in the Bay of Honduras. He responded by explaining that if Spain's right to territory in the Bay of Honduras were sole and absolute, then the persons residing there would be Spanish subjects and could not possibly be considered British subjects. Because Spain had acknowledged by treaty that some of the inhabitants were British subjects, however, Spain's right could not be absolute. Since "such as the subject is such is the jurisdiction," British subjects were entitled to have civil regulations made for them according to the laws of Great Britain, an argument that engaged earlier ones from case law about subjects carrying with them the English laws.[73]

According to Marriott, the bodies of subjects served as a kind of territorial and jurisdictional marker even in territory that had been ceded to the crown of Spain. He also hinted that colonial administrators could extend the sphere of British authority and jurisdiction by acknowledging that diverse peoples were British subjects. In this particular example, Marriott's report, which considered the specific imperatives of shifting imperial rule in the Bay of Honduras, recognized features of subjecthood that did not necessarily have parallels in case law. It is possible to read the opinion as merely extending Cokeian notions of indelible allegiance and its associated protections, but a closer look also indicates that Marriott implied that protection included access to civil regulations and jurisdiction.

A third arena for the development of eighteenth-century understandings of subjecthood centered on the actions and interpretations of numerous administrators, who often operated far from metropolitan oversight and had significant latitude in making decisions about subject status. During a period when territories and peoples were rapidly added to the British Empire and when there was no universally accepted legal ruling about their status, local actors were particularly dynamic in generating novel interpretations of subject status. As a range of administrative, judicial, and other actors drew on generally accessible but often imprecise legal ideas about allegiance and protection, they faced situations and demands in the colonies for which there were no simple answers in case law.

Governors and consuls, among others, often sought guidance about subjecthood, making repeated requests for copies of instructions regarding the colonies under their command and for basic information about the individuals in these territories. Occasionally, they received directions from superiors as to who was or was not a *bona fide* British subject. Sometimes they were given specific instructions about the rights of those under their purview. Nonetheless, the discrepancy between the information they received and that which they required was striking.[74] Frequently without handbooks or relevant precedents at hand, and often waiting in vain for answers from London, many administrators took matters into their own hands, using their personal judgment about what defined subjecthood and the rights of subjects in the new territories. At moments like these they reacted to the best of their abilities, applying and often reworking the definitions of subject status with which they were familiar.

In the absence of formal educational institutions or training for imperial servants in the eighteenth century, the individual backgrounds, experiences, and biases of administrators were especially likely to shape their interpretations of subject status, just as the pressures they faced on the ground might affect their willingness to grant certain privileges to subjects. In the Mediterranean, consuls like Nathaniel Davison were routinely responsible for determining which individuals should be redeemed from captivity as British subjects. Although they sometimes considered an individual's place of birth or allegiance, there were numerous other factors in their decision-making. Some sent lists of individuals they had reclaimed, explaining to London how they had made their determinations based upon subjective factors such as who "looked" or "sounded" British, which no doubt seemed like the most equitable way to make such calculations.[75] There were, of course, periods when the British relied more intensely on the provisions brought into their Mediterranean garrisons by individuals who may not have appeared quite as British as Britons. At times such as these, consuls and governors were more prepared to consider allegiance and protection quite expansively. In the Mediterranean, as elsewhere, the dispositions of particular administrators might also affect whether or not they chose to claim individuals as *bona fide* British subjects. This became particularly clear in the cases of deserters, whom not all officials felt should be redeemed from captivity. Some governors believed in reclaiming these renegades, whereas others, perhaps feeling personally betrayed, argued that deserters had renounced their allegiance and were no longer entitled to protections. The interpretations of local actors, therefore, often played a key role in determinations of allegiance and subjecthood.

In short, by the mid-eighteenth century, colonial administrators and individuals throughout the British Empire might have derived their understanding of "British subject" from a vast and sometimes contradictory array of cases, treatises, opinions, and ideas generated across the arms of officialdom. There was no universally accepted law of subjecthood for the British Empire. There was no centralized court or office whose determinations about subject status were effectuated systematically. Although understandings of allegiance and protection enunciated in *Calvin v. Smith* remained important in this multivalent legal world, they were shaped and reshaped by diplomats, crown counsel, and administrators, each of whom continued to value and develop expansive and flexible notions of subjecthood. Indeed, it was the existence of these multiple legal interpretations that not only enabled colonial administrators to recognize new peoples as subjects but also provided an environment in which many demands for rights could be accommodated.

Divergent Understandings of Subjecthood

If *Calvin v. Smith* had inaugurated expansive possibilities for allegiance, subjecthood was often defined even more inclusively outside the common law courts than it had been within them. And while the rulings of the central common law courts may have had a more recognized "force of law," the understandings of subjecthood that emerged in international treaties and official instructions, reports from attorneys and solicitors general, and the decisions of individual administrators were often generated in immediate response to changing realities in the empire. These understandings remained rooted in Coke's ideas about allegiance and protection and continued to revolve around the relationship between subject and sovereign. But there were some subtly changing inflections in how this allegiance was conceived, which would prove relevant in resolving struggles and debates in the later eighteenth century. Three of the ways in which understandings of subjecthood diverged in layers of legal opinion across the British Empire demonstrate how a reliance on case law alone can lead to a fundamental misreading of the nature and flexibility of subjecthood.

First, unlike case law, neither treaty articles nor the opinions of law officers of the crown defined subjecthood or its protections based exclusively on birth within the king's dominions or allegiance. In *Fabrigas v. Mostyn*, judges had recognized as subjects only natives of Minorca born after the conquest of the island. This was actually a limiting ruling, cleaving carefully to the specific decision regarding the *postnati* in 1608, and it did not unilaterally grant subject status to all inhabitants of Minorca. By contrast, treaty articles and instructions relating to Minorca and other colonies routinely extended subject status to inhabitants who chose to remain in the territory after its conquest. In 1763, for example, inhabitants of Grenada and Quebec were allowed either to sell their estates and depart within eighteen months or to remain as "new Roman Catholic subjects."[76] Indeed, the broader construction of treaties signed for Gibraltar, Minorca, Grenada, and Quebec was that they granted subject status to all inhabitants, whether they had been born before or after the conquest by Britain, and whether they were born within or without the king's allegiance. Because Minorca and Grenada, in particular, changed hands so frequently in the eighteenth century, and because their inhabitants repeatedly went from being foreign to British subjects, documents like treaties and royal instructions provided solutions not otherwise available.

By suggesting that individuals might enter the king's protection, treaties, in particular, endorsed definitions of subjecthood, allegiance, and protection that were inclusive and that could accommodate the peoples added to a continually expanding empire. This subjecthood stemmed neither from "natural allegiance," to use Coke's term, nor from allegiance acquired through denization or naturalization. It was another kind of allegiance. Was it acquired in a new way? Was it local? Was it legal? Sadly, the archival record offers few conclusive answers. But in these other layers of law, where birth as a subject was no longer the only path to belonging, a subject's ability to choose his allegiance and to embrace a relationship of obedience and protection with the reigning monarch had arguably become even more critical. Although the "volitional" nature of allegiance and citizenship in the late-eighteenth-century American context has been contrasted with the "indelible" character of British subjecthood, treaties and responses to treaties provide important evidence that many subjects and administrators, in fact, viewed British subject status as one that might also be chosen.[77]

Second, the understanding of subjecthood that emerged outside the common law courts suggested that subject status was shifting and transient. On the one hand, this contrasted directly with the dominant reading of *Calvin v. Smith*, with the several passages in which Coke and others referred to subject status as unalienable and perpetual.[78] In the colonies, where French subjects often became British, and British subjects sometimes became Spanish, the idea that subjecthood was impermanent gained traction. In 1756, for example, Consul Hyde Parker indicated that Minorcans, once identified as subjects, should not be reclaimed as such since their countrymen had failed to support the British during the French capture of Minorca that same year.[79]

Parker's reading of subjecthood diverged significantly from those passages where Coke or Ellesmere had argued that allegiance could not be severed. Minorcans, according to Parker, were now French subjects because they had alienated themselves from the British monarch. It was because colonial administrators like Parker typically relied on a range of other legal sources that they could challenge notions of indelible subjecthood, embracing as subjects many who had once been aliens and defining subjecthood as either temporary or permanent.

On the other hand, local actors sometimes seemed to be developing and extending Cokeian notions of allegiance, particularly those relating to local allegiance. In Calcutta, for example, the judges of the Supreme Court determined on any number of occasions that defendants were "only temporary subjects of the King." They endorsed notions of a subjecthood that evaporated as soon as a foreign inhabitant left the settlement of Calcutta and the protection of the royal court, but they were careful to refer to this as a temporary rather than a natural subject status.[80] Perhaps because they were well schooled in case law, these judges relied directly on Coke's report, among others, even as they chose to adapt his definition of local allegiance to an imperial outpost. The circumstances of the empire thus prompted varied assertions about allegiance and protection: in some territories, subjects might abandon their status or be recognized merely as temporary subjects; in others, subjects could never renounce their original bonds with the monarch. This variety of approaches to allegiance was more attuned to the circumstances of the eighteenth-century overseas empires—where territories and peoples moved in and out of various monarchs' allegiances—and was more responsive to the realities of subject status as experienced by individuals in the British colonies.

Third, although legal scholars have argued that Calvin's Case conferred a uniform subject status across the king's dominions, several of the law officers' reports articulated a contrasting idea that British subjects' rights might vary between territories.[81] The reports drafted by the attorneys and solicitors general in both 1765 and 1768 concurred that Catholic subjects in the conquered and ceded colonies were not liable to the same penalties as Catholics elsewhere. If inhabitants of the empire were classified as subjects, they were nonetheless subjects whose rights varied from those of their co-religionists within the realm. The king's legal servants formulated a definition of subjecthood that allowed for British subjects in England to have one set of rights, whereas British subjects in the ceded colonies might have another. As administrators would discover, differential rights were essential to accommodating the diverse peoples of the empire. They allowed administrators to reward some inhabitants with specific privileges without worrying that these would be extended throughout the globe and constructed as the rights of subjects more universally.

The fact that case law simultaneously focused on allegiance and protection, but did not establish their specific contours or limits, opened up possibilities. Often finding themselves unable to respond to questions regarding subject status by relying strictly on case law, administrators looked to other sources in which subjecthood became increasingly flexible and expansive. Ambiguity and uncertainty fostered the emergence of other, more inclusive interpretations of subjecthood in the British Empire. Coexisting, sometimes even conflicting, legal interpretations of subjecthood in turn enabled inhabitants of conquered and ceded territories, as well as those born within the king's dominions, to seek recognition as British subjects. They played a central role in struggles over the boundaries and the protections of subject status more generally. Just as many shaped legal understandings of subjecthood in the eighteenth century, so, too, would many become a legal part of the post-1763 empire.

WHAT BECAME OF Lorenzo Canippa and Vincenzo Fiallo, the two captives about whom Nathaniel Davison remained so unsure? Were they ultimately regarded as subjects despite the fact that neither of them had been born within the monarch's allegiance? In their particular case, the archival trail grows cold, leaving us to wonder whether they spent the rest of their lives in captivity. There are, however, countless other individuals whose struggles can be resuscitated from colonial records and whose stories reveal the range of paths to subjecthood for those living in the British Empire after 1763.

As colonial administrators charged with governing the numerous conquered and ceded territories sought answers about the subject status of new peoples, they did sometimes refer explicitly to the decisions of the common law courts, which had considered the boundaries of subjecthood since the early seventeenth century. The definition of subjecthood consistently upheld in case law—one that considered as subjects all those who were born within the allegiance of the monarch of England—had the virtue of accommodating inhabitants throughout the empire and worked to facilitate an empire where subjects might be physically dispersed but remain bound together by their allegiance to the reigning monarch. Nonetheless, a diversity of ideas relating to subject status and its associated rights circulated during this period, emerging both in London and in the colonies themselves, surfacing within and without the formal system of courts, and shaped both by those familiar and unfamiliar with case law. Colonial administrators joined a range of legal practitioners in determining who was or was not a British subject and in responding to conflicts that involved subjects' rights. Their voices and interpretations often affected local outcomes more directly than the opinions of the traditional and distant judiciary. From these other actors, better positioned to respond to local circumstances, new and at times even more inclusive definitions of subjecthood emerged. The space of empire ultimately left colonial administrators with significant room to maneuver.

Traditional analyses of subjecthood, which have relied largely on distinctions based on case law alone, have been unable to capture the multivalence of the eighteenth-century legal world or to address the complexities of subject status. This is also true, however, of a history that fails to analyze how popular ideas about subjects' rights shaped and intersected with legal understandings of subjecthood. If subjecthood was a legal matter, it was also an issue debated on an everyday level in Britain and the British Empire. Moreover, in the absence of precise legal codification of subjects' rights in case law or elsewhere, subjects themselves discovered that they had ample room to maneuver and to assert all kinds of privileges. Uncertainties and inconsistencies in the laws of subjecthood arguably went hand-in-hand with the many rights popularly associated with subject status. In turn, the long-standing tradition of declaring subjects' rights, which is the focus of the next chapter, may simultaneously have made it increasingly difficult to pinpoint the rights of subjects in law or to specify the legal contours of subject status. At the very least, it meant that many in the empire were well versed in demanding privileges and were eager to avail themselves of their relationship to the monarch in making those claims. Between the array of legal understandings and the range of popular ideas about subjects' rights, inhabitants and administrators learned that subjecthood was as much an opportunity for them as it was a matter for legal experts.

2

The Free-born Subject's Inheritance

BRITONS WERE PROUD of their freedoms and often believed themselves to be unusually blessed. Nowhere was this more evident than in the many published commentaries on British liberties. As the author of *British Liberties, or the Free-Born Subject's Inheritance* (1766) wrote, "at present we live under a government, the most perfect in Europe, where being securely landed ourselves we behold the shipwreck of our neighbours; it is the indispensable interest and duty of every true Briton to maintain those privileges, which have been conveyed to us from our ancestors."[1] A few years earlier, *A Critical Review of the Liberties of British Subjects* (1750) had displayed similar sentiments, claiming that "every member of our Community has an indefeasible, hereditary Right to Liberties and Priviledges beyond those of any People upon Earth . . . as far as we excel all other Subjects in Liberty."[2] British rights, liberties, and privileges were superior to those of all other peoples, such treatises argued, and British subjects were responsible for protecting them from any encroachment or threat. Nor were these sentiments expressed only by Britons; both the Baron de Montesquieu and Voltaire believed England to be peculiarly free and its subjects endowed with unusual liberties.[3]

Voltaire famously wrote of the "great Charter which is consider'd as the sacred origin of the English Liberties."[4] Many of the authors who extolled British liberty drew readers' attention to a range of written documents that had been instrumental in securing much-vaunted privileges. Whether these observers cited Magna Carta, the Bill of Rights, or treatises produced in the seventeenth and eighteenth centuries, they praised a rich and varied history of declaring rights. Declarations might appear as humble petitions to the crown, might be cast as statute, might be framed as "declarations of liberties and privileges," or might be discussed in pamphlets that circulated widely. Some were made official by parliamentary enactments, whereas others, though never enforceable, remained etched in the hearts and minds of constituents, inevitably shaping their views about subjects' rights more generally.[5]

But if declarations were intended to "make clear" a set of proposals, and pamphlets purported to catalog subjects' rights for the general public, the astounding variety of such documents provides ample evidence that no single declaration had definitively resolved the matter of subjects' liberties.[6] One author, who praised the 1689 Bill of Rights as "useful and good," nonetheless lamented that it had been "too generally expressed." It seemed that even this famous statute, often thought to have preserved subjects' time-honored rights after 1689, required some elucidation.[7] Similar comments were made during the eighteenth century. In the 1760s, Massachusetts' agent to London, William Bollan, planned to write a book establishing "the native, equal and permanent rights of the colonists against all Opponents," but he found assembling the necessary facts and arguments so challenging that he never completed the task.[8] His contemporaries, including Benjamin Franklin and Thomas Hutchinson, also wished for some definitive overview of subjects' rights and duties.[9] Others readily admitted that to the much-vaunted natural rights of Britons, "no precise idea seems to have been affixed."[10] By 1792, Francis Plowden, an English Jesuit perhaps best known for his sympathies with Ireland and with Catholic emancipation, noted that "no subject . . . ever produced such a variety of discussions, dissertations, and arguments" as the rights of Englishmen.[11] While eighteenth-century observers agreed that British subjects possessed an unusual number of rights, there were few who could agree on what, exactly, those were.

British subjects never seemed to tire of proclaiming their staggering range of "rights," "liberties," and "privileges." In fact, many believed that rights were secure only when spoken and written. Franklin's concern that "we might know what we are & what we have, what our Rights and what our Duties," was shared by others.[12] While some commentators felt that enumerating rights might actually be dangerous, this was typically because they believed that specifying a set of rights necessarily signaled the omission of others and might ultimately limit those available to individuals.[13] But in general, the act of articulating rights was viewed as essential to their preservation.

By analyzing some of the most historically significant declarations of rights, this chapter identifies the recurrent characteristics associated with popular understandings of British subjecthood. The rights cherished by subjects varied across time and place, changing with the needs and circumstances of the individuals who claimed them. The right to petition was viewed as a foundational right by those who wrote *Jura Populi Anglicani* (1701) or

The Rights of the People to Petition (1769) because it allowed subjects not only to express grievances but also to articulate additional rights before the crown or other officials. While some subjects were preoccupied by trial by jury, others focused on the right to representation. And as Britons traveled to the overseas colonies, their declarations demonstrated increasing concern with the right to freedom of conscience or to public meeting. Considering a variety of published declarations reveals how rights were at once astoundingly varied and also intertwined with historical circumstance, local imperatives, and the experiences of those who proposed them.

Regardless of form, most of the declarations produced in the British Isles and empire foregrounded the central relationship of allegiance between subjects and sovereign. Inhabitants and administrators lived in an empire where a personal relationship with the sovereign and a belief in the monarch's protection had long been integral to the fabric of everyday life. British subjects typically claimed their rights, liberties, and privileges as dependent subjects of the king, which worked to differentiate British declarations from those penned by American and French revolutionaries. British declarations were also marked by a persistent and significant tension: most implied that it was the king who granted or upheld certain protections, even as declarations themselves were quite clearly the result of individuals coming together to proclaim their rights. Monarchs were legitimizers of rights, liberties, and privileges, at the same time as those very rights, liberties, and privileges might need to be demanded and shielded from royal power. This tension suggests that British subjects were fusing an older language of privilege stemming from the monarch's protection with an emerging language of intrinsic rights and that the bond between subject and sovereign remained relevant during decades when powerful new ideas about natural rights had also begun to surface.

Finally, published declarations testify to a long tradition of writing and debating rights that flourished across Britain and its empire despite the otherwise notorious absence of a "written constitution." Just as multiple legal interpretations of subjecthood coexisted during the seventeenth and eighteenth centuries, lay understandings of the rights of subjects also abounded. Far from discouraging individuals from making claims, lack of consensus about the meanings of subjecthood merely seems to have precipitated further demands for rights. Moreover, both parliamentary and popular disquisitions on rights suggest that privileges were inconsistently claimed and that the rights deemed "fundamental" had waxed and waned well before they were contested in the colonies after the Seven Years' War. These published declarations ultimately provide a critical foundation for understanding how and why subjects throughout the empire were often themselves able to demand and secure a range of rights.

Declaring Rights

The seventeenth and eighteenth centuries were in many respects the pinnacle for declaring and claiming rights in Britain and the British Empire. Through both official and unofficial channels and in an astonishing number of commentaries, contemporaries struggled to articulate the seemingly limitless number of rights of free-born subjects. Nonetheless, the document that serves as the point of departure in any discussion of rights is Magna Carta (1215). This foundational text was referenced by almost all seventeenth- and eighteenth-century pamphlets detailing subjects' rights and shaped the form of later statutes and published declarations. Even if Magna Carta was endowed with its almost mythical status only because of later declarations of rights, the settlement of 1215 remains crucial to understanding this subsequent history.[14]

In its very framing, Magna Carta offered a powerful reminder of the interconnections between monarchy and rights in British history. Although the document had the appearance of a negotiated settlement and compact between King John and his disenchanted barons, the central role of the king in confirming baronial liberties was evident throughout (figure 2.1). And while the barons actively extracted concessions from the king in exchange for their loyalty, the relationship of allegiance, obedience, and protection shaped the production of this agreement. The settlement began with the king "granting . . . all the liberties written below" on the advice of his loyal subjects and closed with a reminder that concessions were given by the royal hand at Runnymede. Most of its clauses dealt with the barons' specific grievances under the feudal system and against the king, with an emphasis on rights of inheritance, guardianship, and service for feudal lands. Concerns about mismanagement by royal officials were reflected in the clauses dealing with royal forests and with debts. Several clauses addressed the mobility of persons within the king's territories—the right of men to leave and return to the kingdom without harm and the right of merchants to travel freely for the purposes of trade. Most of what was enumerated in Magna Carta reflected the liberties believed to exist and to be essential at the time—but these were liberties that stemmed from the barons' relationship with the monarch and from their place in the feudal order. In an initial analysis, it remains difficult to see in Magna Carta a general declaration of fundamental liberties for all subjects.[15]

FIGURE 2.1 *King John Signing the Magna Carta in 1215*, 1872, engraving. Courtesy of the Victorian Picture Library.

Two clauses, however, would particularly resonate with subsequent generations—one relating to the administration of justice and another relating to judgment by one's peers. Clause 39, which stated that "no free man shall be seized or imprisoned, or stripped of his rights or possessions, or outlawed or exiled, or deprived of his standing in any other way, nor will we proceed with force against him, or send others to do so, except by the lawful judgement of his equals or by the law of the land," was probably intended to confirm the baronial right not to be tried by inferiors. However, it would become an essential precedent for those who argued for the sacred right of trial by jury. Another clause, omitted from reissues of the charter, stated that "no scutage or aid may be levied in our kingdom without its general consent," which was often radically interpreted by later generations to suggest that taxes might not be levied without the consent of the people.[16]

Not only would liberties promised in 1215 reappear in later declarations of rights, but Magna Carta also inaugurated a tradition of casting concessions awarded as rights already in existence rather than as rights recently granted. The first clause, for example, confirmed the existing freedom of the Church, stating: "it shall have its rights undiminished, and its liberties unimpaired." More generally, Magna Carta purported to grant "customs and liberties," implying that it was enforcing customary law rather than proposing radical legal amendments. Whether these were liberties that stemmed from a previous monarch's grant or from time immemorial was open to interpretation.[17] Rights were thus framed as unchanging—already the subject's due rather than newly imagined. Such a rhetorical and strategic move suggested that the king was choosing to uphold long-standing privileges rather than that the barons had managed to extract novel concessions from their sovereign. In this, Magna Carta was the first of many declarations that proclaimed rights to be "ancient" and "indisputable" when they were, in fact, often highly contentious.

Over the course of the seventeenth century, numerous other individuals would rely on the relationship between subject and sovereign and on references to time-honored liberties as they proclaimed rights. The documents they produced would also remain embedded in the popular memory, repeatedly cited by commentators as having irrevocably established the liberties of the people and regarded as part of a common tradition that began in 1215. Two, well-known and frequently cited, merit further discussion: the 1628 Petition of Right and the 1689 Declaration of Rights. They are particularly significant because of a key tension they reveal between subjects claiming liberties as part of a dependent relationship with the monarch and subjects actively negotiating rights.

The Petition of Right was the result of a struggle between the monarch and members of Parliament.[18] It originated as a protest against arbitrary governance by Charles I, lodging complaints against his means of collecting revenues, his prosecution of individuals unwilling or unable to pay those revenues, and his decision to quarter soldiers among civilians. After due consideration, the House of Commons decided that the king was more likely to accept and hear a petition than he was the bill that had initially been proposed; their decision reflected an ongoing calculation about how best to secure royal assent.[19] Choosing to approach the king by petition of right had a very specific meaning. As historian Elizabeth Foster has argued, when Parliament chose to proceed in this way, it was "not asking for leave to proceed at common law to prove a right, but for confirmation by the King of what it conceived had already been demonstrated to be a right."[20]

This suggests two additional points about the relationship between subjects and sovereign in the process of declaring rights. First, while the Petition of Right was worded more boldly than other more deferential and obsequious petitions, it nevertheless reinforced the hierarchical relationship between sovereign and subjects. Precisely because they were a form steeped in languages of loyalty and submission, petitions were effective in asserting the rights and liberties of subjects.[21] The address of 1628, which placed Charles I in the position of power by appealing to him directly, also ensured that members of Parliament were in the subordinate role of subjects who must "humbly show" and "humbly pray" that the king confirm the rights they enumerated. While they challenged royal abuses and actively declared their rights, petitioners in 1628 recognized the crown's role in upholding those liberties. Moreover, as they presented their grievances in a language shrouded in humility, members of Parliament made several radical claims about the rights of the free-born subject: they declared that subjects were free from taxation without the consent of Parliament; free from having companies of soldiers and mariners billeted among them against their will; and entitled to judgment according to the due process of law and by one's peers. Some of these rights echoed the clauses of Magna Carta and were potentially very broad, but others remained rights circumscribed by the grievances and circumstances of elite men of government. Nonetheless, the Petition of Right entered the official record, as well as popular memory, and the rights to which it referred were widely believed to be those due all free-born subjects of the monarch.

Second, the Petition of Right also consistently sought redress for violation of existing rights. The phrasing of the Petition's final paragraph provides an illustrative example of this tradition: petitioners concluded by beseeching the monarch for "their rights and liberties according to the laws and statutes of this realm," suggesting that the rights demanded merely recapitulated ones already codified by law. Moreover, the Petition's opening lines referred to the "inherited freedom" of remaining free from taxes "not set by common consent in parliament," and its third clause spoke very specifically of the rights established by "the Great Charter of Liberties of England," relying on this historic document to establish the antiquity of certain rights. As in 1215, the decision in 1628 to cast the rights sought as existing rather than as new ultimately made these claims seem more conservative than radical. The document also encapsulated a fundamental tension: members of Parliament sought monarchical confirmation of their liberties even as they acted as a group to describe those liberties as ancient and inherited.

If the Petition of Right possessed less force in law than did a statute,[22] the 1689 Declaration of Rights posed no such problems.[23] This declaration was written under very different circumstances, following Prince William of Orange's invasion of England and James II's ignominious flight into exile. A Convention Parliament met and eventually drafted an agreement by which the monarchy would be jointly invested in William and Mary and by which all subsequent monarchs would be expected to govern. During their discussions, members of Parliament used various terms to describe the document they were drafting, including "petition," "address," and "declaration." After several rounds of debate, they eventually settled on "declaration," to give the document added "political force and moral suasion."[24] Initially, the document received William's assent, though not his signature. It would, however, be enacted as the Bill of Rights by Parliament and then as the Act of Rights once it finally received the royal seal.

Like several of its predecessors, the Declaration of Rights was shaped by long-standing conflicts with the reigning monarch and by a quest for certain essential liberties. Its opening lines accused the late King James II of endeavoring to "Subvert and Extirpate the Protestant Religion, and the Laws and Liberties of this Kingdom." Drafters of this declaration determined that allegiance to future monarchs would be contingent upon their protecting a specific set of rights; indeed, members of this Convention Parliament declared William and Mary to be the legitimate "King and Queen" because they had confidence that the Prince of Orange would "preserve them from the violation of their Rights." Although the Declaration of Rights reflected Parliament's increasing ability to influence the course of the succession, it also confirmed that proclamations relating to rights were still compacts with the monarch. For the declaration to gain legitimacy, it needed William's assent. For it to be enacted as statute and as an official statement of rights, a royal signature was required. The Declaration of Rights may have inaugurated a new era of king-ruling-in-Parliament, but it simultaneously embodied the tradition of seeking monarchical confirmation of subjects' rights.

Not unlike the barons at Runnymede or the Commons of 1628, members of the Convention Parliament maintained that they had assembled "in the first place (as their Ancestors in like Case have usually done) for the Vindicating and Asserting their Ancient Rights and Liberties." Drawing on another long-standing practice, the Convention Parliament described the rights violated and subverted by James II as "ancient" rather than as new. Several of the liberties they asserted in 1689—including their attack on the illegality of the king's suspending laws, raising an army within the kingdom, and levying money for the use of the crown without the consent of Parliament—followed the tradition of Magna Carta and the Petition of Right. Others were less familiar. Clauses relating to the free election of members of Parliament and to freedom of speech in regularly held parliamentary debates, as well as those relating to the empaneling of juries and Protestants bearing arms, introduced as "undoubted rights" privileges that had not been the focus of previous grants.[25]

Despite casting the rights described as "ancient," the Declaration of Rights undeniably reflected the changing landscape of the seventeenth century. The increasing concern with freedom of speech and with securing Parliament from royal control loomed large in the wake of royal attempts to curtail Parliament. Additionally, the only clause that referred explicitly to a "right of Subjects" was related to petitioning the king, which had come under attack in the seventeenth century. A long-cherished right in the popular conscience, the right to petition had been abrogated by Restoration statutes such as the 1661 Tumultuous Petitioning Act, which limited the number of individuals who could sign petitions. Earlier declarations of rights had not always made reference to petitions, but in 1689, members of Parliament did so explicitly. Moreover, the Declaration's combination of declarative verbs, used to present certain rights as proven and established, with conditional verbs, used to imply that some rights were desirable and intended rather than already confirmed, was significant.[26] If the document claimed to enumerate the "undoubted Rights and Liberties" of subjects of the realm, its language suggests that drafters did recognize that some of the rights they sought to make part of statute were novel, even quite radical. The Declaration of 1689 drew on earlier traditions and languages: it was framed as a compact between a new sovereign and Parliament, one that necessarily still rested on monarchical confirmation of rights, at the same time as those assembled asserted both "ancient" and "intended" rights.

A third seventeenth-century declaration sits somewhat uneasily with the argument that liberties were sought from, and negotiated with, the reigning monarch. Originally written in 1647 as part of an attempt to "knit army and civilian radicalism together," the Agreement of the People ultimately became the focus of the Leveller movement and was republished in both December 1648 and May 1649, the latter a few months after Charles I's trial and execution.[27] Although it rarely figured in the pantheon of documents said to have established liberties by the eighteenth century, the Agreement of the People (1649) can be seen as firmly enmeshed within the tradition of declaring rights; a number of the rights to which it referred echoed those of earlier declarations, just as many of its clauses would appear in subsequent declarations.[28] Perhaps most important, the Agreement demonstrated that declarations were not merely the province of the high-born or politically powerful.[29] More than any of its predecessors, it proved that anyone might "agree and declare" to certain rights and seek to have them recognized by the nation.

Diverging from declarations that looked to the reigning monarch for confirmation of individual rights, the Agreement still shared many of their conventions, suggesting that rights were part of a compact, or agreement, between parties, and choosing to cast those rights as time-honored. Signatories, who initially addressed Parliament as the guarantor of rights, eventually decided to tender "a peace-offering to this distressed Nation," framing the Agreement as a "settlement" to restore peace and prosperity and to "make this Nation Free and Happy." The use of the term "agreement" was significant, since this lacked the humility of a petition. It evoked the sense of a community, since an agreement typically signaled that a group of individuals had come together for a specific purpose and were acting in unison.[30] The Agreement of 1649 did resemble traditional compacts in its presentation, but it was a compact in which "the free people" agreed to abolish all arbitrary power and set limits on government in order to restore peace. What ultimately made this settlement revolutionary was that it was drawn up between "the free People of England, to whom God hath given hearts, means and opportunity to effect the same," rather than between subjects and their sovereign.

The Agreement continued to cast some of the rights it demanded as already extant, and a number of its clauses resonated with articles penned in 1628 or 1689. It aimed for "the preservation of those safe guards . . . contained in the Petition of Right, made and enacted in the third year of the late King," suggesting that its authors saw themselves as part of a longer tradition that harkened back to at least 1628. Other clauses forbade the raising of armies without the consent of "the representatives," evoking ever-present concerns about billeting and standing armies. Several reiterated that Parliament could not convict individuals and that all inhabitants were subject to the same law; clause 25 echoed statements about juries, arguing that "conviction of life, limb, liberty, or estate" might only happen by "twelve sworn men of the Neighbor-hood." Still another asserted that Parliament could not make laws hindering "persons, from trading or merchandizing into any place beyond the Seas, where any of this Nation are free to Trade," likely reflecting Magna Carta's earlier concern with mobility, as well as the growing attention paid to trade over the course of the seventeenth century.

The vast majority of the Agreement's clauses, however, related to the particular circumstances of the mid-seventeenth century. Those touching the calling and holding of free Parliaments reflected this body's increasing importance, as well as the idea that it might need to be monitored in order to secure the rights and liberties of the people. Several clauses aimed to place limits on the powers granted to Parliament. In addition, some of the most radical clauses concerned freedom of religion, with one proposing that even dissenters should be allowed to serve in positions of trust: "they shall not disable any person from bearing any office in the Common-wealth, for any opinion or practice in Religion, excepting such as maintain the Popes (or other forraign) Supremacy." Such provisions reflected the dissensions and persecutions of the English Civil War (1642–1651), and several clauses were thus an early statement of freedom of conscience. Overall, the diversity of liberties declared in 1649 reflected both an enduring tradition of declaring rights as well as the fact that the subject's rights were determined by time and by the circumstances of those who claimed them.

Thus, by the end of the seventeenth century, a rather "formidable array of liberties of the subject" was already articulated in documents produced by elite men, many of whom were key players in the various political and constitutional struggles of the era.[31] The bond of allegiance described so famously by Lord Coke in 1608 had shaped the production and framing of these declarations of rights, even as it was subtly challenged. Subjects pronounced their loyalty in almost every written declaration of rights, and unlike the American Declaration of Independence, which was itself a powerful statement of rights and was profoundly shaped by its British precursors, most British declarations did not challenge or break with the crown. Rather, those who drafted declarations typically evoked a covenant between monarch and subject to lay claim to an array of rights, with a significant exception to be found in the Agreement of 1649.

As they appealed to the king's sense of benevolence, subjects tended to accept that his goodwill was instrumental in recognizing their liberties. By acknowledging their fundamental dependence on their sovereign, those who enumerated the "rights of Englishmen" were able to avail themselves of the language of protection and privilege. In exchange for their obedience, subjects very clearly sought the rights, liberties, and privileges understood to flow from the monarch's protection. In *A Complete History of England* (1685), Robert Brady would insist that "all the Liberties and Priviledges the People can Pretend to, were Derived from the Crown," making a familiar argument that rights stemmed from the royal person.[32] Although Brady certainly had his detractors, it was not uncommon, particularly after the Restoration, to argue that the ancient rights of Englishmen had somehow been granted or confirmed by the monarch.[33] Many others believed that it was the monarch's coronation oath that implied "a public solemn recognition of the fundamental rights of the people" by the king, an oath that foregrounded the monarch's role in guaranteeing certain rights.[34] Whether they proposed that the royal person was the source of privileges, or embraced a more measured belief that the king protected time-honored liberties, Britons acknowledged that monarchy and rights were intertwined.[35]

Declarations of rights also revealed that a relationship of dependence hardly rendered its subjects passive. Indeed, they foregrounded subjects' roles in securing privileges. The full title of the Declaration of Rights (1689), for example, was "The Declaration of the Lords Spiritual and Temporal, and Commons Assembled at Westminster," underlining the part played by a Parliament assembled together in the struggle for rights. Other declarations of rights, like the Agreement of the People (1649), would be made by "the free people of England," suggesting that a range of individuals, regardless of social status or political credentials, might be actively involved in shaping the rights demanded. As a recent British Library book has shown, Britons of all classes, religious persuasions, genders, and races have contributed to the broader struggle for political, social, and economic rights over the course of time.[36] Declarations also reveal that loyal subjects often sought to revise the rights associated with their status, by asserting that certain liberties were "ancient" or "indisputable," and implying that they were beyond the power of the monarch to rescind. They worked to establish continuity with the past, making potentially radical demands seem less threatening to authorities or to the constituents to whom they were addressed. By electing to cast certain rights as "ancient" and "indisputable," subjects gave them rhetorical and political force in an era when uncertainty still reigned about what the subject's protections actually were. Ultimately, they drew on their relationship with the monarch, as well as on sources like statutes and customs to give their rights the additional weight of history.

If Magna Carta, the Petition of Right, the Declaration of Rights, and the Agreement of the People provide a sense of the tensions within declarations and the range of subjects' rights proclaimed at the official level, the pamphlet literature of the seventeenth and eighteenth centuries and the numerous charters of liberties produced in the colonies highlight the communities of subjects who drafted their own charters and declarations. The rights proclaimed in 1215, 1628, 1649, or 1689 would echo through these other published sources, but so, too, would new ones, as circumstances changed and subjects began to make additional demands.

Popularizing Rights

When historian Forrest McDonald cataloged the "rights of Englishmen" as they stood on the eve of 1775, he relied largely on an array of statutes to identify contemporary understandings of those rights. To familiar ideas about rights to private property and freedom from coerced taxation, McDonald added numerous other rights relating to pasturage, estover, and hunting, rights that are not to be found in the declarations examined thus far.[37] And to his list, still others might have been appended. Those combing Magna Carta or the Declaration of Rights to glean a concrete understanding of why Britons claimed the rights they did have often been stymied in apprehending the "rights of free-born subjects." This is because statutes were not the only places where "ancient liberties" were articulated and enshrined, and because other published sources are essential to providing a fuller picture of popular understandings of subjects' rights.

Commentaries on Britons' rights proliferated in the seventeenth and eighteenth centuries because, regardless of whether they had been confirmed by case law or statute, these rights were believed to be part of the "free-born subject's inheritance" and believed to require protection and elucidation. The existence of such treatises reveals that rights were debated not only within the halls of Parliament but that they were also actively proposed by a range of literate persons in forms ranging from thin pamphlets to massive tomes. Some began by defending particular causes, whereas others were intended to be general overviews of subjects' liberties. They were written as popular guidebooks to rights and as more technical exposés of law. Their numbers and diversity are staggering.[38] Nevertheless, their common emphasis on a vast and vague set of rights passed down from Magna Carta, the Petition of Right, and the Declaration of Rights makes them part of a far longer tradition in which individuals leveraged their subject status to lay claim to new rights at the same time as they relied on history and the "ancient constitution" to do so.

Most treatises aimed to catalog the rights, liberties, privileges, franchises, and immunities due the free-born subject. Commentators promised their readers a succinct and definitive statement of their "divers" or "fundamental" liberties, perhaps attempting to do what contemporaries imagined a Bill of Rights ought to have done. William Penn, for example, explained that his chief goal was to secure "the information and understanding (what is their native right and inheritance) of such who may not have leisure from their Plantations to read large volumes."[39] Readers looked to authors like Penn to synthesize tomes of information about the state of subjects' rights and to present it in an accessible, abbreviated form.

Most authors also provided lengthy overviews of statutes that had rendered liberties sacrosanct. It is in these "histories of law" that the symbolic force of earlier declarations becomes clear and that the resounding importance of declaring rights is manifest. In many editions of *British Liberties, or the Free-born Subject's Inheritance,* the preface announced the author's wish to compile "together in one view those laws that form the basis of our liberties" (figure 2.2). He proceeded to offer a history and commentary on Magna Carta, the Declaration of Right, the Petition of Right, the Law of Appeals of Parliaments, the Habeas Corpus Act, the laws relative to Papists and Protestant Dissenters, and "other statutes in confirmation of the liberties of the subject."[40] Similarly, *A Guide to the Knowledge of the Rights and Privileges of Englishmen* argued that "the surest guide to the knowledge of English Liberty are those very Laws in which the fundamental Rights and Privileges of Englishmen are contained," and also provided an overview of "Magna Charta, the Habeas Corpus Act, The Bill of Rights, and The Act of Settlement."[41] As authors penned these summaries, they ensured that subjects' numerous privileges were regularly put before the public.

Authors hoped that their legal histories would familiarize readers with ancestral struggles for liberty, thereby inspiring them to safeguard that inheritance. Some wrote dramatically of "our brave Ancestors" who "spared neither Blood, nor Treasure in their Defence" at moments when "inestimable privileges" had come under attack. They relied on the language of heroic sacrifice to underline the difficulties with which freedoms had been won, referring to how predecessors had offered "the best and choicest Blood in the Kingdom to the Shrine of Liberty, that we their Posterity might be free and happy."[42]

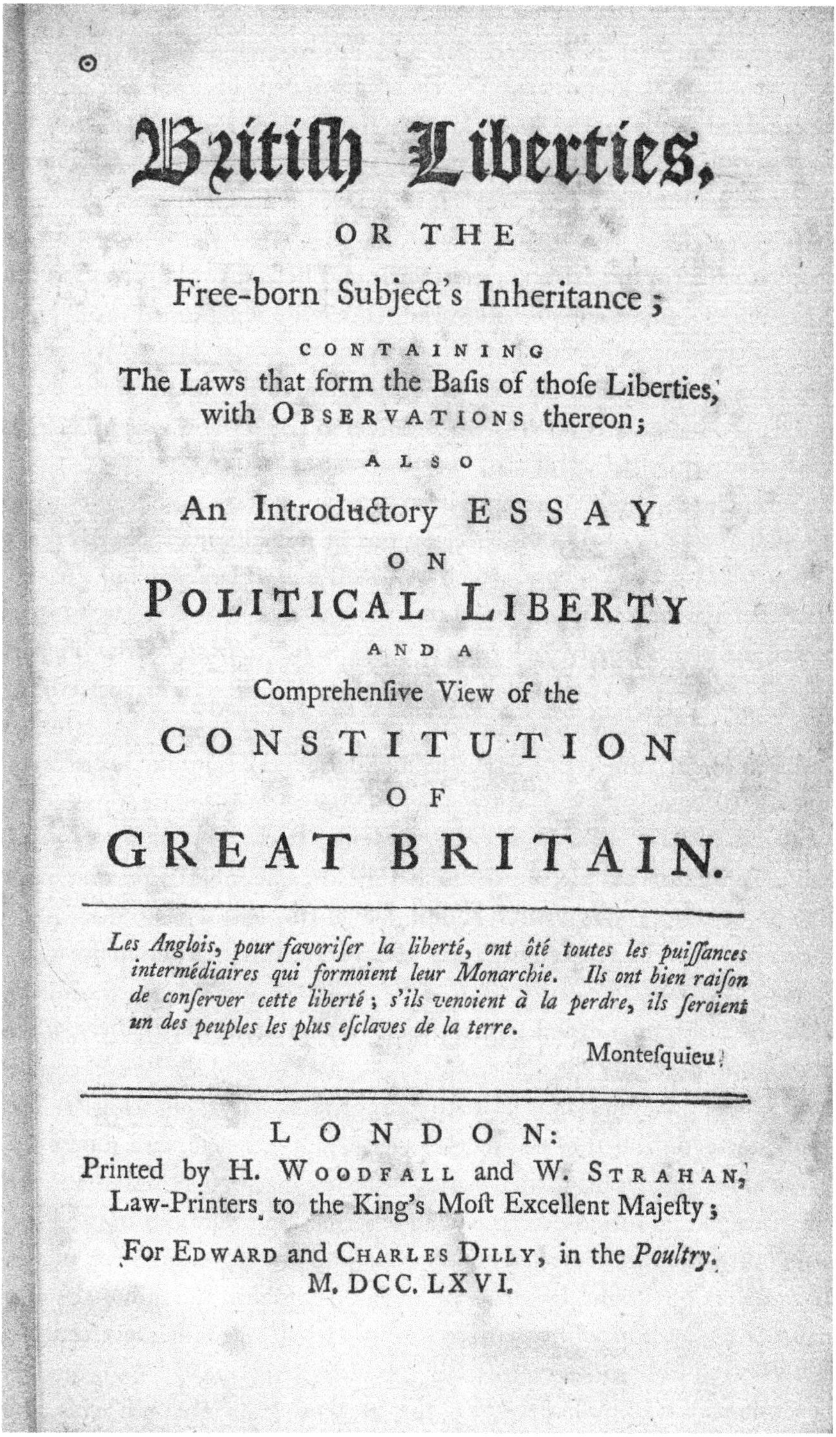

British Liberties,

OR THE

Free-born Subject's Inheritance;

CONTAINING

The Laws that form the Baſis of thoſe Liberties, with OBSERVATIONS thereon;

ALSO

An Introductory ESSAY

ON

POLITICAL LIBERTY

AND A

Comprehenſive View of the

CONSTITUTION

OF

GREAT BRITAIN.

Les Anglois, pour favoriſer la liberté, ont ôté toutes les puiſſances intermédiaires qui formoient leur Monarchie. Ils ont bien raiſon de conſerver cette liberté; s'ils venoient à la perdre, ils ſeroient un des peuples les plus eſclaves de la terre.

Monteſquieu.

LONDON:

Printed by H. WOODFALL and W. STRAHAN, Law-Printers to the King's Moſt Excellent Majeſty;

For EDWARD and CHARLES DILLY, in the *Poultry*.

M. DCC. LXVI.

FIGURE 2.2 Title page, *British Liberties, or the Free-born Subject's Inheritance*. London: Woodfall and Strahan, 1766. Courtesy of Houghton Library, Harvard University (Br 67.25 Lobby IV.2.21).

Penn wrote in 1687, "it is easy to part with or give away great privileges, but hard to be gained, if once lost. And therefore all depends upon our prudent care and actings to preserve and lay sure foundations for ourselves and the posterity of our loins."[43] Penn followed his own admonishments, drawing up a frame of government for Pennsylvania that was designed to protect some of those very rights. Other authors sounded even stronger warnings, exhorting people to reform the existing government and defend the constitution lest their time-honored rights be destroyed. One writer envisioned the "united body of free-born subjects standing forth in support of their privileges."[44] Regardless of individual authors' political agendas, the result of these collected pamphlets was to confirm that subjects had rights worthy of protection and defense.

Seventeenth- and eighteenth-century commentaries on rights echo the characteristics of previous declarations of rights. Some, like Brady's *A Complete History of England*, which was dedicated to James II and a particularly partisan account, continued to stress the connections between royal power and rights. Brady took Magna Carta to be "the sum of the liberties desired," even as he emphasized that "all these liberties and laws were the Grants and Concessions of our Ancient King."[45] He recognized a longer tradition of declaring rights just as he highlighted the centrality of the relationship between subject and sovereign. Other authors focused instead on the distinctiveness of the "rights of Englishmen" and on the subject's "birthright." Penn, for example, wrote of "that inestimable inheritance that every Free-born Subject of England is heir unto by Birth-right, I mean that unparalleled privilege of Liberty and Property, beyond all the Nations in the world beside."[46] *A Critical Review of the Liberties of British Subjects* (1750) similarly spoke of the "unparalleled Constitution" which secured the "lives, liberties, and properties of the Subjects,"[47] while *The Rights of the People Asserted* (1783) echoed Penn's claims by stating that the Britannic constitution "has been esteemed the best of all others, because, in its genuine state, it best preserves to the subject his natural rights."[48] If these authors praised a hallowed constitution that surpassed those of all other nations, they also stressed that that constitution protected rights, liberties, and privileges that were, in fact, the subject's birthright, by virtue of being born within the monarch's allegiance. Even authors without Brady's overtly royalist agenda suggested that rights flowed from subject status.

Commentaries emphasized, too, the "ancient" and "inherited" character of the rights they discussed. Authors routinely implied that they were cataloging long-established privileges for their readers' information rather than introducing new ones. William Prynne argued that his treatise had "sufficiently proved . . . the ancient, hereditary Rights, Liberties, Franchises, Priviledges . . . properly called Fundamental." He also referred to "prudent ancestors in former ages" whose work it had been to declare and instantiate those rights.[49] Another author, evoking the irrefutable nature of historical documents that had stood the test of time, noted: "noble Progenitors found it necessary to have them put into the Order they are now in, that they may be standing Records to Posterity of those Rights and Privileges."[50] By making claims about ancient and ancestral privileges, commentators placed themselves within a well-honed tradition; like the authors of other declarations, they evoked the time-honored nature of rights in order to imbue them with the legitimizing weight of history. References to the "ancient constitution" thus surfaced alongside references to the subject's intensely personal relationship to the monarch.

Finally, published commentaries are essential to both parsing the diverse rights British subjects might have claimed existed and to tracing which rights seemed to attract the most attention over time. Although each author purported to catalog the rights of subjects, each chose to emphasize some rights over others. Even those commentators who explicitly claimed to explicate all of the subject's fundamental liberties still focused on a limited number. In his *A Seasonable, Historical, Legal Vindication and Chronological Collection of the good Old Fundamental Liberties, Franchises, Rights, Laws of all English Freemen* (1654), Prynne identified ten of "the chieftest and most considerable of them." The first two rights identified were that no tax could be levied "but only with and by their common consent and Grant, in a free and lawfull Parliament" and that "no freeman of England ought to be arrested . . . without the lawfull Triall, Verdict and Judgment of his Peers, according to the good old Law of the land," both of which echoed claims made in Magna Carta and the Petition of Right. Like others before him, Prynne argued that no laws could be altered nor wars be fought without the "common advice and consent in Parliament," which was to be "duly summoned, and held for the good and safety of the Kingdom every year." In addition, Prynne declared that subjects could not be forced to leave the country during times of war, just as he insisted on the subject's duty to defend the king and the privileges of the realm against traitors and conspiracies.[51] If Prynne attempted to detail the rights of "English freemen," he nonetheless confined his analysis to the ten he believed were most salient.

Elsewhere, *The Rights of the People Asserted* focused on the fundamental right "that the subject can be bound only by those laws to which he consents;

and such consent is given either by himself, or his Representatives, freely and voluntarily chosen." Its author was concerned more immediately with securing a more equal representation in the Irish Parliament, but chose to cast the argument as one that touched on the fundamental rights of the people.[52] Still other commentaries adopted a similar tactic, defending the actions of particular individuals by framing them as broader discussions of rights. *A Critical Review of British Liberties* had as its subtitle "a comparative view of the Proceedings of the H—e of C—s of I—d, against an unfortunate Exile of that Country; who, in contending for the Rights and Liberties of the Publick, lost his own." Arguing that it would be "tedious, if not endless to recount the manifold Advantages accruing to the Subjects of this most excellent Government," the anonymous author chose instead to focus on the rights "most pertinent to my present purpose"—rights to a fair administration of justice, including bail, fair trial, and trial by jury. If anything, this particular "review of liberties" was used to issue a "seasonable warning to all true Whigs and free Britons."[53]

Some authors recognized the impossibility of addressing all of the subjects' many liberties. Penn acknowledged that there were innumerable privileges "declared and expressed in divers Acts of Parliament" and contended that they were "too large to be inserted in this place." In his own commentary, he chose to focus on the "paramount privileges," the "two grand pillars of English liberty": first, that "no new laws bind the people of England, but such as are by common consent agreed on in that great Council [Parliament]" and second, that no man might be "adjudged to lose life, member or estate, but upon the verdict of his Peers or Equals his neighbours, and of his own condition."[54] Similarly, *A Guide to the Knowledge of the Rights and Privileges of Englishmen* offered extensive commentary on various statutes and their provisions, but drew readers' attention to two in particular. The anonymous author repeatedly exhorted "other electors of Members to serve in Parliament" and mused about "the trust, power, and duty of the grand juries of England." He hoped to underscore that the "birth-right of Englishmen shines most conspicuously in two Things:" "Parliaments" and "Juries."[55] References to Parliament and trial by jury as the ultimate guarantors of liberty became increasingly frequent after the late seventeenth century, suggesting that although the subject's relationship to the monarch remained important in declaring rights, the monarch was not the only source of protection.

While the declarations provided essential material for pamphleteers, these commentators popularized and shaped understandings of these declarations and of subjects' rights more generally. Authors like Brady reminded readers of the monarch's role in granting, upholding, and confirming rights, reinforcing the connections between allegiance, protection, and privilege. Others referred to the "ancient," "hereditary," and profoundly "historical" nature of rights, underscoring their allegedly immutable nature. As authors invoked the legacy of Magna Carta, the Petition of Right, the Declaration of Rights, and a range of other statutes, they worked to enshrine them as repositories of rights. They also ensured that key clauses were not forgotten. Whatever the original intent of Magna Carta or the Petition of Right, their value for later generations was that they could be interpreted broadly; it is because interpretations proliferated and were repeatedly validated that a document like Magna Carta has remained a "sacred text, the nearest thing to fundamental statute that English law has ever had."[56]

By addressing themselves to a general, albeit literate, audience, however, seventeenth- and eighteenth-century commentaries advanced the tradition of declaring rights. While Magna Carta represented a royal settlement with the barons of the thirteenth century and the Petition of Right reflected the grievances of specific members of Parliament in the early seventeenth century, many pamphlets would address the rights of free-born subjects more generally. Most evinced a belief that it was the duty of all subjects, regardless of background, social status, or membership in Parliament, to actively declare and defend their liberties. Pamphlets suggested not only that part of the free-born subject's inheritance was a seemingly limitless array of rights but also that subjects were themselves responsible for shaping and protecting those rights. In the words of one author, liberties and rights "ought to be the daily study of every Man in the Kingdom."[57] Subject status had been declared ripe with promise for all those who could prove themselves to be subjects in allegiance to the monarch.

Rights across the Seas

As Britons crossed the seas, they also produced "charters of liberties" in the colonies, carrying with them the rich practices of statutory enactments, parliamentary petitions, and numerous commentaries. These statements of liberties and privileges initially appeared in the first half of the seventeenth century, often shortly after the establishment of new colonies. Colonists participated in the broader tradition of documenting privileges in order to ensure their ongoing existence. Producing these early declarations of rights may, in fact, have provided a way for colonists to cling to what they conceived to be a distinctly English history. As historian Jack Rakove has also argued, the process of settlement "probably encouraged the colonists to seek formal declarations of their rights, in part to clarify their legal status as settlers, and in part to encourage further immigration."[58] Moreover, debates about whether all, or only some, statutes extended to the colonies and about whether statutes issued within the realm had to refer to the specific colonies, may have furthered settlers' desire to claim as their own a long tradition of rights. Written by groups of settlers, or by assemblies and councils as acts that simultaneously established forms of government, colonial declarations of rights demonstrate that the rights of subjects were being articulated throughout the British Empire well before the struggles over subjecthood that emerged after 1763. Indeed, rights, liberties, and privileges were discussed in the colonies during the same era that they were being debated within the realm.[59] Declaring rights was part of the free-born subject's inheritance, wherever he might settle, but as settlers faced the realities of life in the colonies, they also began to propose a further array of new rights.

One of the earliest such documents was the Massachusetts Body of Liberties (1641).[60] Initially drafted by an individual author, it was then sent to various towns for discussion before being enacted by the General Court, the body endowed with lawmaking power by the Massachusetts Bay Company. The Body of Liberties was the work of men who believed that a public statement of rights was the most effective means of limiting government and preventing potential abuses. It was also an excellent example of a tradition in which individuals debated and discussed rights before enacting them. Like contemporaneous statutes for the realm, this colonial code claimed both to declare and to confirm various rights. Its preamble showcased each of these tendencies: the code claimed to "religiously and unanimously decree and confirme these following Rites, liberties, and priveledges concerning our Churches, and Civill State to be respectively impartiallie and inviolably enjoyed and observed throughout our Jurisdiction for ever." Traditional language about confirming existing rights, liberties, and privileges was present, suggesting that Massachusetts was merely making manifest time-honored rights. But so, too, was a new emphasis on the religious nature of the agreement and the importance of the Church's rights, hinting at the decidedly local inflections that might shape declarations of rights.

The Body of Liberties was far longer and more detailed than Magna Carta or the Petition of Right. It was divided into specific sections addressing "liberties more peculiarlie concerning the free men," "liberties of woemen," "liberties of children," "liberties of servants," "liberties of forreiners and strangers," "capital lawes," and "liberties the Lord Jesus hath given to the

Churches." Its lengthy general overview was concerned with fair trial, the choice of a trial by jury or by the bench, the need for all settlers to have access to the same laws, and the importance of adhering only to decrees issued by the General Court, all of which mirrored the preoccupations of earlier declarations. Other clauses enjoined that no man might be compelled to "any publique worke or service unlesse the presse be grounded upon some act of the generall Court," arguing that labor for government be publicly acceded to and acknowledged. Still others addressed land tenure and inheritance, or disallowed monopolies. As historian Edmund Morgan has observed, these provisions "embodied practices already in existence, but they set down popular rights in black and white for all to see."[61]

The Body of Liberties was intended to publicly clarify fundamental liberties, but it was also a document particularly attuned to the circumstances and needs of a fledgling overseas colony. Most noteworthy were two clauses: the first read, "every man, whether Inhabitant or forreiner, free or not free shall have libertie to come to any publique Court, Councel, or Towne meeting, and either by speech or writeing to move any lawfull, seasonable, and materiall question"; and the second noted that "all freemen called to give any advise, vote, verdict, or sentence . . . shall have full freedome to doe it according to their Judgements and Consciences, so it be done orderly and inoffensively for the manner." Whereas declarations of rights generated within the realm had devoted considerable attention to the importance of Parliament and had become increasingly concerned to protect freedom of speech, the Body of Liberties instead claimed that all men should be allowed to attend public meetings and to make their demands known, reflecting a burgeoning tradition of popular participation in the Massachusetts Bay Colony.

Furthermore, unlike many of the commentaries that sought to delineate the rights of British subjects more generally, the Body of Liberties was a declaration emanating from the particular worldview and needs of colonists who had relocated to secure their religious liberties and practices. The document was one of the first in the British world to enumerate the rights of conscience and worship. Moreover, because it was intended to provide a guiding code for a Puritan colony, a number of its provisions were devoted to the intermingling of civil and religious authority. Civil authorities, for example, were granted the "power and libertie to see the peace, ordinances and Rules of Christ observed in every church according to his word, so it be done in a Civill and not in an Ecclesiastical way" as well as the power "to deale with any Church member in a way of Civill Justice." Thus, the Body of Liberties contrasted with earlier declarations that had been focused on enumerating and protecting existing rights; in Massachusetts, the declaration of rights simultaneously became a frame for government.

Like settlers in Massachusetts, the coalition of English Quakers who purchased the province of West New Jersey and sought to encourage emigration proposed a set of "Concessions and Agreements" in 1677.[62] Drafters stated that "these following concessions are the common law, or fundamental rights, of the province of West New Jersey," demonstrating that this document was both a declaration of rights and a frame of government. Chapters 13–23 of the Concessions detailed the "rights and privileges . . . individually agreed upon by the Proprietors and freeholders." Most clauses related to the administration of justice and to the preservation of liberty and property, as was typical of other declarations of rights. In 1677, for example, freeholders agreed that no one might be "deprived or condemned of life, limb, liberty, estate, property, or any ways hurt in his or their privileges, freedoms, or franchises" without a due trial and judgment by "twelve good and lawful men of his neighborhood first," evoking rights first enumerated in Magna Carta. Several other clauses related to more technical matters in the administration of justice—the issuing of summons, the number of justices, the manner of proof, and the need for free entrance and attendance at the courts.[63]

Although Magna Carta obviously influenced the West New Jersey Concessions and Agreements, so, too, did some of the Leveller ideas from the 1640s. Colonists, for example, proposed to "place nearly all power in a large assembly of 100 deputies who would govern with a weaker plural executive of ten men."[64] That this clause relating to an elected assembly appeared as part of an official and published declaration of rights implies that assemblies were being construed as one of the rights of subjects. The Concessions and Agreements also addressed the matter of freedom of conscience, developing ideas that had surfaced in the Massachusetts Body of Liberties (1641) and the Agreement of the People (1649): "no men, nor number of men upon earth, hath power or authority to rule over men's consciences in religious matters." Pithy and precise, the eleven chapters dedicated to "rights and privileges" in 1677 were cast in the mold of metropolitan declarations of rights, subtly suggesting that colonists were doing nothing more than articulating existing and time-honored rights. However, the Concessions also added the radical rights of assembly and freedom of conscience as they adapted an age-old form to the realities and peculiarities of the North American colonies.

A final document from the province of New York testifies to both the enduring influence of metropolitan declarations of rights as well as to the increasing tendency of colonial declarations to introduce novel rights.

Initially called "The Charter of Libertyes and priviledges granted by his Royall Highnesse to the Inhabitants of New Yorke and its Dependencyes," it was first passed by the legislative assembly in 1683.[65] Along with enumerating liberties and privileges, the Charter imposed an English constitutional system on a colony that was still heavily Dutch in custom and daily practice. Approved by the Duke of York in his capacity as proprietor of the colony, the Charter of Liberties was nonetheless disallowed when the duke acceded to the throne as James II. It took several years, a revolution, and the abdication of James II before it could be reenacted. Only in 1691 was the "Act declaring what are the Rights and Priviledges of their Majesties Subjects inhabiting within their Province of New York" passed when the new governor summoned an assembly, which proposed a slightly modified form of the earlier charter.[66]

Many of the rights declared in 1683 and reiterated in 1691 seem all too familiar, evoking as they did rights hallowed within the realm as well as rights that had become increasingly important in the colonies. Clauses arguing that there be annual sessions of assemblies were supplemented by clauses dictating that representatives be elected without interference. The privileges of assemblymen were enumerated. Clauses addressing justice by due course of law and trial "by the verdict of twelve men," as well as those stating that "no freeman shall be compelled to receive any souldiers or marriners," sounded familiar chords. Still other clauses turned their attention to issues of revenue, stipulating that taxes could not be imposed, levied, or required of his Majesty's Subjects but "by the Act and Consent of the governor and Councill and Representatives of the people in general Assembly meet and Convened." Echoing familiar assertions that taxation could only happen with the "consent of Parliament," the Charter of Liberties adapted such claims to the administrative framework of New York. A few less typical clauses related to land tenure and to the estates of *femmes couvertes*, not unlike those found in the Massachusetts Body of Liberties. Finally, the last clause allowed all persons to enjoy "their opinion persuasions Judgments in matters of conscience and Religion . . . without being hindred or molested," even as it included a subclause specifying that this right did not allow "persons of the Romish Religion to exercise their manor of worship contrary to the Laws and Statutes of their Majesties Kingdom of England." This last right reflected the increasing colonial emphasis on freedom of worship and conscience.

But where the Charter enumerated rights deemed particularly relevant by American colonists, it also retained conventions typical of metropolitan declarations of rights, suggesting that enterprising settlers also clung to familiar conventions and phrasings. Colonists were deliberate about acknowledging the monarch's role in confirming rights. Despite being a "declaration of rights and privileges," the 1691 version opened with an acknowledgment of "their Majesties most gratious favour in restoring to them the undoubted Rights and Priviledges of Englishmen." A few lines later, the Charter began to read more like a petition to the king, when the "Assembly doe with all duty and Submission humbly pray that the rights, Priviledges, Libertyes and francheses . . . may be confirmed unto their Majesties most dutyfull and loyall Subjects." Similarly, the Charter's introduction evoked the ancient constitution: "and that this most excellent constitution soe necessary and soe much Esteemed by our Ancestors may ever continue." In the overseas colonies, as in the British Isles, subjects continued to rely on their relationship with their sovereign as they proclaimed and sought confirmation of rights, just as they acknowledged the significance of the ancient constitution.

While William III rejected the Charter of Liberties in 1697 because it assumed "too great and unreasonable privileges," the document nonetheless provides compelling evidence that declarations of rights proliferated and were subtly reworked as colonists crossed the Atlantic.[67] The Massachusetts Body of Liberties, the West New Jersey Concessions and Agreements, and the New York Charter of Liberties established frames of government for particular provinces, but they also referenced rights that were upheld by the sovereign and were familiar to Britons throughout the realm and empire. Other rights, however, were less familiar, and their presence in these colonial declarations suggested that as colonists faced the particular circumstances of North America, they began to envision and introduce an array of new rights for subjects. As they dispersed across the globe, British subjects engaged and extended the tradition of negotiating the rights that were the free-born subject's due.

Revisiting the Entangled Languages of "Rights," "Liberties," and "Privileges"

Declarations of rights were a diverse and widespread genre in the seventeenth and eighteenth centuries, and they were as likely to make claims about subjects' liberties, privileges, and immunities as they were about subjects' rights. The 1689 Declaration of Rights asserted "ancient rights and liberties," just as pamphlets arguing for a "hereditary Right to Liberties and Privileges" circulated routinely. While these, and others, demonstrate that British subjects claimed their due with verve, they are also noteworthy because they suggest that subjects were fusing languages of privilege and languages of right in framing their demands. These entangled languages raise a number of crucial questions: were rights the equivalent of privileges for British subjects? Or did subjects possess a right to liberties? What did it mean when British subjects referred to their rights, liberties, and privileges, often in a single breath? Above all, why was it historically significant that they did so?

These questions are particularly complex because the specific distinctions between these terms continue to remain elusive. Moreover, the scholars who have analyzed languages of liberties and rights in the Anglo-American context have adopted seemingly conflicting approaches, each of which reveals some of the difficulties inherent in parsing these words. A number of legal historians, for example, have observed that terms such as rights, liberties, and privileges were often regarded as synonyms in the seventeenth century; many call attention to the fact that these words continued to be used virtually interchangeably, particularly in the eighteenth-century American colonies.[68]

But if some scholars have suggested that rights, liberties, and privileges were often substituted one for the other, influential historians of political thought have instead focused on differentiating their usage, identifying fundamental transitions and distinctions in these terms, particularly where "rights" was concerned. They have argued that the seventeenth and eighteenth centuries witnessed crucial shifts as theories of natural rights became more prominent and began to challenge traditional understandings of rights, liberties, and privileges that derived from the sovereign.[69] They have largely focused on tracing a movement away from a "medieval worldview," where liberties and privileges were conceived of as grants or protections, toward a "modern" concept of rights, where rights were increasingly conceived of as belonging to "morally autonomous individuals who are presumed to be capable of choosing how they will exercise their liberty."[70] In this shift from medieval to modern, they note a corresponding tendency to view modern rights as egalitarian, general, even universal, inherent to individuals by virtue of their being human beings, rather than as grants directed toward particular persons.[71]

Declarations of rights, however, can provide an alternative interpretation of subjects' continued and simultaneous use of rights, liberties, and privileges. While it is essential to explore seventeenth- and eighteenth-century understandings of these terms and to revisit the historiographical debates that have arisen around them, declarations of rights reveal an overlooked and historically significant coexistence of traditional languages of privilege with more modern languages of natural rights. When British subjects evoked their rights, liberties, and privileges, they were not necessarily using these words interchangeably, substituting them one for the other. Nor were they simply replacing liberties with more nuanced and modern concepts of rights as the eighteenth century wore on. Something far more complex was occurring.

Instead, as subjects continued to foreground their relationship to the monarch, they used the multiple languages available to them. By virtue of being dependent subjects, they leveraged the traditional bond of allegiance, relying on a concept of the monarch's munificence toward them and protection over them. But they also asserted that they were entitled to certain inherent rights, drawing on languages of natural rights to which they were increasingly exposed. Indeed, for British subjects, notions that rights, liberties, and privileges might stem from the monarch and notions that rights might be intrinsic were not necessarily contradictory, particularly as many subjects believed that it was ultimately the monarch who would uphold those rights. Seeking to maximize the efficacy of their claims, subjects appealed to both hierarchical as well as individual concepts of rights, liberties, and privileges, ultimately using them together in provocative new ways.

The meanings of terms like rights, liberties, and privileges remained unclear and potentially all-encompassing in the seventeenth and eighteenth centuries, rendering them flexible concepts used to embrace a "staggering variety" of claims.[72] In general, "liberties" and "privileges," alongside terms like "immunities" and "franchises," were those used most consistently to refer to the range of protections and freedoms granted by the monarch. Typically, medieval and early modern liberties were conceived of as gifts from the monarch; because they were granted by a "greater authority," these liberties were frequently considered revocable, continuing only so long as the monarch's goodwill.[73] Moreover, most of these grants were understood as directed toward particular persons or entities that could vary considerably across time and place—they were exclusive, even discriminatory. Because liberties were understood to have been granted to subjects who remained dependent on their sovereign, they were perfectly compatible with a belief in inequality and arguably remained an essential prop for states and societies dominated by rank and hierarchy.[74]

Indeed, across English-language dictionaries issued and reissued over the course of the seventeenth and eighteenth centuries, "liberties," "privileges," "immunities," and "franchises" were consistently defined with reference to one another, with the monarch conceived of as the ultimate source of protection. In John Cowell's 1607 legal dictionary, for example, "franchise" was defined as a "privilege or exemption from ordinary jurisdiction, and sometimes an immunity from tribute." "Liberty" or "liberties" were defined as a "privilege held by grant of prescription."[75] Samuel Johnson's *Dictionary of the English Language* (1755) also used these terms as synonyms, with "franchise" defined as an "exemption" and a "privilege, immunity, right granted," and "liberty" defined both as "freedom as opposed to slavery" and "privilege, exemption, immunity."[76] Even the *Encyclopédie* (1751–1772), a hallmark of the Enlightenment, noted that the terms were typically used interchangeably, although several authors did attempt to establish some differences between them.[77]

But even if these terms were used virtually synonymously in various contexts, there were subtle variations in contemporary usages and inflections. "Liberties" and "privileges" were more typically conceived of as grants that enabled the individual or corporation to act, whereas "immunities" tended to be the term used to describe a grant that provided a "discharge from obligation," or an "exemption." What is nonetheless significant about all of these definitions is that neither "liberties," nor "privileges," nor "immunities" were conceived of as belonging to morally autonomous individuals; they existed and were available because individuals inhabited a monarchical society and were granted to some, but not necessarily all, individuals.[78]

By contrast, "rights" was a term far less common on the eve of the seventeenth century, even if scholars have argued that it gradually came to subsume terms like "liberties" and "privileges" during the eighteenth century.[79] While the language of rights had become a virtual "mother tongue" for those engaged in political struggles by the mid-eighteenth century, the term was virtually absent from political discourse during the Elizabethan era and only rarely discussed in seventeenth-century America.[80] Indeed, prior to 1604, "right" or "rights" were typically used in discussions relating to land. In medieval England, a right was a title, which, if validated by a court, conferred ownership of land; rights were associated largely with incorporeal things and almost exclusively with real property.[81] The historical interconnections between rights and ownership of land continued to shape understandings throughout the seventeenth century.[82]

Over the course of the seventeenth century, however, rights were also increasingly associated with freedoms or privileges in both political texts and popular pamphlets. And by the eighteenth century, rights were frequently conceived of as protections against arbitrary government.[83] As late as the 1750s, Johnson revealed his indebtedness to numerous and coexisting understandings of rights; the *Dictionary* defined "right" as "justice" and "freedom," but also continued to rely on a definition of "right" as "property" and "that which justly belongs to one."[84] Nonetheless, across these multiple ideas about rights-as-freedoms, or rights-as-protections, rights were very much still understood to be legal privileges, particularly in the sense that they were offered and upheld by the crown.[85]

Historians of political thought have, of course, devoted considerable attention to tracing shifts in languages of liberties and rights during the seventeenth and eighteenth centuries, relying largely on the works of particular writers. The many "languages of liberty" have attracted considerable attention.[86] Among what he calls the seventeenth-century neo-Roman political thinkers, Quentin Skinner has argued that "liberty" ceased referring merely to liberties-as-grants-from-the-monarch and began to signal new conceptions of freedom from constraint, freedom to live within a free state, and even, on occasion, freedom to live within a state that recognized a set of inherent rights.[87] "Liberties," suggest others, was the term used more generally to evoke a popular set of freedoms, blurring the line between liberties as grant from the monarch and liberties as something to which all were entitled.[88] Just as important were dramatic shifts in understandings of rights that occurred over the centuries and in stages. The most significant of these transitions occurred, according to historians of the seventeenth and eighteenth centuries, as theories of natural rights became more important and challenged existing understandings of rights, liberties, and privileges that derived from the sovereign. Reviewing these arguments illuminates an enduring historiographical disagreement about when this shift occurred, just as it does the numerous and potentially overlapping interpretations of rights-as-property, rights-as-grants, rights-as-freedom, rights-as-protections, and rights-as-intrinsic that British subjects would have had available to them by the eighteenth century.

One group of scholars focused on the Anglo-American context has argued that concepts of rights as natural, inherent to the individual, and inalienable emerged well before the revolutionary upheavals of the eighteenth century as part of a more general challenge to the existing monarchical and constitutional order of the seventeenth century. If the English Civil War is often considered a particularly important moment for rights, the decades of struggle between monarch and Parliament also figure prominently in analyses of modern concepts of rights. Richard Tuck notes that seventeenth-century rights theorists are often credited with inaugurating the concept of man "as the owner of his liberty and other moral attributes."[89] Likewise, Skinner has observed that concepts of rights as natural gained traction in the seventeenth century, and that liberties were increasingly seen not merely as gifts from the sovereign but as inherent birthrights of individuals.[90]

It was also in the seventeenth century that conflicting legal ideas about the origins of English rights secured a broader constituency and became politically relevant. Many contemporaries, including a number who eventually came to identify with the royalist cause during the Civil War, continued to argue that both rights and liberties were the gift of the king, traceable to particular acts of royal authority. The king remained the "fount of justice," the guarantor of all privileges. Another argument popularized by Sir Edward Coke, however, became increasingly important in the early seventeenth century. This argument held that an "ancient constitution" had existed since time immemorial and that it was the source of rights and liberties. If rights and liberties could be rooted in this ancient constitution and shown to predate the advent of royal authority, they might thereby be "rendered independent of the sovereign's interference," free from the prerogative of the king.[91] To suggest that rights and liberties were antecedent to monarchs was, of course, frequently interpreted as a direct challenge to a worldview in which protections were held to derive from the monarch, but this argument also revealed how shifting and unstable notions of rights, liberties, and privileges remained.

Even if the writings of some seventeenth-century theorists suggest that natural rights were becoming increasingly important, earlier understandings of rights and liberties as the grant of the monarch clearly continued to shape the political and constitutional landscape. There was, as J. G. A. Pocock has suggested in his analysis of references to the ancient constitution, an ongoing and unresolved contest between two visions of the origins of rights and liberties: rights and liberties as gifts of the monarch alongside rights and liberties that had existed from time immemorial and could be conceived of as a birthright.[92] The persistence of these visions reflects the understanding of authority so prominent in the English, later British, world. Most subjects, whether lowly or parliamentary, whether contented or discontented, continued to look to the monarch and to the traditional bond of allegiance as an integral part of their daily lives. This was a bond founded on a sense of reciprocity and furthered by a belief that monarchical protection remained a cornerstone of everyday life. Whether British subjects believed that the reigning monarch was the sole fount of rights, liberties, and privileges, or whether they merely sought monarchical confirmation of ancient rights, liberties, and privileges, the monarch and subjects' relationships to their monarch were crucial to their understandings of, and claims to, protections and freedoms. For these protections to be separated from this monarchical frame—and for rights, in particular, to be defined solely as a birthright—would likely have required a severance of the relationship between sovereign and subject, which occurred only very briefly with the English Civil War.

Perhaps this explains why a second group of scholars locates the transition to a modern language of rights in the revolutionary era of the later eighteenth century. According to these historians, as American colonists embraced Enlightenment ideals of both individual and universal human rights, and as they imagined the possibilities inherent in a republic, they increasingly began to appeal to concepts of natural rights. This shift was profound because, for much of the eighteenth century, rights continued to be thought of as restraints on arbitrary government rather than as individual possessions.[93] Few of the civil rights claimed by Britons in the seventeenth century were viewed as natural rights inherent to the individual, or as universal, immutable, and inalienable.[94] It was only over the course of the revolutionary era, argues James Hutson, that colonists abandoned the notion that privileges were granted to them, beginning to see rights as "inherent and indefeasible" and stressing the intrinsic powers within the individual.[95] The American Declaration of Independence and subsequent Bill of Rights, with their references to the "laws of nature" and "unalienable" rights, represent the epitome of this thinking and remain the dramatic expression of a fundamental transition.

This narrative remains appealing, in large part because it clearly identifies the break with monarchy and associated concepts of protections stemming from the monarch as critical in revolutionaries' embrace of modern concepts of natural and individual rights. A number of historians, however, remain less convinced that the revolutionary era was characterized by a clear shift toward natural and individual rights. What instead continued to define the language of rights during the American Revolution was its diversity. Pamphlets produced throughout the revolutionary era did not conceive of individuals as the only rights-holders; rights-holders also included towns, institutions, and the people as a whole.[96] Even at the time of the Founding, rights were seen as deriving from a range of sources, among them nature, history, the common law, contract, right reason, and God.[97] And as Kurt Lash has noted, well into the nineteenth century, the term "rights" remained elusive, including a "rich mix of liberties, advantages, exemptions, privileges, and immunities," and these terms appeared in a variety of contexts and in reference to a range of liberties.[98] Ideas about natural and inherent rights did not necessarily predominate by the revolutionary era.

Thus, although languages of rights may have been in transition, few scholars have been able to agree as to when, exactly, changes occurred and even fewer have been able to identify how widespread those changes were. It is here that documents such as the declarations of rights penned by British subjects can provide another frame for analysis. On the one hand, British subjects positioned themselves as an integral part of a monarchical world in these declarations, embracing understandings of the king's protection and often claiming that privileges flowed from the bond between subject and sovereign. On the other hand, British subjects clearly articulated that they were entitled to certain liberties by virtue of being subjects, and they inhabited a world where ideas about natural and inalienable rights that were intrinsic to all human beings were also becoming increasingly important. Loyal British subjects drew on the many languages of rights, liberties, and privileges available to them, successfully leveraging notions of both bonds of allegiance and time-honored birthrights.

If anything, the traditional relationship between subject and sovereign remained remarkably relevant in the British Empire and for subjects' declarations of rights. As Glenn Burgess has noted, debates over the ancient constitution appeared to divide the English political nation, but inhabitants of Jacobean England possessed an intellectual framework that was broadly consensual.[99] This was a world that remained largely "king-saturated," where most Britons believed that the king was responsible for "doing justice," regardless of which arguments they made regarding the origins of liberties.[100] And it was this worldview—a worldview centered on the personal relationship between subject and sovereign—that allowed British subjects to countenance a variety of seemingly conflicting perspectives and that permitted both fluid and pragmatic use of concepts like rights, liberties, and privileges.

As inhabitants of this world, British subjects would have been aware of arguments that human beings possessed certain natural, intrinsic, and inalienable rights, particularly as those arguments became more commonplace in the writings of Enlightenment thinkers and the pamphlets of revolutionaries. During the moments in which they recognized the king's protection and accepted that privileges flowed from his munificence, subjects often simultaneously articulated that they were entitled to certain inherent, natural rights. It is quite possible, of course, that British subjects were using these multiple languages to maximize the efficacy of their claims and that they were more than happy to avail themselves of the competing ideas about rights, liberties, and privileges, knowing that some superiors would respond to arguments that rights stemmed from monarchical protection and others to the notion that rights were natural. It is also possible that these coexisting languages represented a veiled threat: subjects were happy to ascribe to the notion that a benevolent monarch would grant them their rights, but if that approach failed, they also wished to make clear that they were entitled to those rights by nature and by birthright.

These entangled languages in declarations produced throughout the British world suggest a need to reconsider languages of rights in the context of the British Empire. Although it may be tempting to categorize liberties and privileges as terms evocative of a traditional world where protections stemmed from the monarch, and rights, when used in the sense of natural rights, as a term that signals the birth of the modern individual, such an approach is not necessarily historically productive. Loyal British subjects successfully and simultaneously drew on both traditional bonds of allegiance and protection as well as emerging ideas about time-honored birthrights. Because they did not reject monarchy, they did not have to jettison a concept of the monarch as the "fount of privilege" in favor of a concept of natural rights intrinsic to the individual. Nor did they have to choose or perceive they were choosing between unequal privileges of the medieval era and egalitarian rights of the modern one. For those who remained subjects in the eighteenth-century revolutionary era, there was no "antithesis between the authority of kings and the personally owned rights of the subject."[101] The ideas that rights derived from the king and that rights derived from an ancient constitution did not have to exist in opposition but could be placed on a continuum of familiar ideas.[102] Because their relationship to the monarch remained central in their daily lives and because languages of natural rights were a feature of their increasingly global existence, British subjects were able to fuse two powerful concepts: the idea that protections flowed from the monarch's grant with the idea that individuals possessed an inherent birthright.

Rights were conceived of as a birthright, almost innate, and simultaneously linked to subject status. The vision of rights offered by British subjects in their declarations of rights thus provides an important counterpoint to other languages of rights in circulation during the revolutionary era. Unlike the United States or France, where languages of intrinsic rights gradually displaced earlier languages of rights, liberties, and privileges stemming from the monarch, British subjects continued to avail themselves of these various and powerful languages. Even as British subjects embraced some of the ideas about rights surfacing in the emerging republics, they phrased their claims to rights differently—but no less emphatically—than American colonists or later French revolutionaries.

Well after the conclusion of the American Revolutionary War (1775–1783), for example, both English- and French-speakers in the Province of Quebec would lay claim to the rights and privileges due to the monarch's subjects wherever they might be. As one memorial from "merchants and others of the cities of Quebec and Montreal" asserted in 1788, subscribers sought "to participate in the previous rights and priviledges, which His Majesty's subjects enjoy, in whatever part of the Empire they are situated."[103] A few years earlier, a French-language petition had noted that "your Catholic and Canadian Subjects enjoy, without distinction, all the privileges, immunities, and prerogatives enjoyed by British Subjects in all the parts of the globe that are part of your empire."[104] When they declared their rights, British subjects sought access to protections, not necessarily as individuals entitled to universal or unalienable human rights, but as subjects whose rights either stemmed from, or were protected by, their dependent status. From their bond of allegiance to the monarch and from their loyalty to a monarchical state, rather than from their position as human beings, flowed access to rights, liberties, and privileges. It was as "British subjects" rather than as "men" that they framed their demands, a practice that would flourish in the British Empire after 1763.

There was nonetheless an important parallel in claims made by British subjects and by claims made in the American and French revolutionary contexts. Rights, liberties, and privileges were increasingly described by commentators as rights or liberties of "free-born subjects" or of "true subjects." Rights, whether the birthright of subjects or granted by the monarch to his subjects, were increasingly seen as due to all British subjects. If rights were due to all British subjects, then all those who might prove themselves subjects of the monarch should be able to access those rights by virtue of their subjecthood. If French-speakers in Grenada, or Genoans in Gibraltar, or Dutch inhabitants of Calcutta were recognized as subjects of George III, then they, too, were entitled to the rights, liberties, and privileges of subjects. This conception of rights had powerful implications for new peoples who joined the British Empire after 1763—and it was arguably revolutionary in its own right.

WHEN JOHN PHILIP REID proposed that it was an "easy task" to catalog what the American colonists meant by "their rights as Englishmen," he acknowledged that this was because those rights had been so clearly and so frequently affirmed in the 1760s and 1770s. Reid analyzed yet another declaration of rights—that promulgated by the Continental Congress in 1774—claiming that it represented "the most comprehensive statement of colonial privileges made during the revolutionary war." In this document were crystallized nine principal rights: to life, liberty, and property; to equality, which was defined as granting colonists all the immunities and privileges of the British people; to representation and to elect members of assemblies; to the common law of England; to trial by jury; to the statutes in English law that existed at the time of colonization; to petition; to be free of standing armies; and to free and balanced government.[105] Few of these rights would have come as a surprise to British subjects. Most of them had been articulated throughout the British Isles and empire for well over a century. Loyal subjects had sought—and often gained—royal confirmation of these very liberties. If American colonists were able to identify a specific set of rights due British subjects, it was because they and their predecessors had been delineating and debating those rights for centuries.

But even as Reid succinctly outlined the nine rights upon which colonists supposedly agreed, he noted their "vagueness."[106] Others have been sobered by the overwhelming variety of British rights, liberties, and privileges. The diversity of rights that was associated with British subjecthood by the eighteenth century was a result of centuries of declaring and disputing rights in the halls of Parliament, the bookshops of London, and colonies across the globe. And the landscape of rights was perpetually changing. Even where some rights were given the force of law and even if some charters of liberties were approved by colonial assemblies, legislation could always be abrogated, rescinded, or extended. Moreover, although the numerous commentaries produced in seventeenth- and eighteenth-century Britain and elsewhere attempted to define the inheritance of the free-born subject, their tendency to emphasize some rights over others made the identification of universally accepted rights that much more difficult at the popular level. While declarations of rights may have proposed innumerable liberties and privileges, almost none of them ever emerged as irrefutable. Rights almost always remained contested, something that worked to the advantage and disadvantage of the inhabitants and administrators of the empire, particularly after 1763.

Whatever its limitations and possibilities, the tradition of writing and declaring rights was enduring and widespread. The process of overseas settlement stimulated new types of formal declarations and prompted articulations of rights peculiar to the distant colonies. This same process of rapid expansion also spurred less formal demands for rights, encouraging a parallel and unpublished tradition of declaring and claiming rights that was preserved in the dusty volumes of colonial office files. Far less illustrious and often far less documented, the process by which subjects throughout the empire asserted and sought confirmation of certain rights from colonial administrators mirrored the better-known tradition of formally declaring rights before Parliament or before a colonial assembly. In most overseas colonies, inhabitants and administrators drew on understandings of rights popularized by published documents and treatises, but they also proposed their own ideas about how and where subjects' rights were generated. And, as it turned out, many of these were "new subjects," individuals added to the British Empire by the peace treaties of the eighteenth century, who drew on that status to make provocative and daring assertions about the "rights of subjects" and who ultimately helped to reshape the boundaries of British subjecthood. Like others who publicly proclaimed their rights, these colonial subjects leveraged their relationship to the king and their sworn loyalty to make a staggering diversity of claims. Their stories reveal that echoes of the more hallowed, published tradition of declaring rights provoked redefinitions of rights at the local level.

3

Real and Pretended Subjects

MEDIATING SUBJECTHOOD IN THE MEDITERRANEAN

ARCHIBALD CAMPBELL FRASER, the British consul at Algiers between 1766 and 1773, was not particularly well liked. His enemies accused him of obstructing commerce, arguing that although he was supposed to protect British subjects and their trade, he seemed more determined to ruin them. For his part, Fraser insisted that such calumnies would "only serve to quicken my zeal in his Majesty's Service, and make me to examine yet more stricktly than I have hitherto done, who are Real & who are Pretended Subjects of his Majesty, what Trade is lawful & what is not."[1] Fraser believed not only that his commission required him to verify the qualifications of subjects, but also that ensuring their privileges might mean prohibiting some trade in the region. A Scotsman whose father had been executed for supporting the Jacobite rising in 1745, Fraser no doubt had personal reasons for asserting an unswerving devotion to the crown and for his staunch enforcement of the boundaries of subjecthood.[2] But he also worried that the false assertions of "pretended subjects" might weaken legitimate claims made by "real subjects." He clearly understood that real subjects were entitled to certain protections in the Mediterranean, which he felt duty-bound to safeguard against the spurious claims of aliens.[3] Nor was he unjustified in thinking that his responsibilities as consul required that he determine who was who, however unpopular that might make him.

Fraser was part of an extensive network of administrators in the British Mediterranean, most of whom struggled at one point or another to clarify which individuals were British subjects and which individuals they were obliged to protect as part of their official responsibilities.[4] For all the hostility he provoked, Fraser, like many other consuls and governors, conscientiously worked to uphold the privileges of those he suspected were *bona fide* subjects, seeking advice from secretaries of state when uncertain and carefully explaining his decisions on such matters with reference to orders in council, treaty articles, and official directives. The instructions sent to consuls would have urged that "you will on all occasions, be vigilant for the protection of the Trade, and persons of our Subjects."[5] Consuls also sought to secure provisions for the British garrisons, and, in consultation with the governor of Gibraltar or his counterpart in Minorca,[6] they were typically responsible for determining which British ships warranted protection and which British subjects should be reclaimed from enslavement in the Barbary states.[7] Even if Fraser did so more assiduously than others, he was not alone in fulfilling these responsibilities.

One of the challenges administrators faced in protecting the king's subjects was that it was not always clear who was a British subject in a Mediterranean world where each bay was a "miniature community, a complex world in itself," where migration along land and sea routes was a way of life, and where there were myriad understandings of what was meant by British subjecthood.[8] The inhabitants of British Gibraltar and Minorca did include members of the British garrison and a few English, Scottish, Irish, and Hanoverian immigrants and merchants, whose birth within the monarch's allegiance was generally fairly well established. Both of these strategic outposts, however, were largely populated by civilians of Spanish, Genoese, Livornese, Maltese, Neapolitan, Greek, Jewish, and "Moorish" origin, some of whom had been born in British dominions and within the king's allegiance, but many of whom had taken up temporary residence for the purposes of trade or made a living by provisioning the garrisons. The presence of such diverse inhabitants would require that administrators grapple quite regularly with whether the relationship between subject and sovereign, and its accompanying protections, was determined by birth alone.

Administrative responses would be quite varied. The "List of British Prisoners from the Garrison now held in Spain," preserved in the Gibraltar Civil Secretary's Register for 1780, offers an initial glimpse at some of the competing and coexisting understandings of subjecthood that Governor George Augustus Eliott believed were in existence. By listing individuals as "British Prisoners from the Garrison," Eliott inscribed them into a specific community worthy of his attention—they were "British" and "from the Garrison" rather than "foreign." His list included a soldier from His Majesty's Regiment, a lieutenant from the "Hanoverian brigade," and a London merchant and his servant, some of the usual suspects whose positions and travels were likely to have landed them in Spanish jails. Also listed, however, were Gaspar Grande, Angelo Genaro, Giorgio Baptista Genaro, Giacomo Genaro, Antonio Diaz, Juan Andreu, Vincenso Buzzo, and a certain Portelli, "inhabitants of Gibraltar, employed on the publick service & naturaliz'd by the British Laws." Individuals who had proven their belonging by loyal service and naturalization, their presence on this list suggested that recognition as "British" might be achieved not merely by birth within the king's allegiance but also by other local conventions. Still further down the list were numerous other individuals, classified as members of "crews of two Town Boats" or "inhabitants of this place."[9] These individuals were identified as neither "British subjects" nor "naturalized," but they were included because, as persons responsible for provisioning the garrison, they could not be excluded from protection.

Over the years, inescapable dependence on the motley individuals who populated Gibraltar and Minorca did more than prompt begrudging toleration of foreigners in the garrison's midst. As Eliott's list made clear, not recognizing these men as members of the garrison might have discouraged others whose help the British so desperately needed. Although he may have been unsure about whether these persons were British subjects, Eliott nonetheless recognized that he could not abandon them as foreigners. At least as far as his records were concerned, the protections generally reserved for *bona fide* subjects were imagined to be widely granted. Nor was Eliott alone in holding these views of protection. Directives from London, when combined with accounts gleaned from official correspondence, offer significant evidence that British subjecthood expanded and contracted in ways that reflected the complex histories and realities of life in Gibraltar and Minorca. At times, consuls and colonial governors urged revision of rules and established practices of trade in the Mediterranean. At others, they advocated capacious definitions of royal protection where the ransom of captives was concerned. More generally, the exigencies of life in these strategic outposts prompted a willingness to honor alternative definitions of subject status at the highest levels of imperial governance.

This chapter pays particular attention to these administrators' crucial role in mediating the boundaries and protections of subjecthood. Fraser, like his peers, revealed that he possessed his own ideas about how a subject was to be defined and about what privileges resulted from the bond between subject and monarch. In the absence of a unified official response to questions about subject status in the Mediterranean, Fraser, like many others, reacted to individual requests in light of the circumstances. Indeed, the correspondence between governors of Gibraltar and Minorca, British consuls stationed in the Mediterranean world,[10] the Dey of Algiers, the Emperor of Morocco,[11] and secretaries of state in London, sheds light on how officials contended with the repercussions of subject status in these geopolitically strategic colonies and the variables that shaped their decisions. The day-to-day determinations made by these administrators helped to ensure that British subjecthood remained relatively porous in the eighteenth-century Mediterranean.

Even if local imperatives shaped their ideas about subjecthood, Fraser, Eliott, and other administrators relied on legal cases and treaties in determining subject status, drew on enduring ideas about allegiance and its associated protections, and invoked a familiar language of the rights of free-born subjects. Nonetheless, more pragmatic interpretations of subject status, which did not require a person to have been born in a British dominion or to have achieved formal naturalization by act of Parliament, tended to predominate in the Mediterranean. Indeed, many treaties proclaimed that the inhabitants of Gibraltar and Minorca were to be "looked upon as His Majesty's natural subjects, in the same manner as if they had been born in any other part of Great Britain." Particularly in the years after the Treaty of Utrecht (1713) and the Treaty of Paris (1763), when numerous individuals gained and lost subject status, expansive interpretations of subjecthood tended to emerge; in turn, these revised interpretations found their way into agreements with the Barbary states and into official correspondence.

Perhaps more significant, many of these eighteenth-century treaties insisted not only that inhabitants of Gibraltar and Minorca be looked upon as subjects, but also that they were entitled to the "same liberties and privileges" as those who had been born as British subjects.[12] Nonetheless, if many agreed that loyal subjects were entitled to privileges, few were in accordance about the specific protections that obedience guaranteed. Far from being a fixed concept, subjecthood was constantly evolving, allowing for the emergence of multiple, often new, understandings of rights. Over time, therefore, "liberties and privileges" would acquire their own distinct power in the Mediterranean, particularly because the more celebrated rights to trial by jury or to representative government usually did not occupy center stage in these strategic outposts. What endured across the many discussions of subject status in Gibraltar, Minorca, and elsewhere, however, was the powerful idea that subjects, regardless of how their subjecthood had been attained, were entitled to certain protections.

Two specific rights became nearly synonymous with British subject status in the Mediterranean—access to Mediterranean Passes and redemption from slavery in North Africa. These were, of course, closely linked to what consuls were charged to protect—"the trade and persons of British subjects"—but their association as rights of subjects emerged as part of a symbiotic process. Inhabitants repeatedly asserted that they were entitled to such protections, while administrators, in responding to them, seemed to give official sanction to those very rights. This was a process in which the intertwined languages of allegiance and protection continued to shape discussions of rights and liberties. It was also a process in which the economic protections available to those who could prove themselves to be subjects of the monarch came to dominate understandings of subjecthood.

Administrative Imperatives in the British Mediterranean

As British predominance in the eighteenth century became more dependent on naval prowess, colonial policy grew increasingly attuned to protecting and supporting strategically placed overseas garrisons. After having abandoned Tangier in 1683, the British needed new sites from which to protect trade and monitor the activities of other European powers in the Mediterranean. During the War of the Spanish Succession (1701–1714), the capture of Gibraltar in 1704 and Minorca in 1708 seemed to promise a year-round British presence in the Mediterranean. Occupation of the Rock of Gibraltar, within sight of North Africa and abutting Spain, helped secure British control over European movements throughout the Mediterranean (figure 3.1). The taking of Minorca, at one-day's sailing distance from France and two-days' distance from Spain, put Britain in immediate proximity to her continental rivals. The island's glorious natural harbor, Mahon, boasted a dockyard, victualing area, and the first overseas naval hospital, attractions for ships traveling throughout the region. Recognizing the importance of these new territories, the House of Lords promised King George I that the government would do its utmost "to enable your Majesty to assert and defend your right to Gibraltar and the Island of Minorca, which are of the greatest importance to the preservation of the commerce and naval strength of Great Britain."[13] A French pamphlet from 1756 confirmed this parliamentary enthusiasm; the author succinctly summarized the value of these territories, noting that "the commerce of the whole [Mediterranean] sea was . . . in the hands of England" and lamenting the damages wrought on European trade and shipping more generally since the British occupation of both territories.[14]

FIGURE 3.1 *A View of Gibraltar from the South West, with sailing ships in the Bay of Algeciras seen beyond the New Mole Fort in the foreground* [map], 1779. © The British Library Board (Maps.K.Top.72.48.d).

Officially ceded to Britain by Spain under the Treaty of Utrecht, Gibraltar and Minorca would remain contested, coveted prizes among the various European powers. Gibraltar withstood three sieges and Minorca changed hands five times in the eighteenth century alone,[15] indicating both the perceived and actual importance of these territories.[16] Moreover, the French capture of Minorca in 1756 was a dramatic reversal that toppled a ministry and occasioned a crisis of national morale at the beginning of the Seven Years' War. As one observer wrote, the loss of Minorca put "our ALL in Danger" because "the Nation has lost her Figure in the Eyes of all Europe, along with a valuable possession."[17] When the British managed to retain Gibraltar and Minorca after both the War of the Spanish Succession and the Seven Years' War, they seemed well positioned to remain the most powerful European power in the Mediterranean and elsewhere. Indeed, the possession of these two territories helped to account for the global presence of the British army and navy: before 1750, there were "more British troops stationed in Gibraltar and Minorca than the whole of North America," and by the end of the eighteenth century, there were still "probably as many British ships and crews active in the Mediterranean as there were in the Atlantic."[18]

The structures of governance in these outposts reflected their importance as theaters for waging war. Governors in both were military men and known as commanders-in-chief, even though they were also responsible for their large civilian populations. The fact that these territories were treated predominantly as military outposts and naval bases[19] shaped both the forms of government and administrators' relations with local inhabitants.[20] In Gibraltar, proclamations and standing orders from the governor shaped the day-to-day lives of both military and civilian inhabitants. The legal system available to civilians until the nineteenth century was at least partly supervised by the military governor and the judge advocate, an individual usually associated with courts intended for military personnel. Local assemblies and representative government, forms of civil government permitted in so many other British colonies, were withheld. While some inhabitants protested certain governors' abuses of power,[21] most residents of this garrison city understood that it remained under military rule and that their movements into and out of the fortress would be controlled by the military establishment.[22]

In Minorca, conflicts were common between the local population and the occupying garrison, groups whose needs were often diametrically opposed. The island's civil administration allegedly remained in the hands of the Minorcans, and the commanding officer, at least before 1753, was only responsible for "controlling the civilian population."[23] However, a persistent "reluctance to clarify the parameters of authority of the Governor . . .in civil, as distinct from military, matters" led to ongoing arguments between the colonial governor, who often intervened in civil matters, and the *jurats,* local men chosen by ballot for one-year terms in one of the four administrative districts, who resented all infringements on their long-established *fueros*, or privileges.[24] Furthermore, although Minorcans had been allowed to have their disputes regulated by Spanish law even after 1713, many governors found this arrangement unwieldy when they presided over the courts of appeal and felt that aspects of English law ought to be adopted.[25] Perhaps most problematically, Minorca was Britain's first overseas possession apart from Ireland with a majority Catholic population. Conflicting interpretations of the Treaty of Utrecht, which had permitted Catholicism as far as it was consistent with the laws of Great Britain, plagued British colonial administrators.[26] Minorcans argued that this article permitted them to remain under the jurisdiction of the Bishop of Majorca; the British countered that such jurisdiction was inconsistent with British law. As they struggled to maintain their sway over ecclesiastical administration and law, the Roman Catholic clergy frequently were at odds with their Protestant occupiers and the military government.

Despite the strategic advantages of Gibraltar and Minorca, governors confronted the very real problem of ensuring their garrisons' survival and British naval strength in an undermanned Mediterranean world (figure 3.2).

FIGURE 3.2 *Map showing the Barbary Coast, Mediterranean Sea, and Italy* (image taken from *Atlante Veneto*, originally published in Venice, 1691–1696). © The British Library Board (Maps C.44.f.6.(21)).

Undoubtedly the most pressing day-to-day issue for administrators was securing a steady stream of supplies when production failed to meet demand. Given its minimal fertile land and few natural resources, Gibraltar remained largely unable to produce its own foodstuffs, leaving its military and civilian populations almost entirely reliant on grain, cattle and other livestock, fish, fruit, and vegetables brought into the city.[27] Because Article X of the Treaty of Utrecht forbade "open Communication by Land" with Spain,[28] treaties signed with the Barbary states, which often included clauses permitting British ships with the proper documentation to seek provisions in the harbors of North Africa, became critical to Gibraltar's survival.[29] Consuls stationed in North Africa typically arrived with instructions requiring them to "procure supplies of livestock, corn, vegetables, and water, and all kinds of provisions for his Majesty's fleets, and for his garrisons of Gibraltar."[30] The prospect that the Emperor of Morocco might suspend trade with Gibraltar haunted its commanders-in-chief; similar fears worried their peers in Minorca.[31] Both the civilian and military populations of Minorca experienced frequent shortages of grain and relied on wheat imports from Algiers. Preoccupied with provisioning their garrisons, colonial governors in these Mediterranean outposts had to rely on a diverse group of mariners and complex relationships with neighboring Barbary rulers who had their own competing interests in the region.[32]

British governors of Gibraltar and Minorca also faced a Mediterranean world characterized by perpetual movement and migration and perennial shortages of men.[33] Their situation was aggravated not only because so few British settlers traveled to these outposts but also because significant foreign-born populations actually arrived to meet demands for labor. Predominantly military governments and the unsettled nature of civil administration, combined with their limited size and paucity of available lands, ensured that neither Gibraltar nor Minorca became a colony of British settlement.[34] Despite a 1749 order in council that instructed the governor of Gibraltar to let out "at any easy rent to encourage His Majesty's Protestant Subjects to settle there, which will be a Strengthening to the place," many of the lands granted by the 1749 Court of Enquiry were to the very "Jews, Moors, and Papists of different Nations" the order was intended to sideline.[35] Moreover, several proposals for the settlement of Minorca were circulated in the eighteenth century, including one urging that foreign Protestants from Germany, Switzerland, Piedmont, Geneva, Orange, and Languedoc be encouraged to settle there, but none ever became official policy.[36] British administrators hoped to encourage settlement, but "native British subjects" remained a minority among the civilian populations in these two territories.

Instead of encouraging Protestant immigration, official attention centered on making these colonies commercially viable, handling matters relating to naval prize of war, and, most important, provisioning the garrison and victualing naval ships. Gibraltar was declared a free port in 1706, and a decree of 1712 established that "no duty should be demanded" of goods entering or leaving the ports of Minorca. The intention in making these outposts free ports was to stimulate trade in the Mediterranean, although neither outpost ever became a vibrant commercial center or of significant commercial value to the British.[37] The changing nature of the civilian judicial systems in both locations notwithstanding, Vice Admiralty Courts were successfully established in 1720 and 1739 for Minorca and Gibraltar, respectively, to hear matters relating to prize, letters of marque, and protective passes.[38] Thus, administrative responsibilities were routinely focused on encouraging, monitoring, and adjudicating trade rather than on securing settlers for these outposts.

As a result, the roughly thirty Spanish families who chose to remain in Gibraltar in 1704[39] were soon joined by others of diverse origin, some of whom had been born in British dominions, but many of whom arrived for purposes of trade. Lists of Inhabitants compiled in 1777 and 1791 confirm that a varied population had been allowed to work and settle in the garrison. The 1777 list provides the most compelling evidence of the mixture of peoples living under the purview of the military government. It divided 3,201 documented persons into three categories. First, there were 506 "British or Protestant Inhabitants," only 220 of whom were classified as "Natives" and 286 as "Non Natives." Next, 1,832 "Roman Catholic Inhabitants" were listed, composed of "English or Irish," "Minorkeens," "Natives," "Genoese or Savoyards," "Portugueze," "Spaniards," and "French." Finally, there were 863 "Jews," who were further identified either as "Natives" or "Strangers."[40]

While governors did take action against the presence of "strangers" in the garrison, lists of those being admitted into Gibraltar suggest that officials continued to allow their arrival. Despite the fact that the Treaty of Utrecht forbade the settlement of Jews in Gibraltar, the civil secretary regularly appointed those of both Genoese and Jewish origin to short-term positions "as porters in this Garrison . . . conforming themselves to the Rules and Orders of the Garrison."[41] Boatmen and fishermen were given annual passes and permits to help "carry goods and passengers between the ships in the Bay and the Garrison," most of whom were identified as Genoese or Jewish.[42] Many British administrators found themselves extending royal protection to a range of foreigners.

Similarly, the population of Minorca, though largely Catholic and Catalan-speaking, also included numerous non-native mariners and traders. Commercially minded immigrants became increasingly visible in the 1730s and 1740s. Although the Minorcan clergy worked to prohibit all non-Catholics from establishing themselves on the island, governors and secretaries of state permitted both Greek Orthodox and Jewish inhabitants to settle there in an attempt to nurture a fledgling trade.[43] The population of Greek inhabitants was officially recognized in the 1740s, and that of the Jews in the 1760s.[44] Furthermore, despite ongoing tensions between military and civilians, and despite Minorcan reluctance to assist their occupiers during successive invasions of the island, British governors and administrators relied on the local population to maintain a steady stream of supplies for the garrison, including the scarce commodities of firewood and oil. They also depended on local mariners to bring in cargoes of supplies, and many Minorcans, eager to secure economic benefits enabled by this association with the British, responded to the call.

Over time, these particular demographics would profoundly shape administrators' approaches to local inhabitants in Gibraltar and Minorca. The British governor noted, for example, that he had granted a coveted protective pass to a ship leaving Minorca manned by several foreigners, because "there is not a sufficient number of sailors, natives, to navigate them, so they are under necessity of taking Foreigners as part of their complement."[45] Thirteen years later, the governor of Gibraltar observed that "the vessels, employed in supplying the Garrison with Provisions, from the coasts of Spain and Barbary, are navigated by Spaniards, Genoese, and other foreigners, Inhabitants of this place, and as such reputed subjects of his Majesty; and this trade cannot be otherwise carried on, for want of Native British Subjects."[46] On other occasions, Jews, Moors, and Greeks were allowed to remain in the colonies precisely because they were instrumental to trade.[47] Not only did governors routinely justify extensions of passes to local inhabitants, but they also maintained that the dearth of native British subjects necessitated flexibility in how they regarded alleged foreigners. Many would, in fact, come to favor inclusive definitions of subjecthood in light of perennial shortages of labor.

While such protections became a means for retaining this local population, they also became a source of heated disputes with North African leaders. In their quest to supply the garrisons and to protect British trade and persons more generally, British officials were also drawn into a variety of arrangements with the Barbary states. Beginning in the seventeenth century, England had entered into treaty agreements with the Barbary powers in which both sides pledged to respect ships, goods, and passengers and to release captives. Supplementing these treaties were an array of informal promises made in correspondence between the states of North Africa and the British colonies.[48] British ships were allowed to seek provisions in the harbors of North Africa, though they were expected to carry documents establishing their provenance, most often known as the Mediterranean Passes.[49] Treaties also prohibited the enslavement of all British subjects and provided guidance as to the treatment of subjects, both British and other, captured at sea or enslaved in the course of their travels.[50] Royal and national honor might have required enforcing the terms of treaties and the protective power of the British crown even if British administrators had not needed to retain and reward a local labor force. Captives were frequently released from North Africa with professions of this being "a mark of . . . great regard and esteem for His Majesty and his Subjects."[51] Failure to return captives was regularly said to "give great umbrage to the British Nation," as it also did to officials in Algiers, Fez, or Tangier.[52] But as many of these treaty articles also suggested, the importance of having clear definitions of subjecthood and of being able to prove subject status became paramount: in theory, all British subjects were to be returned if captured.

The corresponding reality was never so straightforward. Given that seizure of ships and captives provided an important source of livelihood and revenue for North African states and corsairs, the Dey of Algiers and the Emperor of Morocco, among others, were loath to part with their prizes too swiftly.[53] In fact, both leaders were repeatedly frustrated with incessant British demands that ships and captives be returned, contending that the British licensed too many foreigners, thereby violating treaty articles. In March 1765, for example, the Privy Council considered the many formal complaints of the Dey of Algiers, who charged that the governor of Minorca was supplying Genoese and Portuguese mariners with passes in contravention of the treaties.[54] Clearly, readings of the treaty articles differed greatly in the Mediterranean, resting in large part on how the term "British subject" was defined.

Thus, in the eighteenth century, consuls and governors walked a fine line between claiming an array of individuals whom they felt were deserving of protection and not wanting to alienate North African rulers who might at a moment's notice refuse to give up any British subjects or supply garrisons. Although the power of the corsairs and the damages they inflicted had lessened by the eighteenth century, British officials were rarely in a position to impose their will. Instead, they tended to engage in a mixture of appeasement, haggling, and, very occasionally, outright demands and shows of force. They vacillated between presenting lavish gifts and sending ships of war. They bargained with their correspondents, reminding the Emperor of Morocco of the "three subjects of Morocco lately sent over" and noting that he could not judge "of what we expect, better than from what we do."[55] On occasion, they refused to provide military supplies in exchange for captives, though at other moments they did so without hesitation.[56]

Sometimes confidently, sometimes cautiously, these British administrators advanced myriad ideas about who qualified as a British subject. Because they were primarily concerned with supplying and securing military garrisons and with protecting the lives and property of a diverse group of crown subjects, consuls and governors tended to advance inclusive definitions of subjecthood that offered many individuals the necessary protections and protections to survive in the Mediterranean.

"To be looked upon as his Majesty's natural born Subjects"

While the consuls and governors who negotiated with the Dey of Algiers or the Emperor of Morocco were significantly influenced by local exigencies, their approaches to the protections due British subjects were also shaped by diffuse legal understandings of subjecthood. Although familiar ideas about allegiance and protection were embedded in reports of case law, legal opinions filtered through the Board of Trade, and the treaties and instructions regularly sent to guide consular and gubernatorial practices, each of these sources differed in how they defined the nature of allegiance and the extent of protections. Consuls and governors might have relied on many of these ideas, just as they also proposed other flexible and inclusive definitions of subject status, some of which challenged those embedded in case law. Many of these administrators then determined how these shifting definitions might most effectively be implemented.

The best known discussion of subject status in the British Mediterranean was found in the case of *Fabrigas v. Mostyn* (1773), which upheld the well-established principle that birth within the king's dominions and allegiance conferred subject status and extended them to Minorca. Anthony Fabrigas, a native of Minorca, brought an action in England against John Mostyn, acting governor of Minorca, for having him arrested, imprisoned, and deported him to Spain without proper trial. He argued that, as a "free-born subject of England," he was entitled to the protection of the laws of England. Over the course of the trial, the court repeatedly upheld Minorcan subjecthood, stating that inhabitants of Minorca, "being born in Minorca since its subjection to the crown of England," were natural-born subjects. The judges confirmed that those who owed allegiance, even if they lived under "the usages and customs of Spain," were entitled to sue in English courts and to the broader protection of the English law.[57]

The idea that birth within the monarch's allegiance was the determining feature of subjecthood had also been apparent in a lesser-known opinion generated by the attorney general and solicitor general in 1752. This opinion preceded *Fabrigas v. Mostyn*, and even if it lay buried in the annals of the Colonial Office, known only to a few administrators in the Mediterranean, it reflected understandings prevalent in legal circles by the mid-eighteenth century. The law officers were asked whether Peter Romero and John de la Rosa, "natives and inhabitants" of the town and garrison of Gibraltar, could be denied certain commercial opportunities and contracts or whether they were instead "intitled to the Privileges of British Subjects at Gibraltar." The ensuing report stated that the two individuals, having been born within a British dominion and to parents living "under Obedience to the Crown of Great Britain," were natural-born subjects and entitled to all related privileges.[58] Counsel extended the familiar idea that birth within the "dominions" and "obedience" conferred subject status to those born at British Gibraltar, just as their phrasing implied that allegiance was understood to bring with it certain privileges.

Despite their willingness to grant the protections of subjecthood to Gibraltarians and Minorcans, both the 1752 and 1773 opinions focused on individuals born after these territories had become British dominions. Given the itinerant nature of populations living in the Mediterranean and the fact that both outposts had been occupied by several European powers, these decisions would prove of limited guidance. Administrators may have been quite willing to honor these decisions, where applicable, but they also regularly dealt with individuals who had been born before conquest or who moved to Minorca and Gibraltar after they had become British. In determining the subject status of those born outside the monarch's allegiance, consuls and governors necessarily looked elsewhere for guidance.

Indeed, the correspondence of administrators provides clues about which sources proved influential in mediating subjecthood in the Mediterranean. In 1768, for example, Archibald Campbell Fraser asked the secretary of state for further instructions regarding the cases of an "inhabitant of Gibraltar" and a "native of Minorca." He prefaced his request by explaining that, in his reading, both were to be defined as subjects "under one of the last additional

Articles of Treaty which seems pretty distinctly express'd that no subject of his Majesty can be henceforward bought, sold, or made a Slave of within the Dominion of Algier."[59] Fraser was far from the only administrator who reported reviewing treaty articles, commissions, and commands issued from London in attempting to determine inhabitants' status. When Governor Eliott sought a definitive ruling from superiors on whether foreign inhabitants of Gibraltar who took the oath of allegiance were to be treated as subjects, he enclosed copies of the treaty articles with Morocco and Algiers that had promised to regard the mariners and fishermen of Gibraltar and Minorca as natural-born subjects and extend to them the corresponding protections.

Both Fraser and Eliott suggested that they were prepared to recognize as subjects many who were, in fact, foreigners. As they sought reassurance about such interpretations, they also revealed the sources that gave legal force to their understandings of subjecthood. Well before opinions were even proffered for Peter Romero, John de la Rosa, or Anthony Fabrigas, the status of inhabitants in territories annexed to the empire under the Treaty of Utrecht had been negotiated in subsequent treaties with the Barbary states. Sent to treat with Algiers in 1715, for example, Vice-Admiral Baker sought advice from superiors about whether the inhabitants of Minorca were to be "esteem'd as Subjects" and began to pressure the Dey of Algiers to recognize inhabitants of both Minorca and Gibraltar as "British subjects."[60] Ultimately, he managed to secure a clause that jointly recognized Minorca and Gibraltar "in every respect, by the government and people of Algiers, to be part of his Britannic Majesty's own dominions, and the inhabitants thereof to be looked upon as His Majesty's natural subjects, in the same manner, as if they had been born in any other part of Great Britain."[61]

Similarly, articles acknowledging that Minorca and Gibraltar were part of the British dominions and their inhabitants "his Majesty's natural born subjects" were inserted into treaties negotiated with Tripoli (1716), Tunis (1716), and Morocco (1721),[62] and they reappeared in subsequent agreements throughout the eighteenth century.[63] Whereas case law defined as subjects those born within the dominions and allegiance of the monarch, treaty clauses instructed that individuals born before a territory had become British also were to be "looked upon as his Majesty's natural subjects." In these other sources, far more inclusive definitions of subjecthood were manifest: all those who could prove that they were inhabitants of Gibraltar or natives of Minorca, even if they had been born before the conquest or had emigrated to these outposts after their respective captures, were henceforth to be considered British subjects.

Furthermore, these treaties frequently accommodated the perpetually shifting nature of subjecthood. As the numbers of people who came within the British empire expanded or contracted following wars in the overseas empires and changing alliances within Europe, clarifying clauses and articles became necessary in many treaties and instructions. The 1729 treaty with Morocco, renewed in 1734 and 1750, referred to the fact that all Hanoverians were to be set free if captured and delivered up to the British consul; in other words, they were to be treated as all other British subjects since the Elector of Hanover was also the British monarch after 1714.[64] Likewise, a slight change was manifest in instructions penned after the French conquest of Minorca in 1756. Like their predecessors, newly appointed consuls were commanded to protect the trade and persons of crown subjects. They were, however, also directed that "the Island of Minorca being now in the possession of the French, the Inhabitants thereof, are not, for the present, to be considered as our subjects."[65] Articles in early-nineteenth-century treaties would continue to extend the protections of subjecthood to inhabitants of Malta and the Ionian Islands, reflecting the shifts in global empire and the fact that the allegiance of these peoples had changed.[66] Additions and revisions to these treaties suggest that British subjecthood was conceived of as flexible, temporary, and able to accommodate the diverse populations of the Mediterranean.

Numerous other official documents repeatedly confirmed that, even if Gibraltarians and Minorcans had not been born within the king's allegiance, they might nonetheless be counted and protected as British subjects. In the aftermath of Minorca's cession, royal instructions sent to James Wishart, commander-in-chief of the Mediterranean Fleet, stated that the people and inhabitants of Minorca were, as of 1713, "to be looked upon as Our Natural born Subjects . . . and to enjoy all the benefits thereof as well as the rest of Our Subjects in our Other Dominions."[67] Colonel Stanhope Cotton's instructions noted that passes were to be given to His Majesty's Subjects or to all those "who tho' they are not born so, are become his Subjects by being Inhabitants at Gibraltar & settled there."[68] Consul Fraser referred to royal commands in which "it seems to be clearly laid down that a person marrying an undoubted British Subject by whom he had acquired property & has children to heir that Property is intituled to His Majesty's Protection"[69] and to letters from the "three last secretaries of state" that corroborated this principle.[70] What this correspondence illustrates is that there were many processes by which individuals might become British subjects in the Mediterranean. Over the years, as London repeatedly directed consuls to obey their instructions and to uphold relevant treaties, these more practical approaches to subjecthood, which brought many new peoples within the king's allegiance and protection, shaped administrators' mediation of subjecthood.

Indeed, although consuls and governors were frequent critics of the instability of Minorcan and Gibraltarian loyalties, they routinely embraced definitions of subjecthood that allowed them to claim these individuals as subjects.[71] As they corroborated the identity of residents, they revealed their indebtedness to international treaties and official instructions. Documents issued at Gibraltar and intended to protect bearers during their travels provide useful examples of the ways in which governors marked individuals as subjects or as somehow "other." In 1775, Governor Boyd issued a certificate stating "that the bearer Blagdon Abbutt is a subject of His Britannic Majesty," and his successor issued a passport to "John Gavino, of Gibraltar Merchant, a Subject of His Britannic Majesty." Not all documents were worded in such a way. Sometimes individuals were identified merely as "inhabitants of Gibraltar" or as "merchants and inhabitants" without being distinguished as subjects.[72] The form of many such certificates is nonetheless significant: individuals were named, then recognized as British subjects, before finally being offered a certificate of belonging that was understood to convey certain advantages. While the more limited definitions of allegiance found in case law were largely set aside, the notion that loyalty to the monarch brought with it certain protections remained alive and well.

Moreover, these evolving definitions of subjecthood were engaged by inhabitants, many of whom were quick to grasp the advantages of such status even if they did not necessarily identify primarily as British. Residents of Gibraltar seem to have been more willing than their Minorcan counterparts to refer to themselves as British subjects. Perhaps the better relations that existed there between members of the garrison and the local population, or the fact that Gibraltar remained British despite repeated sieges, explain this. The persistent threat of attack from Spain, combined with the economic opportunities made possible by the presence of a large British garrison, may also have inclined residents to favor British rule.[73] Petitions such as that from Peter Romero and John de la Rosa, who noted that their fathers had remained obedient to the crown of Great Britain "and were ever after esteemed British Subjects, having thereby shaken off their Allegiance to the Crown of Spain," were not uncommon.[74] If Minorcans were relatively reluctant to identify as British subjects on paper, preferring instead "Inhabitant of the Island" or "Native of Minorca," they nonetheless embraced the language of humble subjection when making requests and readily claimed subject status when it seemed most likely to serve their purposes. Allegiance and residence were consistently invoked in the hopes of securing royal protection even though Minorcans generally remained rather disinclined to assist the occupying power financially or with manpower.

Like so many others across the British Empire, Minorcans and Gibraltarians deployed powerful and familiar understandings of the opportunities inherent in the relationship between subjects and their sovereign. In almost every documented instance, identifying as a British subject involved calculations about access to profits, protections, and privileges. Seeking restitution of two of his ships seized by Algerine cruisers, Salvador Cosino, inhabitant of Minorca and "Subject of his Britannic Majesty," argued that loyal subjects were entitled to a free and protected trade to the coast of Barbary and that his ships ought to be retroactively protected.[75] Pleading to have Patron Pedro Quinbert and his mariners redeemed, Gabriel Pratts and others classified them as "Natives of the said Island of Minorca" who "always have been faithful and loyal subjects to His Majesty King George."[76] These men elicited assistance based on purported allegiance, although a few years later, the vast majority of Minorcans would fail to demonstrate that allegiance and to mobilize when the French invaded the island. Conversely, while many Minorcans invoked their allegiance when it might benefit them, others might deny such affiliation if they stood to gain. One British consul reported a telling example from 1770. A certain Patron Segui, a "Mahoner," hoping to secure permission to load a cargo of wheat from the Emperor of Morocco, was savvy enough to claim that he was Spanish rather than British. At this particular moment in time, the Emperor of Morocco was irritated by the British and eager to curry better relations with Spain. An observer of the situation from Gibraltar attempted to contradict Segui's claims. David Cordosa argued that because Minorca was under British rule, Mahoners were British subjects, whereupon Segui defended himself by insisting that the "Arms of Aragon" were still displayed in Mahon. In the end, the Emperor of Morocco indulged his petitioner, who "by denying his Colours obtained a Cargo of wheat."[77] Like many at the time, Segui took advantage of unstable definitions of subjecthood and of the emperor's favoritism toward Spain, to establish an identity that was most likely to achieve his ends.

Much of the extant official correspondence for the British Mediterranean confirms that administrators relied upon a range of legal sources and on flexible ideas about allegiance in determining which individuals were deserving of royal protection. Many of the treaties signed between Great Britain and the Barbary states, and many official instructions, opened by recognizing that the "British Nation and Subjects" were entitled to certain "Liberties and

Privileges." But the particular liberties and privileges to which they referred were not to be found in case law or in declarations of rights. Treaties and instructions spoke instead of protective passes, protection of trade, and protection of persons who should be redeemed from captivity, as did the administrators who cited them. As inhabitants put forth claims about their subject status and administrators availed themselves of expansive understandings of subject status, they in turn began to sanction certain specific liberties and privileges distinctive to the British subjects around them.

"Suffer the ship to pass unmolested"

Mediterranean Passes were intended to protect subjects who ventured into seas where they might be preyed upon by Barbary corsairs.[78] In an era when cruisers still seized ships and persons each year, these documents had tremendous value. Passes emerged in the seventeenth century as a way for the Algerine corsairs to identify ships that were British and therefore allowed safe passage according to treaty agreements. The 1662 treaty with Algiers allowed two "sitters" to board an English vessel to examine its pass issued "under the Hand and Seal of the Lord High Admiral of England," although ships were also permitted to proceed freely without a pass provided that "the major part of the Seamen of the said ship or vessel, be Subjects to the said King of Great Britain."[79] A less generous subsequent treaty stipulated that after a period of fifteen months, English ships were allowed safe passage only if they had a valid pass.[80] By 1686, the treaty with Algiers no longer mentioned ships that sailed without passes; safe passage was guaranteed only to vessels that had documents proving their Britishness.[81]

In an era before widespread literacy and in a region where numerous languages abounded, a system emerged that did not require mariners to read the documents. Beautifully engraved passes were scalloped to form a "top" and "bottom" that, when placed together, completed the distinctive illustrations (figure 3.3). Copies of these tops were forwarded to consuls in the Barbary ports for distribution to corsair captains, who then placed them next to the bottoms of the passes presented to them when they boarded English ships. Typically, a pass requested that a specified ship be suffered to "pass with her Company, Passengers, Goods & Merchandize, without any Lett, Hindrance, Seizure, or Molestation."[82] In order to secure one, a ship's master had to swear an oath that the ship was British built, belonged to inhabitants of his Majesty's dominions, and was manned by a certain number of "his Majesty's subjects."[83] He usually entered into a bond to deliver up the said pass by a certain date

BY THE COMMISSIONERS FOR · EXECUTING · THE · OFFICE OF · LORD · HIGH · ADMIRAL OF GREAT BRITAIN AND IRELAND ETC. AND · OF · ALL · HIS · MAJESTYES · PLANTATIONS · ETC.

Suffer the Ship or Schooner Providence of Gibraltar Pasqual Dodero Master Burthen Ninety Tons Navigated with Seven Men all His Majesty's Subjects Foreign Built made free and bound to the Mediterranean

to pass with her Company, Passengers Goods & Merchandize without any Let Hindrance Seizure or Molestation The said Ship appearing unto Us by good Testimony to belong to the Subjects of His Majesty and to no Foreigner Given under Our Hands and the Seal of the Office of Admiralty the Twentieth day of May in the year of Our Lord One Thousand Seven Hundred and Sixty six

To all Persons whom these may Concern

A Keppel

C Townshend

J Buller

By Command of their Lordships

Ph Stephens

Five Hundred Sixteen

223

FIGURE 3.3 Mediterranean Pass issued to The Providence of Gibraltar, Pasqual Dodero, Master, 1766. Courtesy of The National Archives, Kew, United Kingdom (ADM 1/3837/2).

"unless the said Ship shall happen to bee taken by Pyrates or be cast away and Shipwrackt."[84] Testifying to the subject status of both captain and crew was thus an essential part of securing these protective documents.

Issued by the Lord High Admiral or by collectors of customs at ports outside of Great Britain, copies of these documents were sent to the governors of Gibraltar and Minorca and to consuls stationed throughout the Mediterranean world for distribution where appropriate.[85] Indeed, by 1714, monitoring the issuance of passes had become part of most administrators' responsibilities in the Mediterranean, and they were routinely informed that it was "the King's Pleasure that His Natural Born Subjects only should be protected by His Colours."[86] When dispensing these passes, consuls and governors inevitably became involved in confirming, sometimes determining, individuals' subject status. In 1777, for example, a certain Mr. Poasqual Scarnichia requested a renewal of his ship's pass, identifying as its master and as a "subject of His Majesty naturalized." Only after verifying with the Vice Admiralty Court that Scarnichia could be "deem'd a British Subject & real Inhabitant of the Garrison" did the governor of Gibraltar approve a Mediterranean Pass.[87] Instructions sent to Consul Charles Logie in 1772 directed that he be given copies of all orders in council and royal proclamations touching on passes in order to "prevent the pernicious practices of Foreigners availing themselves of British Mediterranean Passes." He was also commanded to take all measures necessary to put a stop to such dangerous practices, "which in its consequences is so very prejudicial to the Trade of Our Subjects."[88]

The directions contained in some of the original orders relating to Mediterranean Passes, however, were not always suited to life in Gibraltar and Minorca, where "natural-born subject" proved to be an elusive category. Passes had been a feature of the region well before the British capture of these outposts, and although several immediate adjustments were made to instructions relating to Mediterranean Passes, officials did not initially recognize the peculiar issues relating to subject status that would need to be addressed. The first orders in council and royal proclamations to mention Minorca and Gibraltar, passed in 1714, held the recipients of these passes to the same standards as other British subjects. The "Proclamation for Ships to have an Algerine Pass" noted that "for ye better security of the Ships & Vessels belonging to Minorca they be obliged to wear the same Colours, as Trading Ships of Great Britain do," bringing them within a common framework of royal protection. A concurrent order in council detailed the rules for granting passes at Minorca and Gibraltar, stipulating an oath that inhabitants of Minorca had to take before receiving passes: they must swear that they were "Inhabitants of the Island of

Minorca & Subjects of His Majesty of Great Britain," that the ships' owners also "dwelled in Minorca," and that the mariners did the same.[89]

Within a decade, rules for granting Mediterranean Passes were adjusted in response to the realities of life in Gibraltar and Minorca. Guidelines drafted in 1722 began to make some necessary exceptions for the inhabitants of the Mediterranean colonies. While no pass was usually granted to a ship "whereof the master and three fourths of the mariners are not His Majesty's natural born Subjects or Foreign Protestants made Denizens," orders from the 1720s sanctioned a deviation from this practice, noting that these rules applied "[u]nless it be for the Ships or Vessels belonging to the Island of Minorca or the Town of Gibraltar."[90] Another order in council, responding to concerns that too many foreigners had managed to obtain passes, directed that ships from Minorca and Gibraltar "shall be furnished with Passes of a form peculiar to themselves."[91] This came to be known as a pass of the "settee" form as opposed to passes of the "common" form. By 1750, governors had been instructed to issue both forms as appropriate—the settee to inhabitants of Minorca or Gibraltar and the common to other British subjects who arrived and applied for passes.[92] This later order would suggest that there were at least two distinct categories of persons entitled to passes, but that protections were granted to both. Inhabitants of Gibraltar and Minorca represented a peculiar category of mariners—they were not necessarily all subjects under English law or always recognized as the equivalent of native British subjects, but their ships were to be shielded by passes normally reserved for British subjects. Even in the earliest years of British rule, administrators in London recognized the unusual circumstances and authorized exceptions to the broader rules in force.

Such flexibility in granting the protections of Mediterranean Passes was readily acknowledged by administrators themselves. In 1752, in his correspondence with the *alcayde,* or captain, of Tetuan, Colonel Herbert noted that "Inhabitants of this place are Genoese and other Foreigners, who neither speak our language, nor have the appearance of the Native English, yet, as Inhabitants of Gibraltar, they are deem'd English Subjects. . . . I can not refuse them passes."[93] Although Herbert recognized the incongruities of the situation—the fact that these subjects were not English, did not speak English, and did not have the appearance of being English—he also acknowledged that subjects could not be denied their protections. Similarly, Governor Blakeney noted that foreign mariners tended to marry natives of Minorca, "whereby they claim a privilege of becoming denizens and His Majesty's Subjects, which by the Laws of the Island, I find they are intitled to."[94] A decade later, Governor Cornwallis would comment that many of the vessels responsible for provisioning the garrison were navigated by "Spaniards, Genoese, and other foreigners" who were "Inhabitants of this place, and as such reputed subjects of his Majesty."[95] The choice of words in these missives deserves attention. In each case, administrators identified inhabitants as both "foreigners" and "subjects," hinting at the ongoing slippage between these categories. And in each letter, administrators simultaneously asserted subjecthood and yet also used language that might have contributed to subsequent uncertainties about status: inhabitants of Gibraltar were "deemed" and "reputed" to be subjects. Nonetheless, however fragile and uncertain their subjecthood, British commanders recognized that even reputed subjects could not be denied their protective passes.

Many of the exceptions made to the traditional guidelines for distributing Mediterranean Passes responded to concerns of garrison administrators. Commanders-in-chief frequently argued both that the dearth of native British subjects necessitated an extension of passes to local inhabitants and that recognizing the subject status of locals required certain adaptations of rules and broader extensions of privileges. The Privy Council's 1722 order permitting the governor to issue passes to the inhabitants of Gibraltar "of what Religion soever they be when they apply for them" came in direct response to Lieutenant-Colonel Hargrave's complaint that existing rules for granting passes rendered ineligible Spanish and other Catholic inhabitants of Gibraltar.[96] This exclusion meant that their vessels, instrumental in provisioning the garrison, either lay unused or were captured by cruisers and taken to Algiers. Since there were simply not enough *bona fide* subjects to fill the required jobs, rules for granting passes were gradually adjusted in response to local exigencies. Perennial labor shortages and a pressing need to keep the garrison supplied meant that colonial administrators at Gibraltar, as elsewhere, favored an expansive royal protection that would accommodate the many foreigners upon whom they depended.

Not all complaints were resolved by policy revisions in London. Elsewhere, administrators' desire to extend the protections of subjecthood were revealed through changes they initiated on the ground. For Lieutenant-Governor Boyd, who was well aware of the difficulties raised by the man- and ship-power provided by liminal individuals, that meant altering oaths so that foreigners might qualify for passes. In a letter to the Secretary of the Admiralty, he noted that he had adjusted the words of the oath prescribed for those receiving Mediterranean Passes at Gibraltar. He was persuaded that the Lords of the Admiralty would sympathize with his reasons for so doing. The oaths, on the supposition "that it was as easy to find mariners, who are the King's Subjects, in this place, as it is there," had previously been the same as those issued in England, requiring owners and masters to swear that they and their mariners were subjects. Boyd, however, pointed out that it was "impossible to man a fourth part of the vessels that belong to this place, which are mostly employed to supply us with provisions" without enlisting the help of non-subjects.

Unsure of how, exactly, residents of Gibraltar were to be categorized, Boyd chose to adapt the forms of oaths to allow for flexibility in the rules for granting Mediterranean Passes. He subtly altered them to read: "that no persons shall be employed as Mariners on board the said Vessel but his Majesty's Subjects of the Town of Gibraltar, or those men who have been usually employed in navigating the vessels of this place." Among the men Boyd had in mind were several who had taken the "oath of fidelity" and resided in Gibraltar between ten and thirty years. Although Boyd acknowledged that such persons could not be "properly called his Majesty's Subjects," likely accepting notions that the king's subjects only included those born within the monarch's allegiance, he did seem to believe that the "oath of fidelity" and residence within the king's allegiance rendered an inhabitant subject to a sort of local protection, not unlike that proposed by Coke in 1608.[97] Although it is impossible to know how many oaths unsanctioned by London were administered or to ascertain how often governors granted privileges to those of dubious status whose assistance they needed, it is clear that administrators regularly responded to questions of protection with great care and flexibility.

Indeed, the status of foreigners residing in Gibraltar remained largely unresolved and open to individual interpretation in the eighteenth century. There are necessarily many silences in the archives relating to Mediterranean Passes—the moments or crises when consuls or governors, not wishing to delay by consulting superiors, made decisions in response to individual requests and subsequently neglected to make note of them—and they can only be surmised. But one way to probe the ways that protections were accorded is to compare entries for passes returned at Gibraltar in March 1777 with a "List of Inhabitants" also compiled in 1777. The 46 passes returned in March of that year had all been issued between 1774 and 1776. Of the masters listed as having received passes, more than half were not listed in the 1777 census, suggesting that perhaps they no longer lived in Gibraltar or that they never had. Moreover, of the 22 masters who appeared in the 1777 census, only 10 were identified as being from Gibraltar and therefore as "Natives" actually entitled by regulation to their passes. The remaining 12 were identified as being from Genoa, Lorno, Sarona, Estepona, or Majorca, and were likely considered "Foreigners." Had local administrators been upholding the regulations on the books, these individuals should never have been granted their passes in the first place.[98] In the end, the needs of the garrison trumped widely prevailing case law definitions of subject status that would have required foreign-born inhabitants to have been naturalized through a costly parliamentary process in order to be deemed true British subjects. At Gibraltar, those born in Genoa or Majorca were often admitted to privileges generally reserved for subjects, suggesting that local exigencies and practices sometimes proved more influential than the technicalities of English law.

If some governors were confident about determining who was a subject and who was entitled to protective passes, others were troubled by the uncertainties inherent to existing practice and policy. Governor Eliott seemed particularly concerned with whether having taken an oath of allegiance actually conferred subject status and appealed to the secretary of state in 1784 for an answer about whether foreigners long resident in Gibraltar might legally receive passes. As Eliott noted, the 1783 proclamation regarding Mediterranean Passes had appointed a "peculiar form for Gibraltar" and had instructed that passes were not to be issued to any other "than such as are really our subjects Inhabitants of the said Town & Garrison of Gibraltar." But, Eliott was quick to add, the "bulk of the Inhabitants of Gibraltar are foreigners of different nations, many of whom remained here during the Siege, and several taken prisoner in the war fetching supplies." These foreigners usually equipped vessels, furnished essential funds for the voyages, and secured supplies. Typically, they were allowed to take oaths of allegiance and given passes "agreeable to the invariable practice hitherto observed for the convenience of bringing provisions and supplies to the Garrison."[99] But did an oath of allegiance or loyal service during a war a subject make? Eliott apparently received no specific answers from London on this matter and, like many of his predecessors, he eventually took matters into his own hands, tending to favor more inclusive ideas about subjecthood and its associated protections that allowed him to keep his garrison supplied. Swearing oaths of allegiance or serving during times of siege would not typically have conferred British subject status under English case law, but in the day-to-day experience of the Mediterranean, they did entitle many inhabitants to at least a nominal and local subjecthood.

Although consuls and governors presented clear reasons for employing expansive definitions of subjecthood, they did periodically find themselves having to defend their seemingly capricious granting of Mediterranean Passes. One frustrated consul, for example, lashed out at his fellow-administrators in Gibraltar, charging that there were "hardly one in twenty of the vessels that have their passes at Gibraltar but what belong partly or wholly to Foreigners, particularly to Genoese."[100] Even the governor's secretary in Minorca complained that the Minorcans were "such miscreant perjured Fellows" that they routinely held on to passes longer than they should.[101] Warning of "prejudicial effects on trade" and "misunderstandings with Barbary" if these passes fell into the wrong hands, secretaries of state and of the Admiralty regularly chided governors and consuls and reminded them to strictly enforce the rules relating to Mediterranean Passes. In response to cyclical complaints of fraud, the forms of passes were changed in 1714, 1722, 1729, 1750, 1765, 1776, and 1783.[102] In point of fact, the routine became predictable: abuses were reported, secretaries of state or the Admiralty issued a warning, and consuls or governors responded with defenses of their actions and promises to enforce the terms for granting passes. Little changed. Despite rampant falsification of identity, sales of passes, and widespread failure to return expired documents, the system endured. The Lords of the Admiralty sternly commanded that no passes be issued to a ship that "doth not wholly and bona fide belong to His Majesty's Subjects who constantly inhabit in Gibraltar & that no Foreigner have directly or indirectly any share or concern in them," but these officials likely knew that their directives would often be ignored.[103] After all, neither they nor anyone else could agree on how one identified a *bona fide* subject, nor was it feasible to define subjecthood based merely on birth within the monarch's allegiance.

Ultimately, recurring concerns that Mediterranean Passes were being granted too widely and repetitive inquiries about why foreigners were being accorded such privileges merely furthered the idea that protective passes were a privilege of subjecthood. Extensive official correspondence about these passes illustrates how Mediterranean Passes were gradually constructed as an inherent right of all those who were deemed subjects of the monarch. Although he acknowledged the "pernicious consequence" of foreigners securing Mediterranean Passes, Consul James Sampson also recognized that the persons issuing such passes could hardly be blamed; they typically granted them "under the Appearance that those who get them have a Legal Right." Foreigners practiced "deceitful arts" to obtain these passes, fooling administrators into thinking that they were real subjects by "set[ting] forth that [they] had a Legal Right to a British Pass."[104] By 1784, Consul Nathaniel Davison wrote: "the Right we have to insist on people taken under the Protection of a British Pass is surely incontestable."[105] The languages of protection and right had become entangled, as administrators continued to observe that

Mediterranean Passes had become both distinctive markers and assumed privileges of subjecthood.

In a mutually reinforcing process, administrators in Gibraltar and Minorca came to count an increasing number of inhabitants as subjects given the need for their labor, these individuals began making demands for protections they understood to be their due, and officials who responded to their requests for ships' passes appeared to be upholding Mediterranean Passes as a time-honored right of the British subject. These were interpretations manifest in the correspondence of consuls and governors, but they were also understandings that extended well beyond the realm of local government. The petition of Gideon Duncan, which reached the Privy Council in 1765, clearly illustrates the prevalence of these ideas. A ship's captain, Duncan had applied to the governor of Minorca for a Mediterranean Pass, but had been denied. The Privy Council ruled "that Gideon Duncan the Complainant being, as a British subject, entitled to a Mediterranean Pass," ought to have been given one.[106] At first glance, Duncan's case serves as a reminder that governors of Minorca and Gibraltar, consuls stationed in the Mediterranean, and the Privy Council might all have had different understandings of subject status. However, the language of their decision reveals a far more important assumption gaining traction at the heart of the colonial administration. By juxtaposing "British subject" and "entitled to a Mediterranean Pass," members of the Privy Council agreed that subject status offered its bearers protection in the form of a pass, thereby confirming Duncan's assertion that he was due certain privileges. If pamphleteers lauded many rights of free-born subjects in England, in the Mediterranean, subjects who moved in and out of the monarch's allegiance and the administrators who desperately needed them, would define those rights as including the Mediterranean Pass.

Subjects "unwarrantably put into a state of slavery"

While Mediterranean Passes were a coveted protection, they did not necessarily guarantee safety. Corsairs who preyed upon British ships and trade goods also captured passengers whom they dispatched to the galleys or to agricultural and domestic enslavement in the homes and states of North Africa. The number of British subjects taken captive is difficult to estimate given that so few left written records. Historian Linda Colley has argued that approximately 20,000 Britons were captured during the seventeenth and eighteenth centuries, with the largest percentage removed before 1660.[107] This number represents only a fraction, however, of the total number of enslaved Europeans in Barbary: John

Wolf estimates that somewhere between 200,000 and 250,000 Christians were sold in the slave markets of Algiers alone from 1660 to 1830, averaging about 2,000 per year (figure 3.4).[108] The threat to mariners and to voyagers was real, and it was vividly dramatized by numerous seventeenth- and eighteenth-century captivity narratives that were intended to impress upon readers the physical and spiritual dangers of enslavement in North Africa.[109]

Beginning in the 1640s, English treaties with Algiers included clauses that in theory prevented enslavement of passengers aboard prize ships and shielded any Englishman from being sold into slavery.[110] Treaties signed in 1637 and 1638 stipulated that neither England nor Morocco would take captives and that, if any were held, they were to be freed without payment of ransom.[111] According to a 1662 treaty with Algiers, not only were "no subjects of his Majesty" to be bought, sold, or made slaves, but existing slaves were to be set free "and delivered upon paying the Price they were first sold for in the Market."[112] By 1671 and 1686, Christian slaves who managed to escape aboard a ship of war were considered free.

As subsequent treaties soon included similar clauses, systems of ransom and redemption entered diplomatic correspondence. Sometimes leaders in Algiers or Fez would set captives free without payment as a gesture of respect or in response to British requests. However, more often than not, extended negotiations commenced about whether captives were really British subjects and about what constituted a fair ransom given that "market price" could rarely be established. By international agreement, British subjects were entitled to be set at liberty, but whether or not they were freed was unpredictable given the many competing ideas about subjecthood that muddied the waters.

The formal and informal mechanisms that emerged to broker redemptions of Europeans were many, ranging from religious orders, to charitable organizations, to merchants acting as agents for families or governments, to consuls appointed to treat directly with the Barbary states. Indeed, many consuls and governors in the eighteenth-century British Mediterranean were preoccupied by their ongoing and well-documented negotiations with the Dey of Algiers or the Emperor of Morocco. As part of this incessant back-and-forth, administrators were required to assert—and often to prove—the subject status of the many individuals on whose behalf they acted. Over time, as individuals petitioned for their freedom and administrators worked to secure their releases, redemption from slavery was increasingly assumed to be a right of all who could prove themselves British subjects in the Mediterranean. The relationship of subject and sovereign was once again the site of claims for protections and liberty.

FIGURE 3.4 "Hoe de Slaaven met de Keetenen" ("Christian Slaves in Chains"), engraving, in Pierre Dan, *Historie Van Barbaryen, en des zelfs Zee-Roovers*, vol. 1, opp. p. 390, 1684. Courtesy of the Rare Books Division, The New York Public Library, Astor, Lenox and Tilden Foundations.

Official correspondence relating to redemptions provides one of the best sources for gauging definitions of subjecthood as they operated on the ground. It reveals that consuls typically attempted to reclaim a wide range of individuals from captivity and that, as it did for Mediterranean Passes, the category of British subject was also regularly understood to include the predominantly foreign inhabitants of Gibraltar and Minorca. In records of Captain Millbanke's embassy to Morocco from 1759 to 1760, for example, Millbanke himself noted that there were 334 individuals enslaved in Morocco. Although he was able to secure the release of a certain Captain Barton and his officers with relative ease, his superiors in London were less than satisfied with his results. One indicated that ideally Millbanke would also obtain "the rest of the King's Subjects" and went on to specify that he meant "the Minorquins and British subjects taken under foreign Colours, as well as his Majesty's German Subjects, if any there are." The very wording of these instructions revealed that "the King's Subjects" was a shifting and confusing category; "the Minorquins" and "his Majesty's German Subjects" were clearly identified as part of this group, even as their labels and "national" identifications marked them as different from Barton and his officers. As "the King's Subjects," however, all were entitled to redemption. This more capacious reading of subjecthood, which recognized as subjects those who had moved into the king's allegiance, held sway: in a subsequent letter Millbanke was able to assure his correspondents that he had demanded the remaining captives.[113]

Although many consuls and governors remained uncertain about whom, exactly, they might categorize as subjects, their negotiations with the Barbary states suggest that despite such qualms, they often pursued expansive, sometimes aggressive, definitions of subjecthood based on their readings of treaties. References to Minorcans being reclaimed as subjects, for example, pepper the correspondence. In 1715, "six persons [being Minorcan] . . . were delivered" to the consul. Then, in 1756, the consul wondered whether the captives he had freed were to be landed in England or returned to Minorca. Two Minorcans were released in 1760 as British subjects despite the fact that Minorca was at that point under French rule. Lorens Pons was redeemed from Algiers in 1768 as a "native of Minorca." Finally, in 1779, "eleven Minorkeen sailors taken out of the private ship . . . belonging to Mahon . . . were in consequence delivered up."[114]

Another category of persons redeemed from North Africa and often considered on official lists of "British subjects" or "British prisoners" were individuals originating in the German province of Hanover. Although the personal nature of the union between Britain and Hanover prompted constitutional questions about Hanoverian subjecthood, Hanoverians were nevertheless regularly rescued "in their capacity as subjects of the British king."[115] The secretary of state wrote to the British consul in Morocco as early as 1728 to "acquaint you with His Majesty's further pleasure, that you should inquire whether there are any of his German subjects in captivity in the emperor of Morocco's dominions, and that if you find there are any, you should apply for their discharge," instructions which were confirmed by the 1729 treaty with Morocco.[116] While the numbers of Hanoverians officially rescued were small, administrators were consistent in their treatment of "His Majesty's German Subjects."[117] Overall, references to "Spaniards," "foreigners," "Genoese," "inhabitants of Gibraltar," "Minorquins," and "Hanoverians" abound in correspondence relating to redemptions and suggest that the category of British subject widened to accommodate the many peoples who assisted the British garrisons and who were taken captive on the high seas.

There were also plenty of occasions where British administrators upheld the protections associated with subject status even if they recognized that individuals might not be legally considered subjects. The story of Patron John Podesta illustrates the ambivalence with which many administrators approached questions of subject status, and their willingness to extend protections to those upon whose services they relied. On June 28, 1779, Podesta proposed sailing to Genoa to fetch provisions for the besieged garrison at Gibraltar. A native of Genoa who had resided at Gibraltar for many years, he had regularly navigated ships across the Mediterranean currents to engage in trade and to supply his adopted outpost. This time, however, he sought some guarantees of protection and recognition, asking for a British passport in case he should encounter Algerine cruisers along his journey. After taking a 500-pound security, Governor Eliott granted Podesta a protective pass for the duration of six months. Perhaps hoping to highlight his compliance with official orders, Eliott dutifully noted on the back of this pass that it was "issued to John Baptista Podesta (tho' not a British subject) he being this time solely employed on His Britannic Majesty's service."[118] And yet, even as he labeled Podesta "not a British subject," Eliott argued that his relationship to the monarch—in the form of loyal service—entitled him to protection.

Sometime in September 1780, well after the expiration of his pass, Patron Podesta and his crew were seized by the Algerines while carrying what was ostensibly another cargo of supplies for Gibraltar. Consular correspondence indicates that Nathaniel Davison, the British consul then stationed in Algiers, made repeated attempts to reclaim Podesta and his men from slavery in 1781 and 1782.[119] The dey consistently refused to relinquish them, arguing that they were Genoese rather than English subjects and that they had been sailing under Genoese colors. They were not, in his understanding, entitled to be set at liberty. Despite Davison's persistent pleas for instructions about how to proceed, he was finally authorized in December 1782 to make "serious remonstrance" on behalf of the captives who had been "unwarrantably put into a state of slavery."[120] For several years, Davison worked to free them, but only with the arrival of Sir Roger Curtis's embassy in 1783 was any progress made.[121] By 1785, the secretary of state instructed Consul Charles Logie to apply for ransom money from the Ironmonger's Company to secure the release of these captives,[122] and by 1787 Podesta had finally been set free, awarded 50 pounds for his troubles, as was sometimes the custom for British subjects who had suffered while in captivity.[123]

The significant point here is that Podesta and his crew, identified as Genoese and captured well after the expiration of a legitimate pass, were offered protections generally reserved for British subjects and were ultimately redeemed through official British channels. One consul's letter offers insight into why administrators might have treated these men as entitled to the protections of British subjects when they had elsewhere been labeled "not British subjects." The situation of Podesta "is discouraging to others employed in giving relief to the Garrison . . . especially considered he was an Inhabitant of Gibraltar for upwards of twenty four years . . . navigating under a British pass."[124] In order to maintain confidence in British protection and to keep the garrison supplied, colonial officials needed to extend benefits associated with British subjecthood even to those they recognized to be foreigners.

In addition, there was still confusion in official circles, as Eliott had made clear, about whether Podesta, a longtime inhabitant of Gibraltar, was or was not a British subject. Perhaps in the absence of certainty on this point, it seemed safest to regard him as deserving of protection, given that his services or those of his compatriots might be instrumental in the future. In the negotiations for Podesta's release, administrators understood that they must demonstrate a willingness to shield those who served the garrison as well as *bona fide* subjects, and it was thus that the more traditional understandings of belonging were blurred. If anything, Podesta's case confirms that several paths to securing the protections of subject status existed, particularly where many of the Gibraltarian mariners and suppliers were concerned. Eliott recognized that Podesta was "not a British subject" since he was not born within the dominions and allegiance of the king. Nonetheless, he and other administrators also understood that numerous foreigners who had not been formally naturalized needed to be included under the aegis of protection, and they essentially employed definitions of subjecthood that allowed for local protections and that were attuned to the exigencies of everyday life in the Mediterranean.

From the perspective of many North African leaders, these fluid and generous interpretations of subjecthood and protection arose far too frequently. In 1752, an outraged *alcayde* in Tetuan complained that some Genoese and other foreigners had committed several "piracies" while protected by a pass that had been issued to them at Gibraltar. They were, he argued, under the spurious protection of the English nation. His British correspondent, however, replied with a categorical and confident defense of these individuals, contending that the greatest part of Gibraltar's residents were Genoese and other foreigners who, as inhabitants of Gibraltar, were deemed to be British subjects and recognized as such by treaty.[125] Moreover, in 1788, John Morando, "native of Gibraltar of Genoese parents," was included in a list of eleven deserters who had applied to be reclaimed as British subjects, most of whom were "natives" of Sligo, Dublin, Lancashire, and Falmouth.[126] Although here the British administrators categorically claimed these subjects, probably relying on an expansive interpretation of existing treaties to do so, many may have recognized that the *alcayde* had just cause for critiquing their disingenuousness.

Indeed, if consuls, governors, and their superiors in London were inclined to claim an array of individuals as British subjects, they simultaneously recognized that they had to retain some legitimacy in the eyes of the Barbary powers. In response to the repeated frustrations expressed by North African rulers, colonial administrators negotiating on behalf of enslaved persons often had to prioritize their motley crew and furnish "proofs" of their belonging. On the one hand, they embraced the advantages of a flexible interpretation of subjecthood and demonstrated a broad willingness to protect numerous individuals in the Mediterranean. On the other hand, they sought to avoid the dangers associated with demanding too many as subjects. In the early 1780s, for example, Consul Davison engaged in a delicate balancing act—between attempting to secure the release of all of his Majesty's subjects and not demanding so many that he alienated the Dey of Algiers whose cooperation he desperately needed. Davison repeatedly noted that the dey accused him of "always asking for slaves" or of "always asking for Genoese."[127] He "was very angry at my plaguing him so often about slaves" and apparently insisted that the Hanoverian captives "were not English."[128] Davison's primary consular responsibility was to protect those deemed British subjects, but in order to do so, he had to spend considerable time and energy establishing the legitimacy of subjects' status in the eyes of his correspondents and had to persuade the dey of his integrity. The differences between Davison's and the Dey of Algiers' ideas of British subjecthood threatened to end negotiations altogether.

Sir Roger Curtis's subsequent negotiations with the dey in 1783, which occurred after Davison had failed to secure the captives' release, reveal how the practical realities of redeeming men and women forced many administrators to develop hierarchies among the king's subjects. In approaching the dey, Curtis reported having divided the captives into three groups: subjects whom he demanded as a matter of right, captives whom he felt that he could not "peremptorily claim . . . as a matter of right, yet . . . had hopes of obtaining," and individuals whom he did not attempt to redeem because there was not adequate evidence of their being his Majesty's subjects. He demanded Hanoverians who had proof of their status and "Natives of Gibraltar" whose status had been officially confirmed as a matter of right, no doubt grounding his demands in treaty articles and instructions sent to consuls over the years. Where the second group of captives was concerned, he sought to obtain their release but did so without issuing a categorical claim to them; Curtis no doubt hoped to avoid offending the dey and having him question the legitimacy of requests for the first group. This second group included Patron Podesta and his crew, whom he knew to be Genoese but traveling under British protection, and Patron Cannisso and Vincenzo Fiallo, whom he suspected of being deserters to Spain. These individuals' services were useful to Britain, but their claims to subjecthood were less clear than those of individuals who were obviously protected by treaty. Finally, although he received memorials from Giovanni Ratto, Giovani Antonio Pomlor, and John Baptista Longar imploring his intervention, Curtis felt that none of them "adduced sufficient proof of their pretensions to the right of British Subjects to induce me to make a claim of them."[129] They were likely left to their fates in Algiers. The subtext of this negotiation, like so many others, was that there were numerous individuals who might be requested depending on how expansively subjecthood was defined and on how useful individuals had proven themselves to be.[130] A successful ambassador would know how to prioritize the subjecthood of those whose freedom he sought.

In many of these negotiations, the Dey of Algiers and Emperor of Morocco did not necessarily agree with British consuls' assertions that certain captives were British subjects. The question of "proof" lingered, both spoken and unspoken. Under such circumstances, British administrators might choose either to abandon individuals to their enslavement or to secure verification of their identities. The value of a captive or the strength of his connections in London might prove decisive in determining whether such official documentation was secured. In 1768, Consul Fraser confronted a dey who refused to free two Englishmen "until a certificate of their being English came under his Majesty's seal."[131] Although frustrated by this offensive lack of faith in a consular representative, the secretary of state nonetheless responded with a royal letter to the dey confirming these two men's "Englishness" and giving "more weight & strength" to Fraser's representation.[132] Similarly, in 1761, Consul Aspinwall attempted to claim John Jones by means of "Letters & Papers from the Office . . . whereby he was claimed as a British Subject by his Majesty's Secretary of State."[133] When the consul's word was deemed insufficient, British subjecthood was held to be verifiable by letter or by certificate from the highest levels of officialdom in London.

Securing such documentation often proved difficult and time-consuming in the era before the widespread use of individual passports, but consuls understood that taking these steps might actually strengthen individual claims.[134] When Davison was forced to request "proof" of the Hanoverians' status—something beyond just "their word for being his Majesty's subjects"—he recognized that such verification protected the interests of *bona fide* British subjects. As he explained:

> was I to apply for the release of everyone who comes to me & calls himself a Hanoverian, many who are not would call themselves such with the hopes of getting their Freedom, the consequence would be that if it reached the Dey's knowledge, he would not only insist on a Ransom being paid for them, but likewise make difficulties afterwards about releasing people known to be his Majesty's subjects.[135]

Davison's observations illustrate that even as there were reasons to uphold broad definitions of subjecthood, there were also circumstances under which a more cautious reading actually served the interests of subjects. Perhaps even more important, his remarks pointed to the desirability of subjecthood—many claimants recognized that British subjecthood brought with it certain valuable protections in the Mediterranean.

The hierarchy of "His Majesty's Subjects" hinted at by Curtis was also replicated in the many requests for documentation preserved in official correspondence. Hanoverians, Gibraltarians, and Minorcans seem to have required more concrete proof of affiliation than British subjects who spoke

English and were adduced to be from Great Britain, suggesting that language and self-presentation could be integral markers of subjecthood. In 1783, Sir Roger Curtis personally determined that one captive spoke English well enough to make him legitimate and judged it "proper to require this man."[136] On other occasions, consuls determined that captives' characters entitled them to protection as British subjects.[137] Such informal verifications, however, were not as easily obtained for the non-native English speakers. Very occasionally, individuals might be asked to testify about a given captive's provenance. For example, in determining whether Michael Ache was indeed a native of Minorca and therefore a British subject, Consul Logie summoned a man he knew to be a native of Minorca who established that he knew Ache and had sailed with his father.[138] Although the Dey of Algiers and Emperor of Morocco preferred official documentation, they sometimes accepted a consul's informal confirmation of subjecthood.

More typically, formal proofs were required for consuls to feel comfortable claiming non-native English speakers and for North African officials to release them. On several occasions, "certificates of their being Hanoverian" were required by consuls before they would consider requesting men as British subjects.[139] Proof of residence, familial status, and loyalty to the British Empire might also render someone more easily redeemable, but each nonetheless entailed some kind of official documentation. When Peter Gavarron languished in captivity, the consul stationed in Algiers sought proof of his status and of his eligibility for redemption from administrators in Gibraltar. It came in the form of a certificate reading:

> it appears upon the Books of Record in this Office that Peter Gavarron, about twenty-seven years of age, a naturalized subject of his Majesty & an Inhabitant of this Garrison, where he has a house confirm'd by the Governor & where his wife & children (natives of Gibraltar) have constantly resided with him; that he remain'd in the Garrison during the Siege and has been absent about two months & a half.[140]

Gavarron, whose name did not appear in the 1777 List of Inhabitants for Gibraltar, was likely a more recent arrival of Spanish origin. By 1783, however, he was attached to the garrison not just by property and by family, but had proven his loyalty to Britain and his usefulness to the garrison during the Great Siege (1779–1783). Although the certificate referred to his "naturalization," it did not specify whether this was an official naturalization by act of Parliament, which would have been expensive, or a local naturalization based on his loyal service.

Regardless, the certificate itself points to the range of ways in which an individual might have proven his allegiance and belonging in the British Mediterranean and to the variety of official means by which it was verified. Proofs thus belied both the discretion consuls exercised in patrolling the boundaries of subjecthood and the ways in which captives might rely on acquired languages or character references to persuade consuls of their affiliations.

In all these cases, whether subjects were proven to be "real" or "pretended," whether they returned home or died in slavery, and whether they were set at liberty free of payment or ransomed at an exorbitant price, administrators and captives alike articulated a common understanding that subjecthood brought with it certain protections. In many respects, negotiations in the Mediterranean gave new meaning to the old adage that "Britons never will be slaves," irrevocably linking British subjecthood and redemption from slavery in ways that they were not in the Atlantic or Indian Oceans.[141] The petitions of French captives in North Africa, for example, gradually served to associate ideas about Frenchness with ideas about freedom, as captives sought to define the characteristics that made them truly French and sought redemption as a reward for proven loyalty to the monarch.[142] A similar dynamic was at work in the British case as individuals and administrators employed expansive definitions of subjecthood to make and defend claims to freedom.

By identifying individuals as subjects when they demanded restitutions, administrators also evinced a belief that British subjects were entitled to redemption. Moreover, when consuls intervened for subjects or requested proofs of subjecthood, they seemingly lent official sanction to the notion that subjects were due distinctive economic privileges. If the liberties of free-born subjects were touted throughout the British realm and the relationship between subject and sovereign was widely believed to be a mutual one of obedience and protection, in the Mediterranean these protections became intertwined with the safety and economic well-being of those who served the British monarch. Here, redemption, like protective passes, was construed as a right of the loyal subject, however that subjecthood had been acquired.

IN 1788, a royal proclamation was issued "for recalling and prohibiting seamen from serving Foreign Princes and States." Although this proclamation merely echoed others that had been printed over the course of the eighteenth century, it also suggested that certain specific rights had come to be associated with subjecthood.[143] The proclamation ordered "that if any such Master of Ships, Pilots, Mariners, Seamen, Shipwrights, or other Seafaring Men (being

Our Subject) shall be taken in any foreign service by the Turks, Algerines, or any others, they shall not be reclaimed by Us as Subjects of Great Britain."[144] From the perspective of imperial administrators, this order had repeatedly been necessary in a region where populations were transient, where men and women were of variable loyalty, and where mariners were in such demand that they might easily seek better pay or terms of service elsewhere. Even the British monarchy needed to make a deliberate attempt to keep those it deemed useful subjects within its allegiance by threatening to withdraw coveted privileges.

But the proclamation also hinted that understandings of subjecthood had shifted subtly, influenced by attitudes to royal protection that had emerged in the Mediterranean. The proclamation confirmed that subjects of Great Britain, when taken by Barbary corsairs, were usually entitled to redemption; it also indicated that such privileges could be denied to renegades, revealing that the privileges inherent to the relationship between subject and sovereign might be rescinded and that subjecthood might itself be temporary. While Calvin's Case and subsequent legal treatises had often conceived of subject status as unalienable and indissoluble, the reality of subjecthood was never so straightforward in practice.

By the time this proclamation was issued, the power of the corsairs and their threat to British ships and persons had waned. But in many respects, the occupation of Gibraltar and Minorca had made the British more vulnerable in the Mediterranean, dependent on the assistance and services of a polyglot and itinerant local population in order to maintain their naval and military dominance in the region. Although British governors and consuls were generally more conscientious about redemptions than the crown and state had been in the seventeenth century, they also consistently proved themselves willing to countenance inclusive definitions of subject status as they struggled to keep their outposts provisioned and secure.[145] Drawn into protracted negotiations with the Barbary states over the course of the eighteenth century, many came to view subjecthood as temporary and protean, just as they played a critical role in corroborating and sanctioning the rights of subjects to Mediterranean Passes and to redemption from slavery.

Among the many groups of individuals of shifting loyalties and statuses, however, deserters from the British garrisons, who entered the service of other European powers in the Mediterranean and were subsequently captured by Barbary corsairs, provide a crucial final example of administrators' essential role in mediating the boundaries and protections of British subjecthood. Deserters posed a particular challenge to ideas of "unalienable subjecthood," and their many requests for protection forced administrators to make sometimes-conflicting decisions about whether the relationship between subject and sovereign might ever be severed. In 1757, for example, Governor Tyrawley offered his written opinion that deserters and men who had entered the foreign service were "all born the King's subjects, though bad ones," and that, regardless of their service abroad, the king "does not lose his right over them."[146] Writing in the midst of the Seven Years' War, he may have been desperate for soldiers and hopeful that deserters might be transformed into useful combatants. He also expressed a belief that all those who had been subjects were still entitled to the protections of subjecthood even if their loyalties had been called into question.

But where some administrators were sympathetic to the circumstances that led men to desert and worked toward securing their release, others, like Governor O'Hara of Gibraltar, reacted rather differently. As a military man, perhaps he was more critical of desertion because of the threat it posed to the armed forces.[147] Or perhaps he was aware that the British had far more dependable subjects in Gibraltar.[148] He wrote to Consul Logie, categorically stating that he hoped the British state would not be obliged to claim these deserters. He contended "that deserters should never be re-incorporated into the King's Troops, and as there is still less prospect of their becoming useful members of society in any other line of life, I think it most adviseable leaving them to their fate in foreign service, or slavery, as an example to deter others from such gross villainy and Infidelity to their legal sovereign."[149] For O'Hara, blatant acts of disloyalty signaled that the privileges of subjecthood had been forfeited. Whereas other governors seemed inclined to treat a range of both "native" and "foreign" inhabitants as subjects and to extend various protections to them, O'Hara believed otherwise of deserters. Though it may be impossible to determine exactly how his opinions shaped policy, it is not hard to imagine that O'Hara might have chosen to remain silent where the redemption of certain deserters was concerned and when his support might have swayed a dey or emperor. This was another dark and unpredictable side to subjecthood.

O'Hara was not alone in expressing disdain for deserters. On several occasions during the 1760s, 1770s, and 1780s, British administrators found themselves stymied in their efforts to redeem such men and confronted North African officials who argued that deserters had forfeited claims to the privileges of British subjecthood. The Dey of Algiers made clear that he did not appreciate being "plagued" on behalf of deserters who had "served the Enemies of the State." He posited that such persons were no longer loyal subjects entitled to redemption but enemy captives for whom a substantial ransom must be paid should the British wish to free them.[150] On another occasion, he told the British consul that redeemable captives were those who could be proven to be British and "not to have been in the service of another nation by land."[151] In his correspondence, the Dey of Algiers regularly argued that serving "another nation" transformed subjects themselves into "enemies of the state."

The Emperor of Morocco expressed similar opinions in 1774 and 1775. He refused to believe that Michael Ache, a native of Minorca and British subject, who had deserted from Spanish-occupied Ceuta, could actually still be a British subject. Ache had served a French officer for two years at the conclusion of the Seven Years' War, then been employed in a bakery in Italy for three years, next worked in Barcelona for five years, and ultimately deserted from the regiment he had joined in Majorca.[152] Given this history, perhaps it is not surprising that the Emperor of Morocco questioned Ache's credentials as a British subject. But even the Emperor of Morocco might be persuaded to change his opinions about deserters. When Governor Boyd explained to him that if he refused to return British subjects who escaped Spanish garrisons, the consequence would be that "all those Musulmen who escape from the chains of Christian princes must . . . be returned to their captivity,"[153] the emperor changed his tune, agreeing that "British subjects who escape from Spanish Garrisons in Africa ought to be free and sent to Gibraltar."[154] Although deserters' allegiances and subjecthood might be questionable, the Emperor of Morocco, like his British peers, recognized that he might lose valuable man- and ship-power if loyalty was policed too strictly.

Desertion in the Mediterranean, as elsewhere, triggered provocative questions about whether British subject status was unalienable and unchanging or renounceable and variable. It was nearly impossible to foresee whether deserters would be reclaimed as British subjects or abandoned as renegades. Persistent disagreements over their status only confirm that subjecthood in the Mediterranean remained unclear and unpredictable, often shaped by individual administrators who could determine whether men of shifting loyalties were offered the protections of subject status or left to their fates in Barbary.

But while most negotiations over deserters concerned men who had actually entered the foreign service, the case of John Jones reveals that other kinds of "desertion" were known to occur and to shape the protections associated with subjecthood. Jones, who had been given French papers at Toulon entitling him to sail in a Neapolitan vessel to London, was taken captive during this journey. When the British consul tried to claim him and presented papers from the secretary of state attesting that he was a legitimate subject, the Dey of Algiers refused to release him, arguing that "he was a good for nothing Vagabond, & was turned Maltese & Neapolitan & Roman Catholic too; and that shewd he had deserted his Country's Service & Religion exclusive of Liberty."[155]

Although many of the Gibraltarians and Minorcans redeemed as British subjects in the eighteenth century were themselves Roman Catholics, the juxtaposition of desertion of "country" and "religion" in describing Jones is significant. It suggests not only that religion and loyalty were intertwined but also that Roman Catholics were often believed to be less entitled to the benefits of British subjecthood. And the Dey of Algiers was far from being the only one to hold these views. Enslaved Britons seem to have feared that renouncing their religion might render them "irredeemable."[156] For many captives and their captors, a difference of faith, particularly if that faith was Catholicism, might be viewed as a reason to question which rights were due subjects. Perhaps not surprisingly, then, the protections and rights due Catholic subjects would become particularly contentious during the 1760s and 1770s as territories with large French Catholic populations were added to the British Empire.

4

His Britannick Majesty's New Subjects

THE RIGHTS OF SUBJECTS IN GRENADA AND QUEBEC

IN 1771, GOVERNOR William Leyborne lamented that he was obliged to make an unfavorable report about affairs on the island of Grenada. Apologizing to the secretary of state, he wrote that "the break between His Majesty's Old and New Subjects is of such a nature, so little intercourse between them, such a thorough want of confidence and in short so rooted in Enmity, that I see but very little prospect of a reconciliation."[1] Indeed, prolonged and virulent disagreements between "old subjects," who identified as British-born and Protestant, and "new subjects," who were predominantly French Catholic, threatened to tear apart this British colony throughout the 1760s and 1770s. They challenged even the most patient and capable of colonial governors and secretaries of state. And they were not peculiar to Grenada. At the end of 1764, for example, Governor James Murray sent an emissary to London charged with the unenviable task of providing authorities with a clear account of the "situation in Canada." Facing similar animosities between Protestant and Catholic inhabitants in Quebec,[2] Murray clung to the distant hope that "some remedy may be found out" by consulting with his superiors.[3]

As peace finally returned to the British Empire following the Seven Years' War, recurrent civil tensions repeatedly threatened the economic and political stability of both Grenada and Quebec. In reams of colonial correspondence, administrators consistently provided reports on the "harmony" prevailing or the "factiousness subsisting" between subjects in both these colonies. In Grenada, the number of dispatches between governors and secretaries of state dedicated to the conflicts between old and new subjects was unrivaled, except in a few years when discussion of the island's defenses or its difficulties with runaway slaves seemed particularly relevant. Similarly, letters from the governors of Quebec were preoccupied with the rights and protection of their new subjects, and local officials regularly provided superiors with updates about French Catholic loyalty and allegiance. Administrators in both of these ceded colonies were quite clearly engrossed by such conflicts, aware that these "enmities" threatened to disrupt imperial reconstruction.

Within the formerly French territories acquired by Britain under the Treaty of Paris, inhabitants of Grenada and Quebec became British subjects with "the scratch of a pen."[4] At first glance, these territories seemed quite different. Grenada, an island in the southeastern Caribbean, was a rapidly developing plantation society, with an enslaved population that vastly outnumbered its white minority. Quebec, a far larger province, was a rural society where the European population predominated, although a fur trade involving indigenous peoples remained an important part of the economy. Despite these divergences, Grenada and Quebec shared a crucial demographic parallel. In Grenada, the vast majority of the 1,200 or so white inhabitants were French Catholics, and in Quebec, 60,000 to 70,000 French Catholics dwarfed the population of a few hundred British merchants and traders.[5] It was the presence of these large French Catholic populations that presented administrators with similar challenges in integrating these new territories and that most directly accounted for the struggles that overwhelmed both Grenada and Quebec in the years after 1763.

The loyalties of these French Catholics were, in many respects, doubly suspect—both because they were individuals born within the dominions and allegiance of the French king and also because of their Catholic faith. Britain had been at war with France for much of the eighteenth century, and the distinction between Protestant and Catholic remained an integral part of an emerging British identity.[6] The large numbers of French Catholics in Grenada and Quebec therefore provoked widespread concerns among colonial administrators and the central government more generally about governing Catholics in an empire where non-Protestants were historically treated as second-class subjects. In the 1760s and 1770s, uncertainties about the status of these inhabitants and about whether they could be exempt from the penal laws against Catholics in force within the realm, sit in local assemblies, and retain their own civil laws would bedevil the colonies as they did members of the Privy Council and Parliament.[7] Although the rights of free people of color became a topic of vigorous debate in early-nineteenth-century Grenada, in the decades after the Seven Years' War, it was the rights of white French Catholic subjects that preoccupied colonial administrators.

Whereas the Acadians had been forcibly removed from Nova Scotia in 1755 when their presence was deemed a threat to the "security and protection" of the province, colonial administrators responded very differently to Grenadian and Canadian French Catholics in 1763.[8] Instead of provoking deportations, the presence of these "new subjects" persuaded administrators that French Catholics were individuals whose numbers and skills were essential to imperial survival, whether that was in managing plantations worked largely by slaves or in cultivating lands in climates that many Britons found inhospitable. As it became clear that British-born settlers would flock to neither territory in the postwar era and that French Catholics would likely remain a majority in both, governors and secretaries of state increasingly came to recognize that the allegiance and contributions of non-British-born populations were critical if the ceded colonies were to become productive and well-protected settlements. In certain respects, these colonies seemed to promise that the perennial fear about inadequate manpower might finally be overcome in the British Empire.

One 1763 pamphlet, which extolled expansion in the West Indies, noted that the "bodies and estates of the colonists are as much the riches of our country, as tho' comprehended within the same territory," and that they might, in fact, serve to offset the "smallness of our numbers."[9] Turning to the advantages of Quebec, the same author argued not only that Quebec would serve as a crucial buffer should the French try to attack the continental colonies, but also that "the possession of Canada with its inhabitants" increased security because these individuals became "English subjects."[10] Such sentiments were echoed by high-level colonial administrators, who insisted that nothing was more essential to the king's service "than to retain as many French subjects as possible and to prevent them from leaving their homes to go off to the colonies that may remain in France's possession."[11] Although some feared that the new colonies might drain Britain's population, there were numerous others who proposed that these territories might bolster its numerical strength. As the challenge of Britain's "small numbers" versus France's far larger ones continued to loom large, the transfer of subjects and settlers, even those of suspect faith, was seen as integral to the safety and growth of the British Empire.

In both Grenada and Quebec, then, the needs of an expanding British empire and the limits of British military power meant that the new subjects were widely regarded as capable of making valuable contributions. Even if administrators were wary of the new subjects' religious and linguistic attachment to France, which became especially strong during wartime, most governors found themselves repeatedly trying to conciliate French Catholics. When George Scott first arrived in Grenada as its military conqueror and commander, he wrote to London suggesting that the adopted subjects there be allowed some share in the new government. He recognized, of course, that they might behave like the Acadians of Nova Scotia and be "always a thorn in our Sides," but he also appeared hopeful that concessions to Roman Catholics might provide another path to integration within the British Empire.[12] Similarly, James Murray, the first civil governor of Quebec, wrote to the Lords Commissioners indicating how important it was to win over the French Catholics remaining in his province. The security of the empire depended upon them, and "could they be indulged with a few Priviledges which the Laws deny to Roman Catholicks at Home . . . [the new subjects] might become the most faithfull, and most useful, set of men in this American Empire."[13] Notwithstanding near-constant opposition from influential British planters and traders, most governors in Grenada and Quebec remained in favor of extending rights and protections to French Catholics, whom they understood to be loyal subjects, and the administration at home seems to have upheld their policies.[14]

As Murray's letter to the Lords Commissioners made clear, however, some of the concessions he urged for "new subjects" were "priviledges which the Laws deny to Roman Catholicks at Home." And while a confluence of factors encouraged more flexible approaches to subjecthood and its associated privileges at an administrative level, the constitutional questions raised by the presence of French Catholics were not always so easily ignored. Whereas both French Catholics and British-born Protestants in Grenada and Quebec consistently articulated that the "constitution" and "law" were the British subject's rights, each offered differing interpretations of the character of that constitution. Furthermore, the rights demanded by new subjects usually undermined or contradicted those insisted upon by old subjects. Forced to mediate these constitutional confrontations between new and old subjects, officials grappled with how to secure the allegiance of all "His Britannick Majesty's Subjects." Perhaps predictably, their willingness to grant certain religious freedoms to the French Catholics in an attempt to appease these new and necessary constituents frustrated many of the old subjects, who were determined to maintain a Protestant ascendancy or English law and whose loyalty was also essential to the imperial enterprise.

As administrators wrestled with these difficult questions, they faced the persistent and determined voices of their various constituents. Indeed, both old and new subjects leveraged their positions as much-needed settlers and routinely sought privileges they believed were owed them after years of war and their numerous declarations of allegiance to George III. They emphasized their utility and employed threats to move elsewhere. One Grenada petition noted that discrimination against new subjects might occasion the much-dreaded "departure of many wealthy and industrious inhabitants from an island imperfectly settled."[15] Conversely, a 1765 memorial submitted by the British merchants in Quebec remonstrating against Governor Murray proclaimed that they were "so very unhappy that we must be under the Necessity of removing from [the province] unless timely prevented from it" and simultaneously mentioned that their settlement had contributed to the "advantage of our Mother Country, by causing an additional increase to her manufactures and by a considerable importation of them . . . to promote the commercial interests of this Province and render it flourishing."[16] All of these subjects, though professing a deep loyalty, recognized that colonial administrators relied upon their social, political, and economic contributions, and capitalized on fears about inadequate settler populations to exert pressure on officials.

In the 1760s and 1770s, the subjects who actively and forcefully made claims to certain rights often relied on petitions, addresses, or memorials to do so, and it is these petitions that most concretely reveal the diverse understandings of subjects' rights in existence at the time and the uncertain nature of the constitutional settlements for both Grenada and Quebec.[17] Hailed as the "indisputable right of even the meanest subject," the petition allowed the subject to approach and express grievances to a distant monarch.[18] It was an acknowledged and permitted means for "collective remonstrance" precisely because it was worded in a language of deference, humility, and supplication, and because it "encapsulated the relationship of lordship and dependence that was the core of ideal political relations."[19] For many in the eighteenth century, petitions were the only form of political expression to which they had access, and individuals who were not entitled to elect assembly or council members could nonetheless have their voices heard by submitting them.[20] Often drafted by trained lawyers or writers, the petition was generally accessible to both the literate and illiterate, provided that they had the necessary funds.

In the specific cases of Grenada and Quebec, petitions were widely used by both French- and English-speakers. Questions about the rights of "His Britannick Majesty's New Subjects" were transformed into broader debates about subjecthood because inhabitants availed themselves of outlets such as the petition in order to engage these questions and push them beyond the purview of colonial governors. French Catholics both proclaimed themselves loyal servants and also first asserted their right to vote for and sit in an assembly through a petition to the Grenadian governor, just as British Protestants challenged their claims in a counter-petition. French Catholics in Quebec initially asked the king to restore their "ancient usages" through a memorial, even as those who opposed them also expressed themselves in a variety of addresses. The "enmity" to which governors' letters repeatedly referred was far more than an antipathy between two populations; it was a heated and enduring contest about what a *bona fide* British subject might claim as rights. Perhaps most important, it was a contest sparked by and recorded in petitions, rather than a question that was merely settled by the Board of Trade or the courts.

Across the petitions submitted by subjects themselves and in the official correspondence surrounding those petitions, several questions repeatedly surfaced: Were the rights of British subjects the same across the empire or might they vary from territory to territory? Were British subjects individuals who adhered to a constitution that guaranteed a Protestant ascendancy or were they individuals who had the freedom to live under their own constitutions and laws? Despite similarities in the questions being asked, disagreements about the rights of new Catholic subjects manifested themselves somewhat differently in each of the ceded colonies. In Grenada, the specific debate focused on whether or not French Catholics might sit in the assembly and be elected to public office without having taken the Test. In Quebec, the issue of predominant concern that consistently engaged administrative and ministerial attention was the appropriateness of allowing French civil law when English law had theoretically been introduced wholesale by the governor's commission. Although English law had also been introduced in Grenada, there appears to have been virtually no discussion about maintaining French civil or commercial law for the subjects there. Nevertheless, in both of these colonies, debates centered on the particular privileges the British subject might expect in a transformed empire.

This chapter not only compares the struggles between old and new subjects, but also analyzes the ways in which inhabitants, colonial lobbyists, governors, secretaries of state, and members of Parliament turned to specific understandings of the relationship between subject and sovereign to bolster arguments in favor of, or against, expanded privileges for white French Catholics. It is primarily focused on the role that subjects themselves played in articulating new and controversial ideas about the rights due British subjects in the ceded colonies. By relying on the petition and the familiar idea that subjects owing allegiance were entitled to certain rights, liberties, and privileges, old and new subjects alike generated sometimes radical, alternative definitions of subjecthood. Although their birth in formerly French territories rendered their subject status questionable to those who adhered to strict interpretations of case law, and although their faith meant that any concessions made to them would be repeatedly contested, French Catholics in Grenada and Quebec nonetheless readily engaged their opponents. Through these debates, they gradually redrew the boundaries of subjecthood and secured rights for themselves that diverged from those of Catholic subjects within the British Isles.

Considering the parallels and divergences in the petitions and opinions proffered by individuals in Grenada and Quebec demonstrates some of the ways that various members of the British Empire leveraged notions of obedience and protection and capitalized on local conditions to negotiate the rights of subjects. Indeed, the differing moments at which the French Catholics and their allies were successful hint at how the preponderance of loyal Catholics and their reactions to local and global developments might shape the rights associated with subjecthood. The animosities decried by Leyborne and Murray reflected enduring postwar debates about the position of, and rights owed, British subjects scattered across an empire. Struggles in Grenada and Quebec illustrate not only that definitions of subject status were constantly fluctuating in the eighteenth century but also that subjects were themselves instrumental in negotiating the opportunities provided by a shared subjecthood.

Settlements and Unsettlements in the Ceded Colonies

Throughout the 1760s, many inhabitants and administrators viewed the enmities between old and new subjects in Grenada and Quebec as intertwined, even mutually constitutive. Contemporaries, in fact, commonly invoked circumstances in one ceded territory when making arguments about the other. When they addressed the Privy Council about the possibility of exempting French Catholics in Grenada from the Test, for example, officials in Whitehall referred directly to the situation in Quebec. They noted that in both colonies, the privilege of serving upon juries and acting as advocates in certain courts was granted without requiring a declaration against transubstantiation. But they wondered about the appropriateness of exempting members of the Grenada Council and Assembly from the Test, when these were advantages "that are not allowed to the new subjects in Canada."[21] Similarly, in 1768, petitioners in Quebec asserted that they were emboldened to ask for an assembly "incouraged afresh by His Majesty's Goodness to his Subjects in the Grenadas," where an assembly had been granted several years earlier.[22] Although Grenada and Quebec have been analyzed in relative isolation,[23] observers in the eighteenth century were well aware that questions about the rights of Catholic subjects in both these colonies were intimately connected.[24]

Some commentators even perceived that debates about rights due Roman Catholics were part of broader continuum that involved Ireland and Minorca, among others. In 1765, when the attorney general and solicitor general were approached for their opinion on a plan for the ecclesiastical affairs of Quebec, they asked to consult the papers and reports made "upon the Subject of the Roman Catholick Religion at Minorca" subsequent to its annexation to Britain in 1713, in order to gather information about how predecessors had handled parallel problems.[25] Moreover, in analyzing the Quebec Act (1774), William Knox noted that there were several precedents for how the government might manage a majority Catholic population: "Ireland and Minorca furnished the most striking instances of the treatment, given by our ancestors to a conquered people professing the *Romish* religion."[26] Colonel Isaac Barré, a prominent member of Parliament, lamented the discrepancies in policies toward Catholics across the empire, observing that "it is very singular how this poor Roman Catholic religion has been treated; in Maryland it has been tolerated, in Ireland persecuted, in Canada you choose to give it an establishment."[27] Others were more concerned to ensure that Roman Catholics were consistently accorded lesser rights than Protestants. The argument that "they cannot in reason expect to be put on any other or better footing than His Majesty's Natural Born Subjects of the same Religion" was a familiar refrain among opponents of French Catholics in Grenada and Quebec, as it was elsewhere.[28]

Perhaps it was not surprising, therefore, that those critical of policies favorable toward Roman Catholics tended to excoriate administrative conduct in both Grenada and Quebec. The author of "Strictures on the Conduct of two successive Administrations with Respect to the civil and religious Establishments in Canada and the Grenadines" argued that "popery" was being promoted "by degrees in the distant regions of the British Empire" at a time when administrators should instead be increasingly concerned to "put the civil and religious establishments of all our new acquired settlements on such a footing, as is consistent with the spirit of our free constitution, and is best calculated to secure the loyalty of the inhabitants to our gracious sovereign." Not only did he decry the fact that "his majesty's new adopted subjects in Canada and the West Indies enjoy every right and privilege of free-born protestant subjects" denied to Catholic subjects in Ireland, but he also criticized settlements made for "any part of his majesty's dominions" that violated and subverted "our happy constitution." According to this analysis, policies that upheld the Protestant ascendancy were those best calculated to "secure the loyalty" of inhabitants and to make of them good subjects; all others threatened the security of the relationship between monarch and subject.[29] Nonetheless, for all its obvious animosity toward Roman Catholics, the pamphlet did recognize that a shared history of conquest and cession had generated similar constitutional questions about the position of new subjects in both Grenada and Quebec.

Much of the colonial correspondence from this period also suggests that administrators in London viewed the ceded territories within one overarching framework and adopted a common approach to establishing their constitutions and civil governments after 1763. Like fellow-administrators in St. George or Québec, they were preoccupied by settling the new colonies and by securing British dominance; within five months of the Treaty of Paris, for example, the Board of Trade had written to the governors of Grenada, Quebec, and the Floridas for their opinions on "how the new established colonies in America may be peopled and settled with usefull, industrious inhabitants."[30] By October, the Royal Proclamation of 1763 had announced the king's intentions to establish conditions for "speedy settling our said new Governments," providing remarkably similar constitutional arrangements for each of the various ceded colonies.[31] Unlike some of the earlier North American colonies, whose charters were viewed as foundational to the "settling of government," the constitutions of both Grenada and Quebec were to be found in a range of other documents—the Royal Proclamation of 1763 and the commissions and instructions issued to governors under the royal seals.[32]

While nearly identical documents had effected the constitutional settlements of both Grenada and Quebec, these same documents were also responsible for some of the uncertainties that persisted during the postwar era. However, a number of the critical questions left unanswered by the Royal Proclamation and subsequent instructions to governors had first been introduced by the articles of capitulation, signed prior to the peace, and by the Treaty of Paris itself. Because both Grenada and Quebec initially fell to British forces well before global hostilities had drawn to a close, military leaders were responsible for drawing up capitulations that were viewed as legally binding.[33] Intended to remain in force "until a peace may determine the fate of the island" or "until the possession of Canada shall have been decided between their

Britannic and most Christian Majesties," these capitulations included provisions regarding the departing armies as well as the security of property, freedom of worship, and administration of justice for those civilians who elected to remain behind.[34] Although these capitulations recognized that there would likely be a period of military rule before peace returned and made some effort to entice conquered populations to remain in British territory by reconciling them to their new rulers, each sowed the seeds of future confusions.

For example, when the general capitulation was signed at Montréal in September 1760, Sir Jeffrey Amherst, commander-in-chief of the British army in North America, initially conceded certain rights to the French subjects residing there that "went well beyond the well-known guarantee of the 'free exercise of the Catholic, Apostolic, and Roman religion' " confirmed by the Treaty of Paris three years later. He allowed the Catholic clergy to retain its organizational and ecclesiastical functions, the religious communities to keep their properties and exemptions, and those who wished to leave for France to sell their belongings and take their proceeds with them.[35] As the author of "Strictures on the Conduct of two successive Administrations" made clear a few years later, many believed that "the complete allowance of the Romish superstition," including access to offices of trust, had been established by these articles of capitulation. While he argued that these concessions could not, in fact, have been made, not least because no royal officer could "possibly be vested with a power of making a capitulation expressly contrary to the constitution of the country," he nonetheless acknowledged that misguided readings of the capitulations held powerful sway over popular perceptions.[36]

Similarly, contemporaries were unclear about which laws and rights the capitulations had actually introduced where the new subjects were concerned. The defeated French had initially argued that the "French, Canadians, and Acadians . . . who shall remain in the colony" should remain neutral, but Article XLI of the capitulation signed at Montréal instead determined that they became "Subjects of the King."[37] When the French commander-in-chief also tried to claim that "French and Canadians shall continue to be governed according to the custom of Paris, and the Laws and usages established for this country," Amherst simply referred to the previous article, repeating that they became "Subjects of the King." Because it was the monarch's long-established privilege to bestow laws upon a conquered country, Amherst was unable officially to endorse the retention of French laws, usages, and customs.[38] But a further complication ultimately arose because neither the French nor British signatories to this capitulation specified which laws would apply to "new subjects of the king." Given that during the period of British military rule, from 1759 until 1764, numerous courts of first instance continued to resolve disputes according to French civil law, the silences of the capitulations led many to assume that French law had been accepted wholesale, even where it had not. Thus, uncertainties about what the capitulations had actually established would foment confusion and shape subsequent debates between old and new subjects.

When the Treaty of Paris was finally signed on February 10, 1763, it drew upon these earlier capitulations, and its framers inherited complex questions about the status and rights of new peoples. Throughout this agreement, George III pledged to protect freedom of worship for "his new Roman Catholic subjects . . . as far as the laws of Great Britain permit." Articles relating to Grenada and Canada were nearly identical, with article IX ceding Grenada "with the same stipulations in favour of the inhabitants of this colony, inserted in the IVth article for those of Canada." The king promised that French subjects might safely leave the colonies with their effects for a period of eighteen months if they so wished.[39] Like the preceding capitulations, however, the treaty said nothing about the exact laws by which either Grenada or Quebec was to be administered, nor did it provide further guidance about the status of the Catholic Church.

Eight months later, when the Royal Proclamation of October 1763 defined the territorial limits of the ceded colonies as well as their immediate and future forms of government, the same questions would remain unanswered. In the flurry of activity between February and October, colonial administrators in London were most concerned to assure these colonies' settlement and commercial development, even as they seemed relatively uninterested in their particular demographics or individual customs. East and West Florida, Grenada, and Quebec were treated as part of one common constitutional frame despite their manifestly different histories, economies, and populations. Furthermore, little attention was paid to the condition of the French Catholic inhabitants in Grenada or Quebec, suggesting an administrative assumption that French Catholics in both would eventually be assimilated.[40]

The proclamation was clearly intended to provide the new colonies with a "constitutional model in use in the royal colonies on the Atlantic coast, such as New York or Virginia," allowing governors to convoke assemblies as soon as the situation and circumstances of each colony should permit and stipulating that inhabitants should enjoy the protection of English laws.[41] Promises of representative assemblies, English laws, and favorable grants of land were held out to entice settlers whom administrators expected would be predominantly Protestant. Although the Royal Proclamation was obviously drafted to settle and secure the empire against future French threats and to establish parallel and balanced governments across the new territories, it nonetheless failed to answer questions about the role of Catholicism or of French law that had been raised by the earlier capitulations and treaty.

Commissions issued to Robert Melvill and James Murray, the two governors appointed to introduce civil government to Grenada and Quebec, respectively, represented the final part of the constitutional settlement for these formerly French colonies. Not only were the forms of these commissions remarkably similar, but the questions they both left unanswered provoked parallel problems for their governors. Melvill was instructed, as soon as it was appropriate, to "summon and call general assemblies of the freeholders and planters . . . in such manner as you in your discretion shall judge most proper." He was not, however, given further guidance about who might vote for members of the assembly.[42] Similarly, in the general instructions that accompanied his commission, Melvill was directed to "grant the liberty of the Catholick Religion . . . and conform with great exactness to the stipulation of the said Treaty in this respect."[43] Given that the treaty had said little about what, exactly, liberty of religion was to mean, Melvill's instructions remained rather opaque on this point.

Governor Murray's commission contained analogous instructions about summoning an assembly, but in Quebec clauses about the administration of justice proved most influential in the debates of the 1760s and 1770s. Authorized to make laws for the good governance of the province with the advice and consent of the council and assembly, Murray was also instructed that these laws should "not be repugnant, but as near as may be agreeable" to the laws of Great Britain.[44] He was empowered to constitute courts of judicature so that civil and criminal matters might be resolved according to "law and equity." All those "belonging to the courts," however, were required to subscribe to the declaration against transubstantiation. This requirement suggested that Catholics, most of whom were French Catholics, were to be excluded from the formal judicial system and that English law and equity would likely prevail.[45] Although the commission was relatively clear about which laws were to be implemented, the persistence of French law during the period of military rule encouraged many to question the intent of these provisions.

As the debates of the 1760s would make clear, confusion about what concessions the assorted capitulations, treaty, proclamation, and commissions had actually made to French Catholics surfaced almost immediately. If the proclamation was generally understood to have established English law and forms of government, including the arrangement of governor, council, and assembly familiar to the Atlantic world, this was by no means the only interpretation. A few influential voices argued that the proclamation had not introduced such significant changes. In March 1768, Lord Hillsborough, then secretary of state, claimed that those who drafted the proclamation had never intended to overturn the laws and customs of Canada, and he spoke as one who would have been familiar with their aims since he had served on the Board of Trade in 1763.[46] Given the questions left unanswered, perhaps it is not surprising that debates about which constitution and which laws had been extended to the ceded colonies arose almost as soon as civil government was established in these colonies: Had English law been extended in its entirety? If so, did this mean that the penal laws, which restricted participation in offices of trust within the realm, prohibited French Catholics from assembly or council participation within the empire? And did these English laws necessarily replace French ones or had the conquering monarch permitted some local customs to endure?

Even as inhabitants and administrators often disagreed about what had actually been settled in 1763, most would refer to the capitulations and treaty as they made arguments about subjecthood and about the status of French Catholics. They articulated a common understanding that these foundational documents had transformed new members of the empire into "His Britannick Majesty's Subjects," conferring upon them the rights, liberties, and privileges that stemmed from that relationship of dependence. For example, Francis Seymour Conway, a member of the Privy Council and ambassador in Paris, argued that French Catholics had clearly become British subjects at the transfer of territories in 1763 and that they had been granted certain privileges: "at present as Grenada is part of the British Empire and as a result participates, in common with the other colonies of His Majesty, in the privileges and protection of other ancient British Subjects, no inhabitant of that country can fail to obtain the justice due to him."[47] Memorials in favor of Catholic suffrage in Grenada repeatedly noted that the French Catholics had remained on the island with the understanding that the capitulations and treaty had granted them the privileges, immunities, indulgences, and rights of British subjects.[48] Even opponents of the French Catholics referred to these essential agreements. For British Protestants, a treaty could not transform aliens into subjects any more than it could confer rights; French Catholics could not possibly be *bona fide* British subjects because they must "still in the eye of the law be regarded as Aliens."[49] Nonetheless, old subjects recognized the centrality of these documents in debates over subjecthood, and conflicting interpretations of the capitulations and treaty continued to shape struggles over the protections associated with subject status.

Uncertainties also prompted administrators to seek the opinion of counsel on several matters relating to subject status. In both December 1763 and March 1764, the Lords Commissioners for Trade and Plantations wrote to the attorney general, Sir Fletcher Norton, for his opinion about whether the French and Spanish inhabitants of Canada, Florida, and the islands of Grenada, Dominica, St. Vincent's, and Tobago, "being born out of the allegiance of the His Majesty," were to be considered as aliens and strangers.[50] In June 1764, Norton attended the Board's meeting, after which he delivered a written statement declaring that these new inhabitants, who had taken the oaths of allegiance, were not to be viewed as aliens. They were entitled to the rights promised them under the Treaty of Paris.[51] This ruling clarified that the French Catholics were not aliens, although it was of very limited scope and failed to detail what those rights might be.

A year later, still faced with problems relating to the constitutional settlements of these colonies, the Lords Commissioners again sought outside counsel and received a crucial report that addressed the status of the new subjects and the degree to which English law might be extended to the ceded colonies. In June 1765, the attorney general and solicitor general argued that Roman Catholics in these colonies were not subject to the penal laws in effect against Catholics within the realm.[52] A second report submitted jointly to the Privy Council in January 1768 by the king's advocate, attorney general, and solicitor general confirmed this earlier ruling, noting that the acts of Parliament that imposed penalties upon Roman Catholics did not apply to Quebec.[53] What law officers of the crown conceded was that the Test was not to be extended to the colonies added in 1763.[54] While both of these reports attempted to clarify the position of Roman Catholics and of Catholicism in the colonies, neither tackled the more complicated issue of subjects' rights or the laws applicable to Catholics. Although the reports of crown counsel confirm that questions about subject status were addressed in a range of forums, they also reveal that none resolved them to the satisfaction of inhabitants and administrators and further explain why these issues remained at the forefront of struggles between old and new subjects in the 1760s and 1770s.

Thus, as the formerly French territories of Grenada and Quebec became part of the British Empire, uncertainty persisted about whether French Catholics were entitled to participate in representative government and about whether they might continue to live under the "laws of their ancestors."

Had colonial administrators thought it politic, it might have been possible to implement Article IV of the Treaty of Paris, which guaranteed the French Catholics religious freedom "as far as the laws of Great Britain permit," without necessarily entitling them to a series of rights which their co-religionists in Britain had not yet secured. However, exacerbating the doubts fomented by treaty articles was a postwar landscape in which governors needed to win the support and allegiance of their adopted subjects and were repeatedly instructed to do so by secretaries of state. In 1770, the governor of Quebec was reminded that the king "wishes that every just Ground of discontent in his new Subjects should be removed,"[55] just as his successor was asked in 1782 to show "the tenderest regard to their Rights and Liberties."[56] As fundamental disagreements arose about what it meant to be a "subject of the king" and about what rights, liberties, and privileges stemmed from the bond between subject and sovereign, inhabitants would avail themselves of these myriad uncertainties and of administrative imperatives to assert new and sometimes conflicting visions of subjecthood.

The Rights of Subjects in Grenada

Before Britain formally acquired Grenada in February 1763, pamphlets had already begun to advertise its advantages, seeking to lure prospective settlers to the island. *A Description of the Island of Grenada and Its Different Quarters* (1760), commissioned by the military governor, described the territory as "full of large mountains forming several fertile valleys and producing a great number of fine rivulets, which facilitate the construction of water mills for the use of sugar plantations."[57] Located northeast of Venezuela and northwest of Trinidad and Tobago, Grenada had long been eyed as a valuable prize of war (figure 4.1). Numerous pamphlets praised Grenada's two ports of "incomparable excellence," which not only provided shelter to Britain's largest squadrons but might also "prove very inconvenient" to passing enemy ships or to the neighboring French islands during times of war.[58] Grenada, it was hoped, would increase British "strength and commerce in that part of the globe" and "augment wealth, trade, and navigation."[59] By the time the Treaty of Paris was finalized, many were persuaded that Grenada would prove to be an invaluable addition to the British Empire.

Although Grenada was recognized for its superior harbors and its relative freedom from hurricanes, it was the island's productive capacities that captured the investments and imagination of new settlers. With a good climate, plenty of timber and running water, and developing cocoa and cotton

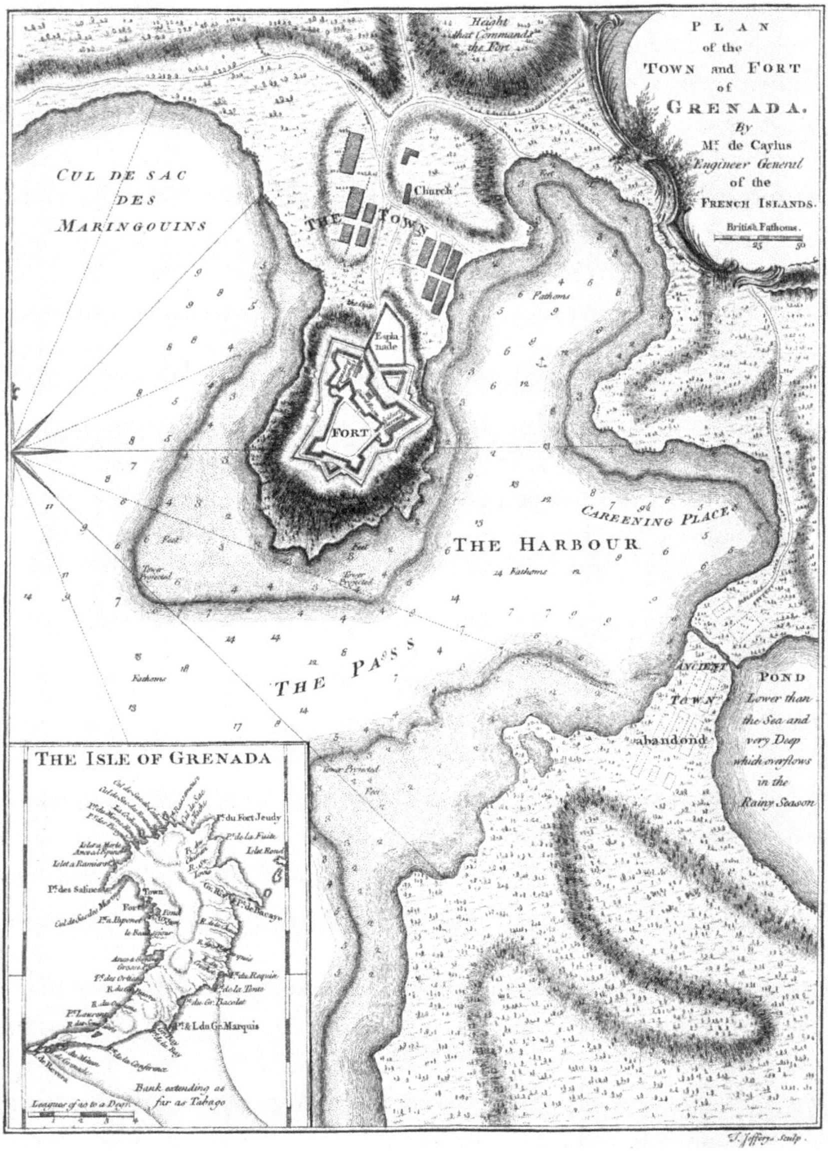

FIGURE 4.1 Thomas Jefferys, *Plan of the Town and Fort of Grenada by Mr. de Caylus, Engineer General of the French Islands, with The Isle of Grenada* [map], 1: 3,800. London, 1760. Courtesy of David Rumsey Map Collection, www.davidrumsey.com (Phillips. Maps of America, p. 303; Cf. LC Maps of North America, 2104).

production, Grenada was touted as a colony whose large tracts of level ground were ripe for improvement, equal if not superior to other lands in the West Indies. According to commentators, tracts in Grenada could be cleared and cultivated with "less expence and fewer negroes" than on some of the other nearby islands, and the sugar that might be produced there was of "fine grain," much more valuable than that produced in Guadeloupe or Martinique. Pampleteers' emphasis on sugar cultivation foreshadowed this crop's growth between 1763 and 1772, when about 43 percent of the island's land was devoted to sugar cultivation. Indeed, within a generation after the Treaty of Paris, Grenada "had attained a sustained growth that made it Britain's second leading West Indian colony" after Jamaica.[60]

Taking advantage of these natural endowments and ensuring that Grenada's plantations remained in working order, however, required propertied and experienced inhabitants. Sir William Young, who was commissioned to survey and grant lands in the ceded islands, observed that the object of government in the new territories was to enable "the speedy population and culture of the islands themselves."[61] Moreover, administrators immediately and routinely recognized how critical it was to retain formerly French settlers and struggled with how to prevent "detrimental emigrations to the French Colonies."[62] Land surveyors recommended that the French Catholic inhabitants should be granted favorable leases and encouraged to keep existing lands because "experience shews, that the possession of property is the best security for a due obedience and submission to Government."[63] Young himself recognized that it was essential to retain inhabitants who would be loyal to the British crown:

> the greatest number of useful and faithful subjects, and the more property can be retained upon these islands, the sooner they will become flourishing and beneficial to Great Britain, and the fewer advantages will accrue to the French King, in the population and settlement of his possessions in these seas . . . upon what terms they can be most safely and best retained, and render'd good and faithful subjects, seems a question of the utmost importance in this business.[64]

From a mercantilist perspective, keeping the production and wealth of these settlers within the British Empire not only advanced Great Britain's growth but simultaneously allowed British administrators to siphon this productive capacity away from the French king and to reduce French power in the West Indies. While Young recognized how critical it was to secure inhabitants for the islands, he also understood that they would need to be appropriately managed. Young himself failed to elaborate on how these subjects were to be "render'd good and faithful subjects" and eschewed any discussion of subjects' rights, but he understood that retaining settlers necessarily brought with it thorny questions about subjecthood.

In the years following the Treaty of Paris, when Young and other administrators encouraged the Board of Trade to hold on to these landholders, Grenada had approximately 1,225 white inhabitants, most of whom were French Catholic.[65] Their skills were essential to keeping the plantations in working order, as was their "knowledge of the Culture peculiar to these Islands."[66] Their experience and numbers were just as crucial in guarding against revolts among a growing slave population,[67] whose numbers more than doubled between the 1760s and 1780s with the rapid development of Grenada's economy.[68] By 1771, the number of white inhabitants had climbed to 1,661, a result of the small but steady arrival of settlers searching for cultivable lands and the retention of formerly French subjects.

Nonetheless, the sense that settlers must be retained shaped a climate in which governors and officials in London favored concessions to French Catholics who chose to remain in Grenada. George III, for example, conferred a knighthood upon Monsieur Laurent in 1768 to emphasize his affection for his new subjects.[69] Advisers recommended that the king appoint two new subjects to the council in 1770 so as to allay any "Doubts and Apprehensions in the minds of Your Majesty's New Subjects."[70] Because the Treaty of 1763 and subsequent instructions had remained vague about how French Catholics were to be treated, this conciliatory approach did not violate international agreements, appeared appropriate given local circumstances, and was in keeping with the generally more tolerant attitudes toward Catholics developing over the course of the eighteenth century.[71] It was abundantly clear that privileges relating to land leases, special honors, and seats in the council and assembly were part of a larger effort to secure the allegiance of new subjects and to preserve their labor, wealth, and expertise in managing a large enslaved population for the British Empire.

Whereas a number of administrators favored concessions to French Catholics who remained on the island after its cession to Britain, this was not the case for all of Grenada's "old subjects," most of whom identified as British-born and Protestant. Almost immediately after 1763, the French Catholic "new subjects" began to share the island with small but increasing numbers of British Protestants, who arrived throughout the 1760s to take advantage of new economic opportunities and to purchase the estates of departing

Frenchmen. Unfortunately for the peace and stability of the island, incoming British Protestant planters had very different ideas from their Catholic counterparts and from many administrators about how representative government should work. The rancorous disagreements that resulted dominated the political life of Grenada throughout the 1760s and 1770s. Documented in numerous petitions, governors' correspondence, and a series of pamphlets, and framed as debates over the contours of representative government and the constitution, these were at their heart struggles over the specific rights, liberties, and privileges due British subjects. Indeed, as British Protestants and French Catholics clashed, each group insisted on their allegiance and drew on the popular and evocative idea that rights stemmed from the relationship between subject and sovereign. As they articulated differing positions on representative government, both old and new subjects proposed conflicting visions of subjecthood and worked to redefine the privileges associated with subject status.

Disagreements between French Catholics and British Protestants were rooted in documents that had established the basic forms of government for Grenada. The Royal Proclamation authorized local government, created legislatures that might pass laws "as near as may be agreeable to the Laws of England," and allowed governors in the ceded territories to summon assemblies "as soon as the state and circumstances . . . will admit thereof."[72] However, it provided no guidance as to how those assemblies were to be constituted or about who might form the electorate. Royal permission to call an assembly was finally sent to Governor Robert Melvill in February 1766, though these instructions were merely the official confirmation of a decision that had been reached far earlier in London.[73] Like the proclamation, these subsequent instructions said little about the assembly's composition. Instead, a local ordinance was passed toward the end of 1765 or in early 1766, enabling all Christians of propertied backgrounds, which presumably included Catholics, who were also subjects, to vote for assembly members. Perhaps tellingly, it did not allow all Christians to sit in this elected body.[74]

But even as royal permission for an assembly was transmitted and rules for election were promulgated locally, tensions between old and new subjects were brewing. In anticipation of the elections, which returned the island's first assembly in April 1766, a bitter debate erupted over which subjects should be permitted to vote.[75] In this preliminary stage of a conflict that would endure until the 1790s, various constituencies vied to establish their credentials as "faithful subjects" and to opine on the proper parameters for representative government. The differing positions in this debate were articulated through several noteworthy petitions submitted to Governor Robert Melvill and attested in February 1766. Although they were framed as addresses of loyalty, these memorials were soon revealed to be documents that sought to define the rights of British subjects in Grenada.

In a first petition, eighteen "British Protestant Inhabitants of Grenada" argued that French Catholics resident on the island were aliens rather than subjects. Faced with a local ordinance that allowed Catholics to vote in upcoming elections, these old subjects contended that Catholic suffrage would endanger the safety of the island and the property of natural-born Protestant subjects. More significant, they maintained that permitting Catholics to vote would violate laws that forbade Catholics from participating in representative government and undermine the "most fundamental and constitutional laws of the Mother Country."[76] They questioned whether foreign Catholics were actually British subjects and relied on the age-old argument that, within the community of British subjects, only those who had sworn the oath against transubstantiation were entitled to vote for assembly members or to sit in the assembly and council. In general, this group of British Protestants believed that their rights as subjects entitled them to a government free from the influence of French Catholics and articulated a vision of subjecthood that rested on a Protestant ascendancy.

Not to be deprived of rights they believed to be their due, thirty-four French Catholics issued a counter-petition (figure 4.2). Claiming that they were "adopted subjects of His Majesty," they expressed alarm at the prospect of being called aliens. They asserted that they were entitled to vote in the upcoming elections, both as subjects and as freeholders.[77] For these planters, all propertied subjects were eligible to participate in representative government regardless of their Catholic faith. According to them, subject status brought with it certain irrevocable rights, rights that could not be abrogated by the religious backgrounds of inhabitants.

Finally, in a third memorial, twenty-five people, styling themselves "His Majesty's Natural Born Subjects," declared their support for the French Catholics around them. This third group of individuals, who identified as British subjects by birth but did not describe themselves as "British Protestant," argued that the "adopted subjects" were entitled to the "name and immunities of British Subjects" and should be allowed to vote.[78] They were inspired to petition by the "dictates of justice and humanity" and believed that many other Grenadians were in favor of wider Catholic suffrage.[79] Like the French Catholics, these "Natural Born Subjects" believed that, in Grenada, the British subject was an individual entitled to participate in representative government irrespective of his religious persuasion.

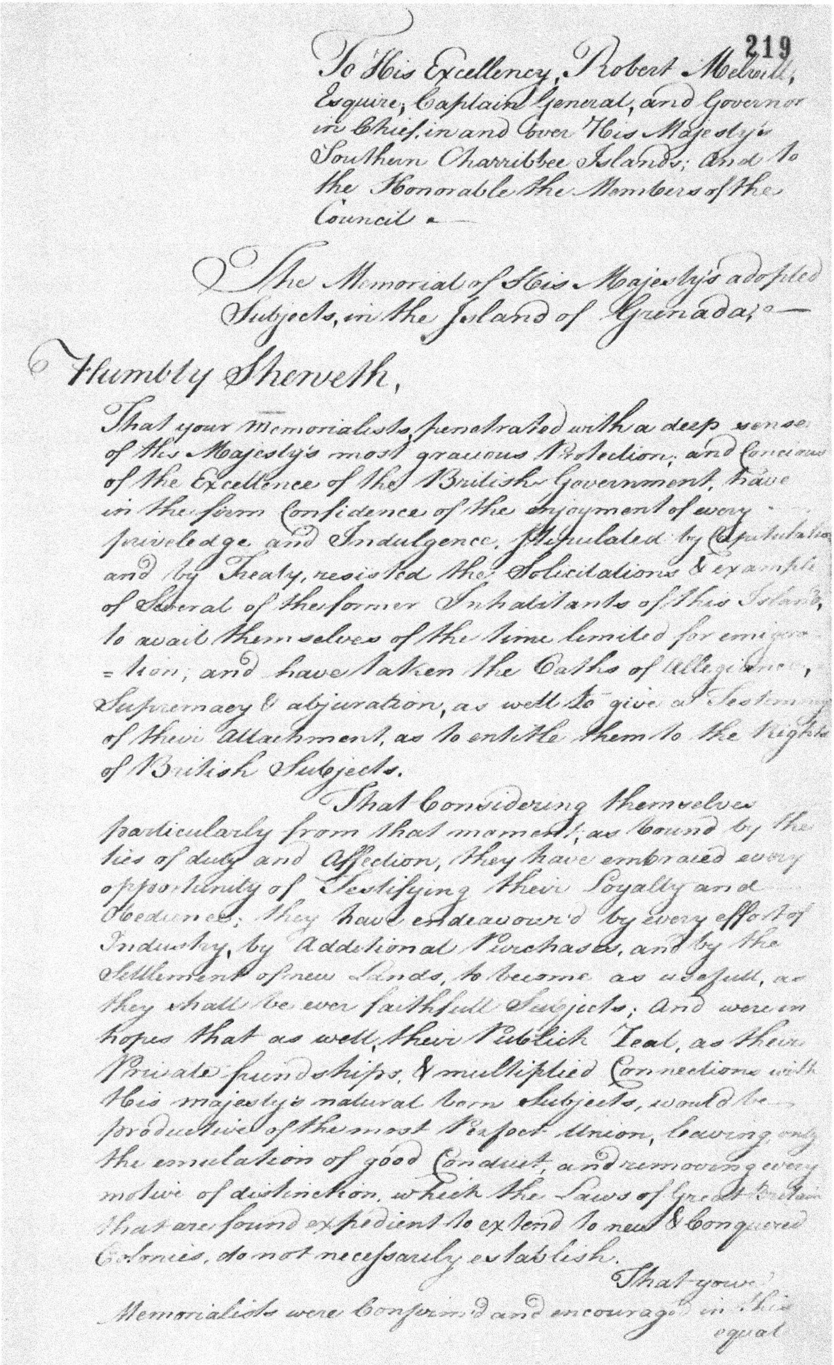
219

To His Excellency, Robert Melvill, Esquire, Captain General, and Governor in Chief, in and over His Majesty's Southern Charribbee Islands; And to the Honorable the Members of the Council —

The Memorial of His Majesty's adopted Subjects, in the Island of Grenada. —

Humbly Sheweth,

That your Memorialists, penetrated with a deep sense of His Majesty's most gracious Protection, and Conscious of the Excellence of the British Government, have in the firm Confidence of the enjoyment of every priveledge and Indulgence, stipulated by Capitulation and by Treaty, resisted the Solicitations & example of Several of the former Inhabitants of this Island, to avail themselves of the time limited for emigra=tion; and have taken the Oaths of Allegiance, Supremacy & abjuration, as well to give a Testimony of their attachment, as to entitle them to the Rights of British Subjects.

That Considering themselves particularly from that moment; as bound by the ties of duty and Affection, they have embraced every opportunity of Testifying their Loyalty and Obedience; they have endeavour'd by every effort of Industry, by Additional Purchases, and by the Settlement of new Lands, to become as usefull, as they shall be ever faithfull Subjects; and were in hopes that as well their Publick Zeal, as their Private friendships, & multiplied Connections with His majesty's natural born Subjects, would be productive of the most Perfect Union, leaving only the emulation of good Conduct, and removing every motive of distinction, which the Laws of Great Britain that are found expedient to extend to new & Conquered Colonies, do not necessarily establish.

That your Memorialists were Confirmed and encouraged in this equal

FIGURE 4.2 The Memorial of His Majesty's Adopted Subjects, in the Island of Grenada, addressed to Governor Robert Melvill and the Honorable Members of the Council, 1766. Courtesy of The National Archives, Kew, United Kingdom (CO 101/1/219).

What is striking about these moments in Grenadian history is not just that diverging ideas about subjecthood occasioned such debate. Rather, for all their antagonisms, French Catholics and British Protestants, new and old subjects, all turned to the tradition of the petition when they wished to express their grievances. In doing so, they expressly assumed the identity of British subjects. Members of contending factions proclaimed their allegiance and their understandings of its meanings in remarkably comparable ways. They relied on their loyalty to instantiate themselves as key participants in a community of British subjects, and they demanded certain rights because of their relationship with their monarch. The battle between old and new subjects would be waged in Grenada and London, in pamphlets and protests, before governors and secretaries of state, but the petitions of subjects are arguably most illuminating. Submitted to the king and to royal governors in Grenada and Quebec during the 1760s and 1770s, these memorials reveal how myriad inhabitants leveraged their subject status as they sought to rewrite the privileges associated with subjecthood.

Indeed, the formulaic quality of the petition provided a certain safety, allowing signatories to articulate conflicting opinions in a template that helped conceal hostilities through similarity of form and a humble language of subjection. Petitions from subjects in Grenada had several essential component parts, each of which was framed by professions of loyalty and claims of subject status, beginning with the address. The 1766 petitions were directed "to His Excellency, Robert Melvill" and to members of the council, all of whom were servants of the crown. In each of these addresses, petitioners characterized themselves as devoted subjects who were thereby entitled to approach the monarch—the Grenadian Protestants stressed that they were "His Majesty's Protestant Subjects"; the Grenadian French Catholics identified as "His Majesty's Adopted Subjects"; and the supporters of the French Catholics claimed that they were "His Majesty's Natural Born Subjects." The very form of the petition required that signatories articulate a hierarchical relationship with their monarch, which had the subtle effect of making them all equal supplicants.

Following the opening address, these memorials proceeded with declarations of allegiance, as constituents detailed their enduring faithfulness as subjects and insisted on their past and present devotion to king, country, and law. Then, petitioners of both French and British descent reflected on the actions that had qualified them to seek royal justice and intervention, often vying with one another to establish their usefulness to the empire. Formalities complete, petitioners proceeded to detail their grievances, arriving at what might be called a statement of rights and a proposed remedy to the injustices they had allegedly suffered. Differing requests notwithstanding, fervent declarations of loyalty reappeared throughout these parts of the memorial, as often-opposing groups described themselves as subjects and clearly, though deferentially, made demands of their monarch for privileges. Contenders from all sides of a debate drew on a familiar and enduring idea that from the bond with the monarch stemmed certain rights, liberties, and privileges.

The closing lines of these memorials were also remarkably similar. Most petitions concluded by reiterating requests and confirming the submission and loyalty of signatories. The entangled languages of allegiance, obedience, and protection were prominent, suggesting the weight they conferred, particularly in the parting lines. The French Catholics, for example, concluded by asking that the government "be pleas'd to confirm and declare the right of your Memorialists, as British Subjects, and as Freeholders, to vote at the ensuing Election of Representatives." Whereas they had begun their memorial by cautiously approaching their superiors as "Adopted Subjects," they had completed it as "British Subjects" whose rights merely needed confirming. The carefully orchestrated narrative of submissive subjecthood that characterized this and other petitions worked to inscribe these individuals as loyal to the king, as critical members of his empire, and as entitled to his protection in the form of various rights and liberties. In Grenada, it was the petitions produced by inhabitants themselves that best illustrated how individuals might rely on their personal relationship to the sovereign, as well as on belonging to a community of British subjects, to articulate conflicting ideas about rights.

While the petitions shed light on fundamentally opposing ideological positions where subjecthood and representative government were concerned, they also foreshadowed a far more widespread and acrimonious debate that gained intensity during the actual elections. According to contemporaneous accounts, the tense situation alluded to in the petitions became more strained as Protestant members of the council and assembly sought to maintain their seats and ascendancy and to garner the support of new subjects. "At this period," wrote one observer, "recourse was had to several Artifices in order to gain the Votes of the new Subjects."[80] Among these ploys was one by Mr. Pigott and Mr. Robertson in late 1766. They requested leave to bring in a bill that declared "all his Majesty's new adopted Subjects capable of enjoying every Liberty and Immunity of natural-born Subjects,"[81] a matter that was reported in the *Grenada Gazette* and led many of the propertied French Catholics to assume that they were going to be allowed not only to vote for representatives, but also to stand for elected office.[82] Continually frustrated in their attempts to obtain a copy of the bill, which was passed on October 14, 1767, the new subjects still had not seen it on the eve of the election. When a certain Mr. Demouchy, a new subject, presented himself as a candidate for election on November 9, 1767, he was unaware of the actual contents of the bill. To his surprise, the returning officer refused to include his name "upon the poll, or to receive any votes for him," determining that Demouchy was a Roman Catholic.[83] Demouchy allegedly responded that "he did not stand as a roman catholic, but as a new subject," an answer which had no effect on election officials, but did illustrate his attempted appeal to a community of subjects loyal to the king.[84]

At this juncture, one Alexandre Cazaud began to read a protest signed by a number of the new subjects.[85] Soon thereafter, both Demouchy and Cazaud were taken into custody, at which point they were told about the actual contents of the bill: it stipulated that only persons "taking the oaths of Allegiance and Supremacy, and subscribing the Test before the Governor and Council, if otherwise duly qualified, had a Right to sit in the Assembly, but refusing to do so was liable to a Penalty of one hundred Pounds."[86] Given these parameters, Demouchy was in violation of the bill, and Cazaud had encouraged him in unlawful action. When brought before the council for questioning, Cazaud refused to answer without the assistance of counsel, for which he was confined in a common prison "surrounded by upwards of forty offenders of different sorts and complexions."[87] Only when he agreed to express concern for having incurred the displeasure of the council and promised to appear before them to answer questions was he released. Almost immediately, Cazaud fled Grenada, traveling by way of Martinique and France to London, where he worked to advance the cause of the new subjects before senior colonial officials.

For his part, Governor Melvill warned superiors about Cazaud's imminent arrival and about the new subjects' machinations to obtain positions in the council and assembly. He noted that the new subjects had "dispatched one Cazaud a Ring Leader in quality of Envoy," but there was little he could do to stop this mission.[88] For their part, opponents of the new subjects began to accuse them of having "insulted the Legislature of the Colony, and having acted in a seditious manner."[89] With the departure of Cazaud, calm temporarily returned to the island. Most British Protestants tried to convince themselves "that notwithstanding all art, solicitations and misrepresentations which may be practiced no Rights or Priviledges unsafe in their nature and exceeding those legally enjoyed in the English Colonies by the British or Irish Catholicks; will ever be granted to Foreign ones."[90] In other words, they fervently hoped that French Catholics would not be granted rights comparable to their own. Once again, what had originated as a debate about participation in representative government had become a question about the rights owed Catholic subjects across the empire.

While Cazaud's mission to England represented one individual's more dramatic response to French Catholic exclusion from potential seats in the assembly, it certainly echoed claims for rights made by a far larger constituency. Indeed, in the months before Cazaud fled Grenada, the new subjects had addressed the Earl of Shelburne, secretary of state, seeking his support for their right to fill offices of trust. They pleaded that "his Majesty will be willing to make no difference between his new and old subjects, by according them without any distinctions all of the rights of English citizens."[91] Framing the debate over representative government as one intimately linked to the rights of subjects, the French Catholics boldly claimed membership in a community of "English citizens." They confidently drew on popular understandings of the central relationship between subject and sovereign, evoking the idea that all subjects were equal before their monarch and that each was entitled to certain mythical liberties that stemmed from that fundamental bond.

British Protestants also continued to appeal to the community of subjects, but often to quite different effect. Another memorial, signed by 337 individuals, was submitted by "his Majesty's most faithful, loyal, and obedient Subjects, born under his Allegiance and resident in the said Island of Grenada" in late 1767. Petitioners protested the "late dangerous and unprecedented attempt by his majesty's French-born subjects, to overturn the constitution of the colony," arguing that even natural-born subjects of the Catholic faith had always been excluded from holding office by the "wisdom of our laws." Emphasizing their own indelible allegiance as well as that of natural-born Catholic subjects, "whose loyalty to their sovereign and affections to their country, have of late been in no instance questioned," they questioned whether the French Catholics were, in fact, loyal subjects. They argued that French requests for seats in the assembly were attempts to overturn the constitutional rights of subjects more generally and that such rights could hardly be "allowed to a people whom the fortune of war only made British subjects." Old subjects demanded the "advantage of our happy constitution in Common with their fellow subjects in other British colonies," contending that allowing Catholics to assume public office destroyed these constitutional privileges and threatened the rights of subjects.[92] Revisiting arguments raised by earlier petitions, they claimed that true British subjects were those who lived under a constitution that prohibited Catholic participation in representative government, just as they questioned whether French Catholics, who had not been born within the king's allegiance and had only been recognized as subjects by treaty, could even really be subjects of the monarch.

Nonetheless, the phrasing of these various petitions revealed that most settlers in Grenada could agree that "new subjects" were "British subjects," even if only by "fortune of war." Few argued that the French Catholics were not British subjects or tried to prevent them from staying in the ceded territories; these were not typically disagreements about who might be called a British subject. Instead, their common references to the inherent rights of Britons made explicit a broader understanding that subjects of the monarch were entitled to certain constitutional rights enabling them to participate in representative government, not unlike those addressed by declarations of rights. Subjects in Grenada, however, diverged in their characterization of that constitution and in their identification of what specific privileges the British subject might expect in a transformed empire. For old subjects, this was a Protestant constitution intended to uphold a Protestant ascendancy. For new subjects, this was a constitution that welcomed all property owners to participate in the business of government, thereby abolishing distinctions between Protestant and non-Protestant. "Factiousness," as it was called in official correspondence, was endemic in the 1760s, and the innumerable pages that detailed responses by governors and councilors merely provided official documentation of a wider social, economic, and political struggle over the rights of subjects.

Grenada might well have remained at an impasse and the rights of subjects unresolved but for the temporary resolution provided by a Privy Council ruling in September 1768. After having reviewed numerous materials from the island, and influenced by petitions from prosperous French Catholics and by the necessity of retaining them to run plantations in Grenada, the Privy Council finally issued its decision on the contentious matter of French Catholic participation in Grenada's representative bodies. They determined not only that French Catholics in Grenada could vote for assembly members, but also that two of their number might actually sit in the assembly and council without having sworn the oath against transubstantiation. While many British Protestants on the island maintained that they were entitled to live under the "happy constitution" and "laws of the mother country," which had always excluded Catholic participation in assemblies, their arguments were overturned. For the time being, the protections of subjecthood had been defined expansively, and the French Catholics had played an active role in shaping the rights deemed fit for British subjects in Grenada.

The Privy Council notwithstanding, fundamental disagreements regarding subject status in Grenada would escalate over the course of the ensuing decade, as the decision from London was met by consistent and sustained protest from a small but vocal portion of the old subjects.[93] On at least two occasions in the 1760s and 1770s, for example, governors suspended British Protestant members of the council who resisted Privy Council orders and refused to take their seats alongside appointed Catholics of French origin. In the autumn of 1769, Lieutenant-Governor Ulysses Fitzmaurice attempted to enforce his instructions by introducing two new subjects, Charles Nicholas Chanteloupe and Paul Mignot Devoconnu, into the Grenada Council. He was prevented from doing so by opposition from existing members who argued that no governor could appoint new members to a council unless fewer than seven were found to be residing on the island.[94] Fitzmaurice responded by suspending six councilors who challenged him. In 1771, Governor William Leybourne again had to suspend council members who refused to allow new subjects into places of trust, including positions in the courts. Even with London's endorsement, the hard-won freedoms of the Grenadian Catholics were thus constantly under attack, underscoring the fundamentally unstable nature of the rights accorded them as subjects.

Having failed to persuade colonial administrators and the Privy Council that British subjects were required to take the Test before they might hold public office, frustrated old subjects varied their approach. While the French Catholics consistently relied on their status as adopted British subjects to advance their rights to participate in representative government, British-born Protestants adopted two differing approaches over the years. With the first, which mirrored the tactics of French Catholics, the British Protestants consistently proclaimed their loyal subjecthood through petitions and correspondence in order to articulate a set of rights they believed to be their due. When this first approach had not succeeded by 1768 and, if anything, had favored their Catholic opponents, British-born Protestants marshaled a second set of arguments with even wider constitutional ramifications for subjecthood.

In January 1772, forty-two "freeholders and merchants" claimed that the Privy Council's decision of 1768 and the ensuing instructions exempting French Catholics from the Test were "wholly illegal because it allows the choice of Roman Catholicks into the Assembly which in our opinion is contrary to the laws of England and to the established Constitution of this Colony."[95] By challenging the Privy Council's authority to make such a decision, these old subjects would insist that only a parliamentary statute could change the constitution and alter the associated rights of subjects. British-born Protestants worked to remove the question of subjects' rights from the purview of the Privy Council and colonial administrators more generally.

Similarly, five councilmen suspended in December 1771 offered a forceful argument for parliamentary intervention. They asserted that Governor Melvill's commission of April 1764, which formed the charter of the colony and had established civil government on the island, required the Test. Neither the king nor his council could alter these laws, which had entitled them to the "full possession of every English privilege and liberty, as our native Birthright." Most important, "the many Acts of Parliament which restrain the Crown from employing in places of Trust and Power all Persons whatsoever who profess the Roman Catholick Religion, are not to be dispensed with by any prerogative of the King . . . [and] can in no wise be removed but by an Act of Parliament of Great Britain."[96] This group of councilmen argued that no body or prerogative power other than a supreme Parliament could rule on a question of such importance as the rights of subjects. This second approach, though constitutionally intriguing and resonant with debates in other parts of the empire, was initially no more successful than the first.[97] Indeed, despite enduring and vocal opposition from influential old subjects, exemption from the Test would remain a foundational paragraph in instructions sent to the governors of Grenada well into the 1790s, reflecting administrative attempts to conciliate and retain their new subjects.[98]

By the 1780s and 1790s, the more expansive interpretation of subjecthood that had temporarily found favor in Grenada was gradually losing ground. Although planters had secured coveted privileges despite being practicing Catholics, their numbers dwindled steadily. From a high of 1,661 in 1771, the number of white inhabitants fell to 1,324 in 1777, and to 996 in 1783.[99] More ominously for the rights of French Catholics, records of land ownership indicated that just over 50 percent of plantations were in the hands of British settlers by the early 1770s,[100] with one report from the mid-1780s suggesting that "there is not at this time above one-tenth of the whole property of the Island which can really be called French."[101]

Perhaps most significant, when the French temporarily reoccupied Grenada between 1779 and 1783, almost all the new subjects deserted to their former sovereign. This betrayal and the bitter conditions experienced by old subjects during this renewed global war did little to encourage toleration of Catholic rights when the British reassumed control in 1783. Anger, mistrust, and suspicion predominated at a local level, and bills eroding Catholic privileges were passed with little resistance. In 1785, a local act stipulated that only marriages, baptisms, and burials performed or registered in the established church were valid. A new election bill was passed by the assembly in 1786 resolving that "none but British Born Subjects professing the Protestant religion and otherwise qualified according to the said Ordinance, can be, or of right ought to be, elected representatives of the Freemen of this Colony."[102] By 1792, a local act was passed requiring all Catholics to take the Test before they could hold political office.

The ultimate reversal to the French Catholics' hard-won privileges came in 1792, when the Privy Council overturned its earlier decision in favor of Catholic representation and stipulated that Catholics in Grenada should be treated like Roman Catholics in Britain rather than like Roman Catholics in Quebec.[103] Rather than being favored with exemptions from the penal laws in force against Catholics, Catholics in Grenada were to suffer the discrimination experienced by their peers in the British Isles, bringing the rights of subjects in Grenada in line with the rights of subjects in Britain itself. Concessions to these planters may have seemed practical immediately after the Seven Years' War, but by the 1780s, they seemed like dangerous bargains with inhabitants who had betrayed their allegiance to the British monarch and were no longer as prominent or desirable as landowners as they had once been. Whereas British subject status had briefly entitled propertied freeholders in Grenada to sit in a representative assembly regardless of religious persuasion, it was soon defined more rigidly, entitling individuals only to an assembly composed of Protestants.

Even as concessions to Catholics were steadily retracted, uncertainties about subjects' rights persisted. Observers would continually opine on whether being a British subject entitled a freeholder of any denomination to vote for his representatives or whether a *bona fide* British subject was someone who participated in representative government only if he had sworn an oath against transubstantiation. In 1787, Alexander Symson, speaker of the Assembly, noted that it was "of the utmost importance to the future welfare and safety of the Colony that the point should be clearly ascertained how far French and other Foreigners who settled here during the Conquest & who remained here after the Peace; are to be considered as Subjects." His concern was an intriguing one—that it must be determined "how far French and other foreigners . . . are to be considered Subjects." Implicit in his letter was the assumption that French inhabitants and other foreigners were subjects, though perhaps not "full subjects," and that their status must be clarified. Sympson also argued that while he personally found it "rather illiberal" to focus on distinctions based upon religious backgrounds, if the French inhabitants were to be subjects, "they must enjoy all the Priviledges of his Majesty's natural born subjects, but no more. Therefore, those professing the Roman Catholic Religion cannot claim or really enjoy Priviledges which natural born Subjects of that persuasion do not enjoy."[104] Here, again, Symson embraced a far more widespread idea that natural-born subjects possessed certain rights, but that such privileges could not be extended differently to fellow-subjects who were Catholic.

Symson's letter and his comments about "illiberal" discrimination based on religious background suggest that not all of the old subjects were simply anti-Catholic. Indeed, over the years, some Protestant inhabitants would side with their French Catholic neighbors and argue for commensurable rights for all subjects. Moreover, Symson's position demonstrates that influential figures and administrators continued to debate the boundaries of British subjecthood, often concluding that "full subjects" were those who lived under a constitution that circumscribed their participation in representative government. Although French Catholics would protest this interpretation in the 1780s and 1790s, subsequent petitions to preserve their rights as British subjects were met by administrative silence. The failure of Fedon's Rebellion between 1795 and 1796, in which many French Catholics, inspired by the principles of the French Revolution, joined slaves and free people of color in open rebellion against British rule, sounded the death knell for any renewed discussion of French Catholic rights in the late eighteenth century.[105] Catholics in Grenada would have to wait until 1832 for their disabilities to be removed and for a full restoration of the rights they deemed to be those of all British subjects.[106]

Nonetheless, for almost two decades after the Treaty of Paris, Grenada provided a terrain in which the rights of subjects were repeatedly contested and successfully extended—often by subjects leveraging their relationship to the reigning monarch. The petitions of new subjects confidently proclaimed the idea that propertied British subjects were entitled to sit in representative assemblies regardless of religious affiliation, and colonial administrators, hoping to retain these valuable settlers, agreed with them for a brief moment in time. Departing from notions of birthright allegiance and indefeasible loyalties made famous by *Calvin v. Smith* and propagated by popular treatises like William Blackstone's *Commentaries on the Laws of England*, new subjects proposed alternative interpretations of British subjecthood.[107] A British subject no longer necessarily meant someone who was born within the monarch's dominions, whose allegiance was unchanging, or who lived under statutes that required all officeholders to take the Test. Instead, the bond between George III and his subjects came to include a wide range of inhabitants—those of various religious backgrounds, those born within the allegiance of foreign monarchs, and those who actively claimed the right to sit in a representative assembly and to petition their superiors to ensure that their myriad rights were upheld.

Just as significant, for those few years, the rights of new subjects in Grenada were allowed to differ from those of their fellow-subjects in Great Britain, where Catholics were barred from seats in Parliament and numerous penal laws were still in effect until 1829. While uneven rights reflected the proactive roles taken by subjects themselves, they also underlined how administrative reliance on Catholic populations could create an environment that was favorable to more expansive understandings of subjecthood. They revealed that subjects' perceived importance to the British Empire might, in fact, affect how flexibly the protections of subjecthood were accorded. The shifting rights of Grenadian Catholics suggest not only that rights might fluctuate at different moments in time across the empire, but also that subjecthood itself might be reshaped in order to accommodate both the needs of administrators and the demands of subjects.

The Rights of Subjects in Quebec

If French Catholics in Grenada were able to choose and define their subjecthood for almost two decades, their compatriots to the north were perhaps even more effective. With the formal cession of New France and its predominantly French Catholic population to the British in 1763, the three districts of Québec, Trois Rivières, and Montréal were united into the Province of Quebec (figure 4.3). Unlike Grenada, which had its steady stream of advocates, this new North American addition was often dismissed as the least desirable of the new colonies and a drain on national coffers. Detractors noted that in 1763 Britain had returned the profitable sugar island of Guadeloupe to France and had instead chosen to keep the "long barren tract of country," a territory that "gave us only furs."[108] In response, advocates stressed Quebec's strategic location, arguing that the French threat had been removed from most of the North American continent by its cession. Others emphasized how much the province might be improved, the potential of its fisheries, the advantages of such vast tracts of land, and the projected increase of its imports and exports.[109] Governors praised the industry and vigor of the French-speaking *Canadiens*, who had managed to carve out an existence from the land despite its inconveniences and challenging winters, and whose influence with indigenous populations and knowledge of the fur trade might prove invaluable.[110] Though it was harder to extol the virtues of Quebec than it was those of Grenada, its inhabitants were clearly among its resources.

Although Quebec had many thousands more white inhabitants than Grenada, it similarly had a far greater Catholic than Protestant population. The French Catholic population of Quebec numbered somewhere between 60,000 and 70,000 during the 1760s, while the population of British merchants and traders hovered between 200 and 300.[111] British administrators initially hoped that they might attract more British-born inhabitants to offset this imbalance, but the predominance of the *Canadiens* only became more pronounced by the 1770s given that only about 1 in 200 of them had chosen to leave the colony after the peace and that few Protestant settlers had arrived.[112] Only with the influx of around 6,000 Loyalists in the 1780s did this demographic imbalance begin to be redressed.[113] Unlike Grenada, the numerical predominance of non-Protestants persisted in Quebec and would profoundly affect the outcome of debates over subjects' rights.

Like Grenada, the presence of this large French Catholic population engendered a climate of relative conciliation toward subjects who were neither British nor Protestant. As General Gage wrote in 1762, "no distinction has been made betwixt the Briton and the Canadian, but [they have been] equally regarded as subjects of the same Prince."[114] Beginning in 1764, Murray wrote to the Lords Commissioners indicating how important it was to win over the new subjects upon whom the empire depended:

> Little, very little will content the New Subjects . . . a Race who could they be indulged with a few Privileges which the Laws deny to Roman Catholicks at home . . . might become the most faithfull, and most useful, set of men in this American Empire . . . and certain I am, unless the Canadians are admitted on Juries, and are allowed Judges and Lawyers who understand their Language that His Majesty will lose the greatest part of this valuable People.[115]

His successor, Guy Carleton, went even further in urging concessions. He recommended trade indulgences so that the *Canadiens* might contribute to British rather than French commercial growth; admission to places of trust that would encourage Catholics to forget their former sovereign; and acceptance of some of the local *noblesse* into the council because the "only way to make them faithful subjects is to place a prudent confidence in and employ them."[116] Similarly, Lieutenant-Governor Hector Theophilus Cramahé, of Swiss Huguenot origin, argued that indulgence of the Catholic religion and

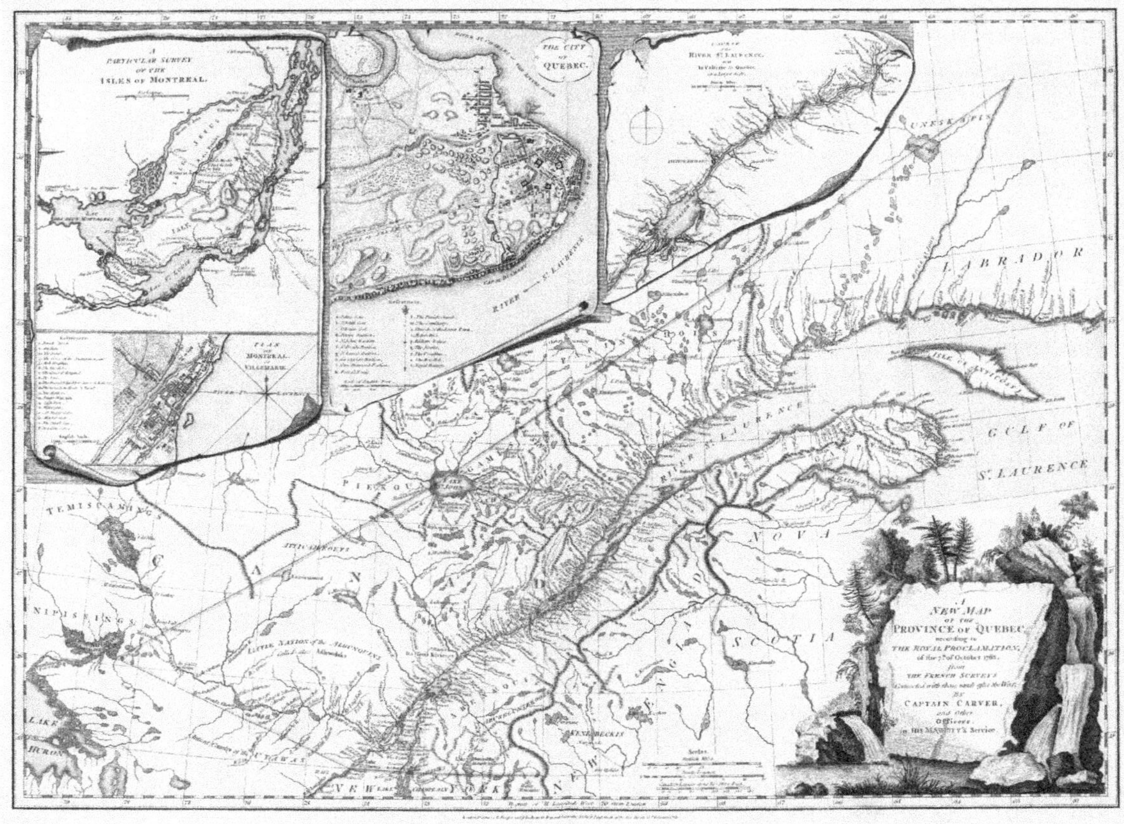

FIGURE 4.3 Thomas Jefferys, *A New Map of the Province of Quebec, according to The Royal Proclamation, of the 7th of October 1763* [map], 1:2,200,000. London: Sayer and Bennett, 1776. Courtesy of David Rumsey Map Collection, www.davidrumsey.com (NMM 361; cf. P 1165, 1166).

confirmation of French laws of property were the only "sure and effectual method of gaining the affections of His Majesty's Canadian Subjects."[117] By the time the Quebec Act was passed in 1774, most governors agreed that the security granted to *Canadien* religion, laws, and property had been instrumental in ensuring relative quiescence over the years.[118] With the return of war to North America in the late 1770s, several administrators proposed that a militia unit officered by *Canadiens* would generate confidence and loyalty, further binding inhabitants to the government.[119] Hopeful that generous concessions might convert the *Canadiens* into faithful British subjects, colonial officials in Quebec thus consistently recommended granting privileges that did not contravene the Treaty of Paris.

Whereas administrators proposed extending rights, liberties, and privileges to the *Canadiens* and were generally sympathetic to allowing them to settle their affairs according to "the laws of their ancestors," few British Protestants were quite so amenable. In the 1760s and 1770s, fierce debates erupted about the rights to be accorded to the new subjects. Although questions about French Catholic participation in representative government were raised in Quebec, other debates also emerged about whether the British subject was an individual who lived under English law or a person who lived under the time-honored customs of his ancestors.[120] Indeed, local accommodations of French civil law and of the "ancient customs" of the *Canadiens* were made beginning in the 1760s and parliamentary approval of French civil law was granted in 1774. Not until 1791 were Upper and Lower Canada granted assemblies and Catholics formally allowed to participate in representative government without subscribing to the Test.

As Governor Guy Carleton noted in one of his letters to the secretary of state, confusion about which law was applicable to Quebec had begun as early as 1763, and disagreements over which law might be used to regulate the affairs of its diverse inhabitants intensified in the years after cession.[121] On the one hand, many believed that French civil law had actually been accorded to the *Canadiens*, since during the period of military rule that lasted from the conquest of Quebec in 1759 until August 1764, various courts of first instance, constituted by officers of the militia, continued to judge disputes according to the customary *Coutume de Paris*.[122] On the other hand, both the Royal Proclamation of 1763 and the commission sent to Quebec's first governor had established English law to the satisfaction of British-born Protestants.

Even as many accepted that the proclamation appeared to have introduced English civil and criminal law, several local ordinances continued to allow numerous French laws and customs.[123] In September 1764, for example, a three-tiered legal system was established in which a second, inferior Court of Common Pleas allowed French law and customs at the same time that a superior court continued to hear and adjudicate all civil and criminal cases according to the laws of England. Over the years, local ordinances were passed that allowed Catholics to sit on juries (1764 and 1766); that enabled the laws and customs of the previous era to prevail concerning tenure, inheritance, and alienation of lands (1767); and that moved the effectual administration of justice out of the hands of justices of the peace and into the hands of the Court of Common Pleas where French law was allowed (1770). The result was a rather murky legal system for everyone involved. While the *Canadiens* were understandably concerned to preserve access to their time-honored customs, based largely on the *Coutume de Paris*, British-born inhabitants were equally worried about maintaining familiar English laws they understood and could navigate. It was thus on the terrain of law, rather than the issue of representative assemblies, that the rights of the new British subject were first successfully renegotiated in Quebec.

Indeed, shortly after Canada's cession, the *Canadiens* began addressing George III and expressing concern about the precarious legal system in the province. Like their Grenadian counterparts, they used petitions not only to entreat the king's intervention but also to proclaim their new status as subjects. Presenting themselves as loyal subjects in each part of their memorials, they similarly underlined their utility to the imperial enterprise as well as their membership in the broader community of British subjects. Also like Grenada's French Catholics, they proposed interpretations of subject status that challenged those put forth by their British and Protestant fellow-subjects.

Initially, the *Canadiens* sought to appeal to George III's humanity, imploring him to administer justice by individuals who understood their language and customs and to confirm the legal system that had been in place under their former sovereign. This request, of course, had profound practical ramifications for those in the province whose lands had been granted under French *seigneurial* tenure and who feared confiscations or changes made to their ownership.[124] As inhabitants testified in an early petition from 1764, they worried that unless their customs were upheld, they would become "veritable Slaves" instead of "favoured Subjects of Your Majesty."[125] Petitioners thus very clearly linked their status as free subjects with their time-honored customs, drawing on familiar ideas that English subjects were distinguished from enslaved persons because of their protected rights to law.

Within a few years, this argument about "ancient laws" and subject status had been developed even further. Petitioners in 1770, for example, argued that restoration of their ancient usages would enable them to understand their rights more fully and render them better able to serve their monarch as loyal subjects.[126] According to this argument, it was access to their ancient laws that allowed individuals to realize their subjecthood. That these customs were influenced by French precedent was immaterial. As they pleaded in 1773 that their privileges and customs be established as the law of the province, the new subjects once again entreated the king "to grant us, in common with your other subjects, the rights and privileges of citizens of England."[127] Like their Grenadian peers, who had asked that "his Majesty will be willing to make no difference between his new and old subjects, by according them without any distinctions all the rights of English citizens," the *Canadiens* beseeched their new monarch to eliminate differences between his subjects.[128] They also evoked membership in a broader community of subjects, all of whom were equal and entitled to time-honored customs by virtue of the bond of allegiance. Throughout the 1760s and 1770s, the French Catholics increasingly and deftly used the language of subjecthood and citizenship to articulate a connection between law and the status of free-born subjects.

In response, other inhabitants, mostly British Protestants, proposed a conflicting vision of subjecthood, insisting that English law was an integral part of subjects' rights. Not only did they attack the inferior courts responsible for administering French law as "tiresome litigious and expensive in this poor Colony," but they maintained that a government that allowed foreign civil law violated the constitution and laws of England, denying the British subject his birthright.[129] These arguments about the subject's birthright were ones the Loyalists would reprise in the 1780s, when they tried to persuade administrators that "they were born British Subjects & have ever been accustomed to the Government & Laws of England." They demanded the blessings of the British constitution and detailed the hardships they feared if forced to live under French laws and land tenures.[130] All of these British Protestant petitioners, however, linked the status of subjects to the question of law. Whereas the *Canadiens* contended that true subjects were those entitled to their ancient laws, many British-born subjects claimed just as passionately that *bona fide* subjects were those who lived under English law. Both positions drew on familiar arguments that British liberties stemmed from the subject's relationship with the monarch and that, among those liberties, the British subject was entitled to time-honored customs and the protections of law; nonetheless, each position offered a radically different interpretation of that "inheritance" and those "ancient usages."

Much as in Grenada, conflicting ideas about law and subjects' rights in Quebec were voiced in the memorials of inhabitants, just as they found their way into official correspondence and contemporary publications.[131] Governors, for example, regularly made suggestions about how loyal subjects might be created, with Governor Murray observing "that in my opinion, the French will be good Subjects if properly managed, but if they are allowed to be led by Ignorant, licentious, factious men, I foresee every bad Consequence to the King's Service and to themselves."[132] By the 1770s, scions of the legal world had begun to articulate that law, even if that meant French law, was part of the subject's inheritance. When Chief Justice Lord Mansfield wrote to the prime minister with his ideas about a legal settlement for Quebec in the early 1760s, he had noted that there was no instance "so rash and unjust" of a conqueror abolishing the laws and customs of a conquered people.[133] In Quebec, where new subjects were accustomed to French law, Mansfield believed that it was a manifest failure of justice to deny them access to the laws with which they were familiar. Perhaps even more tellingly, by 1774, Mansfield had begun to outline the rights of conquered peoples in a King's Bench case originating in Grenada. He ruled, among other things, that "conquered inhabitants once received into the conqueror's protection become subjects" and that the laws of the conquered country continued in force until they were altered by the conqueror.[134] In many respects, Mansfield evoked the age-old principle of protection: the conquering monarch received the obedience of new peoples and, in turn, extended to them a range of protections. Administrators, then, were responsible for protecting the rights of subjects, even if those included access to a law that was not English.

As "anarchy" and "confusion" continued to characterize the legal system of Quebec, both inhabitants and administrators recognized that some official resolution was absolutely essential for the sake of all subjects.[135] In June 1767, the secretary of state had written to Governor Carleton asking him for advice about how "practicable and expedient" it would be to blend the English and French laws, an inquiry that was followed by a series of requests for reports on the constitutional settlement in Quebec.[136] By June 1771, the solicitor general, Alexander Wedderburn, was directed to take into consideration the years of reports and papers relating to laws and courts in Quebec and to prepare a plan that detailed a revised civil and criminal legal administration for the colony. Wedderburn submitted his report at the end of 1772, but both the advocate general and attorney general also forwarded reports in 1773, neither of which was in full agreement with Wedderburn's thoughtful consideration of affairs in Quebec.[137] By 1774, the Board of Trade had therefore considered innumerable proposals for necessary reform of the constitutional and legal system in Quebec, but remained unsuccessful in implementing any of them. As debates between old and new subjects proved inconclusive and local settlements continued to be inadequate, the argument that only an act of Parliament could overturn the legal system in place became more widespread.

Thus, well into the 1770s, opinion still remained polarized about whether granting the French Catholics access to their ancient usages and allowing the Catholic Church there to collect tithes was "cruel and oppressive" or "just and humane." But with growing disaffection for British rule in New England, discontent in Quebec only became an issue of growing concern to the central government, and the loyalty of an ever-increasing *Canadien* population began to seem even more essential. Unlike Grenada, where inhabitants failed to secure a parliamentary statute to settle their disputes, Parliament finally intervened with legislation clarifying the rights of subjects in Quebec. The Quebec Act, which was passed in June 1774 to establish a "more effectual provision for the government" and to adjust the boundaries of the province,[138] drew on the various Board of Trade and legal reports produced in the 1760s and 1770s (figure 4.4).[139] It became the first parliamentary legislation to address the actual government of a specific colony, as well as the first statute to tackle the question of privileges owed to the province's predominantly French Catholic subjects.[140] Among other things, the Quebec Act granted Catholics the free exercise of their religion subject to the king's supremacy and the right to assume offices of trust without subscribing to the Test but by taking an oath designed for those purposes. Perhaps most significant, the act determined that "His Majesty's Canadian Subjects . . . may also hold and enjoy their Property and Possessions, together with all Customs and Usages relative thereto, and all other their Civil Rights . . . as may be consistent with their Allegiance to His Majesty."[141] By finally resolving the question of which laws would apply to the province and by formally allowing the coexistence of English criminal law and French civil law, the act ultimately redefined the rights associated with subjecthood.

Pushed through both houses at the end of the parliamentary session, the Quebec Act attracted both euphoric endorsement and virulent criticism. George III praised it as "founded on the clearest principles of justice and humanity" and believed it would "have the best effect, in quieting the minds and promoting the happiness of his Canadian subjects." By contrast, William Pitt, Earl of Chatham, called it "the most cruel, oppressive and odious measure, tearing up justice and every good principle by the roots," and threatened that it would "shake the affections and confidence of his Majesty's subjects in England and Ireland, and finally lose him the hearts of all the Americans."[142] Although a bill like the Quebec Act had been contemplated for years and Lord North's government had committed itself to resolving problems of

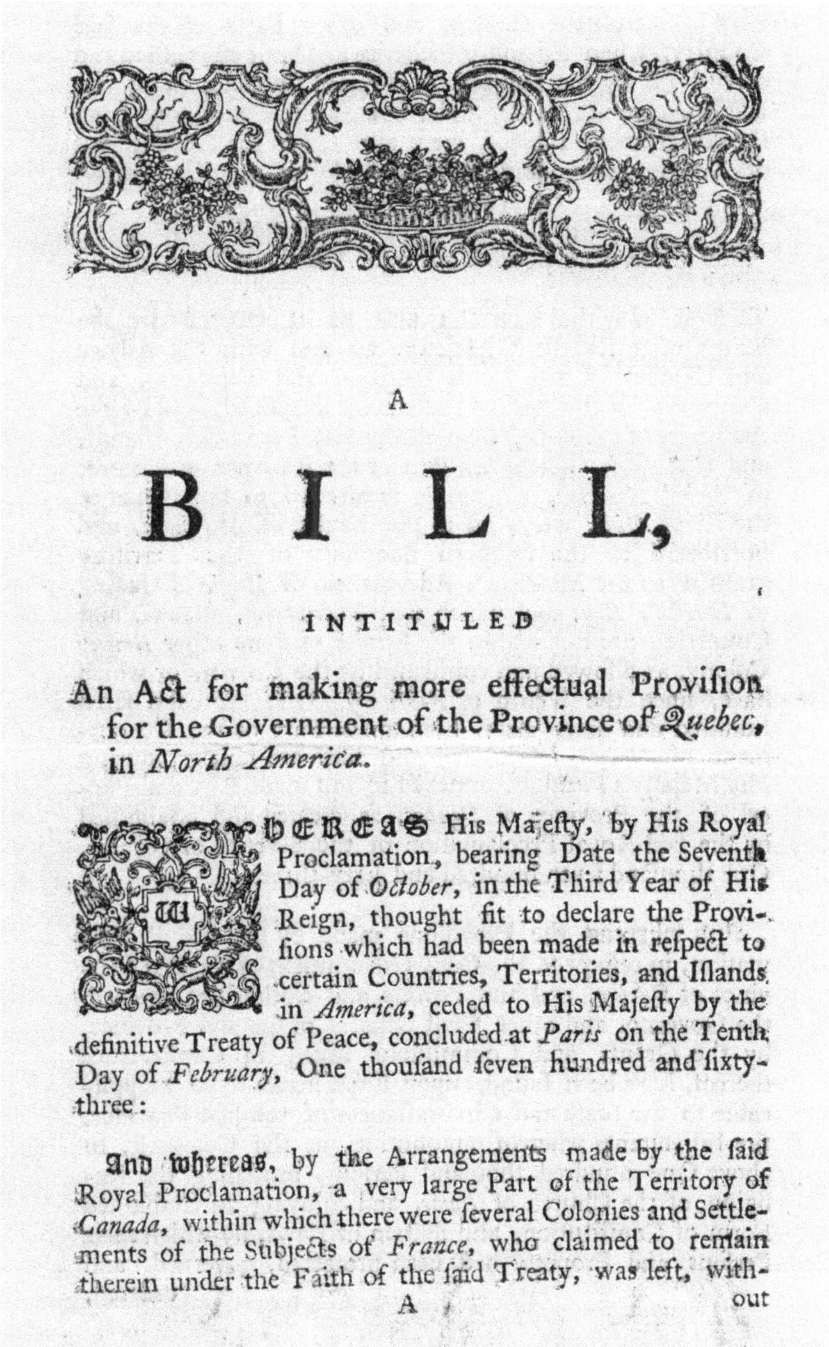

A

BILL,

INTITULED

An Act for making more effectual Proviſion for the Government of the Province of *Quebec*, in *North America.*

WHEREAS His Majeſty, by His Royal Proclamation, bearing Date the Seventh Day of *October*, in the Third Year of His Reign, thought fit to declare the Proviſions which had been made in reſpect to certain Countries, Territories, and Iſlands in *America*, ceded to His Majeſty by the definitive Treaty of Peace, concluded at *Paris* on the Tenth Day of *February*, One thouſand ſeven hundred and ſixty-three:

And whereas, by the Arrangements made by the ſaid Royal Proclamation, a very large Part of the Territory of *Canada*, within which there were ſeveral Colonies and Settlements of the Subjects of *France*, who claimed to remain therein under the Faith of the ſaid Treaty, was left, with-

A out

FIGURE 4.4 *A Bill, intituled An Act for making more effectual Provision for the Government of the Province of Quebec, in North America*. London: Eyre and Strahan, 1774. Courtesy of Houghton Library, Harvard University (EC75.G798L.B791b no.1)

governance in the fall of 1773, many observers on both sides of the Atlantic came to associate the act with the "intolerable acts" passed against the North American colonies earlier in 1774. It was apparent, however, that members of Parliament across the political spectrum believed that the outcome of these debates would determine whether subjects remained consistent in their allegiance to George III.

Because the plan for administering Quebec reached the halls of Parliament, the ensuing discussions were reasonably well documented and reveal that observers actively engaged arguments made throughout the 1760s and 1770s about subjects' rights, particularly those made by old and new subjects themselves. Their discussions suggest that politicians not only weighed questions about an appropriate constitutional settlement for Quebec, but that they were inherently grappling with which concessions were most likely to secure loyal British subjects for the empire. In general, proponents of the act argued that the bill reinforced the constitution because it upheld English criminal law but still permitted the French Canadians to live under the laws they had known for over one hundred years. Indeed, for defenders of the Quebec Act, imposing English laws upon a conquered nation was an "act of the grossest and absurdist and cruelest tyranny," and the bill was intended to remove such a stain of tyranny from the province.[143] Opponents of the bill lamented that it overturned the constitution given to Canada in 1763 and violated promises made to British settlers who had relocated there under the assumption that they would live under English law and the "British constitution."[144] As they discussed the Quebec Act, ministers were attempting to resolve which laws should apply to the province, but they were also debating the meanings of the "ancient constitution" and the rights of subjects more generally.

Perhaps most significant, in the words of pamphleteer William Knox, the Quebec Act was intended to resolve to what extent the French Canadians were "entitled to the common rights of British subjects in that country" and how they might best be "attached to the English government."[145] The problem arose because the rights of British subjects were not well defined and because there were competing ideas about how a government might best create loyal subjects. Those supporting the Quebec Act argued that embracing the French Catholics and allowing them to live under their own laws was the only way to ensure that they became British subjects. Alexander Wedderburn believed that unless the French Catholics themselves wanted to accept English laws, imposing them would have little effect. Rather, leaving the *Canadiens* to their ancient customs and encouraging gradual change "will bring the Canadians much more to the resemblance of British subjects than they are at present."[146]

During his examination in the House of Commons, William Hey, former Chief Justice for Quebec, noted that only "proper indulgence" to the *Canadiens* could turn them away from the French government, bring them to a "perfect submission to the Crown," and make them "good British subjects."[147] Like many colonial governors in Grenada and Quebec, those who supported the bill did so because they believed that concessions were the only means to ensure that French Catholics became "good British subjects." They proposed that subjecthood could accommodate not only those who spoke French or attended Catholic mass, but also those who lived under French laws.

By contrast, most opponents of the bill accused the government of reneging on its sacred duty to promulgate liberty by not requiring that the *Canadiens* live under English laws. As Edmund Burke would assert during the debates of 1774, "it is a violation of the faith of Great Britain held out to the Canadians . . . a violation of a promise to give them the benefit of the laws of England. . . . I would have English liberty carried into the French colonies, but I would not have French slavery brought into the English colonies . . . to deprive the English subject of the benefit of the laws of England."[148] Serjeant Glynn echoed these concerns, noting that it was the government's "duty, by all gentle means, to root those prejudices from the minds of the Canadians." He believed that Parliament, misguided by toleration, was betraying its newest inhabitants: "is it then, wise, I ask, out of compassion to the prejudices of those who have been born under the arbitrary law of another country, to perpetuate a system of government, which will deprive all those who may hereafter be born, from the enjoyment of the privileges of other British subjects."[149] For these critics, instead of transforming *Canadiens* into "British subjects" by introducing English law and fully assimilating them to English liberties, members of Parliament were eschewing their duties and depriving their newest subjects of their rights to English law.

According to these arguments, allowing French Catholics to continue living under French law and French tyranny would result in a failure to create British subjects. Members of the opposition refused to accept that granting French Catholics their "ancient usages" was the best way to turn them into useful subjects. Lord John Cavendish noted that he "would assimilate them as much as possible, that they might become fitter subjects of Great Britain. For that reason, I should think it material not to give them directly their own law again."[150] Edmund Burke would also proclaim: "give them English liberty—give them an English constitution—and then, whether they speak French or English, whether they go to mass or attend our own communion, you will render them valuable and useful subjects of Great Britain."[151] For many of these critics, British subjects might speak different languages and belong to various Christian denominations, but they must be protected by English law in order to become "useful subjects." Not only was the British government sworn to uphold the English law and constitution introduced in 1763, but it was "English liberty" that would secure the allegiance of its newest additions and make "fit subjects" of the *Canadiens*.

Despite popular backlash and an attempted repeal in 1775, the Quebec Act's successful passage upheld a controversial definition of the loyal subject's rights: subjects were entitled to live under their ancient customs and usages even if those were French. Nor was it just the book of statutes that reflected this expanded understanding of British subjecthood. The range of grateful and angry memorials, which reached the king in 1774, clearly regarded the act as having either granted or dismissed the rights of subjects. The ones from French Catholics noted the joy at being granted the "rights, advantages, and prerogatives of British subjects," at having been "adopted as sons of the Nation and as English citizens." [152] The ones from British Protestants decried that, by the act of parliament, individuals had lost the "protection of the English Laws . . . disgraceful for us as Britons."[153] Yet another petition to the House of Commons noted that the Quebec Act "deprives His Majesty's ancient subjects of all their rights and franchises" and pleaded that their liberties be ascertained not by French law but "according to their ancient constitutional rights and privileges heretofore granted to all His Majesty's dutiful subjects throughout the British Empire."[154] In each of these very different petitions, subjects invoked their membership in a broader community of British subjects and asserted that the Quebec Act had impacted their rights as subjects to time-honored customs.

The Quebec Act was ultimately endorsed by a central government that recognized that an inclusive definition of subjecthood was more appropriate for a territory where the French Catholic population continued to grow. The priorities of the central government had also changed between 1763 and 1774. The more assimilative policies of 1763 had lost momentum, and administrators had become more inclined to recognize the diversity of religions and laws across the British Empire as policies of toleration were countenanced.[155] In 1763, treaties and proclamations proposed simultaneous settlements for all of the ceded colonies and sought to integrate them under a broader constitutional model familiar to the Atlantic world—a model that embraced government by representative assembly and judgment according to English law. By the 1770s, the drawbacks of this approach had become clear as the persistent French Catholic majority in Quebec failed to accept English law and continued to favor French civil law. Policies thus increasingly began to consider the particular needs of Quebec and to imagine alternative means of incorporating diverse groups of subjects. At this moment, the rights of subjects, a source of acrimonious dispute for over a decade in Quebec, were debated and at least partially settled within the highest echelons of government in large part because French Catholics remained numerically predominant in Quebec and because their continued loyalty was paramount given discontent brewing in the thirteen colonies to the south. Indeed, Parliament stood fast in its decision regarding subjects' rights in Quebec despite the rising anger of colonists in Philadelphia and New York who maintained that the Quebec Act was part of an intolerable violation of their own rights as subjects.[156]

Although the British government had permitted Minorcans to continue living under Spanish law in the early eighteenth century, the practice of legal pluralism within the empire became a more recognized practice in the years after the Quebec Act officially allowed French civil law. By the 1770s and 1780s, analogous practices and regulations enabled Hindus and Muslims to be judged according to "Hindu" and "Muslim" law, respectively, in East India Company territories. This same move toward legal pluralism also signaled new and flexible understandings of subject status. It was in many respects because definitions of subjecthood were challenged and negotiated by subjects on the ground that official policy began to turn away from assimilating new subjects under English law and a Protestant ascendancy and moved instead toward accepting that adopted populations might live under diverse laws and still remain "consistent in their allegiance." Passage of the Quebec Act thus marked a moment when a truly imperial subjecthood was imagined and realized—a subjecthood that could accommodate the various peoples of the British Empire and that countenanced flexible rights.

DEBATES OVER SUBJECTS' RIGHTS in Grenada and Quebec, which occurred nearly concurrently in the 1760s and 1770s, reveal the crucial role played by subjects themselves in determining the nature and extent of those rights. Benefiting from the legal confusions that welled up in 1763 and the fact that British subjects' rights remained largely unspecified in case law and yet constantly invoked in the public sphere, inhabitants in both of these ceded colonies articulated competing notions of the rights they believed stemmed from their relationship with the monarch and made conflicting demands about the "constitution," representative assemblies, and "ancient laws." Though both French Catholics and British Protestants argued that the rights of the subject were entwined with the constitution and with law, they each interpreted that constitution rather differently. For many of the French Catholics and their supporters, a *bona fide* British subject was entitled to a constitution that permitted him to serve in a representative assembly regardless of his religious beliefs or to live under his chosen set of laws regardless of their country of origin. For their opponents, British subjects were individuals who either embraced a constitution intended to uphold a Protestant ascendancy and to marginalize recusants or who elected to live under English law. Relying on a variety of forms, but particularly on petitions, old and new subjects thus generated their own, alternative understandings of the rights associated with subjecthood.

But French Catholic success at securing privileges they believed stemmed from British subject status varied considerably across the British Empire, hinting at the ways in which the preponderance of loyal Catholics and their responses to local and global developments might also shape understandings of subjecthood. Although the French Catholics of Grenada successfully secured participation in representative government without subscribing to the Test during the 1760s and 1770s, these privileges were gradually eroded. In light of their declining numbers and influence throughout the 1770s and their desertion of the British when the French reoccupied the island in 1779, the tide of toleration began to turn against them. In 1792, law officers of the crown and the Privy Council determined that the "limited privilege . . . granted to the Roman Catholics, cannot take effect," and that henceforth assembly members would be required to make a declaration against transubstantiation.[157] French Catholics had been relegated to second-class subject status.

By contrast, in Quebec, where the *Canadiens* remained a vast majority and did not betray their adopted sovereign during the American Revolutionary War, new legislation granting assemblies in 1791 allowed Catholics to participate without being forced to subscribe to the Test. In 1794, an act passed in Lower Canada further indicated the extent to which the *Canadiens* had been integrated into the broader community of subjects. The Alien Act for Lower Canada, based closely on the Alien Act approved by the British Parliament in 1793, was intended to prevent aliens and others who had resided in revolutionary France from entering the province undetected and disturbing the peace. But in requiring that all aliens declare their arrival in the province, this act simultaneously defined those who were aliens and those who were not obliged to conform to these enactments. Suspect persons—aliens—were those who were not "natural born subjects of His Majesty, nor Denizens, nor persons naturalized by Act of Parliament, nor subjects of his Majesty, having become such by conquest or cession of the province of Canada."[158]

Whereas French Catholics in Grenada had been marginalized by the 1790s, the *Canadiens* were recognized as subjects entitled to the same statutory protections as their natural-born brethren.

In certain respects, the French Catholics' ability to secure these contested rights, however fleeting, suggests that the postwar period was one of openness and toleration. A document like the Alien Act indicates that subjects included not only the "natural-born" or those "naturalized by Act of Parliament," as they had in 1608, but that the peoples added to the British Empire in 1763 were widely acknowledged to be subjects. Certainly, the administrators who recognized the utility and potential contributions of these new subjects were inclined to grant them numerous concessions and to favor more expansive and flexible definitions of subjecthood. Some inhabitants and contemporary observers challenged these notions of subjecthood, arguing for restrictions on the privileges granted to French Catholics. Still others spoke out against the incongruities of policies that allowed Catholics in the ceded colonies to have rights not guaranteed to Catholics in other parts of the empire. Nevertheless, comparing the struggles in Grenada and Quebec illustrates that, while various inhabitants were recognized as subjects, not all subjects had comparable rights across the British Empire. If the rights of subjects were successfully renegotiated by individuals who were non-British and non-Protestant in the 1760s and 1770s, they were also revealed to be unstable and protean. And it was in large part because subjecthood could include so many and yet preserve distinctions between them that subjecthood would remain so important to integrating the British Empire more generally.

5

The Promises and Perils of Subjecthood and Jurisdiction

CALCUTTA

IN 1772, WILLIAM BOLTS called upon the king of Great Britain to assume his role as rightful sovereign of Bengal and asked the legislature to turn its attention to the "concerns of British subjects in the East Indies." This one-time alderman in the Calcutta Mayor's Court found it necessary to explain his terms further, noting that "in speaking of British subjects, we would be understood to mean his Majesty's newly-acquired Asiatic subjects, as well as the British emigrants residing in and establ'd in India."[1] Even though several other commentators concurred that Asians deserved recognition as "British subjects" or "subjects of his Majesty," these views hardly reflected an established consensus about the diverse peoples living in East India Company territories.[2] Future Governor-General Warren Hastings, for example, along with the Calcutta Council, argued that inhabitants of Bengal were "not the subjects of Britain, but aliens and natives of Hindustan."[3] Still others would propose that Christians and continental Europeans were entitled to the benefits of subjecthood, even if native inhabitants were not.[4] For decades, official decisions about individuals' statuses had typically been handled on a case-by-case basis, meaning that the legal status of these residents and their entitlements to political and social protections remained largely unresolved. Thus, by the early 1770s, conflicting views of subjecthood were widespread, and the "ongoing conundrum of subjecthood" persisted across East India Company territories.[5]

However, as the Company's territorial acquisitions increased exponentially, particularly following the Battle of Plassey (1757), and as it assumed responsibility for administering justice with the *diwani* for Bengal (1765), questions about the status of peoples inhabiting its new lands became more urgent and relevant. How many of these individuals should actually fall within the Company's jurisdiction? How many should have access to the protections of subjecthood? At the same time, such expansions also precipitated a growing parliamentary interest in the affairs of the East India Company. Questions about crown and parliamentary control over the East India Company had been raised on numerous occasions over the course of the seventeenth and early eighteenth centuries, but the combination of the Company's hostility to outside interference and the crown's largely *laissez-faire* approach meant that the Company government had managed to elude significant metropolitan oversight until the 1760s.[6] With the end of the Seven Years' War, high levels of government indebtedness increasingly led Parliament to view the East India Company as a means for rescuing national finances, and the parliamentary inquiry of 1767 marked the beginning of a new phase of government supervision.[7] These interventions from London were part of a broader trend toward more authoritarian and centralized imperial rule in the aftermath of global war, but they also provoked changes that would pit the needs of the king-in-Parliament against those of the Company.

While many territories experienced growing scrutiny from London, the legislation that was passed for the East Indies during this period reflected a particular series of concerns and needs that crystallized in the early 1770s. The significant revenues of the subcontinent certainly attracted parliamentary interest, but a number of voices weighed in on the unhappy state of affairs in the East Indies and the neglected welfare of its subjects. Horrific reports about the Bengal Famine in 1770, rumors of rampant mismanagement, and fears that wealthy nabobs returned from India would infiltrate the British political scene each influenced the decisions of a parliamentary select committee organized to review matters relating to the East Indies between 1772 and 1773. Among the issues raised at this time, legislators were particularly anxious that the Company, which had gained the right to govern and gather revenue in Calcutta and the surrounding provinces with the assumption of the *diwani*, was unable to mete out impartial justice given its own economic and political interests. Largely as a result of these concerns, the Regulating Act "for the better management of affairs of the East India Company" was passed in 1773, and it placed both the Company's executive and judiciary under increased parliamentary oversight.

Among its provisions, this landmark legislation created a five-man Supreme Council for governing Company territories and established a new royal court, the Supreme Court of Judicature at Calcutta, in the hopes of improving the administration of justice. Perhaps unsurprisingly, the Regulating Act, which represented crown and parliamentary interference *par excellence*, triggered an array of tensions. A "civil war" raged in the 1770s between members of the East India Company governing council and judges of the new court who were widely perceived to be trying to curb the power of Company officials.[8] Indeed, the founding of the Supreme Court was inherently problematic, in large part because the Regulating Act had allowed two independent and potentially diverging systems of justice: first, the Supreme Court of Judicature in Calcutta, which derived its authority from statute and from the British crown; and second, the hierarchy of Company courts in the *mofussil*, or the surrounding provinces of Bengal, Bihar, and Orissa, which derived their authority from the Mughal grant of *diwani*.[9] As counsel for the East India Company noted in 1780, two powers "distinct and independent of each other" had been established by the 1773 statute, "without providing any means to prevent their collision."[10]

The Supreme Court's destabilizing influence, its place in the plural legal order of the eighteenth century, and its role in extending royal franchises and jurisdiction have received recent scholarly attention. This chapter, however, focuses on how subject status came to represent a particular opportunity for its judges in the struggles that surrounded the Court's founding.[11] Remaining records from the Supreme Court underline the critical role of this court as a site for debates over the limits, meanings, and possibilities of the relationship between subject and sovereign, as well as the ways in which the judiciary engaged familiar legal understandings of allegiance and adapted them to the subcontinent in their daily decisions.

Moreover, in the case of Calcutta, deliberations about subject status were intertwined with questions of jurisdiction in ways that illuminate broader issues of sovereignty. Although the vast majority of the Supreme Court's cases involved a relatively straightforward local jurisdiction over the diverse inhabitants of Calcutta, the Court had also been granted personal jurisdiction over British subjects, Company employees, and servants of British subjects or Company employees, who resided in Calcutta or in the provinces of Bengal, Bihar, and Orissa. It was asserting their jurisdiction over these inhabitants that largely brought the judges into direct conflict with Company officials and courts in the *mofussil*, and ultimately endowed judges' decisions about subject status with a newfound importance. By determining that inhabitants were "British subjects" or "subjects of the king," the judiciary was simultaneously asserting that these individuals were not subjects of the Mughal emperor, not subjects of the East India Company, and not liable to Company courts.

In other words, as judges opined on which individuals were, in fact, "British subjects" and "subject to its jurisdiction," they necessarily made contentious decisions about the reach of royal jurisdiction in the subcontinent over matters previously handled by the East India Company. As they marked subjects and marked their own jurisdiction, judges of the Supreme Court were simultaneously determining the scope of royal authority, often at the expense of an increasingly hostile Company.[12] Because determinations of subject status ultimately represented an interconnected decision about jurisdiction and sovereignty, they remain essential to understanding the significance of subjecthood in the 1770s and 1780s and to parsing the broader contest between crown and Company power.

Although the Supreme Court tended to be eager to label litigants as subjects during its early years, thereby extending its jurisdiction, the rich demography of Calcutta rendered its deliberations about British subjecthood particularly complex. This chapter also aims to document the range of individuals who, at one moment or another, were considered "British subjects" or "subject to the jurisdiction" of the Supreme Court. A vibrant trading community in the eighteenth century, Calcutta was home not only to a large indigenous population but also to merchants and investors of innumerable backgrounds. In the early 1770s and 1780s, the majority of cases before the Supreme Court were brought by Calcutta's Hindu and Muslim inhabitants. Court records and lists of "Europeans residing in Calcutta" also reveal the many non-Indian inhabitants and non-Company-servants of whom administrators were aware.[13] Besides the more predictable English, Scots, and Irish who came before the Supreme Court, natives of Greece, Holland, Denmark, France, Portugal, Manila, China, Armenia, and Persia regularly surface in its proceedings. The varied population of Calcutta enabled and obliged the judges to consider whether non-Christian inhabitants and continental Europeans might legally be considered British subjects under their jurisdiction. Precisely because judges sought to bring this diverse population under their protection and to combat a Company government that they deemed to be oppressive, the Court began to propose and uphold religiously and racially inclusive definitions of subjecthood, allegiance, and protection in the 1770s.

Finally, this chapter relies on a range of archival evidence relating to the Supreme Court, including the papers of Justice John Hyde (figure 5.1), to document a striking change in the judiciary's definitions of subject status between the 1770s and 1780s, arguing that expansive definitions of subjecthood were not always desirable or advisable in East India Company territories.[14] It

FIGURE 5.1 William Sharp, after Robert Home, *John Hyde*, 1814, engraving. © National Portrait Gallery, London (NPG D36431).

situates these shifting ideas about subjecthood against the backdrop of parliamentary statutes relating to Bengal, most notably the Regulating Act of 1773 and the Act of Settlement of 1781. Equipped only with the most malleable of legal definitions and instructions from Parliament in the 1770s, judges of the Supreme Court proposed diffuse interpretations of the relationship between subject and sovereign, relying on arguments about Calcutta as a conquered town and on broad understandings of allegiance and jurisdiction in order to bring considerable numbers of inhabitants under royal protection. By the 1780s, however, these inclusive definitions of subjecthood had mainly disappeared from judicial discussions. Plaintiffs and defendants who came before the Supreme Court were increasingly classified either as "inhabitants of Calcutta" or as "British subjects residing in Bengal." Whereas the judges had initially viewed "British subject" as a potentially all-encompassing category, their deliberations now focused on a largely continental European population and on distinguishing between "temporary" and more "permanent" categories of subjects. Even as they continued to rely on notions of allegiance and protection and to link subject status with jurisdiction, the judges' more limited use of the term "British subject" suggests that parliamentary and Company visions of subject status had become more aligned, more restricted, and more hierarchical by the late 1780s.

Discussions relating to subject status in the Supreme Court of Judicature therefore place Calcutta firmly within an ongoing dialogue about allegiance, obedience, and protection across the British Empire, particularly after the Seven Years' War. As in other territories, a need for subjects in East India Company territories had always predisposed certain administrators to recognize a range of individuals as subjects.[15] As was true throughout the British Empire, the category of British subject was understood to be powerful and evocative, used to make demands and to signify belonging. But while debates about subjecthood centered on inhabitants' claims to economic or constitutional privileges in Gibraltar or Grenada, subject status was most frequently contested in Calcutta because it established an individual's access to the Supreme Court of Judicature and to the protections of the predominantly English law that its judges administered. The example of Calcutta demonstrates how the judiciary's day-to-day decisions about subject status were intertwined with issues of jurisdiction and sovereignty, which arose as crown and Parliament increasingly attempted to supervise the affairs of a company previously operating largely independently.

A Tangle of Sovereignties and Jurisdictions

When the British Parliament reviewed the judicial system that existed in East India Company territories during the early 1770s, the select committee discovered a complex and potentially confusing world of multiple jurisdictions.

Hybrid orders based on local and metropolitan legal practices existed in the three presidency towns of Calcutta, Bombay, and Madras, each of which was nominally supervised by the Company itself.[16] In Calcutta, a Mayor's Court, chartered by the crown in 1726[17] and again in 1753, was authorized to try all civil suits arising within Calcutta or its subordinate factories "except such suits as shall be between Indian Natives which shall be determined among themselves unless both parties consent to the determination of the Mayor's Court."[18] Whereas the Mayor's Court handled civil cases, the governor-general and five senior members of the council remained responsible for criminal matters. Otherwise, a *zamindari* court existed to determine civil and criminal suits involving Indians and was presided over by an English official, known as a *zamindar* or collector, who was also a member of the Governor's Council.[19]

In the eastern part of the Company's territories, the administration of justice was bifurcated between the actual town of Calcutta and the surrounding provinces of Bengal, Bihar, and Orissa, otherwise known as the *mofussil* (figure 5.2). In addition to the various courts in Calcutta, the Company had assumed increasing responsibility for the administration of justice in the *mofussil*, establishing a system of *adalat* courts. Based in large part on the traditional Mughal division of authority between *nizam* and *diwan*, the *adalat* courts administered criminal and civil law throughout the provinces of Bengal, Bihar, and Orissa.[20] In 1772, the Company also established two superior courts above these courts in the *mofussil*, including the chief criminal court of *Nizamat Sadar Adalat* and the chief civil court of *Diwani Sadar Adalat*, over which Company officials maintained a general supervision.[21] The East India Company *adalat* system would operate separately from the administration of justice in Calcutta until the two systems were integrated in 1861.[22]

The act that resulted from Parliament's consideration of this multifaceted judicial system was, in many respects, remarkably targeted. Rather than attempting to reform the entire administration of justice in East India Company territories, the Regulating Act of 1773 tackled only the specific situation in Calcutta, replacing the Mayor's Court with the Supreme Court of Judicature. Although inhabitants of Calcutta remembered the Mayor's Court and existing system of justice longingly after their abolition, Parliament determined that neither could assure the impartial administration of justice where the East India Company or its officials were concerned.[23] First, despite its royal charter, the Mayor's Court was not an independent entity. Many of its aldermen were chosen from the ranks of East India Company

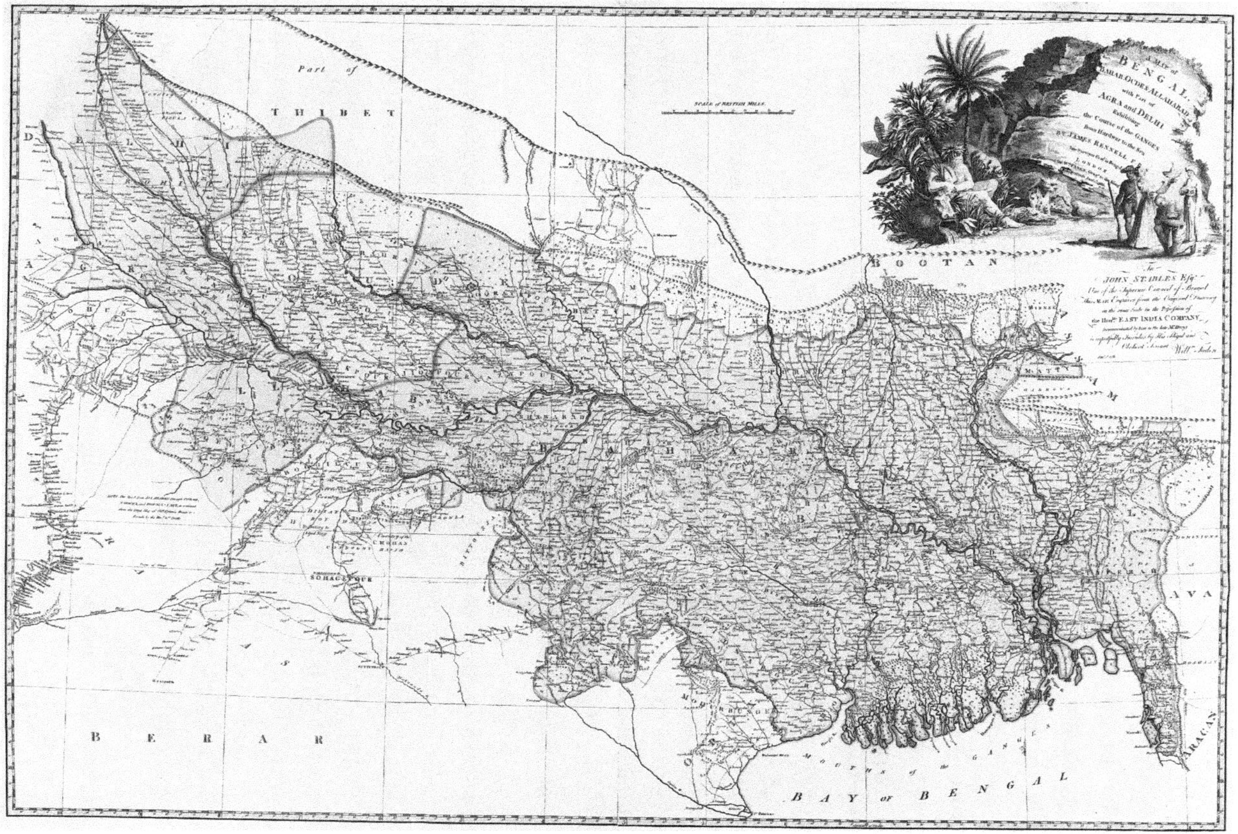

FIGURE 5.2 James Rennell, *A Map of Bengal, Bahar, Oude & Allahabad with part of Agra and Delhi* [map], 1:1,480,000. London: William Faden, 1786. Courtesy of David Rumsey Map Collection, www.davidrumsey.com (Cf. Phillips 6010, 6013, 6047).

junior servants or were private traders dependent on the goodwill of the Company to remain in the subcontinent.[24] Furthermore, the East India Company president and council heard appeals, leaving the executive and judiciary profoundly intertwined in Calcutta. Perhaps more important, the Mayor's Court had only a civil jurisdiction, which meant that criminal cases were heard by the governor-general and five senior members of the council, and the ability of Company officials to be objective in cases that involved abuses committed by their fellow-servants remained an ongoing concern.[25] Finally, the jurisdiction granted to the Mayor's Court did not extend to the rapidly growing British and European population who ventured beyond the limits of Calcutta, a jurisdictional issue that became particularly problematic as Europeans increasingly moved further into the interior and into territorial acquisitions secured after 1757.[26]

The Supreme Court of Judicature envisioned in 1773 was intended to remedy these inadequacies. In most respects, the new court was modeled on the high courts at Westminster, although it singlehandedly exercised civil, criminal, admiralty, and ecclesiastical jurisdiction and dispensed common law, equity, ecclesiastical, and maritime law.[27] Like its predecessor, however, it continued to seek the advice of Hindu and Muslim law officers in cases involving inhabitants of India.[28] The Supreme Court generally continued the work of the Mayor's Court, which had administered civil justice to the polyglot commercial society of Calcutta. The vast majority of its cases, for example, seem to have addressed the everyday concerns of the local population and dealt with actions of debt, bonds and securities, ejectment, trespass, and administration of a deceased's effects. Unlike the Mayor's Court, which had been denied the criminal jurisdiction reserved for the governor and council, the Supreme Court also heard a mixture of civil and criminal cases and therefore became a unified focal point for the administration of justice. Its sessions of Oyer and Terminer and Gaol Delivery were criminal quarter sessions and handled actions of burglary, larceny, forgery, assault, rape, and murder. Other avenues for justice continued to exist in Calcutta, but the Supreme Court became the most visible arena given the wide array of cases and defendants that it considered.[29]

Perhaps most significant, Parliament insisted that the Supreme Court remain completely separate from the executive and that it be a government institution under crown rather than Company control. In stark contrast to its predecessor, the Supreme Court was unequivocally part of an imperial system of justice, with appeals to the king in council rather than to the Company's president and council.[30] The Court was to be run by paid professionals, individuals who were personal representatives of the crown, served during the king's pleasure, and had no ties to the East India Company.[31] By 1774, civil and criminal justice in Calcutta had thus been largely entrusted to a court that was responsible to the British crown and was clearly intended to act as a check on the East India Company, particularly its Supreme Council.

Given the circumstances surrounding its founding, tensions between the Supreme Court and the governor-general and council may have been inevitable. After all, the four reform-minded judges who boarded their ship in Portsmouth on March 30, 1774, and together sailed to Calcutta, believed that they had been appointed to protect the rights of subjects, broadly defined, against a corrupt and oppressive East India Company.[32] They may have been predisposed to assert the jurisdiction of their royal court at the expense of Company traditions.[33] By contrast, Company officials had a vested interest in limiting crown supervision and in maintaining their own existing system of courts, and many feared that undue interference from the Supreme Court would bring Company operations to a standstill. At the root of these tensions, however, lay two unresolved questions: in the 1770s, uncertainty remained both about who was actually sovereign in Calcutta or Bengal and about how exactly the Regulating Act and Charter of Justice had defined the Supreme Court's jurisdiction.

As Company officials made all too clear, the Company's right to govern its factories and settlements had historically stemmed from two competing sources of power—from royal charters and Mughal grants.[34] On the one hand, the city of Calcutta had been reconquered from the *nawab*, or provincial governor of the Mughal Empire, by a joint expedition of East India Company and royal forces in 1757, arguably making it like other conquered territories and a British settlement, albeit one governed by a trading company. On the other hand, the Company had also assumed responsibility for administering civil and revenue affairs when it was granted the *diwani* for Bengal, Bihar, and Orissa by the Mughal emperor. These *diwani* lands lay beyond the city limits of Calcutta in the surrounding provinces of the *mofussil* and had not been declared to be formally part of the British crown's territory. The status of Calcutta and the surrounding provinces of Bengal, Bihar, and Orissa remained largely uncertain.[35] Who was sovereign here? Was it George III? Or the East India Company? Or the Mughal emperor? From the perspective of the East India Company, it remained advantageous to insist on coexisting, sometimes conflicting, authorities in Bengal, including its own.

Company arguments about overlapping sovereignties were difficult for the Supreme Court to refute, in large part because royal and parliamentary sovereignty over East India Company territories was never officially declared in the eighteenth century.[36] Although the attorney general and solicitor general had explicitly been asked in 1757 to determine whether the East India Company might "hold and enjoy" the fortresses, districts, and territories that it had acquired or might acquire, even their ruling reflected the blurred lines between crown and Company sovereignty. Charles Pratt and Charles Yorke argued that places acquired by conquest were vested in the crown by virtue of its prerogative and that consequently "the Company can only derive a Right to them, through Your Majesty's Grant." However, they regarded places acquired through treaty or through a grant from the Mughal emperor slightly differently. In these territories, "Property of the Soil" was vested in the Company via Indian grants, and they remained "subject only to Your Majesty's Right of Sovereignty over the Settlements, as English Settlements, and over the Inhabitants, as English Subjects, who carry with them Your Majesty's Laws, wherever they form Colonies, and receive Your Majesty's Protection."[37] According to this report, Calcutta was a conquered town vested in the crown, but the surrounding provinces were grants vested in the Company.

This widely circulated ruling also pointed to a potentially significant problem: even where land in the provinces belonged to the East India Company, counsel suggested that the crown retained certain rights over those who were its subjects. And it was the bodies of subjects, who carried with them "Your Majesty's Laws" wherever they formed colonies, which also determined the reach of royal protection. Because determinations about subject status essentially represented decisions about the extent and limits of royal authority, as Pratt and Yorke hinted in 1757, the Supreme Court's decisions about allegiance and protection became particularly important and were seen as a threat to other sources of sovereignty.

Early observers of the Supreme Court immediately recognized the potential difficulties that would arise from unresolved issues of sovereignty and the interrelated questions of subjecthood. For example, an unsigned memorandum noted that the Court's charter had authorized all writs issued to run in the king's name, but asked whether "since his Majesty has not assumed the Sovereignty of Bengal & since the Natives of that country owe him no Allegiance, will a writ running in his name be compulsory upon the native?"[38] Philip Francis, a prominent member of the Supreme Council, raised similar concerns in 1776. He emphasized the dangers that arose when jurisdiction was asserted over subjects without any corresponding clarification of sovereignty, noting "we have a Supreme Court of Judicature resident at Calcutta, whose writs run through every part of these provinces in his Majesty's name, indiscriminately addressed to British subjects, who are bound by their allegiance, or to the natives, over whom no right of sovereignty, on the part of the King of Great Britain, has yet been claimed or declared."[39] Francis feared that the Court was blindly seeking jurisdiction over both subjects and non-subjects when, in fact, it ought to have jurisdiction only over those individuals who owed allegiance to the British monarch.

As Francis and others recognized, failure to proclaim royal sovereignty at the time the royal court was established would provoke enduring questions about who, exactly, owed allegiance and was a subject in Calcutta and the surrounding provinces. Terminological vagueness in the parliamentary documents that established the Supreme Court's jurisdiction only exacerbated these uncertainties. Neither the Regulating Act nor the Charter of Justice had clearly defined the extent of the Supreme Court's powers, in large part because neither had offered specific definitions of subject status. What both the 1773 Regulating Act and 1774 Charter of Justice did do was grant the Supreme Court two forms of jurisdiction: a local and a personal jurisdiction, each of which was more extensive than the jurisdictions of the previous Mayor's Court. In different ways, each of these jurisdictions infringed upon the East India Company's administration of justice and systems for controlling its servants, generating widespread confusion and resentment.[40]

The first form of jurisdiction granted was based on the Supreme Court's mandate as the court for Calcutta; it was a local jurisdiction that covered crimes committed in Calcutta and crimes committed by inhabitants of Calcutta.[41] The Court's local jurisdiction therefore extended to all residents of Calcutta, whether Indian or European, a grant which helped to account for the remarkably diverse group of plaintiffs and defendants that appeared before it. As one judge remarked, the Supreme Court had been granted a "compleat local criminal jurisdiction within Fort William and the subordinate settlements, without any Exception as to the Native Inhabitants."[42] Judges were also allowed to hear the cases of all individuals who had entered into written agreements to submit to the Supreme Court's jurisdiction. This local jurisdiction arguably brought a very diverse group within the protection of the king and his law.[43]

More problematically, the Supreme Court was granted a second, more sweeping, personal jurisdiction. This extended to British subjects, servants and employees of the East India Company, and servants and employees of British subjects residing in Bengal, Bihar, and Orissa. Personal jurisdiction over East India Company employees permitted the Supreme Court to try the cases of revenue and legal officials that had previously been handled by Company courts—courts whose primary objective was to maximize profits and collection of revenue. It also brought an increasing number of individuals—British, European, and Indian—within the ambit of this royal court. Such personal jurisdiction meant that the Supreme Court heard cases brought by people who lived in lands well beyond Calcutta, areas that were not formally part of British crown territories and that possessed their own competing judicial systems. This second jurisdiction granted by Parliament thus brought the Supreme Court into direct conflict with the East India Company, whose system of justice in the provinces had not been overturned and whose representatives believed that only Company courts ought to have jurisdiction over inhabitants in the *mofussil*.

The lack of precision in both the Regulating Act and the Charter of Justice immediately provoked problems of interpretation, particularly where the personal jurisdiction of the Supreme Court was concerned.[44] Section 14 of The Regulating Act appeared to use the terms "British subject" and "His Majesty's subject" interchangeably:

> . . . that the said new Charter which his Majesty is herein before empowered to grant, and the jurisdiction, powers, and authorities to be thereby established, shall and may extend to all British subjects who shall reside in the kingdoms or provinces of Bengal, Bahar, and Orissa, or any of them, under the protection of the said United Company . . . and the Supreme Court of Judicature therein and thereby to be established, shall have full power . . . and authority to hear and determine all complaints against any of his Majesty's subjects, for any crimes, misdemeanors or oppressions committed, or to be committed; and also to entertain, hear and determine any suits or actions whatsoever against any of his Majesty's subjects in Bengal, Bahar, and Orissa.

In the same breath that it granted the Court jurisdiction over "all British subjects who shall reside in the kingdoms or provinces of Bengal, Bahar, and Orissa," the act also confirmed the Court's authority to hear and determine complaints "against any of his Majesty's subjects." Legal historian M. P. Jain has suggested that "his Majesty's subject" was intended to be broader than "British subject," perhaps including subjects of British origin who were born in Canada, Australia, and other British possessions, although the clause itself remained inconclusive.[45]

Furthermore, Section 16 gave the Court power to hear suits or actions "whatsoever of any of his Majesty's subjects against any inhabitant of India, residing in any of the said kingdoms or provinces . . . or any of them, upon any contract or agreement, in writing, entered into by any of the said inhabitants with any of his Majesty's said subjects." Here, "inhabitants of India" appeared to be clearly distinguished from "his Majesty's subjects."[46] John Hyde would argue, however, that the parallel clause in the charter, which extended the administration of justice "to our subjects, who shall be resident within the said provinces," meant that the king had "expressly call[ed] all the Inhabitants of Bengal, Bahar, and Orissa his subjects." Hyde recognized, of course, that most Company officials were unwilling to countenance such inclusive interpretations of the clause, but he believed that the documents were intentionally expansive.[47]

Finally, the Regulating Act gave the Supreme Court jurisdiction over individuals "directly or indirectly, in the service of the said United Company, or of any of his Majesty's subjects" at the time the action arose but failed to define what "indirectly in the service" actually meant.[48] In 1781, for instance, Hyde observed that it was still not clear what being "indirectly employed by" the Company or a British subject entailed. In the margins of his notebook, he considered a theoretical problem:

> Suppose a Native British Subject resident in Calcutta should hire three assasins not subject to the jurisdiction to murder a Man and they should murder him in some place out of this Town of Fort William . . . it may possibly be answered that those three assasins would be subject to the jurisdiction by being employed by a British subject . . . but some may wonder of this construction of the Charter.[49]

Through this hypothetical, Hyde highlighted the inadequacies of existing definitions. Because no clause in the Regulating Act specified the differences between "British subjects," "his Majesty's subjects," or "inhabitants of India," or adequately illustrated these categories, the extent of the Supreme Court's jurisdiction over various inhabitants of the subcontinent would remain contested.

The Charter of Justice failed to resolve any of these definitional problems. It referred to both "British subjects" and "our subjects," seemingly interchangeably, and also failed to clarify who was "directly" or "indirectly" in the service of the Company or of British subjects. More significant, in establishing who might sit on a Grand Jury, Section 19 specified that the "principal inhabitants, resident in the said town of Calcutta, being subjects of Great Britain," were to be summoned. On the one hand, the charter seemed to imply that all principal inhabitants of Calcutta were British subjects. On the other hand, the charter might also be read as suggesting that only subjects of Great Britain could be jury members. This second interpretation corresponded to a clause in the Regulating Act, which stipulated that offenses should be "tried by a Jury of British subjects resident in the town of Calcutta, and not otherwise." Nonetheless, the subtle discrepancy between the Regulating Act and Charter, and the possibility that "principal inhabitants of Calcutta" were also "British subjects," would leave considerable room for capacious definitions of subjecthood.

Indeed, these intertwined uncertainties about sovereignty and subjecthood were often the focus of discussions in the Supreme Court. As judges engaged questions about their jurisdiction, they necessarily found that their ability to act also required decisions about subject status, which in turn involved contentious determinations about the source of sovereignty. Sir Robert Chambers, senior puisne judge from 1774 to 1791 and Chief Justice from 1791 until 1798, seems to have had the earlier Pratt-Yorke judgment in mind rather frequently.[50] In one opinion, he claimed that the Supreme Court legitimately held full jurisdiction in Calcutta because the city had officially been claimed by the crown.[51] He remained sensitive, however, to a kind of dual sovereignty in the province of Bengal, recognizing that the Company's original right to govern Calcutta and the surrounding provinces stemmed "partly on the charter of their own Sovereign and partly on the great Mogul's Grant." Rather than being deterred by Pratt and Yorke's understanding of the law, however, Chambers sought to explain why dual sovereignty in the provinces was not necessarily incongruous with an extensive Supreme Court jurisdiction. In making his arguments, he drew on and extended understandings of allegiance from the "ancient common lawyers," including Bracton, Coke, and Hale. Just as these luminaries had claimed that it was possible for individuals to owe both "liege homage," due by native allegiance, and "feudal homage," due to the lord of the land, so, too, according to Chambers, could inhabitants of the provinces recognize two spheres of authority. The Supreme Court's jurisdiction outside of Calcutta was based on individuals' personal subjection to the crown rather than on local subjection and jurisdiction.[52] In other words, even if they resided in territories where they might owe "feudal homage" to Mughal or Company officials, inhabitants could still owe "liege homage" to the British crown. In Chambers's analysis, the Supreme Court needed only to establish that individuals owed some kind of allegiance to the British crown—either local or natural—in order to exercise its jurisdiction.

While both Stephen Caesar Lemaistre and Hyde, puisne judges from 1774 to 1777 and 1774 to 1796, respectively, seem to have favored extending the Supreme Court's jurisdiction beyond Calcutta, they, too, were careful to ground all such claims in theories of subjection and allegiance to the monarch of Great Britain. In justifying the Court's right to adjudicate cases concerning the Company's revenue or other official matters, Lemaistre did so by claiming that Company servants were actually British subjects. They fell within the Supreme Court's jurisdiction because they owed "Allegiance which is due from the East India Company to the King as composed of his subjects owing its existence as a corporation to his Royal Charters and Acts of the British Legislature, which allegiance no subject can by Law transfer or transpose by any change of character or situation whatever."[53] For his part, Hyde argued in 1775 that the king's prerogative "extends as fully over his subjects here as in any part of his dominions."[54] Both Lemaistre and Hyde understood that one of the most effective ways to increase royal authority at the expense of the East India Company was to rely on expansive definitions of allegiance, thereby increasing the number of individuals—be they inhabitants of Calcutta, Company employees, or British subjects—over whom the Supreme Court had jurisdiction. This was the opportunity of subjecthood for the judiciary, since recognizing someone as a British subject meant fundamentally treating him as a subject of King George III rather than of the Mughal emperor or the East India Company. Determining the scope of allegiance, and thereby jurisdiction, thus became a highly charged and inherently political enterprise in the 1770s.

Nor were judges the only ones who noticed the legislative sloppiness of their mandate. Eager to claim expansive definitions of subjecthood, parties before the Supreme Court frequently called attention to the Regulating Act and Charter's failure to adequately define "inhabitants of India," "British subjects," and "his Majesty's subjects." In 1782, one advocate observed that the acts of Parliament referred to "European British subjects," arguing that this suggested that there might be "British subjects" who were not necessarily "European."[55] In the case of *Michael de Rozio v. Chutgeer Gosain*, counsel for both parties remarked on the Charter's confusing language. Counsel for the defendant reminded the Court that the charter simultaneously referred to "British subjects" and "his Majesty's subjects." Even the plaintiff contended that, although the words were used interchangeably, the expression "British subjects" could not be confined to "Native British Subjects." Such narrow readings, the parties seemed to agree, would result in a "manifest failure of justice."[56]

By the 1770s, then, questions of sovereignty and allegiance were embedded in the quotidian judicial determinations about who actually fell within the categories of "British subject," "his Majesty's subject," and "inhabitant of India." Not unlike many of their predecessors, the judges of the Supreme Court drew on a far longer tradition wherein allegiance to the monarch had been used to challenge the authority of the East India Company. Although the crown had granted the Company a commission in 1623 to "chastise, correct, and punish all of the Subjects of Us" employed in the East Indies,[57] questions were perpetually raised about this delegation of sovereign authority to a trading enterprise and about whether individuals were "Company subjects" or "His Majesty's subjects."[58] Throughout the seventeenth and eighteenth centuries, residents would rely on claims of subjecthood and royal protection to critique or attempt to limit the power of the East India Company. The establishment of a royal Supreme Court in 1774 intensified this earlier dynamic, and it meant that the judges' inclusive ideas about subjecthood came to be seen for what they were—a potent and direct threat to Company authority.

Extending Subjecthood and Jurisdiction after 1773

The ambiguities of the Regulating Act and Charter of Justice meant that even as the judges first convened on October 22, 1774, they were faced with numerous decisions about which populations were, in fact, subject to the Supreme Court's jurisdiction (figure 5.3). As they engaged in their day-to-day deliberations and sought to parse the clauses of parliamentary documents, Chief Justice Sir Elijah Impey, Chambers, Hyde, and Lemaistre regularly defined categories like "inhabitant of Calcutta," "in the employ of the Company," and "British subject." As they drew on their knowledge of case law and took advantage of the imprecisions of parliamentary documents, the judges of the Supreme Court brought an increasingly wide range of inhabitants within their jurisdiction in ways that directly challenged the East India Company's authority. And as plaintiffs, defendants, and counsel also endeavored to corroborate status, working definitions of these categories continued to develop, a number of which were religiously and racially inclusive.

Indeed, the demographically varied population that consistently appeared before the Supreme Court provided judges and counsel with an unusual opportunity to consider the boundaries of subjecthood. While the Mayor's Court had clearly been intended mainly for Calcutta's British and European inhabitants and the *zamindari* courts reserved for disputes between Indian

FIGURE 5.3 Thomas Daniell, *The Old Court-house and writer's building, Calcutta*, 1786, etching with aquatint. © The British Library Board (C13588-27, P95).

inhabitants, an increasing number of native inhabitants began to use the Supreme Court.[59] Incomplete bundles of legal records for 1771, for example, indicate that roughly 5 of 170 cases involved an Indian plaintiff and an Indian defendant. However, by the mid-to-late 1770s, at least half of the extant cases appear to have been between Indians, suggesting that the number of suits in this Court brought by Indians against both other Indians and Europeans grew dramatically in the 1770s. Not only had the Supreme Court become the forum to which most constituents in Calcutta turned for justice, but the presence of Indian litigants made necessary wide-ranging discussions about whether "inhabitants of Calcutta" were, in fact, "British subjects."[60] An array of continental Europeans and non-Europeans also relied on the Supreme Court. A varied crew of Britons appeared before the judges, with Scottish and Irish residents joining their English brethren in significant numbers. Natives of Greece, Holland, Denmark, and France also used the system.[61] Natives of Persia and Armenians were frequenters of the Court.[62] In 1794, a "native of Manila" who resided in Calcutta was tried for murder.[63] In both 1778 and 1783, even natives of China, who were in Calcutta for the purposes of trade or who had property in Bengal, initiated suits before the Court.[64]

Many of these cases raised questions of subject status, forcing judges to determine whether plaintiff and defendant fell within the Court's local or personal jurisdiction. Theoretically, either jurisdiction rendered an individual amenable to the Court, and the question may often have remained immaterial for cases originating in Calcutta or involving inhabitants of Calcutta. Nonetheless, the Court's personal jurisdiction—its authority over inhabitants in the provinces outside Calcutta—was determined by whether they were "British subjects" or whether they were in the employ of the Company or of "British subjects." For this reason, resolving whether "inhabitants of India" or "his Majesty's subjects" were also "British subjects" was significant. In general, verifying that defendants were "inhabitants of Calcutta," "employed in the East India Company's service," or "British subjects," however ill-defined these categories were, was similarly essential to establishing the Supreme Court's jurisdiction, just as disproving any of these allowed an inhabitant to escape justice in this particular court and to seek remedy elsewhere.

First, proving or disproving that defendants were "inhabitants of Calcutta" was material to cases throughout the 1770s, since it established that the Court had a local jurisdiction. In the case of *Benud Behary Seat v. Bharotchurn Meter & Mahadeb Dutt*, for example, the defendants were stated to be inhabitants of Calcutta at the time of the action and "therefore no question arose on the Jurisdiction."[65] In the counter-cases of *Nernerain Mitre v. Radachurn Mojumder* and *Radachurn Mojumder v. Nernerain Mitre,* however, Nernerain Mitre argued that the Supreme Court "ought not to consider pleas" because he was "not a British Subject but a Native of Joynagur and not an Inhabitant of Calcutta."[66] In this particular case, because the defendant was neither an inhabitant of Calcutta nor a British subject, he managed to eschew the local jurisdiction of the Supreme Court and secure the right to be tried by courts in the *mofussil*.[67]

Determinations about who qualified as "inhabitants of Calcutta" were not always so clear-cut. In 1787, the *Calcutta Gazette* reported:

> On Friday last, a cause was determined in the Supreme Court, of infinite importance to the commercial inhabitants of this city, as it affords them a certainty of redress against those with whom they may enter into contracts. In the case alluded to, it was decided that a temporary residence in Calcutta, effectually subjects a native to the jurisdiction of the Court.

In this case, the Court ruled that a certain "Gentoo woman" named Ranna Janokee fell within its jurisdiction because she was an inhabitant of Calcutta.

The fact that she was only "occasionally obliged to repair to Calcutta, either on visits of ceremony, or on business," was inconsequential; what mattered was that she was an inhabitant by virtue of her "temporary residence." In a city where itinerant merchants and mariners of many nationalities engaged in business and commerce, the publishers of the *Calcutta Gazette* clearly believed that this elucidation of the Court's jurisdiction over temporary inhabitants was essential, even if they might have disagreed with this definition of what characterized an inhabitant of Calcutta.[68] This ruling was noteworthy because it meant that those who "reside in Calcutta for a few weeks, for the purposes of trade," were liable to the Court's jurisdiction. Even brief periods of residence created a group of individuals subject to the Court's local jurisdiction, which in effect placed them under temporary royal protection.

Second, in order to assert its jurisdiction, the Court might be required to establish that defendants were "in the employ" of the East India Company or of British subjects. In *Rex v. James Clarke*, no written proof was furnished of Clarke being a soldier in the Company's service, but a sergeant swore that he had seen Clarke "muster'd." Verbal testimony about employment was considered sufficient evidence for establishing the Court's jurisdiction, and Clarke was ultimately convicted of murder.[69] In both 1779 and 1793, respectively, Rustom Beg and Mansur Ali Khan were tried for the murder of other Indians because they were proven to be either sepoys or in the militia service of the Company.[70] In 1788, Hoolass Matre was convicted of a murder "committed at Kedderpoor which is in Bengal but not in Calcutta." Although the crime had been committed outside the Court's local jurisdiction, Matre fell within its jurisdiction because he "was in the service of Charles Grant who is a British subject resident in Bengal."[71] As these cases indicate, many of those in the service of the Company or of British subjects were actually native inhabitants of both Calcutta and the surrounding provinces. Prior to 1774, they might have had their cases heard by Company courts, but by the later 1770s, they found themselves summoned before a Supreme Court that was gradually extending its jurisdiction. In this way, the range of those subject to the Court's jurisdiction was broadened, and even though these individuals were not necessarily labeled "British subjects," they were still brought within the scope of royal protection.

Finally, determining that litigants were British subjects owing allegiance to the British monarch provided the clearest means for bringing parties within the Supreme Court's jurisdiction. In December 1785, James Christie was acquitted of murder because he could not be proven a British subject and because "his being a British subject is a question involved in [the] decision."[72] However, in a case of trespass that arose a few years later, the same Christie was proven to be a British subject because he was born in Glasgow, Scotland.[73] On this occasion, the Court ordered that he pay Radacunt Mandell 5,000 rupees.[74] Similarly, in December 1793, William Henry Smith was told that he might be acquitted by the Court if he could prove that he was not a British subject, but that his case would then be handed over to the East India Company's courts. The judges recommended that he assert his subjecthood by admitting to being born someplace in the British Dominions and that he choose to remain within royal protection. Smith appears to have done so, as a verdict of not guilty was handed down shortly thereafter.[75] In each of these cases, the Court was clearly upholding a familiar definition of subject status, arguing that birth within the monarch's dominions and allegiance conferred subjecthood.[76]

What also emerges from the cases considered by the Supreme Court in the 1770s, however, is a judicial willingness to equate "inhabitant of Calcutta" with "British subject." Numerous cases suggest that the Court was inclined to recognize Indian inhabitants and an array of continental Europeans as British subjects and that they were willing to extend subject status and royal protection quite widely. On at least two separate occasions, Hindu petitioners were explicitly treated as British subjects. On December 17, 1776, Hyde referred to the Supreme Court's charter, which had directed that administration be granted to British subjects or for the goods of deceased British subjects. He then noted that the Court had granted administration "to the Estates of Gentoos (as well as other Persons) dying in Calcutta, and to Gentoos inhabiting Calcutta, adjudging them to be British subjects."[77] Similarly, on November 16, 1778, in an action related to the goods of Bindabund Gosain, the judges agreed that they could grant "administrations to Hindoos under the description of British subjects."[78] Identified as "Hindoos" and as "inhabitants of Calcutta," they were, in the minds of the justices, also British subjects. In contrast to this more inclusive approach to subject status, however, another entry for June 28, 1776, noted simply that Hadje Abdulla was "a Mahomedan and not a British subject."[79] Because the record is extraordinarily sparse, it is impossible to assess whether the judges determined that Hadje Abdulla was "not a British subject" because he was Muslim or because he was "not an inhabitant of Calcutta." Although the judges were inconsistent in their categorizations and did not always regard Hindu and Muslim litigants as British subjects, the court record nonetheless suggests that they often equated "inhabitant of Calcutta" with "British subject."

The judges seem most frequently to have defended these interpretations by relying on arguments that Calcutta was a conquered territory and on flexible interpretations of allegiance. Chambers, for example, consistently maintained that Calcutta was a conquered town, which entitled the king to change its laws, and which Chambers also argued meant inhabitants became subjects, much as they had in the conquered territories of Gibraltar, Minorca, Grenada, and Quebec. Hyde would claim something very similar in 1782. He asserted that administration of effects could only be granted if the deceased in question was "at his death a British subject," but also made clear that the only criterion that mattered in establishing the deceased's status was whether he was an inhabitant of Calcutta. As Hyde observed, "we say that Inhabitants of this Town are all British subjects because this Town was conquered by Admiral Watson and Colonel Clive."[80] Although documentation is sparse, both may have relied on legal understandings prevalent in other conquered territories like Grenada or Minorca, where a decision to remain after the conquest was often believed to confer subject status even if the individuals in question had not been born within the monarch's allegiance. For both Chambers and Hyde, the longest serving justices on the Supreme Court, equating "inhabitants of Calcutta" with "British subjects" was not only legally sound, but was also a logical way to increase the reach of their jurisdiction.

Arguments that Calcutta was a conquered town surface throughout Hyde's notes, revealing how interconnected the "incident of birth" and subject status were for the Supreme Court. The case of *David Killican v. Juggernauth Dutt* suggested that individuals born in Calcutta were far more likely to be recognized as subjects than those born in the *mofussil*. Hyde's notes about the decision read: "if the defendant had been proved to have been born in Calcutta, the Court would have considered him a British subject, and therefore subject to the jurisdiction in whatever part of the provinces he might be."[81] Birth in Calcutta was understood to confer full subject status within and without Calcutta, a fact that made the individual subject to the Supreme Court's personal jurisdiction even if he left the city. Analogous cases involving individuals born in Bombay also exist, suggesting that the judges routinely endorsed religiously and racially inclusive definitions of subjecthood for those born in territories they believed were part of the British crown's dominions.[82]

In 1789, birth in the conquered town of Calcutta was once again the central criterion, and counsel in *Michael de Rozio v. Chutgeer Gosain* engaged arguments about conquest and subject status directly. The Court was asked to rule on a bond between Michael de Rozio, who was said to be "a subject of his Majesty the King of Great Britain," and Chutgeer Gosain, who had agreed in writing that any dispute about the bond might be submitted to the Supreme Court of Judicature. Mr. Martin, counsel for the defendant, attempted to prove that de Rozio was not a subject, which would have removed the matter from the Court's hands. Martin argued that de Rozio had been born before the capture of Calcutta and was neither "his Majesty's subject" nor a "British subject." Mr. Dunkin, counsel for de Rozio, made two rebuttals. First, he insisted that the Regulating Act had not intended for "British subject" to be confined to "Native British subjects." Second, he claimed that the conquest of Calcutta entitled those who chose to remain in the city to the privileges of British subjects.[83] Although the archival record does not detail the ways in which counsel made these arguments, Martin may have argued that because de Rozio was born before Calcutta had become a British dominion, he could not have been born within the monarch's allegiance; Dunkin may have drawn on ideas that individuals who remained after the conquest of a territory were often granted the rights of subjects in other colonies or may have referred to Hyde's 1782 argument that inhabitants of a conquered town were all British subjects. Ultimately, however, the judges held that being born in Calcutta before it was conquered in 1757 did not confer British subjecthood, overturning the argument that merely choosing to remain in Calcutta made one a full subject, but suggesting that the conquest of the city often represented a key distinguishing factor in judicial determinations of subjecthood.[84] In the absence of a treaty, like those signed for Gibraltar, Minorca, Grenada, or Quebec, stipulating that all inhabitants who remained in Calcutta after its conquest became subjects, the judges did on occasion reveal themselves to be hesitant to extend subjecthood too broadly.[85]

Whether they offered flexible interpretations of the categories prescribed by the Regulating Act or relied on arguments that Calcutta was a conquered town, the judges did recognize a wide array of individuals as British subjects, a fact that can be further observed in the extant lists of Grand and Petit Juries. Edward Tiretta, by birth a Venetian, was sworn in on December 4, 1777.[86] Antonio D'Conto and Joseph Baretto, likely Italian, Spanish, or Portuguese by birth, were empaneled on June 26, 1781.[87] More provocative, Michael de Rozia was sworn in on June 28, 1781, followed by a Michael D'Rozio on June 29, 1781, though whether this was the same Michael de Rozio whom counsel later tried to claim was not a British subject remains unclear.[88] As Michael de Rozio's attorney would argue in 1789, however, the Court interpreted the words of the Regulating Act and Charter of Justice "in the most extensive sense, in the case of jurymen."[89] Given that the Regulating Act provided for juries of "British subjects resident in the town of Calcutta," the incomplete lists of jurymen suggest that the judges embraced a definition of subjecthood that did not merely require individuals to have been born within the monarch's dominions but that also included continental Europeans.

A December 1777 debate over jury appointments reveals that Impey and Chambers even believed that non-Christian inhabitants of Calcutta might be eligible to serve on juries. Hyde, by contrast, felt that "none but Christians could be jurors," an opinion that carried the day. He did note, nevertheless, that "Portugueze" were acceptable members of a jury, so long as they were Christian. "Portugueze," as he explained, included both descendants of natives of Portugal and "black Fringgees," who were the mixed-race children of Portuguese men and native women.[90] Christopher Hawes, whose research on the Eurasian communities of British India indicates that there were at least two mixed-race members of the jury that convicted the Maharajah Nundocomar in 1775, argues that "educated Eurasians of British stock were considered 'British subjects'" by the Supreme Court at the time.[91] Although no corresponding evidence suggests that native inhabitants of Calcutta were eligible to serve on juries during this period, in practice, "juries of British subjects" tended to encompass a relatively motley crew of Britons, continental Europeans, and inhabitants of mixed race during the 1770s and early 1780s.[92]

Recognizing a wide range of individuals as subjects clearly involved judicial calculations about jurisdiction and about the extent of the Court's influence, but subject status also had deeply individual repercussions, even if these are less evident in the remaining records of the Supreme Court. Because a finding of subject status determined both whether the Court might consider a matter and also which specific conventions and laws it might apply, subject status presented certain distinct advantages and disadvantages, depending on whether a given individual wanted to be subject to the Supreme Court's jurisdiction or preferred to seek justice in another forum. Attempts to eschew classification as a British subject seem to have been more widespread in Calcutta than in other corners of the empire, suggesting that subjecthood was not always desirable in the subcontinent and that avoiding the Supreme Court brought with it an appealing jurisdictional flexibility. Briefly considering what the protection of law from this particular court meant at a practical level may help to explain why subjecthood was not necessarily coveted, just as it helps to elucidate further why determinations of subject status consumed so much of the Court's attention.

From its inception, for example, the Court granted probate and administration of wills only to "British subjects and of the goods of British subjects deceased." On October 22, 1776, the widow of William Bolts applied for an administration to be accorded to her son-in-law. The Chief Justice denied the request because "the person deceased was a Dutch Man not an English Man and the persons applying for Letters of Administration are Dutch and not British Subjects."[93] On January 17, 1782, a petition relating to the goods of the deceased Maharaja Nundocomar was submitted with the claim that he was a British subject who had died intestate. Although records for this particular case are incomplete, it is clear that any chance of resolving this matter in the Supreme Court rested on whether the deceased was judged to be a British subject.[94]

Similarly, over the years the Court addressed issues relating to debts and bonds. Under the Regulating Act, British subjects were prohibited from charging more than 12 percent interest, and the Court was required to uphold the terms of the statute. In January 1792, the judges refused to enforce a bond involving a British subject because the interest on it was greater than 12 percent. Fourteen years earlier, Hyde and Lemaistre had agreed that in cases that did not involve British subjects, they might insist on the interest agreed to by both parties, even if it was greater than 12 percent.[95] The 1797 Usury Act, which established that 12 percent interest was the legal maximum for loans made by British subjects, also forbade British subjects from lending money to Indian princes without the approval of the Court of Directors or the governor-general in council.[96] British subject status regularly determined whether the judges upheld differing interest rates on bonds and whether loans to Indian princes were viewed as legal.

Although few cases addressing land ownership are preserved, British subject status would also have shaped the outcome of any cases relating to land.[97] Technically, despite widespread practice to the contrary, British subjects were prohibited from owning land in Bengal. The East India Company issued an extensive ban in 1790, prohibiting Eurasians, as well as British subjects, from owning land. Most likely directed at British subjects who were evading parliamentary restrictions by buying land in the names of their Eurasian sons, the Company's regulations against Eurasians were not eased until 1831.[98] Classification as a British subject would not only have determined the outcome of cases relating to certain forms of land ownership, but might have encouraged those liable to be categorized as British subjects to seek arbitration or resolution elsewhere.

There were practical reasons that inhabitants of Calcutta might have claimed, or might have sought desperately to avoid, subject status and the jurisdictional privileges associated with allegiance. However, the existing records of the Supreme Court suggest that subjecthood most clearly represented a judicial opportunity and became a political tool in the hands of judges who were determined to assert the subject status of inhabitants in order to extend royal authority and confirm their own jurisdiction. Nonetheless, despite judicial willingness to equate "inhabitants of Calcutta" with "British subjects" in the 1770s, not all inhabitants would remain equal before the Supreme Court for long.

The 1782 case of *Monnickram Chuttopodhie v. Meer Conjeer Alli Khawh* revealed a Court already vacillating on whether inhabitants of Calcutta were truly British subjects. Counsel for the plaintiff tried to argue that Chuttopodhie was a British subject within the meaning of parliamentary statutes because he was an inhabitant of Calcutta. He claimed that the term "city" was used in such a way in parliamentary legislation that "it must mean an English City," and that the use of the term "European British Subjects" revealed that in India there were "other British Subjects who are not European British Subjects." The community of British subjects was expansive, he contended, including both European and non-European. Chief Justice Impey offered a contrasting opinion. He cited an earlier case of usury against an inhabitant of Calcutta in which the Court had determined that the individual "was not that sort of British subject who is within the prohibition of taking more than 12 percent for his Money."[99] Impey revealed that the Court was beginning to establish distinctions between the inhabitants of Calcutta: there were *bona fide* British subjects who were always unable to charge more than 12 percent interest, and there were residents who were "not that sort of British subject" and might not consistently be liable to the laws applicable to subjects.

In a clear statement of some of the jurisdictional problems associated with according inhabitants of Calcutta full subject status, one advocate, Mr. Burroughs, observed in 1794:

> Suppose Mobarek Sheriff to be in some senses a British Subject because he was born in Calcutta after the capture; will it follow that he is a British Subject or a Subject of the King to all intents and purposes? And that he is to be considered in the same light exactly as a British-born subject, who once resided in Bengal but has left it, leaving effects here. If these points are so determined, it will follow that all natives of Calcutta, whether Hindu, Mahomedan, or of any other sect, even such as have entirely deserted Calcutta & live in some remote place, must be subject to the Jurisdiction of this Court . . . this would be an extension of the Jurisdiction of this Court as was never thought of.[100]

If the diverse and itinerant peoples of Calcutta were also British subjects, this meant that they were answerable to the Supreme Court wherever they went. Although Burroughs recognized the argument that Mobarek Sheriff, having been born in a conquered town, was "in some senses" a British subject, he also suggested that this might not grant him subject status "to all intents and purposes." His analysis indicated that strong hierarchies had developed among those once deemed to be "subject to the Court's jurisdiction" and eligible for royal protection.

By the time Burroughs voiced his apprehensions in 1794, he was not alone in believing that the Court had overstepped its bounds and had applied the privileges of subjecthood too broadly. The problems associated with an expansive subjecthood and with extending the Court's jurisdiction had shaken Company administrators, judges, and local residents. Revisions of parliamentary statutes and of the Court's jurisdiction had already been undertaken. The moment when a broad definition of subjecthood might serve the extension of royal authority had passed. The judges, who had seemed to favor a religiously and racially inclusive approach to subjecthood for the conquered town of Calcutta in the 1770s, had grown hesitant about pushing the Court's jurisdiction beyond the city's limits. Resistance to royal authority and to the Supreme Court's jurisdiction, combined with the fact that no explicit claim was made about sovereignty over Bengal, Bihar, and Orissa, meant that expansive understandings of subjecthood were largely in retreat by the time Mobarek Sheriff appeared in the courtroom.

Dividing "inhabitant of Calcutta" from "British subject residing in Bengal"

By the 1780s, the Supreme Court's exploitation of definitional uncertainties to bring an increasing number of inhabitants under its jurisdiction had fostered deep-seated animosities between judges and East India Company officials, threatening to undermine the administration of justice. When combined with local condemnation of the Supreme Court, demand for revision of parliamentary statute became widespread, resulting in new parliamentary legislation in both 1781 and 1786. In light of statutory adjustments, the Supreme Court of Judicature would once again grapple with the interconnected issues of subject status and jurisdiction. This time, however, a subtle division was manifest: inhabitants of the East India Company territories were gradually classified either as "inhabitants of Calcutta," who were subject to the Court's local jurisdiction only when in Calcutta, or as "British subjects residing in

Bengal," who were subject to the Court's personal jurisdiction both within and without the city's limits. These changes not only foreshadowed the emergence of increasingly separate and hierarchical systems of justice across the subcontinent but ultimately meant that the judiciary became progressively more focused on the opportunity provided by notions of local, or temporary, protection, particularly where the Christian and continental European population of Calcutta was concerned.

Mounting resistance to the Supreme Court's extending jurisdiction and political agenda had been evident as early as 1775 with the trial of Maharaja Nundocomar. Encouraged by opponents of Warren Hastings, Nundocomar, a leading Indian official and landowner, brought charges of corruption and bribery against the governor-general in the Supreme Council in March of that year. Hastings was obviously incensed, filing charges of conspiracy against Nundocomar and ensuring that charges of forgery were filed a few days later in the Supreme Court. In rapid succession, Chief Justice Impey and his colleagues found Nundocomar guilty of forgery and pronounced a death sentence. Concerns surfaced almost immediately because of Impey and Hastings's well-known friendship, because important transactions of the case were never published, and because Nundocomar was never allowed to appeal to the Privy Council for a respite of his death sentence, which was carried out in August 1775, less than two months after it had been issued. Furthermore, because forgery was not a capital offense under Hindu or Muslim law, many felt that Nundocomar had been convicted under a law that was not adapted to the "circumstances of Calcutta" and with which the Maharaja was not familiar. It seemed inappropriate for a newly established court to try an "inhabitant of Calcutta" under the relatively harsh English criminal law. All in all, Nundocomar's conviction and subsequent hanging provoked fears about the dangerous personal and political connections between the Court and the governor-general in what was a well-publicized feud between Hastings and members of the Supreme Council.[101]

A few years later, the Supreme Court pitted itself against the Company's provincial council in Patna, some four hundred miles north of Calcutta. In 1777, the provincial council upheld a report made by several Muslim law officers regarding the inheritance of Shabaz Beg's property and its division between his nephew, Behadur Beg, and his widow, Nauderah Begum. After having endured a siege of her living quarters designed to force her to turn valuables over to her nephew, Nauderah Begum approached the Court and lodged a complaint against her nephew and the Muslim law officers for assault and battery, false imprisonment, breaking and entering her house, seizing her effects, and other personal injuries. The Court claimed jurisdiction over Behadur Beg, a revenue farmer in Bihar who was "indirectly in the service of the Company," and over the *qazi* and *muftis,* who had determined the facts of the case, written the original report, and were considered servants of the Company.[102] Viewing Nauderah Begum as an object of "rapine and plunder" in need of protection,[103] the Supreme Court eventually awarded her damages of 300,000 rupees and more than 9,000 rupees for costs.[104] By challenging this provincial council and by ordering that Company servants be brought to Calcutta for trial, the Court undermined the council's authority, attempting to position itself as the defender of Indian inhabitants against the corrupt system of the East India Company. Company lawyers, by contrast, noted that the Court was subjecting natives to imprisonment and trial far from home, which had led to the death of one Muslim law officer en route to Calcutta and an award of damages so high that native officers could never pay.[105]

Most significant, the "Patna cause," when combined with several other rulings against *zamindars* and revenue collectors, fostered a climate of fear among Indian revenue farmers and officials. Company servants, worried that they would be hauled before the Supreme Court for acts committed during official business, were leery of accepting employment.[106] In November 1777, the Court of Directors wrote to Secretary of State Lord Weymouth, arguing that the "exercise of this jurisdiction must inevitably tend to render the collection of the Company's revenues impracticable." A few years later, the Company submitted another petition to Parliament, stressing that the Supreme Court's jurisdiction had created an "embarrassment in the Management and Collection of the Revenues" and threatened to diminish Bengal's usefulness to Great Britain.[107] As many who testified before Parliament between 1781 and 1782 would make clear, numerous inhabitants had lived in "dread" of the new court, and Company fears that Supreme Court proceedings would hinder the smooth operation of government were not unfounded.[108] Company and parliamentary concern about the Supreme Court's interference in official affairs would become central factors in the revision of parliamentary statutes in the 1780s.

Furthermore, a large cross-section of the population in Calcutta, not just Company servants, had come to dislike this royal institution. In January 1779, during a religious festival, native inhabitants rioted in front of the Court House, an act that was widely interpreted as a deliberate attack in response to the "rash and intemperate behavior of the Supreme Court's officers" and was said to portend "a spirit of contempt for its authority, and for Europeans in general."[109] Reports suggested, among other things, that the protesters objected to the rise in legal fees occasioned by the new judicature. A month later, 648 residents, both British and continental European, signed a petition against the Court, appealing to Parliament to protect their liberties as British subjects and complaining, among other things, that the Court did not allow juries in civil cases.[110] By 1780, then, a range of disillusioned residents had organized themselves into committees, and petitions and memoranda from Company officials, European residents, and "native inhabitants" had reached members of Parliament. Despite having enabled Asian and European litigants alike to seek justice against Company servants, British subjects, and servants of British subjects resident in Calcutta and in Bengal, Bihar, and Orissa to an extent that had previously been unimaginable, the Supreme Court had also garnered many enemies.

Although the Supreme Court appeared to be under a united attack less than a decade after its founding, the petitions against the judiciary suggest that inhabitants had also begun to divide along clear-cut lines. The interests of "native inhabitants" were presented separately from those of "British subjects," who defined themselves, at least by their signatures, as broadly European. However, each of the constituencies opposed to the Supreme Court agreed that the powers of the judiciary needed to be circumscribed and that Parliament, not the Supreme Court, must "define, beyond the Power of discretional Distinction, the Persons who are and who are not amenable to the Jurisdiction of the Court."[111]

The 1781 Act of Settlement, which resulted from review by a House of Commons select committee, responded to concerns about the extension of the Supreme Court's jurisdiction and about its dangerous interference in Company affairs. The Act declared that the Court could no longer take cognizance of public acts committed by Company servants, including *zamindars*, tax collectors, or law officers serving in Company courts, who were acting on written orders of the council. In addition, although the 1781 legislation reaffirmed the Supreme Court's local and personal jurisdictions, it made a few significant adjustments. The Court was to have unhindered local jurisdiction over "all manner of actions & suits against all and singular the inhabitants of the said city of Calcutta," with one central caveat.[112] Matters of inheritance, succession, and contract involving Hindu and Muslim inhabitants were henceforth to be judged by personal law, and judges were to take into account the manners and customs of the native population. To ascertain more properly "those of the natives who shall be subject to the jurisdiction of the Supreme Court, on account of their being employed by any of his Majesty's British Subjects," legislators required that both the Company and British subjects register the name, description, and place of abode of all natives in their employ.[113] This stipulation suggested that Parliament was increasingly concerned with monitoring the number of native inhabitants who might appear before the Court.

As far as the Court's personal jurisdiction was concerned, the Act of Settlement reiterated that it had jurisdiction over inhabitants of Bengal, Bihar, and Orissa who were employed by the East India Company or by British subjects, but with several important changes. Whereas the Regulating Act had indiscriminately placed all Company servants, including Hindu and Muslim employees, under the civil jurisdiction of the Supreme Court in matters of inheritance, succession, and contract, the 1781 legislation relieved these servants from the expense and difficulties of appearing before the Supreme Court and allowed them to submit to Company courts in the *mofussil* for judgment.[114]

If the Supreme Court's influence over East India Company servants was limited in 1781 and its local jurisdiction was clearly confined to Calcutta, its personal jurisdiction was increased in 1781, as well as in 1786 and 1793. This extension reflected the realities of trade in the East Indies, where subjects of the king and servants of the Company frequently roamed far from Calcutta and might otherwise have remained beyond the pale of jurisdiction. In 1786, Company servants and his Majesty's subjects resident in India were declared to be amenable to the Court for criminal actions committed "in any of the countries or parts of Asia, Africa, or America, beyond the Cape of Good Hope to the Streights of Magellan within the limits of the exclusive trade of the said United Company."[115] Even more tellingly, legislation in 1793 stipulated that his Majesty's subjects and servants of the East India Company were liable to be tried for offenses committed "in any of the Lands or Territories of any Native Prince or State, or against their Persons or Properties, or the Persons or Properties of any of their Subjects," which foreshadowed an extension of jurisdiction into the lands of foreign rulers.[116]

At the same time that acts expanding the Supreme Court's personal jurisdiction were passed, other statutes attempted to limit the movements of British subjects, hinting once again at how important determinations of subject status would be. In both 1781 and 1793, clauses instructed that it was unlawful for "any British subject or subjects, in the service of the said United Company, or licensed by them to proceed to India, to reside in any other place in India than in one of the principal settlements belonging to the said United Company, or within ten miles of such principal settlement, without the special license of the said United Company."[117] Parliamentary revisions of jurisdiction thus reflected a deep ambivalence after 1781. On the one hand, they recognized that the Supreme Court's personal jurisdiction over British subjects must be enlarged given the continued movement of these individuals beyond Calcutta and beyond the provinces of Bengal, Bihar, and Orissa. On the other hand, they sought to limit the chances that this personal jurisdiction would ever be exercised and to avoid the problems of competing jurisdictions by stipulating where subjects might settle.

As the Court's personal jurisdiction expanded beyond Calcutta and the surrounding provinces and as subjects moved into the territories of other sovereign authorities, it theoretically became even more urgent to determine who was a subject of the crown and thereby subject to the Court's more sweeping personal jurisdiction. But despite the obvious difficulties presented by the terms "British subject," "his Majesty's subject," "inhabitant of India," and "directly or indirectly employed by the East India Company" throughout the 1770s, subsequent legislation failed to clarify who fell within these categories. Judges were clearly preoccupied by questions of subject status and by the entangled issue of extending the king's protection into East India Company territories, but clarifying the boundaries of subject status apparently mattered far less to members of Parliament. Perhaps because state resources were already stretched by the American Revolutionary War in 1781, Parliament seems to have been more concerned to resolve the problems associated with the Court's jurisdiction over, and interference with, Company revenues and to maintain Company government and revenue wherever possible.

Nonetheless, the tensions of the 1770s had certainly spurred some elucidation of the Court's jurisdictions, and the 1781 Act of Settlement curbed several of the Court's earlier powers. The local legal record indicates that there were corresponding procedural changes within the Court itself. Recognizing that the legislation of 1781 had "materially varied" its jurisdiction, the Supreme Court passed a little-known order in 1782, stipulating that all plaints, bills, libels, and articles used to initiate suits not only aver that the defendant was subject to the jurisdiction of the Court, which had been part of established practice since 1774, but also specifically state "by what means the defendants are subject to the jurisdiction."[118] In light of parliamentary revisions, litigants, writers, advocates, and judges began to categorize individuals as either "inhabitants of Calcutta" or as "inhabitants of Calcutta and British subjects residing in Bengal." Without definitive clarification from Parliament about whether "inhabitants of Calcutta" were "British subjects" when they left Calcutta, perhaps it seemed safest for legal professionals to distinguish those who unquestionably fell within its more restricted local jurisdiction from those who fell within its broader personal jurisdiction.

Regardless, with little debate or fanfare, "inhabitants of Calcutta" and "inhabitants of Calcutta and British subjects residing in Bengal" became separate and well-understood categories that seemed to require little explanation. Indeed, this shift in classification is manifest in the court records. In the 1760s and 1770s, individuals filing suits described themselves and referred to defendants as "Inhabitants of Calcutta subject to the Jurisdiction of the Court," regardless of whether they were of British, European, or Indian origin. Although incomplete, bundles of eighteenth-century paperwork preserved in the Calcutta High Court, which encompass indictments, depositions, bills, and affidavits, reveal that "inhabitant of Calcutta" was an inclusive and default legal category that brought a range of individuals within the Supreme Court's jurisdiction and, on some occasions, was held to be synonymous with "British subject." By the 1780s, these same documents reflect a subtle shift. They indicate that the Court increasingly distinguished between "inhabitants of Calcutta" and "inhabitants of Calcutta" who were also "British subjects residing in Bengal." Between 1780 and 1782, a few defendants were described as "British subjects residing in Bengal," with the vast majority still being classified as "inhabitants of Calcutta." By 1783, those with surnames that were obviously Irish, Scottish, and English were categorized as "British subjects," and those of Asian or continental European origin remained "inhabitants of Calcutta." By the late 1780s and early 1790s, this division in the legal record had become commonplace.[119]

This tendency to specify whether individuals were simply "inhabitants of Calcutta" or whether they were simultaneously "British subjects residing in Bengal" was also reflected among the judges of the Supreme Court. In 1788, Hyde recorded that "Mr. Morris is stated to be a British subject residing in Bengal & an Inhabitant of Calcutta & Ramlochun to be an Inhabitant of Calcutta."[120] Plaintiff and defendant, both within the Court's jurisdiction, were so for different reasons. Each was a resident of Calcutta, but Ramlochun Sircar could secure the Court's protection only while in Calcutta, a local and temporary protection. Edmund Morris, a British subject, was eligible for a more sweeping and inalienable protection when he was well beyond city limits.[121]

The practical effect of these categorizations was to limit the number of individuals described by the Court as "British subjects" by the 1780s and to increase the number of individuals who were "inhabitants of Calcutta." Put another way, by the mid-1780s, there were two more clearly defined classes of individuals: "inhabitants of Calcutta," who fell within the Court's jurisdiction only when in Calcutta, and "British subjects residing in Bengal," who remained subject to its jurisdiction even when outside the city's limits. Although the judges may have been inclined to conflate "inhabitants of Calcutta" with "British subjects" in the 1770s and to embrace a more inclusive definition of subjecthood, they gradually seem to have revised these definitions, agreeing that "inhabitants of Calcutta" were subject only to a local jurisdiction and lost their protected status when they left the confines of the town.

Christians, Continental Europeans, and the Concept of Temporary Subjecthood

If parliamentary revisions seem to have encouraged a growing distinction between "inhabitant of India" and "British subject residing in Bengal" at the level of judicial practice during the 1780s, however, official statutes still had not clarified whether other Christian and continental Europeans were "his Majesty's subjects" or "British subjects." These populations had lived within East India Company settlements for decades and had typically fallen within the Company's jurisdiction. Despite the fact that the Supreme Court had often regarded the Armenian Christian population of Calcutta as *bona fide* British subjects, for example, their status continued to prompt judicial deliberation. Particularly as the distinction between "inhabitant of Calcutta" and "British subject residing in Bengal" became more pronounced, key questions arose as to whether inhabitants like the Armenians remained subjects once they left Calcutta and whether the Supreme Court maintained its personal jurisdiction over them. As the judges grappled with these issues, they began to formulate new and legally significant arguments about the temporary and permanent subjecthood of non-native inhabitants residing in Bengal, Bihar, and Orissa.

In 1788, when a case relating to an Armenian Christian came before the Court, Hyde offered his view on the Armenians' status: "it seems reasonable to give so much latitude of construction to the words British Subject dying within the provinces, as to include a class of Christians who are strangers and foreigners here, and who consider themselves, whether they live in the Town of Calcutta, or out of it, as residing under the protection of the British Government, and not of the Subakdar." He went on to cite a 1688 deed which had given the Armenians the right to live in any of the Company towns and to "buy, sell & purchase house & land & to be capable of all civil offices as if they were Englishmen born." Most of the judges clearly concurred in the opinion that Armenians were to be treated as British subjects because letters of administration were granted for the goods of P. Johannes, and letters of administration could only be awarded for British subjects.[122] In this instance, the Supreme Court was willing to recognize Armenian Christians as British subjects, liable to its jurisdiction not only if they resided in Calcutta, but also if they moved beyond the Court's local jurisdiction.

A few years later, Mariam Khanun Cachick, an Armenian, sought to have her case addressed by the Supreme Court. She requested that Moses Cachuck, also an Armenian, be ordered to file his suit against her in the Supreme Court rather than in the *adalat* of the *mofussil* where he had initiated proceedings. In her petition, she stated that because they were both British subjects, the case ought to be tried only by the Supreme Court. The Court granted her request, noting that the Armenian Christians living in Calcutta and Bengal did so under the protection of the British flag and that they did not "acknowledge any other sovereign than the King of Great Britain," which in effect made them British subjects.[123] In a 1792 case, the judges would note, once again, that Armenians had submitted to the law of England, and the Armenian defendant in question was referred to as a "liege subject" of the monarch of Great Britain.[124] These various rulings suggest that the judges regularly evoked Armenians' allegiance to the monarch in order to classify them not merely as "inhabitants of Calcutta" but also as "British subjects residing in Bengal" over whom the Supreme Court retained a more sweeping personal jurisdiction.

Despite these determinations, Armenians were not always granted the Supreme Court's protection, and the instability and impermanence of their subject status became all too obvious. In 1796, the administration of P. Johannes's goods again came before the Court. This time, it was proven that, though he had resided at Calcutta and traded there as a merchant, he had left Calcutta over thirty years earlier and had died in Canton. Because he had resided in Calcutta largely before its conquest, the judges determined that he was not a British subject and that the protection generally accorded to Armenians was no longer applicable given that he had died outside the three provinces. The judges, who seem to have been willing to recognize the subject status granted to Armenians in 1688, were not prepared to extend these protections beyond the terms of this earlier decree. Like many others, Armenians faced the prospect that they were subjects only if they remained inhabitants of Calcutta and that the inclusive subjecthood once accorded them might be rescinded.

Particularly after the 1781 Act of Settlement had restricted its powers, the Supreme Court needed to determine whether its jurisdiction included continental Europeans once they moved beyond Calcutta. The presence of French prisoners of war, who remained in Calcutta and the surrounding provinces after the global wars between the French and British, provoked recurrent questions about the expansiveness and duration of British subjecthood.[125] In the case of *Boqbaun Gose v. Peter Verle*, the defendant was a French prisoner of war living in Calcutta on his "parole of honor." The cause, however, had arisen when the prisoner lived in the French settlement at Chandernagore. Counsel for the plaintiff contended that Verle was a British subject, citing Blackstone's description of local allegiance as well as other treatises stating that prisoners living on parole were subjects of the king. Counsel for the defendant disagreed. First, he argued that Verle was not a British subject since parole of honor did not confer full subjecthood. To convict Verle for a crime committed outside of Calcutta, the plaintiff needed to prove that he was a British subject and not merely someone who owed temporary allegiance. Second, he argued that the cause had arisen well before the time anyone might have claimed Verle was, in fact, a subject. No final judgment appears to have been handed down, but the case reveals that the Court was beginning to consider at least two different types of subjecthood—one that might be thought of as "temporary" and another that was more "permanent."[126]

A second and more complete case involving another French prisoner of war came before the Court in 1783. John Princep filed suit against "Francois Fairie of Chandernagore in the Province of Bengal, Inhabitant, being a British subject." Fairie, a Frenchman by birth, had taken the oath of allegiance and had vowed not to serve against the king of Great Britain. He had been released upon his parole of honor after having been imprisoned in 1781. Fairie's attorney argued that taking the oath of allegiance did not make a person a British subject, "for if it did, the statutes which are yearly passed to make persons denizens would never be applied for, because it would be much easier to take the oaths." Although the Court had been granted jurisdiction over British subjects in the provinces of Bengal, Bihar, and Orissa, it had never assumed a jurisdiction over those who were, in fact, "Natives of France" residing there. Agreeing that the oath of allegiance did not confer subject status, Impey, Chambers, and Hyde determined that Fairie could not be considered a British subject once he left the confines of Calcutta.[127] Though Frenchmen and French prisoners of war might be his Majesty's subjects while in Calcutta, this was a temporary or locale-specific subjection, and they lost this status once in the *mofussil*.

Notions of temporary subjecthood may ultimately have limited the Supreme Court's jurisdiction over continental Europeans once they moved into the provinces, but they remained instrumental in assisting judges who needed to resolve cases involving the transient European population of Calcutta. The 1789 case of *Rex v. Peter Horrebow* perhaps best exemplifies the opportunity provided by these notions of local and temporary allegiance in the town of Calcutta, and the ways in which both prosecution and defense might use them to differing effect. Peter Horrebow, a Dane, was prosecuted for "manstealing or kidnapping" after he loaded slaves onto his ship in the French settlement of Chandernagore and then sold them in Colombo. Counsel for Horrebow maintained that the case should not come before the Supreme Court because the slaves in question had been subjects of the French king and boarded while in a French settlement. Furthermore, the crime had not been committed within the limits of Calcutta, and Horrebow was not a British subject at the time the act had been committed. Counsel for the defense accepted that Horrebrow had been a "subject of the king by residence in Calcutta," but he contended that "an alien who comes here is a subject for the time but as soon as he leaves the settlement he is a subject no longer." Continental Europeans described as "subjects of the monarch" were really only local subjects when in Calcutta—not throughout the Company's limits of trade—suggesting that subjecthood might be temporary and alienable.

In response, the prosecution cited William Blackstone's definition of subjecthood, arguing that every man was a subject of his Majesty while he resided in the king's dominions. Horrebow, who lived with his family in Calcutta and had sailed from Calcutta under the British flag when he embarked on his trip to sell slaves, was therefore a British subject. The prosecution clinched the argument by proving that the order for enslavement had been given in Calcutta and that the slaves were imprisoned there briefly on the journey to Colombo, making the crime one that fell within the Supreme Court's local jurisdiction and making the question of subjecthood immaterial. In the end, Horrebow was convicted but received a relatively light sentence because of his personal character and his "ignorance of the law of England." Perhaps most interesting, the rigor of the law was relaxed because he was "only a temporary subject of the King."[128] Both the debates between counsel and the final ruling endorsed the notion of a temporary subjecthood that evaporated as soon as a foreign inhabitant left the settlement of Calcutta.

The 1797 trial of a continental European in the military service of the East India Company also turned on the permanence or impermanence of

British subjecthood. Francisco Jose, alias Joseph Moore, was indicted for an offense committed outside Calcutta and the surrounding provinces. Born in Portugal, he had served in the Company for fifteen to sixteen years. During his tenure, argued counsel for the plaintiff, Jose had been entitled to the protection of the king and of the Supreme Court, and since protection and allegiance were reciprocal, Jose had contracted a temporary allegiance. Much as the Company itself was subject to the king, so too "every Company's servant is a subject of the King." Although this attorney acknowledged that "an alien" would cease to be a subject at the conclusion of his employment by the Company, he argued that temporary allegiance contracted during service was extensive and encompassed crimes committed outside Calcutta and its surrounding provinces.

By contrast, counsel for the defense argued that the Act of 1786, which had extended the Supreme Court's jurisdiction to crimes committed outside Calcutta and the provinces of Bengal, Bihar, and Orissa, only encompassed crimes by British subjects. As a servant of the Company, Jose may have been subject to the Supreme Court while in Calcutta, but he was not a subject of the king beyond Calcutta and was therefore not subject to the Supreme Court for an act committed outside the three provinces. Jose was ultimately acquitted because two justices determined that the exact phrasing of the Act of 1786 did not "make the prisoner a subject of the King because he is a servant of the Company." The Act of 1781 had clearly made Company servants liable to Supreme Court jurisdiction in the three provinces, but Chambers and Royds did not believe that the Act of 1786 had intended to make Company servants liable to the Court throughout the limits of the Company's trade. The judges thus upheld a crucial distinction between permanent British subjects, who might be tried by the Supreme Court for crimes committed throughout Asia, and temporary subjects, over whom the Supreme Court had a more limited jurisdiction.

By the 1780s, Hindu and Muslim inhabitants were no longer marked as "British subjects" in the court record, and the Court's jurisdiction over them ceased to be a significant day-to-day issue. However, the status of other Christians and continental Europeans continued to preoccupy the judges, and they proposed a range of ideas about local and temporary allegiance as they tried to envision and uphold a variety of forms of subjecthood across the East India Company territories. Even as early as 1775, Justice Lemaistre had reminded the Grand Jury that there were two kinds of allegiance. The first was "natural allegiance," owed to the crown based on birth within its territories, and held to be "unalienable & perpetual." The second was "local allegiance," due from a foreigner while he resided in the territories of another sovereign. It differed from natural allegiance "in being of no longer duration than during such time as the foreigner shall reside under the protection of the laws of such sovereign." Lemaistre had not explained which inhabitants fell within which category, but he clearly believed that there were several forms of subject status and allegiance in Calcutta.[129]

Indeed, in their ruminations on subjecthood, the judges of the Supreme Court revealed their indebtedness to familiar legal arguments about subjecthood, allegiance, protection, and conquered territories. Hyde's notebooks demonstrate the bench's repeated reliance on both Coke and Blackstone's "doctrines of allegiance."[130] Like Lemaistre, Hyde's reading divided allegiance into two forms. There was a perpetual, indelible allegiance, which Hyde recorded was prescribed according to the law of England, and which others would have recognized because of Calvin's Case and popular legal treatises. But there was also a temporary allegiance owed by foreigners residing in Great Britain, Ireland, and the overseas British dominions, or by persons who chose to remain in a conquered city after it had passed into royal hands. Hyde, for example, noted that allegiance was due to the king from Natives of Hanover, from British subjects whether natural-born, naturalized, or endenizened, and from persons born in acquired territories provided that they were born after acquisition.[131]

These were understandings of allegiance whose seeds could be found in Coke, but which assumed a new importance as notions of indissoluble subjecthood became less and less practicable given the diverse inhabitants who came within the Supreme Court's jurisdiction and the challenges posed by competing sovereignties. The records of the Supreme Court thus reveal not only that Hyde and his fellow justices were profoundly interested in documenting types of subjects, but that the judiciary extended some of the well-established understandings of allegiance found in case law and began to envision varieties of subjecthood that diverged significantly from their metropolitan counterparts.[132]

With its polyglot and transient population, its royal court with both limited and also potentially expansive jurisdictions, and its justices determined to protect purported subjects, Calcutta thus provided innumerable opportunities for judges to explore the varieties of allegiance and subjecthood. While racially and religiously inclusive definitions of subject status were contemplated and advocated in the 1770s as a means to enlarge the Court's jurisdiction, they had largely disappeared from the records of the judiciary by the 1780s. Gradually, "British subject" was defined as an exclusive and permanent category, whereas "his Majesty's subject" became a flexible and temporary one. Expansive approaches to subjecthood were replaced by new formulations about temporary and permanent subjecthood that pertained largely to the Christian and continental European populations long resident in East India Company territories. Hierarchical visions of allegiance increasingly gained ground.

FRANCIS GLADWIN, oriental scholar and publisher of the *Calcutta Gazette*, was described as an "inhabitant of Calcutta" and "subject to the jurisdiction of the court" in a case where he was the defendant in 1777. Ten years later, he was referred to as an "Inhabitant of Calcutta and British subject residing in Bengal" by the same court.[133] He had, it would appear, been marked as a British subject during the intervening decade. Gladwin's slightly varied appearances in the legal archive might at first be attributed to the sloppiness of overburdened clerks. But further examination of records from the Supreme Court of Judicature in Calcutta reveals that judges were routinely preoccupied by the meanings of subject status and engaged in sustained judicial efforts to clarify the meaning of "inhabitant of Calcutta" and "British subject residing in Bengal."[134] The judiciary emerged as a central site for negotiations over subjecthood, just as subjecthood became a malleable tool in the hands of judges who sought to extend royal jurisdiction in a landscape still dominated by the East India Company.

As Gladwin's evolving categorization suggests, the 1770s and 1780s were particularly important decades for developing concepts of British subjecthood in the Indian subcontinent. Expansive rulings on subjecthood initially represented an opportunity to strengthen royal power at the expense of East India Company authority during a period when Parliament was becoming progressively more interventionist in the affairs of the empire. Recognizing individuals as "British subjects" rather than "Company subjects" effectively extended the Supreme Court's jurisdiction and the scope of royal authority, and during the 1770s, the judges welcomed many of the racially and religiously diverse inhabitants of Calcutta within their protection. Inclusive definitions of subjecthood seemed to portend benevolent royal jurisdiction in the 1770s, but noticeable shifts had occurred by the 1780s. Indeed, the Supreme Court found its powers severely curtailed by the 1781 Act of Settlement, and both the failure to declare royal or parliamentary sovereignty over Bengal and growing resistance to the Court's jurisdiction meant that more limited concepts of subjecthood and a more limited jurisdiction over the inhabitants of Calcutta began to seem more appropriate.

While the judges retreated from their previously expansive claims of subjecthood, they nonetheless turned their attention to other matters of subjecthood, focusing instead on clarifying the legal differences between "temporary" and "permanent" subjecthood among the diverse Christian and continental European populations of Calcutta. In the process, they gradually introduced powerful new hierarchies between subjects. "British subject" began increasingly to refer only to those Britons who were subject to the jurisdiction of the Court outside of Calcutta. "His Majesty's subject" or "subject of the king" was used to refer to Christians and continental Europeans who owed a kind of temporary allegiance while in Calcutta or other conquered territories claimed by the crown, but who renounced that allegiance as soon as they left such territories. Finally, "inhabitant of Calcutta," once held to be potentially synonymous with "British subject," came to have two very separate meanings. First, it referred to "British subjects" or "his Majesty's subjects" who resided in Calcutta. More typically, however, it came to designate the Hindu and Muslim inhabitants of this conquered city whose subject status did not accompany them when they left Calcutta. "British subject," which had been an inclusive category, even if briefly, became a concept plagued by fractures and fissures.

Where the Supreme Court and the East India Company had clashed over definitions of subjecthood in the 1770s, they moved into greater alignment by the 1780s and 1790s. The East India Company, which had often engaged in clarifying concepts of "subject" and "family" through its own courts and charitable institutions, also began to issue directives that threatened expansive interpretations of "British subject" and revealed that hierarchies were being imposed upon the various inhabitants of the subcontinent.[135] Eurasians, who were a growing and increasingly visible group, were among the first directly affected by these more exclusive classifications. In 1784, the Company decreed that the illegitimate children of its servants, most of whom were Eurasian, could no longer return to Britain for their education, as had previously been the custom. In 1791, the Company disqualified Eurasians from covenanted civil and military service on the basis that they were "Natives of India," and in 1795, orders passed in Bengal barred all Eurasians from combatant service in the East India Company army. From the Company's perspective, exclusive definitions of subjecthood were viewed as necessary to maintaining imperial control.[136] Thus, at the level of both judiciary and executive, a narrow subjecthood had come to seem necessary, even advantageous, by the late eighteenth century.

Where subject status had been intimately linked to questions of jurisdiction since the Supreme Court's founding, it also continued to be a determining factor in which legal protections were accorded to individuals in both royal and Company courts. With the 1781 stipulation that Hindus and Muslims still subject to the Supreme Court have matters of inheritance, succession, and contract settled according to "Hindu" and "Muslim" law, respectively, jurisdiction became more and more personal. Henceforth, only "British subjects" would have access to "English law" as administered by the Supreme Court, and hierarchies of law became *de rigueur*. Parallel but separate systems of justice were emerging, even if they were typically administered by the same legal personnel. Inhabitants were effectively "divided by classes of juridical subjects,"[137] later to be divided by racial and religious difference, a process which had begun as the Supreme Court first attempted to establish the boundaries of subjecthood.[138]

Despite repeated judicial and Company attempts to clarify subject status, definitions would remain in flux throughout the late eighteenth and nineteenth centuries, shaping the lives of many in the subcontinent. Unanswered questions about the intertwined problems of subjecthood and jurisdiction continued to arise, and uncertainty persisted because of the various available understandings of "British subject." In 1830, the East Indians of Calcutta, children of British men and Indian women, submitted a petition to Parliament requesting the rights of British subjects. They noted that failure to recognize them as British subjects meant that they had recourse only to Hindu and Muslim law in the country courts rather than to English law via the Supreme Court. Although they might choose to have their affairs settled by English law as Christians while they resided in Calcutta, they lost those privileges once they resided in the *mofussil* because of their liminal status as children of both "British subjects" and "Natives of India." Like the Armenians and continental Europeans, the East Indians possessed only a temporary subjecthood, and they sought parliamentary intervention to secure a more permanent status. Yet well after select committees had considered their petition, their exact status would remain unresolved.[139] For all the efforts justices of the Supreme Court had made to clarify subjecthood both within Calcutta and beyond, a definitive determination remained elusive.

Although these indeterminacies engendered tensions at a local level, failure to fully define "British subject" and the corresponding reach of crown authority over Calcutta and the surrounding provinces may actually have been part of what enabled royal and Company power to coexist until 1858, when the crown officially assumed control over territories formerly controlled by the East India Company. A flexible and unspecific understanding of subject status may have been appealing, particularly as it enabled the crown to expand or limit the number of its subjects in the future depending on shifting political, economic, or diplomatic needs. The crown and Parliament may consciously have shied away from concrete definitions, leaving such decisions to the judges in an attempt to minimize their own conflict with a powerful trading company and to avoid setting precedents that might then have been applied elsewhere in the empire. Indeed, precisely because there was little clarification from London on these matters, the East India Company would continue to interpret "British subject" as it saw fit in its dealings, and subject status would continue to be defined in the Supreme Court despite ongoing revisions to its jurisdiction.

In her 1858 proclamation to the princes, chiefs, and people of India, Queen Victoria called upon "all our subjects within the said territories to be faithful." At the moment royal authority was unequivocally proclaimed over territories that had previously been "administered in trust for us by the Honorable East India Company," the monarch finally bound herself "to the natives of our Indian territories by the same obligations of duty which bind us to all our other subjects."[140] Inhabitants of Calcutta and the now-numerous provinces had been officially welcomed as subjects. But the proclamation, like parliamentary acts before it, still revealed definitional slippage. On the one hand, the people of India were welcomed as "our subjects." On the other hand, they were "natives" entitled to the same protections as "our other subjects." The queen's words seemed to foreshadow new differentiations that would be made between subjects in the subcontinent. This time, the difference between temporary and permanent subjects, between Christian and other subjects, or between an expansive and a restricted subjecthood would be less important than a new distinction that was emerging between subjects who were deemed capable of self-government and subjects who were not. Once again, the flexibility of subjecthood had proven itself well suited to the imperatives of rule in British India, just as it had in eighteenth-century Calcutta and across the British Empire.

Conclusion

FROM MEMBERS OF the House of Lords, who routinely addressed the reigning monarch as humble subjects, to lowly villagers, who regularly beseeched their king for relief or privileges, many believed that powerful protections flowed to those who were obedient. From indigenous peoples who sought protection from the encroachments of colonists, to colonists who themselves pleaded for assistance against the attacks of their "savage neighbors," many described themselves as loyal subjects.[1] Across outposts in North America, the Mediterranean, the Indian Ocean, and elsewhere, a dizzying range of peoples proclaimed their allegiance and relied upon the bond between subject and sovereign to assert an array of rights, liberties, and privileges.

There were, however, always moments when claims of subjecthood became more prevalent, when inhabitants dispersed through the British dominions insisted on their rights with particular vigor. Debates that erupted in one particular territory appeared to reverberate from those in neighboring ones. Administrators' responsiveness to memorials in Grenada seemed to encourage petitioners in Quebec. The three decades after the Seven Years' War were punctuated by such moments. These were years when questions about the status of populations added to the British Empire in 1763 arose repeatedly and when contemporaries were prepared to acknowledge that these new peoples were essential resources. In 1772, Solicitor General Alexander Wedderburn assessed the crucial role of new subjects: "in more civilized times," he observed, "the object of war is dominion . . . *subjects* and not slaves are the fruits of victory."[2] Along with numerous other administrators, Wedderburn recognized that British victories in the global wars of the eighteenth century had yielded new subjects whose inclusion in the polity might ultimately strengthen the British Empire.

Indeed, the examples provided by Gibraltar, Minorca, Grenada, Quebec, and Calcutta confirm that a wide range of individuals sought the protection of George III and were regarded as subjects in the aftermath of the Seven Years' War. Whether they invoked their subjecthood from captivity in Barbary or wrote of their loyalty through petitions penned in Quebec, many sought to leverage their relationship with the sovereign. Whether they were "real" or "pretended" subjects, "old" or "new" subjects, "temporary" or "permanent" subjects, they articulated wide-ranging and sometimes conflicting ideas about rights. Even where illiteracy, lack of access to administrators, and religious and racial prejudices limited their opportunities, they benefited from the empire's dependence on them, using their allegiance to George III to secure an array of controversial privileges. Arising in these colonies during times of both war and peace, struggles over the meanings of subjecthood were recurrent and indicate that subjects themselves actively shaped the rights they were accorded.

As new subjects soon discovered, however, willingness to accept and accommodate them was inextricably linked to the ebb of war and peace and was intertwined with the pragmatic maneuverings of colonial officials. In peacetime, administrators tended to remain hopeful about their ability to secure allegiance and to successfully use subjects to improve the fortunes of Britain. In Quebec, successive governors argued that "the Canadians . . . are an honest good people" and that the "Canadians are tractable and submissive," especially when granted a few concessions.[3] During the 1760s and early 1770s, administrators usually regarded the French Catholics of Grenada as valuable and loyal subjects. Unfortunately, as soon as international conflict broke out again, such perspectives were liable to change. Most of the privileges accorded to French Catholics in Grenada were rescinded after a renewed war with France. Moreover, officials remained anxious about French Canadian loyalty throughout the American Revolutionary War. Governor Haldimand noted that with the exception of the noblesse, the clergy, and some of the bourgeoisie, the "Canadians are not to be depended upon, especially if a French war breaks out."[4]

But the recurrence of global war could also intensify reliance on and suspicion of new subjects in ways that were far from predictable. War with France saw George III authorize the governors of Minorca and Gibraltar to grant letters of marque and reprisal to "any of our subjects that they shall think fitly qualified," enabling inhabitants of both outposts, regardless of their countries of origin, to seize ships and goods belonging to the French king and to benefit from the spoils of war in 1793.[5] And yet, some of the first statutory restrictions passed against aliens entering Britain were enacted that very same year, requiring foreigners to register their arrivals, obtain passports, and limit their movements.[6] Military exigencies might mean that foreign-born inhabitants were enlisted to combat the French on the high seas, but they did not necessarily dispel fears that other foreign-born infiltrators were threatening national security or lead to inclusive definitions of subjecthood everywhere. The likelihood that subjects would find a sympathetic and receptive audience often depended on officials' responses to a precarious and unpredictable balance of power in the eighteenth-century overseas empires.

In general, however, during the three decades after the Seven Years' War, the relationship between subject and sovereign, a relationship typically characterized by its dependence, was one that held untold promise. The path of allegiance and the traditional bond of obedience and protection represented powerful opportunities for inhabitants and administrators well into the revolutionary era. Certainly, American colonists found themselves unable to acquire rights they believed to be their due as British subjects and chose to sever ties with their onetime sovereign, and French *citoyens* ultimately decided to define their liberties as members of a new republic rather than an *ancien régime*. Nonetheless, the vast majority of individuals in the late eighteenth century remained subjects who navigated relationships with sovereigns. Demands for rights were not the exclusive province of revolutionaries, but frequently had their roots in the monarchies of Europe and the ancient covenant between subject and monarch. Bonds of allegiance would remain remarkably relevant even during an era usually remembered for its tremendous change, upheaval, and revision of existing sources of sovereignty.

In the legal, popular, and administrative understanding, subjecthood was endowed with both a critical expansiveness and a noteworthy imprecision. Because allegiance lay at the heart of legal definitions of subjecthood and because so few rights were associated with subject status in case law, inclusive and diverse understandings of subjecthood proliferated throughout the empire, ultimately providing numerous opportunities for inhabitants and administrators. Moreover, the long tradition of declaring rights in both public and published fashion in Britain and the British Empire was developed and adapted in significant ways by the new peoples added to the empire in the 1760s. Exploiting multiplicities and ambiguities in legal and popular understandings of subjecthood, subjects were able to propose and obtain various economic, political, and legal privileges by virtue of their allegiance to George III.

Indeed, the flexibility of subjecthood was manifest across the globe. Members of Parliament might continue to speak of their "fellow-subjects," hoping to rally communities of constituents by appealing to notions of fellowship that transcended separate territories and peoples. Pamphleteers might persist in invoking the mythic qualities of the "free-born subject," demanding an array of rights unconfirmed by formal law. Individuals like Salvador Cosino, a Minorcan by birth, might write to his local governor, claiming that he, too, was a subject and that "all His Britannick Majesty's Subjects are entitled to a free trade to the Coast of Barbary."[7] Groups of subjects in Bengal, a territory under East India Company jurisdiction and surrounded by lands still ruled by Indian *nawabs*, might appeal to Parliament, arguing that they "humbly conceived" trial by jury to be their indefeasible birthright.[8] The capaciousness of subjecthood and the ever-growing number of rights associated with subject status were profoundly shaped by these debates and others that occurred in the colonies between the 1760s and 1780s.

The British Empire was realized and unified by common understandings of the relationship between subject and sovereign, just as it was by shared texts and taxes.[9] A shared subject status provided an essential means of connecting individuals living under disparate religions, laws, and societies precisely because common allegiance to a king or queen could transcend the confines of the body politic or the limits of newly emerging colonies. A shared belief that innumerable rights, liberties, and privileges flowed from the relationship between subject and sovereign continued to make that bond relevant across the British Empire (figure C.1). Ultimately, subjecthood provided a shared opportunity, which was essential to the workings and character of an expanding empire.

Appeals to subjecthood were calculated acts undertaken by inhabitants and administrators, but these shared appeals also had a less tangible and more abstract significance. In fact, whether or not they personally identified as British or as British subjects, when individuals as diverse as Spanish mariners, French Catholic planters, and inhabitants of Calcutta defined themselves as subjects, they were positioning themselves as part of a global community of subjects. During an era when fealty to a monarch who governed from afar remained one of the only commonalities between peoples who lived under various systems of law, spoke a range of languages, and practiced different religions, subjects' relationship to the sovereign figured centrally in these appeals. Each individual maintained a personal relationship to the monarch as his or her subject and related to others as fellow-subjects, whatever the varied rights accorded across the empire.

The Grenadian Catholics, for example, did not portray themselves merely as inhabitants of Grenada, as wealthy planters, or as former subjects of France. Instead, as they noted repeatedly, their sense of loyalty had been transformed

FIGURE C.1 Benjamin West, *John Eardley Wilmot* (detail), 1812, oil on canvas. Courtesy of The Yale Center for British Art, Paul Mellon Collection.

when they became "adopted subjects" of Great Britain and of King George III.[10] Similarly, although their compatriots to the north described themselves as "principal Inhabitants of Canada," they were far more inclined to attest to their "unalterable fidelity to Your Majesty" and to conclude memorials by inscribing themselves as "the most faithful subjects" of their new king.[11] Even if it might take months to travel between colonies and even if few inhabitants of Grenada or Quebec ever visited colonies outside the Atlantic World, their common bond to the monarch mattered. Individuals in Grenada or Quebec shared at least one thing with those in Minorca or Bengal. Wielded by peoples throughout the globe, the relationship between subject and sovereign worked to forge symbolic links across the empire. Subjecthood, which provided both a common language and status, thus also imbued an empire that spread from the Atlantic to the Mediterranean to the Pacific with a degree of coherence that it might otherwise have lacked.

In this respect, subjecthood was instrumental in forging community among dispersed individuals who shared a status and access to certain protections. Repeated evocation of subject status by so many individuals and in so many written sources allowed subjects to imagine themselves as part of a broader monarchical and imperial community. Historian H. V. Bowen has suggested that a sense of simultaneity emerged in the mid-eighteenth-century empire as Britons read reports of battles happening on the same days in the Americas and in Asia and began to conceive of them as part of one imperial frame.[12] This extends some of Benedict Anderson's arguments that novels and newspapers, among other forms, allowed people to situate themselves within one field of exchange and communication, within one "imagined community."[13] Likewise, the written assertions of subjects were instrumental in forging global communities: while there were numerous peoples, nationalities, religions, and races across the empire, they were all encompassed by one expansive label and one shared opportunity—"British subject." Each time inhabitants proclaimed their loyalty, they were reinforcing the bonds of allegiance that tied them to their monarch and were reiterating their belonging to a far larger community of fellow-subjects.

By sheer force of repetition and print, claims of loyal subjecthood and its associated rights so common to memorials and addresses could generate a sense of belonging and often encouraged a sense of loyalty among their proponents. The act of writing their allegiance and proclaiming their subject status meant that inhabitants actively participated in a dynamic process of inscribing and re-inscribing themselves in the British Empire, just as it worked to "covenant communities" of individuals who were dispersed around the globe. As individuals subscribed to addresses, petitions, and even compacts, they bound themselves to "communities of adherents," joining others "whose names are underwritten."[14] George III had spoken of the broader community of subjects and had included many among that number; similarly, by affixing their marks and signatures to documents in which they claimed to be subjects, inhabitants were quite literally claiming their places among a global community held together by its monarch.

Had the benefits of subjecthood been only symbolic, however, debates over its contours might well have been dismissed, viewed merely as a drain on colonial resources and on officials' time. The elasticity of subjecthood proved advantageous in the colonies, making it appealing not only to inhabitants who perceived its utility in security rights and membership, but also to numerous administrators who sought to harness the labor and manpower of new populations. Subjecthood worked to integrate a diverse and disparate empire at a functional and day-to-day level as well, and the very absence of a uniform definition of subjecthood and inability to agree upon a set of rights due subjects, in fact, provided administrators with tremendous flexibility in responding to demands in the individual colonies. The dual expansiveness and imprecision of subjecthood was ultimately what rendered subjecthood so crucial in managing and organizing the British Empire.

Inhabitants who articulated their belonging to a wider community of fellow-subjects, for example, participated in a process of binding themselves to the empire in ways that facilitated the work of colonial officials. Since one of the only codified rights of subjects was the fundamental right to petition or appeal directly to the crown, an expansive interpretation of subjecthood meant that numerous inhabitants could claim that right. Petitioning, like appealing, inherently involved recognition of sovereign authority and of certain hierarchies of power (figure C.2).[15] When subjects throughout the empire were permitted to approach the monarch directly, they confirmed their allegiance each time they chose to do so, thereby reinforcing the framework of royal authority.

Furthermore, if large numbers of inhabitants could petition the monarch, this meant that they had access to nonviolent means to voice complaints and had outlets for dissatisfaction. When individuals proclaimed their belonging and then relied on subject status to articulate claims or grievances, colonial administrators, Parliament, and the crown had a written means to gauge problems or frustrations in the empire. Administrators presumably had an opportunity to respond with concessions as necessary before mere discontent erupted into violence or threatened to disrupt imperial unity. Allowing myriad subjects to engage the monarch worked effectively to defuse tension in the empire and preserved an illusion of equality and integration.[16] Thus, expansive definitions of subjecthood served to uphold power structures across the colonies and to bind the empire in both an abstract and practical way.

Inclusive approaches to subject status also strengthened the position of individual administrators in the colonies. British officials understood that by recognizing numerous inhabitants as subjects, they might secure valuable conscripts for future wars with their European rivals. Strategic extensions of subjecthood were widespread, as both Lord Cathcart's proclamation to inhabitants of the Spanish colonies in 1740 or flexible grants of letters of marque in 1793 have suggested. The enticements of subject status were recognized to be useful during peacetime as well. Acknowledging that the lands, expertise, and slaves of myriad settlers were essential to the survival and cultivation of new colonies, administrators endeavored to retain them as British subjects. Furthermore, Sir William Young, responsible for surveying and granting lands in Grenada in the 1760s, argued that persuading French settlers and planters to stay in the British Empire meant that the French King would suffer property and population losses.[17] As governors, secretaries of

FIGURE C.2 Mr. Cooper after Thomas Strothard, *The King relieving the prisoners in Dorchester jail*, 1820, etching and engraving. London: Thomas Kelly, 1820. © The Trustees of the British Museum (1872, 1012.542).

state, and even judges everywhere recognized, retaining Spanish, French, even Company subjects was essential to the king's service. Profiting from the trade and property of subjects marked as British bolstered the global economic position of the British vis-à-vis the French or Spanish.

Moreover, the bodies of subjects might themselves serve to demarcate, and sometimes establish or extend, the sphere of British jurisdiction.[18] When asked whether the king might establish any kind of civil government or jurisdiction over British subjects residing in the Bay of Honduras, which was nominally Spanish, the advocate general offered a provocative opinion. He determined that "such as the subject is such is the jurisdiction," arguing that British subjects were entitled to civil regulations according to the laws of Great Britain.[19] The persons of British subjects could therefore carry British law and authority into territories ceded to the crown of Spain. By welcoming inhabitants as British subjects, judges on the subcontinent could subtly extend the sphere of royal authority and jurisdiction. Even as they often remained uncertain about which rights they might grant, colonial administrators nonetheless continued to claim numerous individuals as subjects, always recognizing the necessity of additional settlers and additional bodies.

The imprecision of subjecthood would allow administrators to respond as needed to demands and crises in the colonies. They might extend the privileges of suffrage to French Catholics in Grenada when this was perceived to be useful in the 1760s and 1770s, but then rescind those privileges when those same French Catholics were viewed as a liability. Governors might cultivate the goodwill of the *Canadiens* by allowing them to live under French civil law in Quebec well before an Act of Parliament formally upheld this right. Even fellow Catholics in Britain, against whom suspicions of a majority Protestant population ran high, did not obtain parallel rights until the nineteenth century. The uncertainties of subject status acted to preserve differential rather than uniform rights across the British Empire, strengthening the hand of administrators who did not necessarily feel that all subjects should have the same rights and who might, on occasion, have to reward some subjects at the expense of others.

Precisely because common allegiance to a king or queen was potentially so expansive, subjecthood allowed both inhabitants and administrators to envision the British Empire as a single entity from a new perspective. However fragile this entity was, the relationship between monarch and subject was central. It was an entity held together by the bonds between subjects and sovereign and yet inhabited by myriad subjects each with individual identities and sets of often-conflicting rights. As one prominent observer wrote of the new colony of Quebec, "the King makes no distinction between a man born in Canada and one born in Middlesex—we are all His Majesty's subjects—He is the fountain of honor—His Royal favor will extend to the worthy, be they new, or be they natural born subjects."[20] Subjecthood acted to integrate the later-eighteenth-century British Empire because its shifting and expansive parameters were best poised to bind—symbolically and functionally—a constantly changing group of colonial territories and peoples. For an empire that was increasingly concerned to be seen as espousing and protecting liberty and that had a vested interest in suggesting that all of its inhabitants were equal while simultaneously maintaining distinctions, British subjecthood was a crucial concept and tool.[21]

Though often dedicated petitioners and loyal subjects, those who wielded the language of subjecthood were not always successful in securing their ends. For the French Catholics of Grenada whose political privileges were gradually eroded during the 1780s and 1790s, or in the case of some captives who were not deemed British and were therefore left to their fates in Barbary, subjecthood was protean and its protections porous. While a capacious subjecthood meant that a vast array of inhabitants were legally recognized as subjects, it was also the case that the rights of Protestant subjects or of those who spoke English were more often upheld than those of non-Anglican or non-European inhabitants.

The promises of subjecthood lay in its flexibility and imprecision, but so, too, did the perils. Individuals living across disparate territories and under a variety of legal systems might all lay claim to it. At the same time, since the rights of subjects remained relatively undefined by law, the privileges due subjects were variously interpreted and granted to greater and lesser extents across the colonies. Subjecthood remained so important because it did not guarantee equality and did not assure administrative uniformity. It could both unify and divide, both include and exclude. In this duality lay its greatest utility.

The later eighteenth century has often been portrayed as a period of increasing centralization of power and more uniform patterns of rule, but the struggles over subjecthood across the British Empire suggest another trajectory.[22] Subjecthood in the colonies was unstable and temporary, a far cry from the immutable and unalienable status set forth by Sir Edward Coke or Sir William Blackstone in the seventeenth and eighteenth centuries, or from that officially viewed as "indelible" until nationality laws were changed in 1870.[23] It was not dictated by a central government, administrators acting in unison, or a uniform body of law. Rather, the experience of subjects in the empire suggests that there were paths to belonging that differed from those espoused by case law or by jurists within the realm. This was an empire in which inhabitants and administrators were constantly choosing, challenging, and extending definitions of allegiance and protection. This was a world where claims made in the colonies did not merely replicate those made in the imperial metropolis but developed existing ideas about rights in distinct new ways. This was a period in which subjecthood, like authority more generally, was negotiated rather than imposed.[24]

An expansive and imprecise subjecthood thus provided innumerable opportunities for subjects and for the empire, and its importance correspondingly endured well beyond the eighteenth century. In 1813, a group of free colored inhabitants, "with assurances of the truest loyalty toward His Majesty," appealed to the Grenada House of Assembly. One John Mitchell had been seized, publicly flogged, and confined without benefit of trial by executive order of the vice-governor and without the civil judicature's approval. The Assembly responded by acknowledging the inappropriateness of the vice-governor's actions and by pledging to support the men "in common with His Majesty's other subjects in the Assertion of their Rights and Privileges, and their claims to the Protection of the Laws."[25] Seventeen years later, a committee representing the East Indians of Calcutta, who were the children of British men and Indian women, petitioned Westminster in the hopes of securing recognition as British subjects and access to English law, although their requests, debated at length, ultimately went unanswered.[26] And in 1847, Don Pacifico, a Portuguese Jew, sought the British government's protection for property damages incurred during anti-Semitic riots in Greece, claiming that he was a British subject born in Gibraltar. Although his request for compensation was widely considered to be inflated,[27] the foreign secretary, Lord Palmerston, argued in 1850 that "a British subject, in whatever land he may be, shall feel confident that the watchful eye and the strong arm of England, will protect him against injustice and wrong," famously justifying the fact that a fleet had been authorized to blockade several Greek ports until restitutions were made to this subject.[28]

Well after the eighteenth century, individuals throughout the colonies continued to invoke their allegiance and rely on their identities as subjects to claim protections. Even as "citizen" became the cry adopted by liberals and by those in the burgeoning republics, "subject" remained the term used by those seeking rights and privileges in Britain and the British Empire. The appeal of subjecthood would endure, and many who were neither originally "British" nor initially "subjects" would continue to shape the contours of subjecthood. In the nineteenth and twentieth centuries, subjects would seek British passports and protection when traveling abroad and claim entry and right of abode in England. In numerous struggles for civil rights, non-European inhabitants would employ claims of subjecthood in asserting equality before the law and demanding access to political office.[29] The rights associated with subject status were no more codified in subsequent centuries than they had been in the eighteenth when the myriad ways in which inhabitants would use the language of subjecthood had only started to become apparent. The relationship between subject and sovereign, a bond that had proven remarkably resilient during an age of revolution, would remain so in the centuries and debates yet to come.

Notes

INTRODUCTION

1. "Declaration of Independence, July 4, 1776," http://avalon.law.yale.edu/18th_century/declare.asp (accessed November 2, 2016).
2. "Petition to the King, July 8, 1775," in *Journals of the Second Continental Congress*, http://avalon.law.yale.edu/18th_century/contcong_07-08-75.asp (accessed November 2, 2016).
3. See references from newspaper articles and pamphlets compiled by Jack P. Greene, *Peripheries and Center: Constitutional Developments in the Extended Polities of the British Empire and the United States, 1607–1788* (New York: Norton & Co., 1990), 22, 54, 95.
4. A significant number of these colonists, however, remained loyal subjects throughout the revolutionary years and chose exile from their American homes and lands rather than breaking with the British crown. See Maya Jasanoff, *Liberty's Exiles: American Loyalists in the Revolutionary World* (New York: Knopf, 2011).
5. Thomas Paine, *The Rights of Man, Part I* (1791), in *Paine, Political Writings* ed. Bruce Kuklick (New York: Cambridge University Press, 1989), 143.
6. For the classic narratives, see Eric Hobsbawm, *The Age of Revolution, 1789–1848* (New York: Vintage, 1996); and R. R. Palmer, *The Age of Democratic Revolution: A Political History of Europe and America, 1760–1800* (Princeton: Princeton University Press, 1959). More recently, see David Armitage and Sanjay Subrahmanyam, *The Age of Revolutions in Global Context, c. 1760–1840* (New York: Palgrave Macmillan, 2010); and Sarah Knott, "Narrating the Age of Revolution," *William and Mary Quarterly* 73, no. 1 (2016): 3–36.
7. Hobsbawm, *The Age of Revolution*, 112.
8. In *The Royalist Revolution: Monarchy and the American Founding* (Cambridge, MA: Harvard University Press, 2014), Eric Nelson has provocatively shown the extent to which patriots like John Adams, James Wilson, Alexander Hamilton,

and others, in fact, embraced royalism. For Nelson, royalism is defined not as an idealization of kingly title or hereditary right but is associated with the belief that prerogative power is compatible with protecting subjects' liberties. Nelson shows that many thinkers believed monarchical power might further subjects' interests.

9. For the role played by the British monarch and the centrality of monarchical culture in the British Empire, see Richard L. Bushman, *King and People in Provincial Massachusetts* (Chapel Hill: University of North Carolina Press, 1992); James Joseph Caudle, "Measures of Allegiance: Sermon Culture and the Creation of a Public Discourse of Obedience and Resistance in Georgian Britain, 1714–1760" (PhD diss., Yale University, 1996); Stephen Constantine, "Monarchy and Constructing Identity in 'British' Gibraltar, c. 1800 to the Present," *The Journal of Imperial and Commonwealth History* 34, no. 1 (2006): 23–44; Eliga H. Gould, *The Persistence of Empire: British Political Culture in the Age of the American Revolution* (Chapel Hill: University of North Carolina Press, 2000); Paul Halliday, *Habeas Corpus: From England to Empire* (Cambridge, MA: Harvard University Press, 2010); Jasanoff, *Liberty's Exiles* (2011); Brendan McConville, *The King's Three Faces: The Rise and Fall of Royal America, 1688–1776* (Chapel Hill: University of North Carolina Press, 2006); Nelson, *The Royalist Revolution*; and Hannah Smith, *Georgian Monarchy: Politics and Culture, 1714–1760* (Cambridge: Cambridge University Press, 2006). The role of the monarch and the uses made of the king's image are topics also explored by historians of the Spanish and French empires. See Kenneth J. Banks, *Chasing Empire Across the Sea: Communications and the State in the French Atlantic, 1713–1763* (Montreal: McGill-Queen's University Press, 2002); Alejandro Cañeque, *The King's Living Image: The Culture and Politics of Viceregal Power in Colonial Mexico* (New York: Routledge, 2004); John H. Elliott, *Empires of the Atlantic World: Britain and Spain in America, 1492–1830* (New Haven: Yale University Press, 2006); Malik Ghachem, *The Old Regime and the Haitian Revolution* (Cambridge: Cambridge University Press, 2012); Brian Owensby, *Empire of Law and Indian Justice in Colonial Mexico* (Stanford: Stanford University Press, 2008); Anthony Pagden, *Lords of All the World: Ideologies of Empire in Spain, Britain, and France, 1500–1850* (New Haven: Yale University Press, 1995); Jacob Soll, *The Information Master: Jean-Baptiste Colbert's Secret State Intelligence System* (Ann Arbor: University of Michigan Press, 2009); and Michael Wintroub, *A Savage Mirror: Power, Identity, and Knowledge in Early Modern France* (Stanford: Stanford University Press, 2006).

10. Timothy Blanning, *The Pursuit of Glory: Europe, 1648–1815* (New York: Viking, 2007), 288.

11. Blanning, *The Pursuit of Glory*, 319.

12. According to Lawrence Gipson, oaths of allegiance were an accepted part of international law in the seventeenth and eighteenth centuries. See Lawrence Henry Gipson, *The Great War for the Empire: The Years of Defeat, 1754–1757*, vol. 6 (New York: Knopf, 1959), 244. See also Robert Michael Morrissey, "Bottomlands

and Borderlands: Empires and Identities in the Illinois Country, 1673–1785" (PhD diss., Yale University, 2006).

13. For a recent discussion of this "tacit compact" and "contractual relationship between the ruler and the ruled" in two empires, see Elliott, *Empires of the Atlantic World*, 131–133. For a wide-ranging analysis of oaths and covenants, including the "covenant" between king and subjects, see Edward Vallance, *Revolutionary England and the National Covenant: State Oaths, Protestantism, and the Political Nation* (Woodbridge: Boydell Press, 2005), 77–78. See also Owensby, *Empire of Law*.
14. These historians have generally worked to document legal definitions of subjecthood at specific moments in time and changes in the "law of subject and alien." Examples include Caitlin Anderson, "Britons Abroad, Aliens at Home: Nationality Law and Policy in Britain, 1815–1870" (PhD diss., University of Cambridge, 2004); M. Page Baldwin, "Subject to Empire: Married Women and the British Nationality and Status of Aliens Act," *The Journal of British Studies* 40, no. 4 (October 2001): 522–556; Andreas Fahrmeir, *Citizens and Aliens: Foreigners and the Law in Britain and the German States, 1789–1870* (New York: Berghahn, 2000); Rieko Karatani, *Defining British Citizenship: Empire, Commonwealth, and Modern Britain* (London: Frank Cass, 2003); James Kettner, *The Development of American Citizenship, 1608–1870* (Chapel Hill: University of North Carolina Press, 1978); Keechang Kim, *Aliens in Medieval Law: The Origins of Modern Citizenship* (Cambridge: Cambridge University Press, 2000); and Sudipta Sen, "Imperial Subjects on Trial: On the Legal Identity of Britons in Late Eighteenth-Century India," *The Journal of British Studies* 45, no. 3 (July 2006): 532–555.
15. Some cultural theorists have been interested in the positioning of the subject and in questions of subjectivity. See, for example, Etienne Balibar and Immanuel Wallerstein, *Race, Nation, Class: Ambiguous Identities* (London: Verso, 1991).
16. Rogers Brubaker, *Citizenship and Nationhood in France and Germany* (Cambridge, MA: Harvard University Press, 1992), 51. Although Brubaker refers to this ideological antithesis, his goal is, in fact, to highlight some of the similarities between the codifications of citizenship and subjecthood.
17. See Ann Dummett and Andrew Nicol, *Subjects, Citizens, Aliens and Others: Nationality and Immigration Law* (London: Weidenfeld & Nicolson, 1990); John Salmond, "Citizenship and Allegiance," *The Law Quarterly Review* 67 (1901): 270–282; and Gershon Shafir, ed., *The Citizenship Debates: A Reader* (Minneapolis: University of Minnesota Press, 1998). In her review essay, "Rights and Citizens in the Old Regime," *French Historical Studies* 20, no. 2 (1997), Gail Bossenga observes that the French Revolution not only created modern citizenship but that it also "made individuals bearers of rights" (222).
18. See Carolee Ruth Pollock, "His Majesty's Subjects: Political Legitimacy in Quebec, 1764–1791" (PhD diss., University of Alberta, 1996), 106.
19. Rodney Baker, *Political Legitimacy and the State* (Oxford: Clarendon Press, 1990), 3.

20. In *Law and Citizenship in Early Modern France* (Baltimore: Johns Hopkins University Press, 1995), Charlotte C. Wells notes that others have placed undue emphasis on the evolution from subject to citizen. In *The Development of American Citizenship,* Kettner traces Americans' evolution from British subjects to American citizens who embraced an active, contractual, volitional, and contributory citizenship. Similar points are also made by Jerry Bannister and Liam Riordan in "Loyalism and the British Atlantic, 1660–1840," in *The Loyal Atlantic: Remaking the British Atlantic in the Revolutionary Era* eds. Jerry Bannister and Liam Riordan (Toronto: University of Toronto Press, 2012).
21. In *Citizenship in the Western Tradition* (Chapel Hill: University of North Carolina Press, 1992), Peter Riesenberg argues that *civis* and *subditus* had become interchangeable by the fourteenth century. He notes that "subject" had, in fact, become dominant by the sixteenth century, generally replacing the concept of "citizen," even if the idea of the active citizen, once so prevalent in Greece and Rome, continued to exist.
22. Wells, *Law and Citizenship*, xvii.
23. Denis Diderot and Jean le Rond d'Alembert, eds., *Encyclopédie, ou dictionnaire raisonné des sciences, des arts et des métiers, etc.* (University of Chicago: ARTFL Encyclopédie Project [Spring 2011 Edition]), Robert Morrissey, ed. http://encyclopedie.uchicago.edu, see vols. 3 and 15. A *citoyen* was defined as "a member of a free society of several families, who shares in the rights of this society and who benefits from its franchises," although the historical references were largely drawn from classical Greece and Rome (3:488). *Sujet* described "all the members of the state, in contrast to the sovereign, either when sovereign authority has been entrusted to one person, as in a monarchy, or to a number of men, as in a republic" (15:643). *Sujet* was clearly used to describe members of both monarchical and republican states who lived under the protection of some kind of sovereign authority.
24. Diderot and d'Alembert, *Encyclopédie*, 15:643.
25. For example, one author claimed that "citizen must refer to all those who are entitled to all of the advantages, to all of the privileges of the association & who are properly members of the state, either by birth or in some other way; all the others are merely simple inhabitants or foreigners passing through rather than citizens." He appeared to suggest that citizens were members of the state with an even greater number of privileges than others. A few paragraphs later, however, subjects were also described as being due "all advantages common to members of the state," implying that perhaps the differences between citizens and subjects were not so great. Diderot and d'Alembert, *Encyclopédie*, 15:643.
26. Samuel Johnson, *A Dictionary of the English Language* (London: 1755).
27. For an important study of the ideal and practice of the "city commonwealth" and of what it meant to be a "freeman" and "citizen" in early modern England, see Phil Withington, *The Politics of Commonwealth: Citizens and Freemen in Early Modern England* (Cambridge: Cambridge University Press, 2005).

28. Jean Bodin, *Six Books of the Commonwealth*, trans. M. J. Tooley (Oxford: Seven Treasures Publications, 2009), 62, 59.
29. John Locke, *Second Treatise of Government*, ed. C. B. Macpherson (Indianapolis: Hackett Publishing Company, 1980), 62.
30. Nannerl O. Keohane, *Philosophy and the State in France: The Renaissance to the Enlightenment* (Princeton: Princeton University Press, 1980), 6.
31. Robert Brady, *A Complete History of England, from the First Entrance of the Romans . . . unto the End of the Reign of King Henry III* (Savoy: 1685).
32. Vallance, *Revolutionary England*, 78. In 1750, *A Critical Review of the Liberties of British Subjects*, like numerous other pamphlets, described the coronation oath as the moment at which the king renewed the "original compact" between the king and the people.
33. For another overview of the terms "subjecthood," "citizenship," and even "nationality," see Caitlin Anderson, "Old Subjects, New Subjects, and Non-Subjects: Silences and Subjecthood," in Jane Rendall, Nicholas Guyatt, and Richard Bessel, *War, Empire, and Slavery, 1770–1830* (Houndsmills: Palgrave, 2010), footnote 1.
34. For an important discussion of the origins and significance of the concept of "free-born Englishman," see Rachel Foxley, *The Levellers: Radical Political Thought in the English Revolution* (Manchester: Manchester University Press, 2013). Foxley argues that before John Lilburne, a prominent figure in the Leveller movement, the "collocation" of "free-born Englishman" was not common. Lilburne attached a strong political message to the "free-born Englishman," arguing that such men had a uniform set of liberties.
35. David Armitage, *The Ideological Origins of the British Empire* (Cambridge: Cambridge University Press, 2000), among others.
36. P. J. Marshall, *The Making and Unmaking of Empires: Britain, India, and America, c. 1750–1783* (Oxford: Oxford University Press, 2005), 6–7.
37. For a printed copy of the Treaty of Paris, see Adam Shortt and Arthur G. Doughty, eds., *Documents relating to the Constitutional History of Canada, 1759–1791* (Ottawa: Printed by J. de L. Taché, 1918), 113–122. The treaty itself was framed in a language of subjecthood, an agreement between monarchs and between "subjects" of their "Britannick, Most Christian, Catholic, and Most Faithful Majesties." Signatories vowed that no articles would be infringed by their "respective subjects." The Treaty of Paris drew on capitulations signed in Quebec, Montreal, and Grenada, among others—capitulations that had pledged to regard French Catholic inhabitants who remained as "Subjects of the King" and were viewed as legally binding. For more on capitulations, see Shortt and Doughty, *Documents relating to the Constitutional History of Canada*, 33; Pollock, "His Majesty's Subjects," 32, 171.
38. *The History, Debates, and Proceedings of Both Houses of Parliament of Great Britain from the Year 1743 to the Year 1774*, vol. 4 (London: 1792), 101, 140, among others.
39. The connections between the wider European indebtedness that resulted from the Seven Years' War and the conditions that enabled the American and French

Revolutions have been widely studied. For a small sample of recent works that assess the impact of this indebtedness, see Fred Anderson, *Crucible of War: The Seven Years' War and the Fate of Empire in British North America, 1754–1766* (New York: Vintage Books, 2000); Colin Calloway, *The Scratch of a Pen: 1763 and the Transformation of North America* (New York: Oxford University Press, 2006); Gould, *The Persistence of Empire*; Marshall, *The Making and Unmaking of Empires*; Simon Schama, *Citizens: A Chronicle of the French Revolution* (New York: Vintage, 1989); and Gordon S. Wood, *The American Revolution: A History* (New York: The Modern Library, 2002).

40. A predominant concern in settling and defending the disparate territories of the British Empire was the very real shortage of manpower in Great Britain. By the 1770s, the population of England was about three and a half times smaller than that of France, which boasted 25 million inhabitants and was the most populous country in Europe. For further information, see Pierre Tousignant, "The Integration of the Province of Quebec into the British Empire, 1763–1791," in *Dictionary of Canadian Biography*, vol. 4 (Toronto: University of Toronto Press, 1979), xlvii. Pamphlets published in the 1760s also revealed this fear of "small numbers," but many suggested that the colonies might bolster England's numerical strength. For an excellent summary of eighteenth-century debates regarding depopulation and the empire, see Bernard Bailyn, *Voyagers to the West: A Passage in the Peopling of America on the Eve of Revolution* (New York: Vintage Books, 1988). For further numerical analysis and the debate relating to a national census in Britain, see D. V. Glass, *Numbering the People: The Eighteenth-Century Population Controversy and the Development of Census and Vital Statistics in Britain* (London: D. C. Heath, 1973).

41. A significant percentage of the Pennsylvania population was of German extraction prior to 1755. In *Crisis of Empire: Great Britain and the American Colonies, 1764–1783* (London: Arnold, 1966), Ian Christie notes that the British government welcomed these foreigners and the human resources they could provide. Indeed, the 1740 "Act for Naturalizing Foreign Protestants" (13 Geo. II, c. 7) provided that foreign Protestants who had resided in the American colonies for seven or more years should be deemed natural-born subjects.

42. A particularly interesting example of this rhetoric can be found in the "Letter from the Committee of the British Subjects residing in Bengal, to the Right Honorable Lord North dated May 25, 1779," in *The Several Petitions of the British Inhabitants of Bengal, of the Governor-General and Council, and of the Court of Directors of the East-India Company to Parliament* (London: 1780).

43. See Peter Marshall, "Britain and the World in the Eighteenth Century: The Turning Outwards of Britain," *Transactions of the Royal History Society* 6th ser., vol. 11 (2001), 3.

44. For emerging work on the subject status of enslaved and indigenous peoples in the British Empire, see Christopher L. Brown, "From Slaves to Subjects: Envisioning an Empire Without Slavery, 1772–1834," in *Black Experience and the Empire* eds.

Philip D. Morgan and Sean Hawkins (Oxford: Oxford University Press, 2004), 111–140; Ann Curthoys and Jessie Mitchell, "Bring this Paper to the Good Governor: Aboriginal Petitioning in Britain's Australian Colonies," in *Native Claims: Indigenous Law Against Empire, 1500–1920* ed. Saliha Belmessous (New York: Oxford University Press, 2011), 182–203; Gregory Evans Dowd, "Domestic, Dependent, Nations: The Colonial Origins of a Paradox," in *Backcountry Crucibles: The Lehigh Valley from Settlement to Steel* eds. Jean R. Soderlund and Catherine S. Parzynski (Bethlehem: Lehigh University Press, 2007), 125–157; Brooke N. Newman, "Contesting 'Black' Liberty and Subjecthood in the Anglophone Caribbean, 1730s–1780s," *Slavery & Abolition* 32, no. 2 (2011): 169–183; Jenny Hale Pulsipher, *Subjects unto the Same King: Indians, English, and the Contest for Authority in Colonial New England* (Philadelphia: University of Pennsylvania Press, 2005); and Craig Bryan Yirush, "Claiming the New World: Empire, Law, and Indigenous Rights in the Mohegan Case, 1704–1743," *Law and History Review* 29, no. 2 (May 2011): 333–373.

45. Richard Pares, *War and Trade in the West Indies* (Oxford: Clarendon Press, 1936), 71–75.

CHAPTER 1

1. This is not to argue that subjecthood was only a matter of law. Indeed, the expansiveness of many legal interpretations actually encouraged the emergence of additional definitions of subjecthood at the interstices of law and everyday life. See Tamar Herzog's call for scholarship that looks at definitions of community that emerge between "formal legal categories" and "social practices," in *Defining Nations: Immigrants and Citizens in Early Modern Spain and Spanish America* (New Haven: Yale University Press, 2003), 166.
2. See Charles S. Maier, "Consigning the Twentieth Century to History: Alternative Narratives for the Modern Era," *American Historical Review* 105, no. 3 (2000): 807–831; and John Salmond, "Citizenship and Allegiance," *The Law Quarterly Review* 67 (1901): 270–282. Writing in 1901 and clearly influenced by the waves of nationalism in Europe, Salmond argued that the "primitive conception of the state as a personal and permanent union of determinate individuals" was gradually giving way to territorial definitions of the state (271). Maier focuses on the significance of "territoriality" in defining the twentieth century. By contrast, in *Defining Nations*, Herzog argues that as the French kings asserted their sovereignty in the seventeenth century, there was a shift away from territoriality to subjecthood.
3. For the legal tie, see J. Mervyn Jones, *British Nationality Law and Practice* (Oxford: Clarendon Press, 1947).
4. William Blackstone, *Commentaries on the Laws of England*, ed. Stanley N. Katz (Chicago: University of Chicago Press, 1979), 230, 354.

5. Some have gone so far as to suggest that the "subject" is defined by reference to his antithesis, the "alien." In *British Nationality Law and the History of Naturalization* (Milano: Guiffrè, 1954), Clive Parry notes how frequently experts have looked at individuals who are "naturalized" or "endenized" in order to draw conclusions about who was *e contrario* a "subject".
6. "Calvin's Case," in *The Seventh Part of the Reports of Sir Edward Coke* (London: 1738), 5.
7. Yale, D. E. C., ed., *Sir Matthew Hale's The Prerogatives of the King*, vol. 92 (London: Selden Society, 1976), 54.
8. For the importance of local actors and imperial agents in shaping the "law" that developed in the empire, see Douglas Hay and Paul Craven, eds. *Masters, Servants, and Magistrates in Britain and the Empire, 1562–1955* (Chapel Hill: University of North Carolina Press, 2004); and Daniel Hulsebosch, *Constituting Empire: New York and the Transformation of Constitutionalism in the Atlantic World, 1664–1830* (Chapel Hill: University of North Carolina Press, 2005). See also Lauren Benton and Benjamin Straumann, "Acquiring Empire by Law: From Roman Doctrine to Early Modern European Practice," *Law and History Review* 28, no. 1 (2010): 1–38.
9. Many legal historians now regard "law" as a multiplicity of practices rather than a set of fixed doctrines and analyze the meanings of law in everyday life. See, among others, Laura Edwards, *The People and Their Peace: Legal Culture and the Transformation of Inequality in the Post-Revolutionary South* (Chapel Hill: University of North Carolina Press, 2009); Amy Louise Erickson, "Common Law versus Common Practice: The Use of Marriage Settlements in Early Modern England," *Economic History Review* 43, no. 1 (1990): 21–39; Robert W. Gordon, "Critical Legal Histories," *Stanford Law Review* 36, no. 1–2 (1984): 57–125; Robert W. Gordon, "Introduction: J. Willard Hurst and the Common Law Tradition in American Legal Historiography," *Law & Society Review* 10, no. 1 (1975): 9–55; William E. Forbath, Hendrik Hartog, and Martha Minow, "Introduction: Legal Histories from Below," *Wisconsin Law Review* 4 (1985): 759–766; John Phillip Reid, *Law for the Elephant* (San Marino: Huntington Library, 1997); Austin Sarat and Thomas R. Kearns, eds., *Law in Everyday Life* (Ann Arbor: University of Michigan Press, 1993); and Christopher L. Tomlins and Bruce H. Mann, eds. *The Many Legalities of Early America* (Chapel Hill: University of North Carolina Press, 2001).
10. Clive Parry, *Nationality and Citizenship Laws of the Commonwealth and of the Republic of Ireland* (London: Stevens, 1957), 41, as quoted in Ann Dummett and Andrew Nicol, *Subjects, Citizens, Aliens, and Others: Nationality and Immigration Law* (London: Weidenfeld & Nicolson, 1990), 59; and Polly Price, "Natural Law and Birthright Citizenship in Calvin's Case (1608)," *Yale Journal of Law and the Humanities* 9 (1997), 73. In "The Ancient Constitution and the Expanding Empire: Sir Edward Coke's British Jurisprudence," *Law and History Review* 21, no. 3 (2003), Daniel Hulsebosch asserts that Sir Edward Coke "was on the verge of recognizing a new kind of imperial subjectship" (466).

11. The law officers of the crown included the attorney general (who was traditionally the primary representative of the sovereign in the courts), the solicitor general (who was the attorney general's deputy and assistant in all responsibilities), and the advocate general (who served as a standing adviser to the government on matters relating to questions of international, maritime, and ecclesiastical law). In general, the crown tapped its law officers for a range of services, from legal opinions on domestic and international law, to decisions about litigation, to advice in drafting bills proposed to Parliament.
12. Keechang Kim, *Aliens in Medieval Law: The Origins of Modern Citizenship* (Cambridge: Cambridge University Press, 2000); and Price, "Natural Law and Birthright Citizenship," 93. For more developed arguments about the importance of the "alien," see Kim, *Aliens in Medieval Law*. Kim argues that the legal status of foreign merchants was an important consideration in the fourteenth century and would reorient understandings of personal status. Kim documents an important shift at the end of the Middle Ages from an emphasis on the personal status of free versus unfree to an emphasis on allegiance versus nonallegiance and subject versus alien.
13. John Cowell, *The Interpreter: or Booke containing the signification of words wherein is set foorth the true meaning of all, or the most part of such words and termes, as are mentioned in the lawe writers, or statutes of this victorious and renowned kingdome, requiring any exposition or interpretation* (1607). The same definitions persisted in editions of *The Interpreter* published well into the eighteenth century.
14. Denization was granted by the monarch through letters patent and allowed the denizen to hold but not to inherit property. However, only an act of Parliament could naturalize a subject, putting him "in exactly the same state as if he had been born in the king's ligeance." Although naturalized subjects were initially granted the same privileges as natural-born subjects, the political rights of naturalized persons were restricted by the Act of Settlement in 1701. The Act stipulated that anyone born out of the dominions, even if naturalized, was no longer able to sit in the Privy Council, become a member of Parliament, or capable of enjoying any office or place of trust. By the mid-eighteenth century, when Blackstone described the several statuses of those who owed allegiance to the monarch, he noted that the "denizen" represented a kind of "middle state" between the alien and natural-born subject.
15. "Calvin's Case," in *The Seventh Part of the Reports of Sir Edward Coke* (1738), 4. Henry de Bracton's thirteenth-century treatise, which linked subject status to an individual's allegiance, was cited in this report. In addition, the defendants and plaintiffs themselves referred to Sir Thomas Littleton and to the statute of 1351. Various additional published versions of Sir Edward Coke's report were available to contemporaries and remain readily accessible to scholars, including *Calvin v. Smith* 7 CO. REP. 1b, 77 *English Reports* 377; "Lord Coke's Report of Calvin's

Case," in T. B. Howell, *The Complete Collection of State Trials* (1816), 607–658; *The Famous Case of Reobert Calvin, A Scotsman, as contain'd in the Reports of Sir Edward Coke* (1705); and *The Selected Writings and Speeches of Sir Edward Coke*, ed. Steve Sheppard (2003), 166–232, which includes English translations of sections originally published in Latin. Unless otherwise indicated, *The Seventh Part* will be cited in this chapter.

16. Both the Commissioners of Union appointed by James I and a separate parliamentary committee wrestled with the legal status of James's Scottish subjects, mulling over various proposals for naturalization. Whereas the Commissioners declared that Scots born after the union, or *postnati*, ought to be considered subjects, and that Scots born before the union, or *antenati*, ought to be formally naturalized, a committee drawn from both houses of Parliament debated the issue in 1606 and decided that subjects of one kingdom were not necessarily subjects of the other. Perhaps in large part because many in Parliament were unsympathetic to a full legal union between England and Scotland and feared the influx of Scottish migrants, the issue remained unresolved for several years. For details of the commission convened, the parliamentary debates, and the reports produced, see Keechang Kim, "Calvin's Case (1608) and the Law of Alien Status," *Journal of Legal History* 17 (1996): 155–171; Hulsebosch, "The Ancient Constitution and the Expanding Empire, 443–445; and Price, "Natural Law and Birthright Citizenship."
17. In the account of Calvin's Case in *A Complete Collection of State Trials* (1816), T. B. Howell reported that after the House of Commons challenged the Commissioners' proposals, a decision was made to settle the point out of Parliament by bringing two suits. In "Natural Law and Birthright Citizenship," Price asserts that most scholars agree that the case was contrived (81), just as Kim argues in "Calvin's Case (1608)" that the case was brought as an attempt to bypass Parliament (156). Bacon, Coke, and Ellesmere, for example, had shown themselves willing to naturalize well before 1608 and many of the arguments they later published first appeared in parliamentary discussions. See "Case of the Union of the Realm of Scotland with England," in Howell, *A Complete Collection*.
18. Sir Thomas Egerton, *The Speech of the Lord Chancellor of England, in the Eschequer Chamber, touching the Post-nati* (1609); "Speech of Lord Bacon as Counsel for Calvin, in the Exchequer Chamber," in Howell, *A Complete Collection of State Trials* or in James Spedding, ed., *The Letters and the Life of Francis Bacon, including all his occasional works* (1868), vols. 3 and 4; and Coke, *The Seventh Part*.
19. James H. Kettner, *The Development of American Citizenship, 1608–1870* (Chapel Hill: University of North Carolina Press, 1978), 17. In "Natural Law and Birthright Citizenship," Price also notes that Coke's report was typically included as part of standard legal treatises published in early America (139).
20. These three arguments are outlined most clearly in *The Seventh Part*, 3.
21. *The Seventh Part*, 5.
22. *The Seventh Part*, 10; Ellesmere, *The Speech of the Lord Chancellor*, 101.
23. *The Seventh Part*, 6; Ellesmere, *The Speech of the Lord Chancellor*, 63.

24. Price, "Natural Law and Birthright Citizenship," 83. As to the association of Calvin's Case with *jus soli*, it is important to note Kim's observation that the rise of *jus soli* "can only be understood when one remembers the double meaning of ligeance, which allowed the question of political subjection to be discussed under the guise of birthplace." See Kim, *Aliens in Medieval Law*, 210.
25. *The Seventh Part*, 19. In fact, Coke used this example on two occasions in his report of Calvin's Case. See also *The Seventh Part*, 6.
26. *The Seventh Part*, 8. As Coke wrote, "faith and truth " were the "member parts" of ligeance and could not "be circumscribed within the predicament of *ubi*." As Brian Levack also argues, it is possible to view Calvin's Case as having minimized the subject's ties with the territorial state in favor of the "community of allegiance." See *The Formation of the British State: England, Scotland, and the Union, 1603–1707* (Oxford: Clarendon Press, 1987), 84.
27. *The Seventh Part*, 9.
28. Coke's observations were echoed by Bacon and Ellesmere. Both noted the dangers of trying to separate the allegiance due to the natural person of the king from that due to the political body.
29. *The Seventh Part*, 13.
30. *The Seventh Part*, 13–15.
31. *The Seventh Part*, 5. The translation of "dual and reciprocal tie" is taken from Sheppard, *The Selected Writings and Speeches of Sir Edward Coke*, 176.
32. *The Seventh Part*, 5.
33. Philip Hamburger, "Beyond Protection," *Columbia Law Review* 10, no. 8 (2009): 1823–2001.
34. Paul Halliday, *Habeas Corpus: From England to Empire* (Cambridge, MA: Harvard University Press, 2010), 208.
35. Not all legal historians would agree with this reading of Calvin's Case or of subject status more generally. For scholars like Ann Dummett, Andrew Nicol, and Christopher Vincenzi, subjecthood has always been about duties and obligations rather than about rights. Others, like Polly Price and Daniel Hulsebosch, have cautiously suggested that subjects possessed a limited number of rights or that there were a few core liberties that traveled with the subject. See Dummett and Nicol, *Subjects, Citizens, Aliens, and Others*, 62; Hulsebosch, "The Ancient Constitution," 1, 16; Price, "Natural Law and Birthright Citizenship," 88; and Christopher Vincenzi, *Crown Powers, Subjects, and Citizens* (London: Pinter, 1997), 283.
36. "Case of the Union of the Realm of Scotland with England," in Howell, *The Complete Collection*, 564.
37. "Speech of Lord Bacon as Counsel for Calvin, in the Exchequer Chamber," in Howell, *The Complete Collection*, 582–583.
38. Ellesmere, *The Speech of the Lord Chancellor*, 103.
39. Ellesmere did not spend significant time on these various types of allegiance, noting that others had, but he did discuss "legal allegiance" as distinct from "alta allegiance by birthright" (natural allegiance). Similarly, Bacon spent considerable time

explaining the "degrees" of persons and the differences in protections due alien enemies, alien friends, denizens, and natural-born subjects. Both were aware of the arguments made by Coke.

40. "Speech of Lord Bacon," in Howell, *The Complete Collection of State Trials*, 596.
41. *The Seventh Part*, 5. See also Paul Halliday and G. Edward White, "The Suspension Clause: English Text, Imperial Contexts, and American Implications," *Virginia Law Review* 94 (2008), 642.
42. *Craw v. Ramsey* Vaughan 274, 124 *English Reports* 1072.
43. T. B. Howell, *A Complete Collection of State Trials* XX (London: 1816), 82–238.
44. As Jack P. Greene has noted, the question of whether common law, and English law more generally, followed the subject was never really resolved for the extended territories of the British Empire. See Jack P. Greene, *Peripheries and Center: Constitutional Development in the Extended Polities of the British Empire and the United States, 1607–1788* (New York: W. W. Norton & Company, 1990).
45. See *Dutton v. Howell* (1693) (Shower 24, 1 *English Reports* 17). Judges decided that Barbados was a "plantation or new Settlement of Englishmen by the King's Consent in an uninhabited country," which meant that settlers must abide by the same laws as England. In a non-conquered country, the common law was deemed the "birthright" of subjects who "no more abandoned the English laws than they did their Natural Allegiance, which they did not." For histories of Barbados, see Hilary McD. Beckles, *A History of Barbados: From Amerindian Settlement to Nation State* (Cambridge: Cambridge University Press, 1990); Larry Gragg, *Englishmen Transplanted: The English Colonization of Barbados, 1627–1660* (Oxford: Oxford University Press, 2003); and F. A. Hoyos, *Barbados: A History from the Amerindian to Independence* (London: Macmillan, 1978).
46. See *Blankard v. Galdy* (1694) (4 Mod. 222, 87 *English Reports* 359) and *Smith v. Brown and Cooper* (1702) (2 Salkeld 666, 91 *English Reports* 566). In *Smith v. Brown and Cooper*, judges, for example, determined that the laws of England did not extend to Virginia because it was a conquered country and was subject to whatever law "the king pleases." This then allowed the court to rule that slaves were, by the laws of Virginia, "saleable as chattels."
47. See *Anonymous* (1722) 2 P. Wms 75, 24 *English Reports* 646 and *Rex v. Cowle* (1759) 2 Burr. 834, 97 *English Reports* 587. More specifically, in 1722, the Privy Council decided that in an "uninhabited country newly found out, and inhabited by the English," subjects were to be governed by the laws of England since that law was "the birthright of every subject."
48. *Christian v. Corren* (1716) 1 P. Wms. 329, 24 *English Reports* 412.
49. Some scholars contend, of course, that England already possessed an internal empire. See Nicholas Canny, *Kingdom and Colony: Ireland in the Atlantic World, 1560–1800* (Baltimore: Johns Hopkins University Press, 1988); Michael Hechter, *Internal Colonialism: The Celtic Fringe in British National Development, 1536–1966* (Berkeley:

University of California Press, 1975); and Neil Longley York, *Neither Kingdom nor Nation: The Irish Quest for Constitutional Rights, 1698–1800* (Washington, D.C.: Catholic University of America Press, 1994). Such scholarship renders the omissions of Calvin's Case surprising. Jurists in the early seventeenth century would surely have been familiar with issues that arose over the status of those born before or after a conquest. Furthermore, Coke, who had been involved with drafting the Virginia Company's original charter, made no mention of North America in his report. And although Coke mentioned Ireland, Berwick, and the Norman provinces, he did so briefly, simply noting that "all men know that they [those born in Ireland] are natural-born subjects, and capable of and inheritable to lands in England." Given that these were the early years of a renewed and intensified English settlement in Ireland, Coke's neglect of Ireland is striking. The likely conclusion is that made in this chapter: that judges in 1608 were concerned with the particular matter at hand and not with the repercussions of subjecthood in the broader empire.

50. Coke's report made very clear that those born in other conquered territories had historically been viewed as subjects, but he drew his examples largely from those born after territories had been conquered and thus born under the king's allegiance. He did, however, note that denization of aliens occurred in three ways: by Parliament; by letters patent; and "by Conquest, as if the King and his Subjects should conquer another Kingdom or Dominion, as well *Antenati* as *Postnati* . . . are all Denizens of the Kingdom or Dominion." See *The Seventh Part*, 6. Did Coke intend to suggest that aliens were endenizened by the act of conquest itself? And were they endenizened in just the conquered dominion or also in England itself?
51. *The Seventh Part*, 28.
52. As Daniel Hulsebosch has argued, Calvin's Case was concerned more with the rights of people entering England than with the rights of Englishmen emigrating elsewhere, and England was envisoned as an "importer" rather than an "exporter" of people. See Hulsebosch, *Constituting Empire,* and Hulsebosch, "Ancient Constitution."
53. *Christian v. Corren* (1716) 1 P. Wms. 329, 24 *English Reports* 411.
54. In the seventeenth century, statutes such as the 1661 Tumultuous Petitioning Act were passed, which put limits on petitions but which nonetheless confirmed the subject's right to petition. In 1689, the Bill of Rights confirmed that the subject was entitled to petition the monarch for redress.
55. As Colin Calloway notes, however, a copy of the treaty signed on February 10, 1763 did not reach the British commander-in-chief in North America until May 1763. See Colin Calloway, *The Scratch of a Pen: 1763 and the Transformation of North America* (New York: Oxford University Press, 2006), 19.
56. CO 42/24—Letter from Egremont to Murray dated May 21, 1763.
57. CO 101/9—Letter from Egremont to the commanding officer at St. Vincent dated August 13, 1763. Egremont wrote to instruct the commanding officer of the

"nullity" of certain purchases from the departing French inhabitants there, enclosing the ninth article of the treaty.

58. CO 102/1—In his General Instructions dated November 3, 1763, Robert Melvill was ordered to explain two articles from a seventeenth-century treaty to inhabitants.
59. CO 102/1—See, for example, the additional instructions sent to Robert Melvill and dated October 6, 1768.
60. CO 101/1—Memorial of His Majesty's Adopted Subjects and Memorial of His Majesty's Natural Born Subjects attested February 14, 1766.
61. CO 102/1—Additional Instructions to Robert Melvill dated October 6, 1768.
62. For a printed copy of the Treaty of Paris, see Adam Shortt and Arthur G. Doughty, eds., *Documents relating to the Constitutional History of Canada, 1759–1791* (Ottawa: Printed by J. de L. Taché, 1918), 113–122.
63. CO 91/31—Letter from Eliott to Sydney dated June 25, 1784.
64. This is an argument also made by C. R. Pennell in "Treaty Law: The Extent of Consular Jurisdiction in North Africa from the Middle of the 17th to the Middle of the 19th Centuries," *The Journal of North African Studies* 14, no. 2 (2009): 235–256. Pennell notes that treaties were part of a general consular practice and that they were essential components of the socio-legal order.
65. CO 389/54—Instructions for our trusty and welbeloved Sr. James Wishart given at Our Court at St. James's on February 28, 1713.
66. CO 91/31—Copy of the Second Article of the Treaty of Peace and Commerce concluded between Great Britain and Algiers dated October 29, 1716.
67. For more about law officers of the crown, see George Chalmers, *Opinions of Eminent Lawyers on Various Points of English Jurisprudence, Chiefly concerning the Colonies, Fisheries, and Commerce of Great Britain* (London: 1814); J. Edwards, *The Law Officers of the Crown* (London: Sweet & Maxwell, 1964); and James Oldham, *English Common Law in the Age of Mansfield* (Chapel Hill: University of North Carolina Press, 2004).
68. Chalmers, *Opinions of Eminent Lawyers*, xxi–xxii.
69. CO 323/18/1—Report of His Majesty's Attorney General dated July 27, 1764 on the question whether those Subjects of the Crowns of France and Spain, who remain in the ceded Countries in America, are to be considered as Aliens.
70. In Grenada, many inhabitants would echo these understandings, arguing that because French Catholic planters had taken oaths of allegiance, they were entitled to the rights of subjects. See CO 101/1—The Memorial of His Majesty's Adopted Subjects in the Island of Grenada attested February 14, 1766 and The Memorial of Several of His Majesty's Natural Born Subjects attested February 14, 1766. Moreover, one of the main reasons given for removing the Acadians from Nova Scotia in 1755 had been that they had refused to swear unqualified oaths of allegiance and were not, therefore, British subjects. For more on this, see John Bartlett Brebner, *New England's Outpost: Acadia before the Conquest of Canada* (New York: Columbia, 1927); N. E. S. Griffiths, *From Migrant to*

Acadian: A North American Border People, 1604–1755 (Montreal: McGill–Queen's University Press, 2005); Christopher Hodson, *The Acadian Diaspora: An Eighteenth-Century History* (New York: Oxford University Press, 2012); and Geoffrey Plank, *An Unsettled Conquest: The British Campaign against the Peoples of Acadia* (Philadelphia: University of Pennsylvania Press, 2001). By contrast, judges in the Calcutta Supreme Court of Judicature would argue that having taken the oaths of allegiance did not, in fact, confer subjecthood. See the case of François Fairie in HP Reel 2—March 17, 1783. Although many believed that the oaths of allegiance confered subjecthood, this was not a universally accepted legal understanding.

71. CO 42/2—Letter to the Lords Commissioners for Trade & Plantations dated Lincoln's Inn, June 10, 1765, signed Norton and de Grey. This report is reproduced in many other locations, including Shortt and Doughty, eds., *Documents relating to the Constitutional History of Canada.*
72. CO 42/7—Report from Marriott to the Privy Council dated January 18, 1768.
73. CO 123/1—Letter from James Marriott to John Pownall in response to April 21, 1766 letter referred to His Majesty's Advocate General from the Lords of Trade and Plantations. I am grateful to Peter Silver for having referred me to this volume of correspondence.
74. There are, of course, many reasons for this, some related to the distance between metropole and colony, some related to the fact that other issues often preoccupied administrators in London, some related to administrative overload. Additionally, because the colonial offices themselves were not very professionally managed, gaps in knowledge between administrators were significant. The work of secretaries of state and their ability to communicate with their subordinates suffered from the fact that the correspondence of their predecessors had been treated as private and therefore not part of the administrative archive until George III ended this detrimental practice (see Hulsebosch, *Constituting Empire*, 132–136).
75. See FO 113/3—Report of the Transactions at Algiers between the Dey & Regency & Sir Roger Curtis dated November 20, 1783. Sir Roger Curtis personally determined that one captive spoke English well enough to make him a legitimate object of redemption and therefore attempted to claim him.
76. See Articles IV and IX of "The Treaty of Paris," in Shortt and Doughty, *Documents relating to the Constitutional History of Canada*, 113–122.
77. Kettner, *The Development of American Citizenship*; Nathan Perl-Rosenthal, *Citizen Sailors: Becoming American in the Age of Revolution* (Cambridge, MA: Harvard University Press, 2015).
78. In *The Seventh Part*, Coke noted that naturalization vested by birthright could not be taken away by any subsequent separation of the crown, just as *The Speech of the Lord Chancellor* argued that neither faith nor obedience could be severed. More than a century later, in his *Commentaries on the Laws of England*, vol. 1, William Blackstone argued that natural allegiance was owed in perpetuity and could only

be altered by the "united concurrence of the legislature" (257). The problems caused by "perpetual allegiance" have often been examined vis-à-vis the impressment controversies between the United States and Great Britain in the late eighteenth and early nineteenth centuries. For details on these controversies, see Denver Alexander Brunsman, *The Evil Necessity: British Naval Impressment in the Eighteenth-Century Atlantic World* (Charlottesville: University of Virginia Press, 2013); James Kettner, "Subjects or Citizens? A Note on British Views," *Virginia Law Review* 62 (1976): 945–967; Kettner, *The Development of American Citizenship*; and Perl-Rosenthal, *Citizen Sailors*.

79. SP 71/20—Letter from Parker dated August 25, 1756.
80. See HP R4074—vol. 26—July 27, 1789; HP R4074—vol. 33—April 28, 1791; and HP R4071—vol. 13—March 22, 1792.
81. See, for example, William Searle Holdsworth, *A History of English Law*, vol. IX (London: Methuen: 1922), 80.

CHAPTER 2

1. *British Liberties, or the Free-Born Subject's Inheritance* (London: 1766), 161. This is the 1766 edition of Henry Care's *English Liberties, or the Free-Born Subject's Inheritance*, first published in 1682 and then republished numerous times, including in the colonies in 1721 and 1774. See Lois Schwoerer, *The Ingenious Mr. Henry Care, Restoration Publicist* (Baltimore: Johns Hopkins University Press, 2001), for a history of its publication.
2. Anonymous, *A Critical Review of the Liberties of British Subjects* (London: 1750).
3. In *The Spirit of the Laws* (Cambridge: Cambridge University Press, 1989), Montesquieu dedicated an entire book to analyzing the English constitution, arguing that "the monarchies we know do not have liberty for their direct purpose as does the one we have just mentioned" (166). Voltaire apparently often joked with visitors who visited his estate in Ferney that "if ever I smell of a Resurrection, or come a second time to Earth, I will pray God to make me be born in England, the Land of Liberty." See Voltaire, *Letters concerning the English Nation* (Oxford: Oxford University Press, 1994), ed. and with an intro. by Nicholas Cronk, vii.
4. Voltaire, *Letters concerning the English Nation*, 39.
5. As Jack N. Rakove has argued, there was "no single model" for declarations but rather a "set of possibilities." See *Declaring Rights: A Brief History with Documents* (Boston: Bedford Books, 1998), 27.
6. Lois G. Schwoerer, *The Declaration of Rights, 1689* (Baltimore: Johns Hopkins University Press, 1981), 11–29. Schwoerer argues that "declaration" had strong connotations and a rich history. In ordinary usage, it meant "making clear" or "telling," and was typically a "proclamation in emphatic, solemn or legal terms." In law, "declaration" referred to the statement of charges against a defendant. And in political usage, the term had occasionally been applied to describe public statements on contested issues.
7. Schwoerer, *The Declaration of Rights*, 289.

8. As quoted in James H. Hutson, "The Emergence of the Modern Concept of a Right in America: The Contribution of Michel Villey," *American Journal of Jurisprudence* 39: 185 (1994): 217.
9. See John Phillip Reid, *Constitutional History of the American Revolution: The Authority of Rights*, vol. 1 (Madison: University of Wisconsin Press, 1986), 200, 3.
10. See "John Dickinson Appeals to William Pitt," in Edmund Morgan, ed., *Sources and Documents on the Stamp Act Crisis, 1764–1766* (Chapel Hill: University of North Carolina Press, 1959), 123.
11. Francis Plowden, *Jura Anglorum: The Rights of Englishmen* (Dublin: 1792), 1.
12. Reid, *Constitutional History: Authority of Rights*, 200.
13. As Rakove notes in *Declaring Rights*, many federalists were suspicious of the idea of compiling a list of rights and opposed the Bill of Rights, fearing that the enumeration of some rights would relegate those not mentioned to an "inferior, less-than-constitutional status" (144).
14. See J. C. Holt, *Magna Carta: Second Edition* (Cambridge: Cambridge University Press, 1992), Chapter 1. Holt argues that "the 'myth' of the Magna Carta, that interpretation of it which gives it qualities which the men of 1215 did not intend, was part of the document's potential" (9).
15. The text of Magna Carta (1215) can be found in both Latin and English in Holt, *Magna Carta*, Appendix 6, 448–473.
16. This was Clause 12 of Magna Carta (1215), which disappeared from subsequent charters. For a useful listing of clauses subtracted from subsequent issues of Magna Carta, see http://legacy.fordham.edu/halsall/source/magnacarta.asp (accessed October 28, 2015).
17. Indeed, as J. G. A. Pocock's foundational study, *The Ancient Constitution and the Feudal Law: A Study of English Historical Thought in the Seventeenth Century* (Cambridge: Cambridge University Press, 1957), demonstrates, arguments that liberties stemmed from the monarch's grant and arguments that liberties stemmed from time immemorial shaped the various interpretations of the Norman Conquest and of Magna Carta, particularly in the seventeenth century.
18. The text of "The Petition of Right" can be found in J. P. Kenyon, *The Stuart Constitution: Documents and Commentary*, 2nd ed. (Cambridge: Cambridge University Press, 1986), 68–71.
19. The medieval practice whereby Parliament submitted petitions to the king, the king gave his assent to them, and a favorable royal endorsement authorized the judges to draw up a statute, had waned well before the 1620s. Although the petition continued to be used to express grievances, offer counsel, or raise concerns regarding the royal prerogative, the bill was the more accepted way to present legislation, which then must be accepted by the crown before becoming statute. For more on this history, see Elizabeth Read Foster, "Petitions and the Petition of Right," *Journal of British Studies* 14:1 (1974): 21–45; and Frances Helen Relf, *The Petition of Right* (Minneapolis: Bulletin of the University of Minnesota, 1917).
20. Foster, "Petitions and the Petition of Right," 43.

21. For more about the argument that the petition reinforces and upholds hierarchy and the monarchical order, see Hannah Weiss Muller, "Bonds of Belonging: Subjecthood and the British Empire," *The Journal of British Studies* 53:1 (2014): 29–58; and Hannah Weiss Muller, "From Requête to Petition" (forthcoming, *The Historical Journal*).
22. The debate about whether Charles I's assent to the Petition of Right gave it the force of law is a long and complex one. Here, I follow the interpretation of Foster and Relf, who argue that the Petition of Right did not have the weight of law.
23. The text of "The Declaration of Rights" can be found in Schwoerer, *The Declaration of Rights*.
24. Schwoerer, *The Declaration of Rights*, 14.
25. This is what Schwoerer has referred to as constitutional change "clothed in conservative dress." See *The Declaration of Rights*, 283.
26. Schwoerer, *The Declaration of Rights*, 22.
27. Rachel Foxley, *The Levellers: Radical Political Thought in the English Revolution* (Manchester: Manchester University Press, 2013), 78.
28. The text of the "Agreement of the Free People of England" can be found in William Haller, ed., *The Leveller Tracts, 1647–1653* (Gloucester: P. Smith, 1964), 318–328. Originally, the Agreement was drawn up in 1647 by Levellers in the army. The Agreement constituted the Levellers' basic platform and was revised, improved, and expanded between 1647 and 1649. The Agreement analyzed here is that of 1649.
29. As Foxley has argued, the Levellers were noteworthy for issuing documents and demands in the name of "many thousands" of people and for using those documents to mobilize their supporters and to define their movement. See Foxley, *The Levellers*, 4.
30. Stephen Schechter, ed., *Roots of the Republic: American Founding Documents Interpreted* (Madison: Madison House, 1990), 6.
31. Forrest McDonald, *Novus ordo seclorum: The Intellectual Origins of the Constitution* (Lawrence: University Press of Kansas, 1985), 38.
32. Robert Brady, *A Complete History of England, from the First Entrance of the Romans under the conduct of Julius Caesar unto the End of the Reign of King Henry III* (Savoy: 1685), preface, no pagination.
33. For more on these arguments made by royalist historians and polemicists, see Pocock, *The Ancient Constitution,* Chapter 8.
34. *London Magazine* 34 (1765), as quoted in Reid, *Constitutional History: Authority of Rights*, 140.
35. This is a point also made by historians of France. See Nannerl Keohane, *Philosophy and the State in France: The Renaissance to the Enlightenment* (Princeton: Princeton University Press, 1980), among others.
36. Mike Ashley, *Taking Liberties: The Struggle for Britain's Freedoms and Rights* (London: The British Library, 2008).

37. McDonald, *Novus ordo seclorum*, 36–38.
38. A preliminary list of such pamphlets and commentaries can be found in Reid, *Constitutional History: The Authority of Rights*, 243–315.
39. William Penn, "The Excellent Priviledge of Liberty and Property Being the Birth-Right of the Free-Born Subjects of England" (1687), reprinted in Philip Kurland and Ralph Lerner, eds., *The Founders' Constitution*, vol. 1 (Chicago: University of Chicago Press, 1987), 432.
40. *British Liberties*, preface (unpaginated).
41. *A Guide to the Knowledge of the Rights and Privileges of Englishmen* (London: 1757), 6.
42. *A Guide to the Knowledge*, 5.
43. Penn, "The Excellent Priviledge," 432.
44. Anonymous, *The Rights of the People Asserted and the Necessity of a More Equal Representation in Parliament Stated and Proved* (Dublin: 1783).
45. Brady, *A Complete History of England*, xxx, xxxiv.
46. Penn, "The Excellent Priviledge," 431–433.
47. *A Critical Review*, 15.
48. *The Rights of the People Asserted*, 12.
49. William Prynne, *A Seasonable, Historical, Legal Vindication and Chronological Collection of the good old Fundamental Liberties, Franchises, Rights, Laws of all English Freemen* (London: 1654), 54.
50. *A Guide to the Knowledge*, 6.
51. Prynne, *A Seasonable, Historical, Legal Vindication*.
52. *Rights of the People Asserted*, 12.
53. *A Critical Review*, title page, 15–18.
54. Penn, "The Excellent Priviledge," 432.
55. *A Guide to the Knowledge*, 1–2.
56. Bernard Schwartz, *The Great Rights of Mankind: A History of the American Bill of Rights* (Madison: University of Wisconsin Press, 1992), 7.
57. *A Guide to the Knowledge*, vii.
58. Rakove, *Declaring Rights*, 14.
59. In this, my argument in this chapter parallels that of John Phillip Reid, who argued in *Constitutional History of the American Revolution: The Authority of Rights* that rights asserted by Americans were English rights. The arguments of this book, however, are ones of simultaneity and seek to broaden Reid's conclusions; British subjects throughout the empire were asserting rights they identified as "English" or "British."
60. The text of this code can be found in Edmund S. Morgan, ed., *Puritan Political Ideas, 1558–1794* (Indianapolis: Bobbs-Merrill, 1965), 178–203.
61. Morgan, *Puritan Political Ideas*, 178.
62. For a text of the "West New Jersey Concessions and Agreements" see http://www.westjersey.org/ca77 (accessed October 28, 2015).
63. Interestingly, the "Concessions and Agreements" were more radical than some of their counterparts where the administration of justice was concerned. The gave

juries power over both fact and law and left judges very little discretionary authority. See Schechter, *Roots of the Republic*, 53.

64. Schechter, *Roots of the Republic*, 53.
65. The text of the 1683 Charter can be found in Schechter, *Roots of the Republic*, 65–75. As Dan Hulsebosch notes in *Constituting Empire: New York and the Transformation of Constitutionalism in the Atlantic World* (Chapel Hill: University of North Carolina Press, 2005), drafters of this particular charter drew on both the English constitutional canon and the charters of neighboring colonies.
66. The text of the 1691 Act can be found in Schechter, *Roots of the Republic*, 76–82 or *The Colonial Laws of New York from the year 1664 to the Revolution* (New York: 1896), 244–248.
67. As quoted in Hulsebosch, *Constituting Empire*, 54.
68. See, among others, Jack Rakove, *Declaring Rights*; Kurt Lash, *The Fourteenth Amendment and the Privileges and Immunities of American Citizenship* (New York: Cambridge University, Press, 2014); and Philip Hamburger, "Equality and Diversity: The Eighteenth-Century Debate about Equal Protection and Equal Civil Rights," *The Supreme Court Review* (1992): 295–392. Though Americanists, these scholars make this observation for the seventeenth-century English context as well.
69. See, in particular, Quentin Skinner, *Liberty before Liberalism* (Cambridge: Cambridge University Press, 1998); and Richard Tuck, *Natural Rights Theories: Their Origin and Development* (Cambridge: Cambridge University Press, 1979).
70. Rakove, *Declaring Rights*, 21.
71. See J. C. D. Clark, *The Language of Liberty, 1660–1832: Political Discourse and Social Dynamics in the Anglo-American World* (Cambridge: Cambridge University Press, 1994); and Ann Dummett and Andrew Nicol, *Subjects, Citizens, Aliens, and Others: Nationality Law and Immigration Law* (London: Weidenfeld and Nicolson, 1990), 29. See also Rakove, *Declaring Rights*; Skinner, *Liberty before Liberalism*; Tuck, *Natural Rights Theories*.
72. See Rakove, *Declaring Rights*.
73. For more on concepts of "liberties" in early modern England, see Paul Halliday, *Habeas Corpus: From England to Empire* (Cambridge, MA: Harvard University Press, 2010).
74. Rakove, *Declaring Rights*, 29.
75. John Cowell, *The Interpreter: or Booke containing the signification of words wherein is set foorth the true meaning of all, or the most part of such words and termes, as are mentioned in the lawe writers, or statutes of this victorious and renowned kingdome, requiring any exposition or interpretation* (1607).
76. Samuel Johnson, *Dictionary of the English Language* (London: 1755).
77. See, for example, Denis Diderot and Jean le Rond d'Alembert, eds, *Encylcopédie, ou dictionnaire raisonné des sciences, des arts et des métiers, etc.* (University of Chicago: ARTFL Encyclopédie Project [Spring 2011 Edition]), Robert Morrissey, ed. http://encyclopedie.uchicago.edu, 8:578. The entry for "Immunités" is particularly revealing, as the author notes: "in our usage we frequently join together the

terms franchises, liberties, privileges, exemptions, and immunities. These terms, however, are not synonyms. A franchise consists of not being subject to certain obligations or duties; liberties are also more or less the same thing as franchises; a privilege consists of some right which is not common to all; exemptions and immunities which signify the same thing, represent the freeing from a particular obligation or duty given to a person who without this exemption would have been subject to it." The entry for "Libertés" in 9:474 is also intriguing; it seeks to differentiate "libertés" from "privileges" and "immunités," noting that they have usually been used interchangeably. The author argues that privileges were "exemptions and particular graces accorded to some against the common right," whereas liberties were determined by observing ancient laws. Many contributors to the *Encyclopédie* were clearly attempting to distinguish between these various terms and to endow words like "libertés" and "droit" with their more "modern" associations; nonetheless, they acknowledged that at the time of publication, these words were still used virtually synonymously.

78. Phil Withington, who focuses on the ideal and practice of the "city commonwealth," has also drawn the link between liberties and the territorial jurisdiction of individual cities. He notes that this early modern conception did not see liberties as innate to the person but as attributes of a place. See *The Politics of Commonwealth: Citizens and Freemen in Early Modern England* (Cambridge: Cambridge University Press, 2005), 89.
79. Scholars disagree about when "rights" became predominant. In *Declaring Rights*, Rakove maintains that "rights" and "liberties" were used interchangeably in 1689, but from that time forward, "rights" slowly began to eclipse "liberties" (21). In "The Emergence of the Modern Concept of a Right," James Hutson argues that "liberty" was replaced by "right" over the course of the seventeenth and eighteenth centuries, although he acknowledges that confusion over the distinction existed well into the 1760s (216).
80. James H. Hutson, "The Bill of Rights and the American Revolutionary Experience," in *A Culture of Rights: The Bill of Rights in Philosophy, Politics, and Law – 1791 and 1991*, ed. Michael J. Lacey and Knud Haakonssen (Cambridge: Cambridge University Press), 62.
81. Hutson, "The Emergence of the Concept of Right," 198–200; Rakove, *Declaring Rights*, 19.
82. Cowell's dictionary, for example, though among the more famous, was not unusual in defining "right" as "not only a Right, for which a Writ of Right lies, but also any Title or Claim, either by Virtue of a Condition, Mortgage, or the like." See Cowell, *The Interpreter*.
83. Reid, *Constitutional History: The Authority of Rights*. It should be noted, of course, that the "right" to property was viewed as essential to protecting against arbitrary government and seizures of land. Ideas of "right-as-property" and "right-as-freedom" remained profoundly interconnected.

84. Johnson, *Dictionary of the English Language.*
85. See, among others, Rakove, *Declaring Rights*, and Reid, *Constitutional History: The Authority of Rights*. I should note that Reid has argued that although "language can be found from the eighteenth century saying that rights were grants from the sovereign, we have no way of knowing whether these statements represented serious constitutional theory . . . even if serious, they were the minority view" (68). Although this section will not explore the range of constitutional debates regarding the origins of rights, it is important to emphasize that the idea that rights were grants from the sovereign was certainly present in seventeenth-century documents. As Alan Ryan notes, even someone like Jeremy Bentham believed that stable government was based on a "clear understanding that rights were the gift of the sovereign" (389). See Alan Ryan, "The British, the Americans, and Rights," in *A Culture of Rights*. Ryan is referring to H. L. A. Hart's discussion of "Bentham and the United States of America."
86. See, among others, Clark, *The Language of Liberty.*
87. See Skinner, *Liberty before Liberalism.*
88. Hutson, "The Emergence," 203.
89. Tuck, *Natural Rights Theories*, 3. Tuck, of course, traces the existence of this idea back to the fourteenth century but agrees that by the seventeenth century "rights have come to usurp the whole of natural law theory" (67) and that eighteenth-century notions of the inalienable rights of mankind can, in fact, be found among seventeenth-century theorists (150).
90. Skinner, *Liberty before Liberalism*, 65.
91. Pocock, *The Ancient Constitution and the Feudal Law*, 37.
92. Pocock, *The Ancient Constitution and the Feudal Law*. These competing understandings were clearly on display in 1604, when the House of Commons drew up the Form of Apology and Satisfaction. Professing their dutiful submission and enduring loyalty as subjects of James I, the House of Commons described their privileges and liberties both as a birthright and inheritance and also noted that such rights had been cherished "from time immemorable." In addition, they argued that James had been misinformed when he was told that "we held not privileges of right, but of grace only." Although the House of Commons appeared to be distinguishing between privileges held "of grace" and "of right," they continued to use both of these concepts loosely and multiply. A text of the "Form of the Apology" can be found in J. R. Tanner, *Constitutional Documents of the Reign of James I, 1603–1625* (Cambridge: Cambridge University Press, 1960), 217–230. For more on these arguments, see Hannah Weiss Muller, "Languages of privilege, languages of right" (unpublished paper).
93. See Rakove, *Declaring Rights*, 22; Reid, *Constitutional History: The Authority of Rights*, 73.
94. Reid, *Constitutional History: The Authority of Rights*, 89.
95. Hutson, "The Emergence of the Concept"; and Hutson, "The Bill of Rights."
96. See, among others, Rakove, *Declaring Rights.*

97. Richard Primus, "An Introduction to the Nature of American Rights," in *The Nature of Rights at the American Founding and Beyond*, ed. Barry Alan Shain (Charlottesville: University of Virginia Press, 2007).
98. Lash, *The Fourteenth Amendment*, 13–14.
99. Glenn Burgess, *The Politics of the Ancient Constitution: An Introduction to English Political Thought, 1603–1642* (University Park: Pennsylvania State University Press, 1992).
100. Alan Cromartie, *The Constitutionalist Revolution: An Essay on the History of England, 1450–1642* (New York: Cambridge University Press, 2006), 90.
101. Reid, *Authority of Rights*, 106.
102. In this sense, these conclusions nuance the conclusions drawn by J. G. A. Pocock in *The Ancient Constitution*. I would suggest that not only did the visions he refers to coexist, but that they were often used deliberately in order to achieve the greatest possible effect with superiors.
103. CO 42/63—The Memorial and Petition of the Subscribers, Merchants and Others of the Cities of Quebec and Montreal to Lord Dorchester dated December 1, 1788 (enclosed in Letter from Dorchester to Sydney dated December 8, 1788).
104. See CO 42/63 for a copy of this petition, enclosed in Instructions to Adam Lymburner dated December 8, 1788. The petition appears to have been from 1784.
105. Reid, *Constitutional History: The Authority of Rights*, Chapter 2.
106. Reid, *Constitutional History: The Authority of Rights*, 10–11. Reid writes that "most rights asserted in eighteenth-century Great Britain or British North America were more vague" (10), and in the next paragraph notes that "vagueness, whether deliberate or unintentional, was not a consideration when claiming eighteenth-century constitutional rights" (11).

CHAPTER 3

1. Fraser was likely referring to the complaints filed against him by the Jurats of Mahon who charged that he had tried to obstruct the trade of "his Majesty's Minorqueen Subjects at Algiers" (FO 3/4—Letter from Rochford to Fraser dated August 4, 1772). Secretary of State Rochford notified Fraser in a letter dated February 12, 1773 (FO 3/5) that his name had been cleared of these charges.
2. Archibald Campbell Fraser was the son of the infamous Simon Fraser, 11th Lord Fraser of Lovat, who was impeached by the House of Lords and executed in 1747 for his involvement in the Jacobite rebellion of 1745. For more information, see Lawrence Goldman, ed., *Oxford Dictionary of National Biography* (Oxford: Oxford University Press, 2009).
3. FO 3/4—Letter from Fraser to Rochford dated October 7, 1772. He vowed, for example, that he would never put a protective pass into "the hands of an Alien."
4. For more on the role of consuls in the Mediterranean, see D. B. Horn, *The British Diplomatic Service, 1689–1789* (Oxford: Clarendon Press, 1961), particularly

237–258; Hilda Lee, "The Supervising of the Barbary Consulates, 1768–1836," *Bulletin of the Institute of Historical Research* 23 (1950): 191–199; C. R. Pennell, "Treaty Law: The Extent of Consular Jurisdiction in North Africa from the Middle of the Seventeenth to the Middle of the Nineteenth Century," *The Journal of North African Studies* 14, no. 2 (2009): 235–256.

5. For sample instructions to British consuls in the Mediterranean, see SP 71/20 and SP 71/11.
6. By the mid-eighteenth century, most consuls were informally reporting to the governor of Gibraltar. This occurred even before the 1764 instructions to one consul in Morocco that stated: "you do not take any step till after you shall have consulted the Governor of Gibraltar and received his opinion and direction." See Lee, "The Supervising of the Barbary Consulates," 196. In practice, many consuls also consulted with the governor of Minorca on these matters.
7. The term "Barbary" referred originally to the Berbers, North Africa's indigenous people. When the British used the term "Barbary," it was generally used as a blanket term for the entire North African region and for all of its diverse peoples. The term "Barbary states," most in usage between 1520 and 1830, referred to Morocco, Algiers, Tunis, and Tripoli, all of which were autonomous provinces of the Ottoman Empire.
8. Fernand Braudel, *The Mediterranean and the Mediterranean World in the Age of Philip II* (New York: Harper & Row, 1972), 110, 276–277.
9. GGA—Civil Secretary's Register 4 (1779–1786)—List of British Prisoners from the Garrison, now in Spain, dated January 30, 1780.
10. British consuls were stationed at ports, European, Ottoman, and other, throughout the Mediterranean world. Many were in regular correspondence with the governors of Gibraltar and Minorca in addition to the secretaries of state during the eighteenth century. Incomplete records in the Government of Gibraltar Archives (GGA) indicate that the governor there was in correspondence with consuls at Algiers, Tetuan, Tangier, Tripoli, Tunis, and Malaga.
11. I use these titles since they are the ones used in official correspondence. The Dey of Algiers, the ruler of the regency of Algiers, was under the nominal if not effective control of the Ottoman sultan, and Algiers remained, in theory, a province of the Ottoman Empire. The Emperor of Morocco, whose position was usually referred to as that of "sultan," inherited his title through the male line. Morocco managed to maintain its independence from the Ottoman Empire.
12. For a useful compendium of treaties that refer to the status of inhabitants of Minorca and Gibraltar, see "Barbary States" in Lewis Hertslet, ed., *A complete collection of the treaties and conventions, and reciprocal regulations, at present subsisting between Great Britain and foreign powers* (London: 1841).
13. Quoted in Sir William Jackson, *The Rock of the Gibraltarians: A History of Gibraltar* (Rutherford: Fairleigh Dickinson University Press, 1987), 127.
14. Ignace Hugary de La Marche-Courmont, *Essai politique sur les avantages que la France peut retirer de la conquête de l'isle Minorque: dedié à son altesse sérénissime*

Monseigneur le prince Louis de Wirtemberg (Port-Mahon: 1756), 3. The original French reads: "tout le commerce de l'Océan étoit, ainsi qu'il l'est encore, dans les mains de l'Angleterre."

15. Gibraltar was besieged in 1704–1705 (a counteroffensive after its capture in 1704), 1727, and 1779–1783. Minorca was under British rule (1708–1756), French rule (1756–1763), British rule (1763–1781), Spanish rule (1781–1798), and British rule (1798–1802) before being returned to Spain in 1802.
16. Historians have emphasized that neither Minorca nor Gibraltar proved all that profitable to the British. Neither became a significant trading center, and the costs of maintaining their garrisons were more than once criticized as a drain on national revenue. Nonetheless, both outposts remained critical to victualing and refitting ships throughout the eighteenth century, and though "informed opinion" may have viewed Gibraltar as being of negligible value, its popular appeal should not be underestimated. For more about views of Gibraltar, in particular, see Stetson Conn, *Gibraltar in British Diplomacy in the Eighteenth Century* (New Haven: Yale University Press, 1942).
17. *Considerations on the addresses lately presented to His Majesty, on occasion of the loss of Minorca. In a letter to a Member of Parliament* (London: 1756).
18. Linda Colley, *Captives: Britain, Empire, and the World, 1600–1850* (New York: Anchor Books, 2004), 70, 24.
19. David W. Donaldson, "Britain and Menorca in the Eighteenth Century" (PhD diss., Open University, 1994), 121; and Constantine, *Community and Identity*, 178. Although estimates of civilians vary for each of these territories, a recent publication by Tristan Stein notes that the civilian population in Gibraltar grew from 1,113 in 1725 to 3,201 in 1777, whereas the civilian population in Minorca grew from 15,000 in 1720 to 25,000 in 1763. See Tristan Stein, "Passes and Protection in the Making of a British Mediterranean," *The Journal of British Studies* 54, no. 3 (2015): 602–631.
20. For an excellent overview of the existing judicial system and its challenges, see Donaldson's important dissertation, "Britain and Menorca," Chapter 4.
21. See CO 91/30—Petition from the Committee of Inhabitants of Gibraltar to Lord North dated May 23, 1783, and Petition from the Agents of the Inhabitants of Gibraltar to Lord North dated October 23, 1783. Both leveled complaints against Governor Eliott.
22. Donaldson, "Britain and Menorca," 534.
23. Desmond Gregory, *Minorca, the Illusory Prize: A History of the British Occupations of Minorca between 1708 and 1802* (Rutherford: Fairleigh Dickinson University Press, 1990), 99. Gregory argues that governors had to stop short of using martial law in their quest to maintain order.
24. Donaldson, "Britain and Menorca," 120. The local *jurats* and counselors were chosen by ballot for a one-year term in the *universitats*. Four *universitats* governed the four administrative districts of Minorca.
25. See Donaldson, "Britain and Menorca," Chapter 4.

26. Article XI had stipulated that both the ecclesiastical and secular inhabitants "might safely and peaceably enjoy all their estates and honours, and the free use of the Roman Catholic religion shall be permitted . . . provided the same be consistent with the civil government and laws of Great Britain." See "Treaty of Peace and Friendship between Great Britain and Spain signed at Utrecht the 13th July 1713," in *The Consolidated Treaty Series*, vol. 28, ed. Clive Parry (Dobbs Ferry: Oceana Publications, 1969).
27. Indeed, historians have speculated that Queen Anne declared Gibraltar a free port in 1706 in the hopes that merchants and traders might be induced to settle there and might be attracted by the prospect of supplying the garrison and by broader opportunities for trade in the Mediterranean. This was, as Constantine notes, a proclamation published locally. Free port status meant that most goods could be shipped into and out of Gibraltar without the payment of additional duties, although port duties and service charges might still be collected.
28. See Article X of the "Treaty of Utrecht" in Israel, *Major Peace Treaties*, 223. The same article, however, did allow for "Communication by Sea with the Coast of Spain."
29. See Article II of the *Treaty of Peace and Commerce between the King of Great Britain and the Emperor of Morocco dated July 28, 1760*.
30. P. G. Rogers, *A History of Anglo-Moroccan Relations to 1900* (London: Foreign and Commonwealth Office, 1991), 129.
31. Indeed, a recurring issue in governors' correspondence is the problem of provisioning and the various threats to a steady supply of grain or cattle. See CO 91/23; CO 91/33; CO 91/35 for examples of such letters. Sidi Mohammed, the formidable sultan of Morocco between 1757 and 1790, occasionally vowed to suspend shipments of grain or cattle to the garrison of Gibraltar when British governors or consuls did not comply with his wishes, a threat that usually worked and enjoined administrators to pay further ransoms or damages.
32. In 1713, Parliament approved the cost of maintaining seven regiments in the Mediterranean for the purposes of defending the overseas dominions, four of which were to remain in Minorca and three of which were to be housed in Gibraltar. In "Britain and Menorca," Donaldson estimates that there were between 2,400 and 4,000 soldiers in Minorca during the eighteenth century (273). Stephen Constantine estimates that garrison numbers in Gibraltar varied from a minimum of 1,100 to a maximum of 5,000 during the same period (15).
33. Braudel, *The Mediterranean*, 147, 1239.
34. Minorca is about thirty miles long and eight to twelve miles wide. Although it has certain areas with more fertile soil, in the eighteenth century, it was generally only able to feed its own population in good years, and unable to meet the needs of both the civilian and military populations. It did not draw settlers and land speculators in the same way that many of the Atlantic colonies did. Gibraltar, though nearly 1,400 feet high, is merely three miles long and half- to three-quarters of a mile in width. In the eighteenth century, it was an outpost largely devoid of natural resources, a rock on which little could be harvested.

35. GGA—Crown Lands Series A—General Bland's Court of Enquiry in 1749.
36. See Donaldson, "Britain and Menorca," 214, in particular.
37. In "Britain and Menorca," Donaldson does note that the trade in grain from Minorca may have benefited from its free port status, 533–534.
38. Of the ten courts in existence in Minorca when British rule began, the Vice Admiralty Court was the only one that changed significantly and began administering British maritime law as opposed to the maritime laws of Aragon. Similarly, up until 1739, the civil court instituted in Gibraltar in 1721 and composed of a judge advocate and two English Protestant merchants, enforced issues relating to bonds and passes according to "common law" that was largely based on Spanish commercial law. For further details, see Tito Benady, "The Settee Cut: Mediterranean Passes Issued at Gibraltar," *The Mariner's Mirror* 87, no. 3 (2001): 281–296; or Constantine, *Community and Identity*.
39. This is the number traditionally cited by historians of Gibraltar. In *Rock of Contention: A History of Gibraltar* (London: Hale, 1974), George Hills notes that its provenance is a November 1712 report made by Joseph Bennett, the Engineers Colonel, preserved in Add. MS 10034, f. 136 at the British Library, who claimed that "there remained about 30 families . . . and six clergymen, but the whole number of men, women and children did not exceed seventy in all" (177). Constantine estimates that 5,000 Spanish civilians fled Gibraltar and went into exile when it was captured in 1704 (35).
40. GGA—List of Inhabitants (1774). It should be noted that there were 13 "English and Irish" included within the 1,832 "Roman Catholic Inhabitants." Overall, the numbers point to a preponderance of "Roman Catholics" and "foreigners."
41. Article X of the Treaty of Utrecht forbade the settlement of Jews in Gibraltar. For the full text of this article, see Israel, *Major Peace Treaties,* 223–224.
42. GGA—Civil Secretary's Register No. 3—List of Porters for this Garrison for 1774 and 1775. GGA—Civil Secretary's Register No. 3—Orders & Regulations concerning the Boatmen & Fishermen dated January 26, 1774.
43. CO 174/2—Letter from Wynard to Newcaste dated January 25, 1746. A 1745 order in council promised all Greeks "who should settle in this place, such Privileges, Libertys and Immunitys as his Majesty's Subjects now enjoy . . . the Liberty of erecting a Church with a burying place . . . a priest of their own communion." The Minorcans opposed this, and another order was issued in 1749 reiterating that the Greeks were to be allowed into Minorca. For more information about the Greek and Jewish communities in Minorca, see Donaldson, 227–228, 240. The Greeks were expelled by the French in 1756, re-established themselves in 1763, and were then expelled again by the Spanish in 1781. The Jews were banished by the Spanish in 1781, at which point there were said to be 450 of them residing in Minorca.
44. The 1750 census for Minorca noted 21,619 civilians, of whom 546 were non-native (a figure that excluded Britons). See Donaldson, 225–228.
45. CO 174/2—Letter from Blakeney to Bedford dated January 14, 1750/1.
46. CO 91/14—Letter from Cornwallis to Egremont dated September 11, 1763.

47. See CO 389/55—Report from Monson et al. dated July 5, 1744. The report submitted to the king by counsel argued that Greek inhabitants ought to be allowed to settle in Minorca and allowed a church because it would encourage others of their religion to settle there as well, thereby encouraging trade.
48. In 1783, for example, the Emperor of Morocco ordered that provisions for Gibraltar might be exported free of duty for "a certain time," and the governor of Gibraltar responded by licensing ships to make the crossing. See GGA—Civil Secretary's Register No. 4 (1779–1786)—License to Barbary Vessels dated April 28, 1783.
49. Some treaties even specified the duties to be paid by British naval and merchant ships upon landing in the North African ports. See Article II of the *Treaty of Peace and Commerce between the King of Great Britain and the Emperor of Morocco dated July 28, 1760* (London: 1763) or Article II of "Treaty between Great Britain and Algiers, signed April 10, 1682," in Hertslet, A *complete collection of the treaties*, 58–59. Other treaties were more specific about the nature of this trade, including the "Treaty between Great Britain and Morocco, signed July 28, 1760," also in Hertslet, which specified the goods and provisions English subjects were allowed to purchase, in addition to the stipulated duty for those items (106–107).
50. In the "Treaty between Great Britain and Algiers, signed April 10, 1682," for example, Article XII specified that after the ratification of the treaty, "no subjects of His said Majesty shall be bought or sold, or made slaves in any part of the Kingdom of Algiers." See Hertslet, *A complete collection of the treaties*, 61. The first two articles of the "Treaty between Great Britain and Morocco, signed December 15, 1734" provided guidance as to how captured individuals were to be treated by both signatories. See Hertslet, 95.
51. CO 174/2—Letter from Blakeney to Bedford dated July 18, 1750.
52. GGA—Letters to Consuls and Ambassadors—Letter from Raleigh to Houghton dated May 27, 1772.
53. The literature about the Barbary corsairs is extensive. For a particularly useful study of the ways in which corsairing was interlinked with the economies of North Africa, see Ellen G. Friedman, "Christian Captives at Hard Labor in Algiers," *The International Journal of African History* 13, no. 4 (1980): 616–632. See also Sir Godfrey Fisher, *Barbary Legend: War, Trade and Piracy in North Africa, 1415–1830* (Oxford: Clarendon Press, 1957); and John B. Wolf, *The Barbary Coast: Algiers under the Turks, 1500–1830* (New York: Norton & Company, 1979).
54. PC 1/7/147—Records of the Committee of Lords of His Majesty's Most Honorable Privy Council dated March 25, 1765.
55. GGA—Letters to Consuls and Ambassadors—Letter from Raleigh to Houghton dated May 27, 1772.
56. As one secretary of state wrote to the governor of Gibraltar in 1749, the idea of having either to pay the Emperor of Morocco for captives or to break diplomatic relations with him entirely was "not altogether suitable to the dignity of his Majesty's Crown and Character." See CO 389/56—Letter from Bedford to Bland dated

October 19, 1749. But on balance, the British continued to pay ransoms and seek treaties, the king's dignity notwithstanding.

57. T. B. Howell, *A Complete Collection of State Trials*, vol. 20 (London: Hansard, 1816), 82–238.
58. CO 389/56—Letter from Holdernesse to Mr. Attorney and mr. Sollicitor General dated July 14, 1752 and Report upon the case of Peter Romero and John de la Rosa dated [July 26/8?], 1752.
59. FO 3/3—Letter from Fraser to Shelburne dated July 23, 1768.
60. CO 174/15—Letter from J. Baker dated April 27, 1715 and Letter from J. Baker to the Dey of Algier dated August 13, 1715.
61. See Article II of the "Treaty between Great Britain and Algiers, signed October 29, 1716," in Hertslet, *A complete collection of the treaties*, 76–77.
62. See Hertslet, *A complete collection of the treaties*, 137–142, 159–163, 89–92.
63. See *Treaty of Peace and Commerce between Great Britain and the Kingdom of Tripoli concluded September 19, 1751* (London: 1752) and *Treaty of Peace and Commerce between Great Britain and the State of Tunis concluded October 19, 1751* (London: 1752).
64. SP 71/20—Copy of Captain Milbanke's Treaty with Morocco with corresponding articles in former treaties. For the treaties themselves, see Hertslet, *A complete collection of the treaties*, 93–99. For a history of Hanover and the British Empire and of the "personal union," see Nicholas Harding, *Hanover and the British Empire, 1700–1837* (Woodbridge: Boydell Press, 2007).
65. SP 71/20—Fifth Article of Instructions to James Read dated July 26, 1757.
66. See "Treaty between Great Britain and Algiers, signed March 18, 1801" and "Treaty between Great Britain and Algiers, signed April 3, 1816," in Hertslet, *A complete collection of treaties*, 84–85, for Malta and the Ionian Islands.
67. CO 389/54—Instructions for James Wishart dated February 28, 1713.
68. CO 389/54—Letter from Methuen to Cotton dated March 7, 1716/17.
69. FO 3/4—Letter from Fraser to Rochford dated October 7, 1772.
70. FO 3/4—Private Letter from Fraser to Mostyn dated July 25, 1772.
71. In the late 1740s, for example, Secretary of State Bedford was writing to Lieutenant Governor Blakeney, urging him to be particularly watchful of the Catholic clergy in Minorca who would lose no opportunity to overturn the British government (CO 389/56—Letter from Bedford to Blakeney dated February 23, 1748/9). In 1778, there was discussion of using Minorcans in the subterranean defenses of Saint Philip's Castle, but commanders worried that the Minorcans would fail in their duties and desert to enemy lines (CO 174/11—Letter from Skinner to Amherst dated July 3, 1778). Even Gibraltarians were suspected of furnishing intelligence to Britain's enemies (GGA—Letters to Consuls and Ambassadors—Extract of letter from Fraser to Cornwallis dated January 20, 1769).
72. GGA—Civil Secretary's Register 3 (1774–1778)—Certificate given to two British Subjects from Morocco dated October 12, 1775; GGA—Civil Secretary's Register 4 (1779–1786)—Passport for Mr. Gavino dated May 1, 1782.

73. Writing of his travels to Gibraltar in the 1880s, Henry Field also commented on the significant number of Spanish political prisoners and ordinary criminals who had fled Spanish jurisdiction and escaped to Gibraltar. For such individuals, of course, British rule was far preferable to Spanish annexation.
74. CO 389/56—Correspondence between Holdernesse and Attorney and Solicitor Generals dated July 1752 and referring to petition from Peter Romero and John de la Rosa.
75. CO 174/16—Memorial of Salvador Cosino to William Blakeley dated January 31, 1754.
76. CO 174/16—Humble Petition of Gabriel Pratts, Mathias Fabrigas, Francisco Hernandes and Maria Quinbert (wife to Patron Pedro Quinbert) on behalf of themselves and the said Patron & Mariners now Captives in Morocco dated January 31, 1754.
77. CO 91/17—Letter from Lucas to Raleigh dated February 1, 1770.
78. Mediterranean Passes remain an under-explored topic, though Stein's recent piece, "Passes and Protection in the Making of the British Mediterranean," marks a significant step in remedying that historiographical lacuna. For some earlier pieces about British Mediterranean Passes, see Anderson, "Great Britain and the Barbary States"; Benady, "Settee Cut"; and Richardson, "Mediterranean Passes."
79. *Articles of Peace between his Sacred Majesty Charles the II and the City and Kingdom of Algiers* (London: 1664).
80. Benady, "Settee Cut," 281.
81. *Articles of Peace and Commerce between James II and the City and Kingdom of Algiers* (Savoy: 1687).
82. ADM 7/76—Entry dated December 1686 and entitled The Severall Reules, now in Force for the Granting Passes, made since the Peace with Algire in Aprill 1682.
83. The fractions of British seamen required to secure a Mediterranean Pass varied, ranging from two-thirds to three-fourths. At times, the form of the oath merely asked the master to state how many of his seamen were his Majesty's subjects.
84. ADM 7/76—Forme of the Pass and Forme of the Bond directed by the several articles of the preceding rules dated December 1686.
85. The amount charged for these passes at Minorca and Gibraltar was not to exceed twenty-five shillings. For Gibraltar, see Benady, "Settee Cut," 286. For Minorca, see PC 2/88—Orders in Council regarding Mediterranean Passes dated June 14, 1722.
86. FO 3/4—Letter from Fraser to Mostyn dated July 25, 1772.
87. GGA—Diary of Occurrences, Secretary's Office (1777–1778)—Entries for June 15, 1777 and June 17, 1777.
88. FO 52/3—Instructions for Charles Logie dated May 27, 1772.
89. PC 2/85—See various Orders in Council and Proclamations dating from 1714.
90. GGA—Admiralty Book 1—Copy of Order in Council with Instructions for the delivery of Mediterranean Passes at Gibraltar and Port Mahon dated June 14, 1722.
91. PC 2/91—Orders relating to Mediterranean Passes dated December 18, 1729.

92. ADM 2/1321—Letter to Burges dated August 22, 1750.
93. CO 91/11—Letter from Herbert to the Alcayde of Tetuan dated September 2, 1752.
94. CO 1714/2—Letter from Blakeney to Bedford dated January 14, 1750/1.
95. CO 91/14—Letter from Cornwallis to Egremont dated September 11, 1763.
96. PC 2/88—At the Court at Kensington—Orders to the Admiralty and Treasury about calling in old passes and issuing new ones dated June 14, 1722.
97. CO 91/16—Letter from Boyd to Stephens dated August 14, 1769.
98. GGA—Admiralty Book No. 1—Passes returned in March 1777; GGA—List of Inhabitants (1777). Those responsible for these lists tended to classify inhabitants as being from certain hometowns or provinces, including Genoa, Lorno, Sarona, Estepona, and Majorca, which were the names of towns, provinces, or islands within present-day Italy or Spain.
99. CO 91/31—Letter from Eliott to Sydney dated June 25, 1784. The letter encloses several observations and documents relating to Mediterranean Passes.
100. ADM 2/1320—Letter from Burchett to Sabine dated April 30, 1739.
101. ADM 2/1322—Letter from P. S. to Collins dated January 16, 1769.
102. See ADM 2/1320; ADM 2/1321; ADM 2/1322; ADM 2/1323; GGA—Admiralty Book 1.
103. ADM 2/1320—Letter from Burchett to Sabine dated June 13, 1738.
104. FO 3/2—Letter from Sampson to Shelburne dated October 6, 1766.
105. FO 3/6—Letter from Davison to Sydney dated February 25, 1784.
106. PC 1/7/146—By a Committee of the Lords of His Majesty's Most Honorable Privy Council dated March 25, 1765.
107. Colley, *Captives*, 89.
108. Wolf, *The Barbary Coast*, 151. Gillian Weiss offers an extraordinary and more particular documentation of the numbers of Christians enslaved in Algiers, Tunis, Tripoli, and Morocco drawn from references to captives in official correspondence, captivity narratives, the records of religious groups, and secondary sources more generally. See Appendix I in Gillian Weiss, *Captives and Corsairs: France and Slavery in the Early Modern Mediterranean* (Stanford: Stanford University Press, 2011).
109. For a bibliography of English language captivity narratives for the seventeenth and eighteenth centuries, see Colley, *Captives*, 381–382. For an extensive list of French-language captivity narratives for the seventeenth and eighteenth centuries, see Weiss, *Captives and Corsairs*, 326–334.
110. Fisher, *Barbary Legend*, 211–212. Wolf notes that a treaty signed by "those of Algiers" and by Sir Thomas Roe, England's ambassador to the Ottoman Empire, allegedly established peace and allowed English slaves to be freed by purchase as early as 1622 (187). Fisher, however, argues that there is only incomplete information about the 1622 negotiations (195–198).
111. Rogers, *A History of Anglo-Moroccan Relations*, 35.
112. *Articles of Peace between his Sacred Majesty Charles the II and the City and Kingdom of Algiers* (London: 1664).

113. CO 91/13—Copy of an account of His Britannic Majesty's Subjects, Slave to the Emperor of Morocco dated April 30, 1759; Letter from Home to Pitt dated May 24, 1760; Letter from Milbanke dated May 14, 1760.
114. CO 174/15—Letter from Dey of Algier to Baker dated August 26, 1715; SP 71/20—Letter from Parker to [Fox?] dated May 11, 1756; CO 91/13—Letter from Home to Pitt dated August 4, 1760; FO 3/3—Letter from Shelburne to Fraser dated September 30, 1768; FO 3/6—Letter from Woulfe to Weymouth dated August 18, 1779. Interestingly, the redemption of Minorcans continued quite consistently, despite their changing and uncertain status as Minorca moved from French to British control.
115. See Nicholas Harding, "North African Piracy, the Hanoverian Carrying Trade, and the British State, 1728–1828," *The Historical Journal* 43, no. 1 (2000): 25–47; and Nicholas Harding, *Hanover and the British Empire, 1700–1837* (New York: Boydell Press, 2007) for more about the Hanoverian union and about the integrative elements of trade policy between Britain and Hanover. Harding argues that even if the protections accorded to Hanoverians were not necessarily commercially and economically very significant given the small numbers of Hanoverian ships and seamen in the Mediterranean, they were constitutionally significant and an important symbol of the personal union.
116. Harding, "North African Piracy," 31.
117. In "North African Piracy," Harding refers to two specific "rescues" of Hanoverians: according to *Fog's Weekly Journal* No. 98, 8 Hanoverians were rescued in 1730; according to Governor Bland's official correspondence with the secretary of state, 4 Hanoverians were rescued in 1751 (31). In my own research, I have documented several other negotiations over Hanoverians, particularly between Millbanke and the Emperor of Morocco in 1759 and 1760, and between both Nathaniel Davison and Sir Roger Curtis and the Dey of Algiers in 1782 and 1783.
118. CO 91/27—Letter from Eliott to Hillsborough dated May 2, 1781.
119. Correspondence relating to this case can be found in CO 91/28; CO 91/29; CO 91/30; FO 3/6; and FO 113/3. An extract in FO 3/6 lists Podesta and others as "taken by the Algerines the 27 September 1780." Davison's letter to Fox dated June 6, 1782, also in FO 3/6, notes that Podesta and his crew were taken "near two years ago."
120. CO 91/29—Letter from Townshend to Eliott dated December 31, 1782.
121. For the details of Sir Roger Curtis's embassy, see FO 113/3.
122. FO 3/6—Letter from Sydney to Logie dated May 20, 1785. The Worshipful Company of Ironmongers, originally known as the Ferroners, were incorporated by Royal Charter in 1463. One of the first livery companies in the City of London, the Company was a trade association of iron merchants and, to this day, remains a charitable institution. In the eighteenth century, the Ironmongers often provided funds for ransoming slaves from North Africa.
123. CO 91/34—Letter from Eliott to Sydney dated May 28, 1787.
124. FO 3/6—Letter from Davison to Eliott dated May 25, 1782.
125. CO 91/11—Letter from Herbert to the Alcayde of Tetuan dated September 2, 1752.

126. FO 3/6—List of Eleven Deserters from Oran who have applied to Consul Logie enclosed in Logie's letter dated February 17, 1788.
127. CO 91/28—Extracts of letters from Davison to Eliott dated August 16, 1781; FO 3/6—Letter from Davison to Eliott dated May 7 1782.
128. CO 91/28—Extract of letter from Davison to Eliott dated January 3, 1782.
129. FO 113/3—Report of the Transactions at Algiers between the Dey & Regency & Sir Roger Curtis dated November 20, 1783.
130. It is hard to pinpoint the variables that shaped consular negotiations. Many consuls were likely under the impression that they could ask for only a certain number of captives, an approximate number that might have been determined by how many men and women were actually enslaved, how much the dey or emperor needed ransom money or how willing he appeared to be to part with captives, how many North African slaves had recently been freed in Europe, the current state of relations between the Barbary states and Great Britain, and whether or not the consul had arrived with a costly gift.
131. FO 3/3—Letter from Fraser to Shelburne dated April 14, 1768.
132. FO 3/3—Letter from Shelburne to Fraser dated July 8, 1768. Shelburne enclosed the letter from the king but asked Fraser not to deliver the royal letter to the dey unless absolutely necessary.
133. GGA—Letters from Consuls—Letter from Aspinwall to Pitt dated June 12, 1761.
134. For more on the emergence of passports issued by central governments, see John Torpey, *The Invention of the Passport: Surveillance, Citizenship, and the State* (Cambridge: Cambridge University Press, 1999). For an account of the significance of Customs House certificates in the early American republic, see Nathan Perl-Rosenthal, *Citizen Sailors: Becoming American in the Age of Revolution* (Cambridge, MA: Harvard University Press, 2015).
135. FO 3/6—Letter from Davison to Eliott dated August 16, 1781.
136. FO 113/3—Report of the Transactions at Algiers between the Dey & Regency & Sir Roger Curtis dated November 20, 1783.
137. FO 3/6—Letter from Logie to Sydney dated February 17, 1788.
138. FO 52/3—Letter from Logie to Rochford dated September 18, 1775.
139. Consul Davison required proof by certificate of Hanoverian affiliation. See CO 91/28 and FO 3/6.
140. GGA—Civil Secretary's Register Book 4 (1779–1786) —Secretary's Office, entry for December 10, 1783.
141. See *The Complete Poetical Works of James Thomson*, ed. J. Logie Robertson (Oxford: 1908), 420, as quoted in Linda Colley, *Britons: Forging the Nation, 1707–1837* (New Haven: Yale University Press, 1992), 11.
142. Gillian Weiss, "Barbary Captivity and the French Idea of Freedom," *French Historical Studies* 28, no. 2 (2005): 239, 253. See also Weiss, *Captives and Corsairs*, Introduction.
143. See among others PC 2/85—Proclamation for recalling & prohibiting seamen from serving Foreigners read and approved on June 5, 1716. Proclamations relating

to recalling seamen appear consistently in the Privy Council Registers, particularly during times of war.

144. CO 91/35—By the King a Proclamation for recalling and prohibiting seamen from serving Foreign Princes and States given at Our Court the 22nd March 1788.

145. Colley, *Captives*, 53. The English state was well known for its "meanness." As Colley notes, ransoming captives "received low governmental priority" before 1700. The fact that the governors of Gibraltar, in particular, became involved with redemptions beginning in the early eighteenth century may have improved captives' chances of being freed.

146. CO 91/12—Letter from Tyrawley to Barrington dated February 18, 1757.

147. He was also aware that deserters were shot by the sentence of a court-martial at Gibraltar. See GGA—Civil Secretary's Register 3—Entry dated March 16, 1776, where David Hicky was sentenced to be shot to death for desertion.

148. On at least one occasion, O'Hara expressed sympathy for the "fate of poor Patron Migone" from Gibraltar and suggested to Consul Logie that he could "second" his representations to the dey, presumably in the hopes of freeing him. See GGA—Letters to Consuls & Ambassadors—Letter from O'Hara to Logie dated September 27, 1789.

149. GGA—Letters to Consuls and Ambassadors—Letter from O'Hara to Logie dated November 28, 1787.

150. FO 3/6—Letter from Davison to Hillsborough dated July 7, 1780.

151. FO 3/6—Letter from Logie to Sydney dated July 10, 1786.

152. FO 52/3—Letter from Logie to Rochford dated September 18, 1775.

153. CO 91/20—Letter from Boyd to the Emperor of Morocco dated April 6, 1774.

154. CO 91/20—Numerous letters in this volume relate to promises made to return British deserters. The August 26, 1774, letter from Rochford to Boyd signals the conclusion of these negotiations.

155. FO 3/1—Letter from Aspinwall to Pitt dated June 12, 1761.

156. These beliefs were also prevalent among the consuls. See among others GGA—Letters from Consuls—Letter from Fraser dated April 24, 1765.

CHAPTER 4

1. CO 101/5—Letter from Leybourne to Hillsborough dated November 22, 1771.

2. I will use the term "the Province of Quebec" or "Quebec" to refer to the Province of Quebec as it was defined after the cession of "Canada" to the British in 1763. The three districts of Québec, Trois Rivières, and Montréal remained united in the British "Province of Quebec." This new British territory encompassed lands on both banks of the St. Lawrence River from Ottawa River to Anticosti Island with a western point at Lake Nipissing. When appropriate, I will also use the term "Canada" to refer to this same region during the period of French rule. "Canada" was one of the French territories in North America known as "New France," which also included

Acadia, Hudson Bay, Newfoundland, and Louisiana at various points in the seventeenth and eighteenth centuries. Although "Canada" and "New France" are sometimes used interchangeably, namely because Canada was the most important of the French territories in North America, I prefer the term "Canada" for clarity's sake. During the period of French rule, "Québec" referred either to the district of Québec or to the city of Québec.

3. CO 42/2—Letter from Murray to the Lords Commissioners dated October 29, 1764.
4. Colin Calloway, *The Scratch of a Pen: 1763 and the Transformation of North America* (New York: Oxford University Press, 2006), xi. The expression is one originally used by Francis Parkman.
5. Population figures for Grenada are drawn from Raymond Devas, *Conception Island: The Troubled Story of the Catholic Church in Grenada* (London: Sands and Co., 1932), 38; Javier A. Gonzalez, "A Strange Discordant Mass of Heterogeneous Animals: The Role of Ethnic Divisions in British Grenada, 1763–1779" (Harvard University: unpublished BA thesis, 1994), 19–21. Population figures for Quebec are estimated based on several sources: Philip Lawson, *The Imperial Challenge: Quebec and Britain in the Age of the American Revolution* (Montreal: McGill–Queen's University Press, 1994); Pierre George, *Le Quebec* (Paris: PUF, 1979); and Pierre Tousignant, "The Integration of the Province of Quebec into the British Empire, 1763–1791," in *Dictionary of Canadian Biography*, vol. 4 (Toronto: University of Toronto Press, 1979), xxxii–xlix. Tousignant puts the number of French Catholics at 60,000 in the early 1760s; George at 65,000 in 1763; Lawson at 70,000 for the 1760s.
6. Traditional hostility toward Roman Catholics in Great Britain has usually been attributed to their perceived untrustworthiness and potential threat to the establishment, as well as to the ongoing wars that were fought against the Catholic powers of Europe. For classic accounts of anti-Catholicism in Britain during the eighteenth century, see Colin Haydon, *Anti-Catholicism in Eighteenth-Century England, c. 1714–80: A Political and Social Study* (Manchester: Manchester University Press, 1993); C. D. A. Leighton, *Catholicism in a Protestant Kingdom: A Study of the Irish Ancien Regime* (New York: St. Martin's Press, 1994); and Edward Norman, *Roman Catholicism in England from the Elizabethan Settlement to the Second Vatican Council* (Oxford: Oxford University Press, 1985). The most influential argument about the ways in which wars with the Catholic powers of Europe, particularly France, shaped British national identity, Protestantism, and sense of distinctiveness, remains Linda J. Colley, *Britons: Forging the Nation, 1707–1837* (New Haven: Yale University Press, 1992). Caitlin Anderson makes the argument that both Catholics and religious non-conformists in Britain and its empire were often viewed as being of "compromised allegiance" (204). See Caitlin Anderson, "Old Subjects, New Subjects, and Non-Subjects: Silences and Subjecthood," in *War, Empire, and Slavery, 1770–1830* eds. Jane Rendall, Nicholas Guyatt, and Richard Bessel (Houndsmills: Palgrave, 2010), 201–217.

7. The assorted penal laws were designed to protect Britain against the possibility that Catholic subjects might nurture and abet plans for a foreign invasion of the British Isles, might seek to restore the deposed Catholic Stuarts to the throne, or might more generally subvert the government by obtaining positions of trust. Although the specific penal laws varied from kingdom to kingdom, they generally outlawed the Catholic clergy and holding of mass, curtailed Catholic education and landholding, barred Catholics from military service and restricted their right to bear arms, and blocked Catholics from legal, acadmic, and political offices. The question of whether these various penal laws extended to the colonies was therefore particularly thorny.
8. John Bartlett Brebner, *New England's Outpost: Acadia before the Conquest of Canada* (New York: Columbia University Press, 1927); N. E. S. Griffiths, *From Migrant to Acadian: A North American Border People, 1604–1755* (Montreal: McGill–Queen's University Press, 2005); Christopher Hodson, *The Acadian Diaspora: An Eighteenth-Century History* (New York: Oxford University Press, 2012); and Geoffrey Plank, *An Unsettled Conquest: The British Campaign against the Peoples of Acadia* (Philadelphia: University of Pennsylvania Press, 2001). The Acadians were descendants of the seventeenth-century French colonists who settled in Acadia, a colony of New France. They were predominantly, though not always, Roman Catholic.
9. Ignotus, *Thoughts on trade in general, our West-Indian in particular, our Continental colonies, Canada, Guadeloupe, and the preliminary articles of peace addressed to the community* (London: 1763), 5, 12.
10. Ignotus, *Thoughts on trade in general*, 44.
11. As quoted in Calloway, *The Scratch of a Pen*, 114.
12. CO 101/1—Letter from Scott dated May 15, 1763.
13. CO 42/2—Letter from Murray to the Lords Commissioners dated October 29, 1764.
14. The only governor who was recognizably hostile to some French demands in his official letters was Grenada's Robert Melvill. However, it would appear that he helped push through a 1766 ordinance that gave French inhabitants the right to vote for assembly representatives despite Andrew Jackson O'Shaughnessy's claim that he had been part of an anti-Catholic club in Edinburgh (see *An Empire Divided: The American Revolution and the British Caribbean* [Philadelphia: University of Pennsylvania Press, 2000], 125). He seems to have turned against the French Catholic planters when a small group of them demanded the right to sit in the assembly and sent Alexandre Cazaud to London with a petition to that effect in 1767. Many of the pamphlets published in the late 1760s demonized Melvill, but official correspondence suggests that Melvill tried to cleave a middle path between the conflicting demands made of him.
15. CO 101/1—Memorial from His Majesty's Natural Born Subjects in the Island of Grenada attested February 14, 1766.
16. CO 42/25—1765 memorial with charges against Governor James Murray.

17. Petitioners from both Grenada and Quebec used the terms "address," "memorial," and "petition" when entitling their submissions to the monarch. I tend to favor the term "petition," because of the humility it implies and because the "right of petition" was that asserted by contemporaries, but the terms were often used interchangeably. As the work of both Mark Knights and James Bradley suggests, however, "address" sometimes had a more specific meaning, referring to addresses of loyalty presented to the monarch. These might be offered at moments such as the accession or during political crises; the "addresses" in favor of coercion and the government's position were contrasted with the "petitions" for peace during the American Revolutionary War. See Mark Knights, "Addressing the monarch" (unpublished paper) and James E. Bradley, *Popular Politics and the American Revolution in England* (Macon, GA: Mercer University Press, 1986).
18. David Zaret, *Origins of Democratic Culture: Printing, Petitions, and the Public Sphere in Early-Modern England* (Princeton: Princeton University Press, 2000), 86.
19. Zaret, *Origins of Democratic Culture*, 86; and Geoffrey Koziol, *Begging Pardon and Favor: Ritual and Political Order in Early Medieval France* (Ithaca: Cornell University Press, 1992), 44–45.
20. Nira Wickramasinghe, "La Petition Coloniale: Objet de Contrôle, Objet de Dissidence," *Identity, Culture & Politics: An Afro-Asian Dialogue* 7, no. 1 (2006): 1–16.
21. CO 102/1—Letter to the Privy Council from Clare, Dyson, and Fitzherbert dated November 20, 1767.
22. CO 42/7—Letter from Merchants trading to Quebec to Hillsborough dated New York Coffee House the September 20, 1768.
23. Indeed, clashes over Catholics' admission into the Grenada Council and Assembly and over their right to French civil laws finally guaranteed by the Quebec Act (1774) are documented in just about every text written about Grenada and Quebec, respectively. See George Brizan, *Grenada, Island of Conflict: From Amerindians to People's Revolution, 1498–1979* (London: Zed Books, 1984); Reginald Coupland, *The Quebec Act: A Study in Statesmanship* (Oxford: Clarendon Press, 1925); Devas, *Concepcion Island*; Gonzalez, "A Strange Discordant Mass"; Lawson, *The Imperial Challenge*; Peter Marshall, "The Incorporation of Quebec in the British Empire, 1763–1774," in *Of Mother Country and Plantations: Proceedings of the Twenty-Seventh Conference in Early American History*, eds. V. B. Platt and D. C. Skaggs (Bowling Green, OH: Bowling Green State University, 1970), 42–64; Karl David Milobar, "The Constitutional Deveopment of Quebec from the Time of the French Regime to the Canada Act of 1791" (PhD diss., University of London, 1990); Hilda Neatby, *The Administration of Justice under the Quebec Act* (Minneapolis: The University of Minnesota Press, 1937); Carolee Pollock, "His Majesty's Subjects: Political Legitimacy in Quebec, 1764–1791" (PhD diss., University of Alberta, 1996); and Beverley A. Steele, *Grenada: A History of Its People* (Oxford: Macmillan Caribbean, 2003). Few historical works have attempted to compare these animosities with those that occurred virtually

simultaneously in Quebec during the 1760s and 1770s, and which continued in both colonies well into the 1780s and 1790s.

24. For that matter, they were also aware that the rights of Catholic subjects in North America more generally, might also be relevant. In Grenada, petitioners noted instances in other colonies where Roman Catholics and Dissenters had been permitted to elect representatives. See CO 101/1—Memorial of His Majesty's Adopted Subjects in the Island of Grenada attested February 14, 1766.
25. CO 174/16—Letter from Robert Walpole on behalf of the Council requesting that a copy of the Archbishop of Canterbury's report relating to the Church Government of Minorca in 1718 be transmitted to the Council Office dated November 12, 1765. From this letter, it appears that the Archbishop of Canterbury had taken the question of the Catholic Church's position in Minorca into consideration, but that the report of 1718 was missing. Nonetheless, the desire to consult previous reports and to compare Minorca and Quebec seems evident.
26. William Knox, *The justice and policy of the late act of Parliament for making more effectual provision for the government of the province of Quebec, asserted and proved: and the conduct of administration respecting that province stated and vindicated* (London: 1774), 20, 26. For Knox, the marginalization of Irish Catholics had not worked to convert or attach them to England, whereas the more lenient policies in Minorca "were more promising."
27. J. Wright, ed., *Debates of the House of Commons in the year 1774, on the Bill for Making More Effectual Provision for the Government of the Province of Quebec* (London: 1839), 41.
28. CO 101/12—Letter from Melvill to Hillsborough dated May 25, 1768, for example. This was also the repeated refrain of entries in *The Political Register* hostile to the new subjects in Grenada and Quebec. See in particular "Strictures on the Conduct of two successive Administrations with Respect to the civil and religious Establishments in Canada and the Grenadines," in John Almon, *The Political Register*, May 1769, No. 26, 268.
29. "Strictures on the Conduct," in Almon, *The Political Register*, 257–273.
30. R. A. Humphreys, "Lord Shelburne and the Proclamation of 1763," *The English Historical Review* 49, no. 194 (1934), 252; *Journal of the Commissioners for Trade and Plantations*, vol. 70.
31. Adam Shortt and Arthur G. Doughty, *Documents relating to the Constitutional History of Canada, 1759–1791* (Ottawa: J. de L. Taché, 1918), 165.
32. Lawrence Henry Gipson, *The British Empire Before the American Revolution*, vol. 9 (*The Triumphant Empire: New Responsibilities within the Enlarged Empire, 1763–1766*) (New York: Knopf, 1956), 19.
33. See Pollock, "His Majesty's Subjects," 32, 171.
34. For copies of capitulations for Québec and Montréal, which fell in 1759 and 1760, respectively, see Shortt and Doughty, *Documents relating to the Constitutional History of Canada*. In the case of Grenada, French armies surrendered without a shot

having been fired on March 5, 1762, with the understanding that soldiers and inhabitants would be granted the protections and privileges accorded to Martinique, captured that same month, and Guadeloupe, which had capitulated in 1759. A copy of the capitulation signed for Martinique can be found in Robert Beatson, *Naval and Military Memoirs of Great Britain*, vol. 3 (London: 1790), 368–379. See Gipson, *The Triumphant Empire*, 239, for more about these capitulations.

35. Tousignant, "The Integration of the Province of Quebec," xxxii–xxxiii.
36. "Strictures on the Conduct," in Almon, *The Political Register*, 268.
37. Shortt and Doughty, eds., *Documents relating to the Constitutional History of Canada*, 33. Amherst could not allow the *Canadiens* to remain neutral in case of another conflict with France, articulating instead that they were "subjects."
38. The monarch's prerogative to bestow laws upon a conquered country was discussed in numerous cases, including *Calvin v. Smith* (1608), *Blankard v. Galdy* (1694), and *Smith v. Brown and Cooper* (1702).
39. Shortt and Doughty, *Documents relating to the Constitutional History of Canada*, 113–122.
40. See Humphreys, "Lord Shelburne and the Proclamation of 1763," 241–264. Attorney-General James Marriott commented on how "hurried" the provisions of 1763 seemed, and Robert Henley, Lord Northington, who was Lord Chancellor at the time, called the proclamation a "very silly document."
41. Tousignant, "The integration of the province of Quebec," xl.
42. CO 102/1—Draught of a Commission for Robert Melvill Esquire to be Governor of Grenada dated October 4, 1764. The commission did specify that persons elected to the assembly would be required to take the various oaths "for extinguishing the hopes of the pretended Prince of Wales and his open and secret abettors" and that they would be required to make various declarations to that effect. The same was not said, however, of the freeholders who would elect those assembly members.
43. CO 102/1—Representation to His Majesty with draught of General Instructions . . . for Robert Melvill dated November 3, 1763.
44. For a comparative analysis of the "repugnancy principle" so important to the Atlantic world, see Mary Sarah Bilder, *The Transatlantic Constitution: Colonial Legal Culture and the Empire* (Cambridge, MA: Harvard University Press, 2004).
45. See "Commission appointing James Murray Captain General and Governor in Chief of the Province of Quebec dated November 21, 1763," in Shortt and Doughty, *Documents relating to the Constitutional History of Canada*, 126–132.
46. CO 43/8—Letter from Hillsborough to the Lieutenant Governor of Quebec dated March 6, 1768.
47. SP 78/268—Letter from Conway to Le Marquis de Blesset dated October 3, 1763.
48. See CO 101/1—Memorial of several of His Majesty's Natural Born Subjects in the Island of Grenada attested February 14, 1766; Memorial of His Majesty's Adopted Subjects in the Island of Grenada attested February 14, 1766.

49. CO 101/1—Memorial of the British Protestant Inhabitants of the Island of Grenada attested February 14, 1766. Although the individuals who signed the petition did not develop the argument that French Catholics were still aliens "in point of law," it is quite possible they believed that only individuals born within the dominions of the monarch or naturalized by act of Parliament were true subjects.
50. *Journal of the Commissioners for Trade and Plantations*, vols. 70–72 (London: Published by His Majesty's Stationery Office, 1935).
51. CO 323/18/1—Report of His Majesty's Attorney General dated July 27, 1764 on the question whether those Subjects of the Crowns of France and Spain, who remain in the ceded Countries in America, are to be considered as Aliens. Although the Lords Commissioners further considered this report between November and December 1764, it is unclear whether they ever acted directly upon this legal ruling.
52. CO 42/2—Letter to the Lords Commissioners for Trade and Plantations dated June 10, 1765, signed Norton and de Grey. This report is reproduced in many other locations.
53. CO 42/7—Report from Marriott to the Privy Council dated January 18, 1768.
54. These rulings were in line with the determinations in 1722 and 1759 that held that acts of Parliament made after the English had inhabited a colony must specifically name that colony in order to be applicable there. In *The Imperial Challenge*, Lawson references legal rulings in Maryland that determined that Elizabethan anti-Catholic legislation applied only to colonies under English rule when those acts had been passed (45).
55. CO 43/8—Letter from Hillsborough to Carleton dated June 12, 1770.
56. CO 42/42—Letter from Shelburne to Haldimand dated April 22, 1782.
57. Thomas Jeffreys, *Description of the Island of Grenada and Its Different Quarters* (London: 1760), as quoted in Mark Quintanilla, "The World of Alexander Campbell: An Eighteenth-Century Grenadian Planter," *Albion: A Quarterly Journal* 35, 2 (2003), 235.
58. John Campbell, *Candid and impartial considerations on the nature of the sugar trade* (London: 1763), 177; Young, *Some observations which may contribute to afford a just idea of the nature, importance, and settlement, of our new West-India colonies* (London: 1764), 1.
59. Young, *Some observations*, 25.
60. Quintanilla, "The World of Alexander Campbell," 245.
61. Sir William Young, *Some observations*, 35; and Sir William Young, *Considerations which may tend to promote the settlement of our new West-India colonies, by encouraging individuals to embark in the undertaking* (London: 1764), 14. Young believed that Grenada would be settled principally by "persons already in the West Indies" who lived on neighboring islands, as well as by a few adventurers and laborers from Great Britain and Ireland. See 10–15, 50.
62. CO 101/10—Letter from Melvill to Halifax dated February 17, 1765; CO 101/1—Letter from Melvill to the Lords Commissioners dated February 7, 1765.

63. CO 102/1—Representation to His Majesty upon the method of disposing of Lands in the islands dated November 3, 1763; CO 101/1—Report of the Privy Council dated February 10, 1764.
64. Young, *Some observations*, 43.
65. Population figures for Grenada are drawn from Devas, *Conception Island,* 38; and Gonzalez, "A Strange Discordant Mass of Heterogeneous Animals," 19–21. Gonzalez notes that Governor Scott reported 3,500 white inhabitants living under French rule. This may reflect inflated French projections or Scott's own desire to emphasize the dangers of depopulation to his superiors. The number agreed upon by most scholars is 1,225.
66. PC 1/59/5/2—Representation of the Board of Trade upon a Plan for the Disposal of His Majesty's Lands in Grenada, St. Vincent's, Dominica & Tobago dated November 3, 1763. In this report, Yorke, Gascoyne, Hillsborough, Jenyns, and Bacon noted that many of the French planters currently in the British islands might be induced to leave for the neighboring French islands where they would be welcomed with open arms given the slaves they would bring with them.
67. This argument is made most persuasively for Grenada by Edward Cox, *Free Coloreds in the Slave Societies of St. Kitts and Grenada, 1763–1833* (Knoxville: University of Tennessee Press, 1984), 80–81. He suggests that in an attempt to maintain control over its non-white population, the government was willing to make certain concessions to its new subjects.
68. In 1763, historians estimate that there were approximately 12,000 slaves in the island of Grenada; this number had more than doubled to 24,620 by the mid-1780s. See, in particular, Cox, *Free Coloreds in the Slave Societies of St. Kitts and Grenada*, 13–14.
69. CO 102/15—Letter from Hillsborough to Melvill dated March 8, 1768.
70. CO 102/1—Letter from Jenyns, Rice, Roberts, Fitzherbert, and Lisburne to the King's Most Excellent Majesty dated March 2, 1770.
71. As numerous authors have noted, even if popular antipathy to Catholics remained strong and might suddenly be transformed into dangerous animosity, as it did with the Gordon Riots in 1780, the deadliest riots in London's history, a spirit of toleration was emerging more generally among the British elite by the second half of the eighteenth century. Colin Haydon, in particular, examines how popular hostility might coexist with an elite and "official" tendency to move toward policies of toleration. This tolerant inclination was made possible not only by the spirit of the Enlightenment but also by an alignment of factors within Great Britain and the British Empire, including the waning of the Jacobite threat, the involvement of Irish, Scottish, and other Catholics in the imperial enterprise, and the perceived unlikelihood of an imminent French attack in the 1760s. See Haydon, *Anti-Catholicism*; and Ole Peter Grell and Roy Porter, eds., *Toleration in Enlightenment Europe* (Cambridge: Cambridge University Press, 2000).
72. Shortt and Doughty, *Documents relating to the Constitutional History of Canada*, 165.

73. CO 102/1—Additional Instructions to Melvill dated February 27, 1766. The Additional Instructions gave official confirmation of an earlier decision reached in London. The February 14, 1766 petitions from Grenada indicate awareness of discussion relating to this Assembly, as does the Ordinance for regulating elections of the General Assembly, attested February 14, 1766 and included in Robert Melvill's March 1, 1766 letter in CO 101/1. Prior to receiving his official instructions, Melvill had obviously already supervised the drafting of ordinances for regulating elections.
74. The date of this "Ordinance for Regulating the Elections for the General Assembly of Grenada," found in CO 101/1, is unclear. Attested on February 14, 1766, and included in Melvill's letter of March 1, 1766, it was likely produced several months earlier. The petition from British Protestants residing in the island of Grenada was dated December 28, 1765 (though it was only attested on February 14, 1766), and it queried whether permitting French Catholics to vote was not striking at the root of the constitution itself. This led Lawrence Henry Gipson to conclude that Roman Catholics who had taken the oath of allegiance and been confirmed in the possession of lands were admitted to exercise the franchise in Grenada as early as 1765 (see Gipson, *The Triumphant Empire*).
75. For a list of the members of this first assembly, see "A List of the Members chosen Representatives to serve in the Assembly" included in the appendices of Anonymous, *Audi alteram Partem, or a Counter-Letter to the Right Hon. The E—l of H—ll—gh* (London: 1770).
76. CO 101/1—Memorial of the Undersigned British Protestant Inhabitants of the Island of Grenada, attested February 14, 1766. A printed copy of this petition can also be found in the appendix of *Audi alteram Partem* and is dated December 28, 1765.
77. CO 101/1—Memorial of His Majesty's Adopted Subjects in the Island of Grenada, attested February 14, 1766.
78. The religious identities of these petitioners are difficult to ascertain. They were likely a diverse group: some may have been Catholics of Irish or Scottish origin; some were likely nonconformists or dissenters with a vested interest in seeing rights extended to non-Anglicans; some may have been Anglicans but chose to differentiate themselves from the "British Protestants" who attacked the French Catholics.
79. CO 101/1—Memorial of several of His Majesty's Natural Born Subjects in the Island of Grenada, attested February 14, 1766.
80. Anonymous, *The Grenada Planter: or, a Full and Impartial Answer to a Letter in the Gazetteer of October 22, 1768* (London: 1768), 10.
81. Anonymous, *The Grenada Planter*, 15.
82. See Anonymous, *Audi alteram Partem*, 15 of appendices. The author notes that the motion made by Mr. Pigot and seconded by Mr. Robertson was inserted in the *Grenada Gazette*.
83. Anonymous, *The Grenada Planter*, 17.
84. Anonymous, *Audi alteram Partem*, 16 of appendices.

85. A copy of this protest can be found in Anonymous, *Audi alteram Partem*, 18–19 of appendices. As *The Grenada Planter* makes clear, the new subjects acted "conformable to the Civil Law, to which the new Subjects had formerly been accustomed" (so French civil law) when they read the protest. See 17–18.
86. Anonymous, *The Grenada Planter*, 18–19.
87. Anonymous, *The Grenada Planter*, 20.
88. CO 101/2—Letter from Melvill to the Right Honorable Lords Commissioners dated January 31, 1768.
89. Anonymous, *The Grenada Planter*, 19.
90. CO 101/2—Letter from Melvill to Hillsborough dated May 10, 1768.
91. CO 101/2—Tres Humble Adresse des Nouveaux Sujets de Sa Majeste de l'Isle de la Grenade au tres Honorable Comte de Shelburne (received October 1767 but undated).
92. This petition can be found as Appendix VI in Anonymous, *Audi alteram Partem. The Grenada Planter* notes that it was signed by 337 persons on page 24.
93. Both governors Melvill and Fitzmaurice were recalled in order to answer charges against them in their handling of struggles between Grenadian inhabitants, illustrating the widespread anger of many in the island and their influence in London. The inquiry against Robert Melvill was well documented, particularly in pamphlets such as Anonymous, *A Narrative of the Proceedings Upon the Complaint against Governor Melvill* (London: 1770) and Anonymous, *Audi alteram Partem*. Articles of complaint were sent to England in late October 1769 and Melvill was called to answer those charges before the Privy Council on February 20, 1770. He was informed of his acquittal in April 1770. See CO 101/14—Letter from Hillsborough to Melvill. The inquiry against Ulysses Fitzmaurice was less publicized and revolved around his confusion as to when he should admit two new subjects to the Grenada Council. See CO 101/3—Letter from Hillsborough to Fitzmaurice dated May 13, 1769; and CO 101/14—Letter from Hillsborough to Fitzmaurice dated April 21, 1770.
94. CO 101/3—Letter from humble subjects in Grenada to Hillsborough dated October 4, 1769 and Minutes from the Meeting of the Council at St. Georges dated September 25, 1769.
95. CO 101/5—Petition of the freeholders, merchants and others to Leyborne dated January 30, 1772.
96. CO 101/16—Statement of those suspended from the Council Board dated December 6, 1771.
97. See, for example, the discussion of a parliamentary act for Quebec. The arguments made in Grenada might also be contrasted with arguments made in the thirteen colonies for royal protection against parliamentary incursion into rights.
98. It should be noted, of course, that instructions sent to governors rarely show much change or change only very slowly. Nonetheless, the instructions sent to Melvill (1768), Fitzmaurice (1769), Leyborne (1771), Macartney (1775–1776), and Green (1796) still included the paragraph(s) noting that a certain number of new subjects were entitled to sit in the council and assembly and to be exempt from the Test.

99. Cox, *Free Coloreds in the Slave Societies of St. Kitts and Grenada*, 13–14.
100. Devas, *Conception Island*, 38; Gonzalez, "A Strange Discordant Mass," 19–21.
101. CO 101/26—Private information on the present state of the Island of Grenada and its Value and Importance to the Crown of Great Britain. It should be noted, however, that this undated report enclosed with other documents from 1786 was submitted by "British Merchants" who likely had an interest in suggesting that the French presence was negligible.
102. CO 101/26—Resolutions dated March 2, 1786. A letter dated April 1, 1787, referred to the "new election bill, passed some months since by the Assembly" (CO 101/27).
103. This date for the Privy Council ruling is taken from secondary sources about Grenada and from an incomplete draft of the Attorney General's report on the status of Roman Catholics in the Privy Council papers. I have been unable to locate the text of the original ruling. The correspondence for Grenada indicates awareness that this matter was before the Privy Council. A letter sent to Governor Mathew, dated May 22, 1790, noted that the claims of the new subjects were "still under consideration of the Privy Council" (CO 101/30).
104. CO 101/27—Copy of the Honorable Alexander Symson's letter dated January 11, 1787.
105. For an account of Fedon's Rebellion, see Edward L. Cox, "Fedon's Rebellion, 1795–96: Causes and Consequences," *The Journal of Negro History* 67, no. 1 (Spring 1982): 7–19. For an account of how convictions for treason during and after this rebellion worked to "define the convict as a British subject," see Anderson, "Old Subjects, New Subjects, and Non-Subjects."
106. Beverley A. Steele, "Grenada, an Island State, Its History and Its People," *Caribbean Quarterly* 20 (1974): 5–43.
107. Sir William Blackstone, *Commentaries on the Laws of England*, ed. Stanley N. Katz (Chicago: University of Chicago Press, 1979).
108. Lawson, *The Imperial Challenge*, 4, 7. Several pamphlets considered the relative worth of Canada versus Guadeloupe, including: *The reasons for keeping Guadaloupe at a Peace, preferable to Canada, explained in five letters from a gentleman in Guadaloupe to his friend in London* (London: 1761); *A detection of the false reasons and facts, contained in the five letters, entitled Reasons for keeping Guadaloupe at the peace, preferable to Canada, by a member of Parliament* (London: 1761); Benjamin Franklin, *The Interest of Great Britain considered: with regard to her colonies, and the acquisitions of Canada and Guadaloupe* (London: 1761); and Ignotus, *Thoughts on trade in general, our West-Indian in particular, our Continental colonies, Canada, Guadaloupe, and the preliminary articles of peace addressed to the community* (London: 1763).
109. Ignotus, *Thoughts on trade*.
110. Administrators also recognized that French influence with indigenous peoples might be a double-edged sword. While Carleton argued that admitting some of the Canadian noblesse to the council would greatly assist the council in their

management of Indian affairs, Murray and Halifax recognized the dangers of Canadians joining the Indians "over whom they have great influence." See CO 42/7—Letter from Carleton to Hillsborough dated March 15, 1769; CO 42/25—Letter from Murray to Halifax dated March 9, 1764; CO 42/1—Letter from Halifax to the Lords of Trade dated May 21, 1762.

111. See supra 5.

112. Tousignant, "The integration of the province of Quebec," xxxiv. In *The Scratch of a Pen*, Calloway notes that only 270 French Canadians left the colony after the peace (114). Article IV of the Treaty of Paris gave inhabitants eighteen months to emigrate from the colony "with all safety and freedom."

113. See Maya Jasanoff, *Liberty's Exiles: American Loyalists in the Revolutionary World* (New York: Alfred A. Knopf, 2011), 354. The demographic imbalance was still evident in 1774, when observers noted that there were anywhere from 80,000 to 150,000 French Catholics as opposed to a few thousand British Protestants. Studies of the Quebec Act tend to concur that there were approximately 90,000 inhabitants in "Canada," of whom the vast majority were of French origin in 1774. However, contemporaries offered a range of other estimates. Tousignant notes that the reports of law officers in the 1770s suggested that there were more like 80,000 "new subjects" (See "The integration of the province of Quebec," xlvii). Examined by the House of Commons in 1774, both Francis Maseres and Guy Carleton stated that there were 150,000 *Canadiens* then in the province. Carleton also referred to a 1770 return that listed 360 Protestants in the province of Quebec. For more information about these hearings and an analysis of the population of Quebec in the 1770s, see Wright, *Debates of the House of Commons in the year 1774*, 103–131.

114. As quoted in Coupland, *The Quebec Act*, 19.

115. CO 42/2—Letter from Murray to the Lords Commissioners dated October 29, 1764.

116. CO 42/27—Letter from Carleton to Lords Commissioners of Trade dated March 28, 1767; CO 42/7—Letter from Carleton to Shelburne dated January 20, 1768; CO 42/27—Letter from Carleton to Hillsborough dated March 15, 1769.

117. CO 42/8—Letter from Cramahé to Dartmough dated June 22, 1773 and CO 42/33—Letter from Cramahé to Dartmouth dated December 12, 1773.

118. Although governors were repeatedly frustrated by French Canadian failure to mobilize for war efforts, the *Canadiens* did not desert to the American or French causes.

119. CO 42/38—Captain Foy's letter dated February 6, 1778, and Haldimand's letter dated July 25, 1778.

120. For various reasons, however, governors did not encourage representative institutions, and assemblies allowing Catholic participation were not secured until 1791. Much of this stemmed from the fact that there were only a few hundred merchants and traders of British origin in the province and that the vast majority of *Canadiens* were said to be rarely in favor of representative bodies they feared

would breed trouble and raise taxes. Linked to this were also very real fears about whether an assembly involving only Protestant members could be representative in Quebec. Protestant merchants and traders may have believed such an institution to be representative, but the governors of Quebec astutely realized that it would provoke tension and that it could not possibly satisfy the *Canadiens*. As the years passed and no assembly was granted in response to the demands of Protestants, petitioners changed their approach and began to suggest that Catholics might be admitted to this body. By 1784, memorials in favor of an assembly frequently included both French Catholic and British Protestant signatories. For important pamphlets about the debate regarding assemblies during the 1760s and 1770s, see Francis Maseres, *An Account of the Proceedings of the British and other Protestant Inhabitants of the Province of Quebeck in North America in order to obtain an House of Assembly in that Province* (London: 1775); Francis Maseres, *Additional papers concerning the Province of Quebeck: being an Appendix to the Book entitled An Account of the British and other Protestant Inhabitants* . . . (London: 1776); Francis Maseres, *The Canadian Freedholder: in two dialogues between an Englishman and a Frenchman settled in Canada, shewing the sentiments of the Bulk of the Freeholders of Canada concerning the late Quebeck Act* . . . (London: 1777). Many of these treatises simultaneously addressed the issue of a house of representatives and questions about which law should be administered in the province of Quebec.

121. CO 42/7—Letter from Carleton to Shelburne dated December 24, 1767.

122. Tousignant, "The Integration of the Province of Quebec." See also Michel Morin, "The Discovery and Assimilation of British Constitutional Law Principles in Quebec, 1764–1774," *Dalhousie Law Journal* 36, no. 2 (2013): 581–616.

123. The scholarship about the legal system in the province of Quebec during the 1760s and early 1770s is extensive. For recent and innovative treatments of this topic, see Donald Fyson, *Magistrates, Police, and People: Everyday Criminal Justice in Quebec and Lower Canada, 1764–1838* (Toronto: University of Toronto Press, 2006); and Donald Fyson, "The Conquered and the Conqueror: The Mutual Adaptation of the Canadiens and the British in Quebec, 1759–1775," in *Revisiting 1759* (Toronto: University of Toronto Press, 2012). See also the work of Michel Morin.

124. Land in New France was most commonly granted in *fief et seigneurie*. A seigneur claimed honorary and real rights based on written titles to land, but he was obliged to cede acreage to a certain number of *censitaires*, or holders of plots who paid *cens* to the seigneur, and to encourage settlement. This system inherently made transfer of land difficult and expensive, and it was not designed, in the words of Marcel Trudel, for the "rapid industrialization of society." (For further information, see Marcel Trudel, *The Seigneurial Regime*, Canadian Historical Association Booklets 6 [Ottawa, 1976].) By contrast, English land was granted in free and common socage, whereby an individual landholder paid a fixed annual sum. Land

held in free and common socage was alienable and could be bought and sold as long as the new landholder fulfilled his obligations (usually a payment) to the donor (usually the king).

125. "Address of French Citizens to the King regarding the legal system," in Shortt and Doughty, *Documents relating to the Constitutional History of Canada*, 228. The petition was read on January 7, 1765, suggesting that it had been composed in late 1764.
126. "Petition for the Restoration of French Law and Custom (dated sometime in 1770)," in Shortt and Doughty, *Documents relating to the Constitutional History of Canada*, 419–422.
127. "A Petition of diverse of the Roman-Catholick Inhabitants of the Province of Quebeck to the King's Majesty (signed December 1773 and presented February 1774)," in Shortt and Doughty, *Documents relating to the Constitutional History of Canada*, 504–508.
128. CO 101/2—Tres Humble Adresse des Nouveaux Sujets de Sa Majeste de L'Isle de la Grenade au tres Honorable Comte de Shelburne (received October 1767 but undated).
129. "Presentments of the Grand Jury of Quebec," in Shortt and Doughty, *Documents relating to the Constitutional History of Canada*, 212–215.
130. CO 42/47—The Petition of Sir John Baronet and others . . . Loyalists, their Associates, who have taken Refuge in Canada, dated April 11, 1785.
131. See, for example, Maseres, *An Account of the Proceedings of the British and other Protestant Inhabitants of the Province of Quebeck;* Maseres, *Additional papers concerning the Province of Quebeck;* Maseres, *The Canadian Freedholder*.
132. CO 42/1—Letter from Murray to Barton dated April 11, 1764. Nearly two decades later, Governor Haldimand would observe that it was the protections and rights guaranteed by the Quebec Act (1774) that had preserved the *Canadiens* in their allegiance to the crown of Great Britain. See CO 43/14—Letter from Haldimand dated October 25, 1780.
133. Lord Mansfield to George Grenville dated December 24, 1764, *Grenville Papers* 2:476–477, as quoted in Lawson, *The Imperial Challenge*, 58.
134. For an accessible version of Mansfield's decision in *Campbell v. Hall* (1774) and his propositions at large, see Shortt and Doughty, *Documents relating to the Constitutional History of Canada,* 525–526.
135. These were the words of Thomas Townshend in 1774. See Wright, *Debates of the House of Commons in the year 1774*, 3.
136. In August 1767, the Privy Council requested a report from Quebec on its constitutional settlement. By July 1769, the Board of Trade had responded to the Privy Council's request with a report that duly criticized the lack of a constitutional settlement for Quebec. A few local ordinances, including the 1770 ordinance "for the more effectual administration of justice," temporarily ameliorated the access of French Canadians to their own laws, but also succeeded in alienating many of the British-born Protestants.

137. For details about these many reports and discussions, see Pollock, "His Majesty's Subjects"; and Lawson, *The Imperial Challenge*.
138. "The Quebec Act (1774)," in Short and Doughty, *Documents relating to the Constitutional History of Canada*, 370–376.
139. See, in particular, Lawson, *The Imperial Challenge*; Marshall, "The Incorporation of the Province of Quebec in the British Empire"; and Pollock, "His Majesty's Subjects." The December 1772 report of Alexander Wedderburn was particularly influential in shaping the Quebec Act.
140. Marshall, "The Incorporation of Quebec in the British Empire," 63. It should be noted that the Regulating Act (1773) made comparable provisions and established an administration of justice for Bengal. However, Bengal was technically a territory governed by the East India Company rather than by colonial administrators such as the Lords Commissioners, the secretaries of state, and the governors who were responsible for Quebec.
141. "The Quebec Act (1774)," in Short and Doughty, *Documents relating to the Constiutional History of Canada*, 373.
142. Wright, *Debates of the House of Commons in the year 1774*, iv.
143. Wright, *Debates of the House of Commons in the year 1774*, 29. More generally, proponents of the bill insisted that government by governor and council was best suited to introduce slow change in accordance with the habits of the *Canadiens*. Finally, they argued that the Catholic Church had not been established, given that it was still subject to the king's supremacy; the government was committed to supervising a church that accepted Canadian born-and-bred priests rather than alienating clergymen and thereby encouraging them to look to France for succor.
144. More generally, opponents worried that by allowing the collection of tithes, the Quebec Act was perceived to have established the Catholic Church in Canada. Overall, critics believed that the act introduced a language of despotism and that, by failing to institute an assembly, it had introduced tyrannical government, a fear that was echoed in representations from the Continental Congress and the Assembly of New York.
145. Knox, *The justice and policy of the late act of Parliament*, 30, 18.
146. Wright, *Debates of the House of Commons in the year 1774*, 57.
147. Wright, *Debates of the House of Commons in the year 1774*, 160.
148. Wright, *Debates of the House of Commons in the year 1774*, 213.
149. Wright, *Debates of the House of Commons in the year 1774*, 264.
150. Wright, *Debates of the House of Commons in the year 1774*, 44.
151. Wright, *Debates of the House of Commons in the year 1774*, 289.
152. CO 42/34—Petitions of 1774.
153. CO 42/34—Petitions of 1774.
154. Copy of Petition to the House of Commons dated November 12, 1774, in Francis Maseres, *An Account of the Proceedings of the British and other Protestant Inhabitants*, 258.

155. This is an argument made by: Coupland, *The Quebec Act*; Lawson, *The Imperial Challenge*; Marshall, "The Incorporation of the Province of Quebec in the British Empire"; David Milobar, "Quebec Reform, the British Constitution and the Atlantic Empire: 1774–1775," *Parliamentary History* 14, no. 1 (1995): 65–88; David Milobar, "The Origins of British-Quebec Merchant Ideology: New France, the British Atlantic, and the Constitutional Periphery, 1720–70," *The Journal of Imperial and Commonwealth History* 24, no. 3 (1996): 364–390; and David Milobar, "The Constitutional Development of Quebec from the Time of the French Regime to the Canada Act of 1791" (PhD diss., University of London, 1990).
156. "Address to the Inhabitants of the Province of Quebeck," in *Journals of the Continental Congress, 1774–1789*, vol. 1, eds. Worthington C. Ford et al. (Washington, D.C.: Government Printing Office, 1904–1937); "The Representation and Remonstrance of the General Assembly of the Colony of New-York," in *Parliamentary History of England from the Earliest Period to the Year 1803*, ed. T. C. Hansard, vol. 18 (London: 1812–1820); "Declaration of Independence, July 4, 1776," http://avalon.law.yale.edu/18th_century/declare.asp (accessed October 2, 2016).
157. CO 102/16—Letter from Dundas to Home dated October 5, 1792.
158. "An Act for establishing regulations respecting Aliens and certain subjects of his Majesty," in *The Provincial Statutes of Lower-Canada*, vol. 1 (Quebec: 1795).

CHAPTER 5

1. William Bolts, *Considerations on India Affairs; particularly respecting the present state of Bengal and its dependencies* (London: 1772), iv.
2. See *A Letter to the Right Honourable Lord North on the East-India Bill now depending in Parliament* (London: 1773), 27.
3. As quoted in Arthur Mitchell Fraas, "'They Have Travailed into a Wrong Latitude': The Laws of England, Indian Settlements, and the British Imperial Constitution, 1726–1773" (PhD diss., Duke University, 2011), 434.
4. In the 1750s, for example, the East India Company executive began to claim that Christians more generally had many of the same benefits as British subjects. For details, see Fraas, "They Have Travailed," 402.
5. Durba Ghosh, *Sex and the Family in Colonial India: The Making of Empire* (Cambridge: Cambridge University Press, 2006), 12. See also Lauren Benton, *Law and Colonial Cultures: Legal Regimes in World History, 1400–1900* (Cambridge: Cambridge University Press, 2002), Chapter 4; Fraas, "They Have Travailed"; Sudipta Sen, "Imperial Subjects on Trial: On the Legal Identity of Britons in Late Eighteenth-Century India," *The Journal of British Studies* 45, no. 3 (2006): 532–555.
6. For recent studies of the East India Company's position relative to that of the crown and British state more generally, see Fraas. "They Have Travailed"; and Philip Stern, *The Company-State: Corporate Sovereignty and the Early Modern*

Foundations of the British Empire in India (New York: Oxford University Press, 2011). As H. V. Bowen noted in *Revenue and Reform* (Cambridge: Cambridge University Press, 1991), 58, the crown was notoriously hesitant to assert its right over Company territories given its limited resources.

7. Philip Lawson, "Parliament and the First East India Inquiry, 1767," *Parliamentary History* 1 (1982): 99–114. In *The East India Company in Eighteenth-Century Politics* (Oxford: Clarendon Press, 1952), Lucy Sutherland also argued that the period from 1763 to 1784 reflected an era of gradual "encroachment" by the British state over the affairs of the East India Company.
8. Thomas M. Curley, *Sir Robert Chambers: Law, Literature, and Empire in the Age of Johnson* (Madison: University of Wisconsin Press, 1998), 188. Although this "civil war" was for the most part a struggle of words and ideas, marked by mutual criticism, stalemate, and inertia, it did occasionally involve show of force. See, for example, IOR L/L/6/1—No. 279. George Rous, counsel for the East India Company, noted in 1780 that a military force had been required to resist the Supreme Court. Rous was likely referring to events surrounding the Kasijora Case (1779–1780) when the East India Company sent a party of sepoys to prevent the arrest of one of its *zamindars*.
9. This is a point made most clearly by M. P. Jain, *Indian Legal History* (Bombay: N. M. Tripathi, 1966), 116. A quick note on terms: *mofussil* technically refers to the "hinterland" or the "interior of the country." It was generally used to refer to the regions outside the three principal East India Company settlements of Calcutta, Bombay, and Madras. Thus, the *mofussil* for Calcutta encompassed the provinces of Bengal, Bihar, and Orissa in the 1760s, 1770s, and 1780s.
10. IOR L/L/6/1—No. 279 dated December 5, 1780.
11. Robert Travers, *Ideology and Empire in Eighteenth-Century India: The British in Bengal* (New York: Cambridge University Press, 2007); and Robert Travers, "Contested Despotism: Problems of Liberty in British India," in Jack Greene, ed., *Exclusionary Empire: English Liberty Overseas, 1600–1900* (Cambridge: Cambridge University Press, 2010), 191–219; Benton, *Law and Colonial Cultures*; and Paul Halliday. *Habeas Corpus: From England to Empire* (Cambridge, MA: Harvard University Press, 2010).
12. For other recent scholarship that considers jurisdiction as the "power to do justice" or the "power to decide" and that also examines the ways in which jurisdiction works to constitute and contest authority, see Bradin Cormack, *A Power to Do Justice: Jurisdiction, English Literature, and the Rise of the Common Law, 1509–1625* (Chicago: University of Chicago Press, 2007); and Shaunnaugh Dorsett and Shaun McVeigh, *Jurisdiction* (Milton Park: Routledge, 2012).
13. IOR O/5/26—Lists of Europeans residing in Calcutta in 1793 and 1804. The Court of Directors instructed its officials in Calcutta to produce such lists for several decades before the list of 1793 was compiled and sent to England.
14. The only extant record of judicial deliberations after 1774 are the Hyde Papers, which encompass seventy-two volumes of notes taken on cases and the day-to-day

transactions of the Supreme Court between 1775 and 1798. Over time, there has been some disagreement as to how many actual volumes have survived. Here, I cite Thomas Curley's estimate, though Walter K. Firminger claimed there were seventy-three volumes and S. C. Nandy wrote that there were seventy-four. The disappearance of several volumes in the Victoria Memorial Collections, Calcutta, combined with the fact that the microfilm reels at the National Library, Calcutta are incomplete, may help to explain these discrepancies. For more information about this set of volumes, see Curley, *Sir Robert Chambers*; Walter K. Firminger, "Selections from the Note Books of Justice John Hyde," *Bengal Past and Present* 3, no. 1 (1909): 27–64; and S. C. Nandy, "A Second Look at the Notes of Justice John Hyde," *Bengal Past and Present* 97, no. 184 (1978): 24–35. Sir Robert Chambers was responsible for at least nine of the volumes after John Hyde's death on July 8, 1796, though a range of handwriting in the volumes suggests that other judges may have made contributions. Although these can hardly be considered a perfectly accurate or comprehensive record, they do capture the tensions that plagued the Supreme Court, particularly during its early years. When considered alongside reports of counsel for the East India Company and summaries of the Court's activities documented in the *Calcutta Gazette* from March 1784 onwards, the Hyde Papers offer critical insight into judicial attempts to clarify British subjecthood in Calcutta and into the ways in which expansive subjecthood was at times the result.

15. For example, Armenians had been granted the "liberty to live in any of the Company's Cities, Garrisons, or Towns in India and to buy, sell, and purchase Land or Houses and be capable of all Civil Offices and preferments in the same manner as if they were Englishmen born" in 1688 in the hopes that they would direct more of their profitable trade toward East India Company settlements. The grant of full legal subjecthood to the Armenians was cited by Justice John Hyde in the Supreme Court in 1788. See HP Reel 9—vol. 20—August 21, 1788. H. Beveridge referred to the original deed in *The Trial of Maharaja Nanda Kumar, a Narrative of a Judicial Murder* (Calcutta, 1886) when discussing the status of Armenians who had appeared before the Supreme Court. The text of this document can be found in R. W. Ferrier, "The Agreement of the East India Company with the Armenian nation, 22 June 1688," *Revue des Etudes Armeniennes* NS 7 (1971): 427–443. Similarly, despite prohibitions against their serving in covenanted positions or as combatants in the East India Company armies, Eurasians were regularly recruited into armed militia forces. See C. J. Hawes, *Poor Relations: The Making of a Eurasian Community in British India, 1773–1833* (Richmond: Curzon, 1996), 37.
16. For more about the diversity of these legal orders and the accommodations that resulted in Calcutta, Bombay, and Madras, see Fraas, "They Have Travailed."
17. Mayor's Courts had been authorized to hear civil suits arising within the presidencies of Calcutta, Bombay, and Madras in 1726 in response to complaints that there

was a lack of "speedy and effectual administration of justice." (As quoted in B. B. Misra, *The Judicial Administration of the East India Company in Bengal, 1765–1782* [Delhi: Montilal Banarsidass, 1961], 133.) These were to be courts of record presided over by a mayor and nine aldermen, seven of whom had to be natural-born British subjects, and who theoretically applied the laws of England, though few of them had anything but a passing knowledge of those laws. In Calcutta, jurisdiction was limited to the town, district, and subordinate factories, though the Mayor's Court exercised jurisdiction over British subjects, natives in their employ, and any persons who had voluntarily submitted to its jurisdiction, adjudicating between many of the religiously, nationally, and racially diverse inhabitants of Company towns. For details of these courts' operation, see Fraas, "They Have Travailed," Chapters 2, 3, and 4.

18. As quoted in Misra, *The Judicial Administration,* 135. Indeed, it is important to note that the Mayor's Court in Calcutta heard numerous cases involving Indian litigants with the consent of the parties, and the Court retained a Brahmin on its staff to advise on issues of Hindu law. For more details, see Misra, *The Judicial Administration*, 137.
19. Authority to superintend this court and to settle disputes between native inhabitants stemmed from the East India Company's purchase of *zamindari* rights for the three villages of Sutanuti, Govindpur, and Calcutta in 1698, which included the administration of civil justice.
20. Authority to administer this vast system of courts stemmed from the East India Company's assumption of the *diwani,* or civil and revenue administration, in 1765. Traditionally, however, authority in the provinces of the Mughal Empire was divided between the *nizam* and the *diwan*, in an attempt to maintain a system of checks and balances. The *nizam*, or *nawab*, was the head of the *nizamat*, which was responsible for the military, maintenance of law and order, and administration of criminal justice. The *diwan* was responsible for collecting revenue and for determining all civil cases. When the East India Company assumed the *diwani* in 1765, it technically became responsible only for civil justice and criminal justice remained under the purview of the *nawab*. However, given the waning power of the *nawab* and the fact that military power effectively rested with the East India Company, Company officials became increasingly involved with criminal justice in the *mofussil.* Although the judicial plan of 1772 left the administration of criminal justice to Muslim law officers, it provided for collectors to supervise them at the district level and allowed the superior court of *Sadr Nizamat Adalat* to serve as a court of appeal.
21. The *Sadr Nizamat Adalat* consisted of an Indian judge assisted by a chief *mufti* and three *moulvies*, all of whom were formally appointed by the *nawab*, who, in turn, was advised by the East India Company. The *Sadr Diwani Adalat* was made up of the governor and members of the council, who acted as a court of appeal for *diwani* courts in the *mofussil.* The traditional division between criminal and civil

justice was thus preserved in these superior courts, but the East India Company maintained its general supervision over both areas. See Jain, *Indian Legal History*, 61–62.

22. Jain, *Indian Legal History*, 155
23. Peter J. Marshall, "The Muharram Riot of 1779 and the Struggle for Status and Authority in Early Colonial India," *Journal of the Asiatic Society of Bangladesh* 50, no. 1–2 (2005): 305. Many inhabitants cited the Mayor's Court's flexible application of law and sensitivity to the conventions and practices of the city's commercial community.
24. "Some Records Relative to the Mayor's Court," *Bengal Past and Present: Journal of the Calcutta Historical Society* 8 [1913?]: 6–7; Jain, *Indian Legal History*, 51.
25. Jain, *Indian Legal History*, Chapter 6.
26. Indeed, the parliamentary committee concluded that the existing system of corporations and justices of the peace was inadequate to administer law to a British and European population that was quickly moving beyond the reach of the existing Calcutta Mayor's Court and the supervision of Company courts. See 13 George III, Cap. 63, Section 13, in *A Collection of statutes concerning the incorporation, trade, and commerce of the East India Company, and the government of the British possessions in India* (London: 1794). In abolishing the Mayor's Court in Calcutta, the parliamentary act stipulated that the charter for this earlier court did not provide sufficiently for the administration of justice in the presidency.
27. Despite adhering to most standard proceedings in criminal and civil prosecutions, however, the Supreme Court did hear civil cases without benefit of jury and had the option to adapt conventions to local circumstances.
28. Travers, *Ideology and Empire*, 185.
29. In his article on the Muharram Riot of 1779, for example, Peter Marshall notes that as late as 1777, justices of the Supreme Court had discovered that the *faujdar* (usually a member of the Muslim service gentry who were responsible for maintaining law and order in their districts) and *daroga* (magistrate of the criminal court) of Chitpur had been exercising their authority within Calcutta. I am also grateful to Peter Marshall for clarifying that Indians could use the *zamindari* courts in Calcutta in addition to the Supreme Court of Judicature. In *Calcutta: Essays in Urban History* (Calcutta: Subarnarekha, 1993), S. N. Mukherjee indicates that at least two *dals* had existed in Calcutta since the mid-eighteenth century alongside the British Indian administrative system. The *dals*, which were made up of various castes and were headed by the leading families in town, were often used to settle disputes relating to inheritance, marriage, caste, rank, or intercaste relationships.
30. This is not to say that individuals could not appeal to the Privy Council prior to 1774. A number of cases reached the Privy Council from the Mayor's Courts. However, after 1774 appeals went directly to the Privy Council rather than first to the council and then to the Privy council. For more about appeals to the Privy Council from the Mayors' Courts, see Fraas, "They Have Travailed."

31. Judges in the Supreme Court of Judicature served during the king's pleasure whereas judges of the English high courts could only be removed by Parliament via impeachment hearings. The Charter of Justice noted that justices served during the king's pleasure (Section 3). In *Ideology and Empire*, Robert Travers notes that judges represented a "new breed of 'king's men' in India" (183).
32. In *Sir Robert Chambers*, Curley notes that these four judges were "reform-minded" and made certain assumptions about Company "misadministration" (Chapter 5).
33. The junior judges, John Hyde and Stephen Caesar Lemaistre, were known for their "contempt" of the Company's administration, going so far as to claim that the Court had criminal jurisdiction in the three provinces outside of Calcutta and that royal sovereignty should extend to Bengal, Bihar, and Orissa. Even Chief Justice Sir Elijah Impey and the well-established Sir Robert Chambers seem to have been willing to uphold royal over other forms of sovereignty in Calcutta and to have eagerly asserted the jurisdiction of their royal court. See Curley, *Sir Robert Chambers*, 288; Nasser Hussain, *The Jurisprudence of Emergency: Colonialism and the Rule of Law* (Ann Arbor: University of Michigan Press, 2003), 81.
34. For arguments about "dual sovereignty" in Bengal, see Sudipta Sen, *Distant Sovereignty: National Imperialism and the Origins of British India* (New York: Routledge, 2002); and Sen, "Imperial Subjects on Trial."
35. As Curley explains in *Sir Robert Chambers*, even though the landmark 1773 Regulating Act confirmed the Company's right to maintain law, order, and commerce in the East Indies, it did not explicitly disavow Mughal dominion over East India Company territories, a fact that would continue to engender confusion regarding sovereignty and jurisdiction in Calcutta and the surrounding provinces.
36. See Travers, *Ideology and Empire*, 144. Travers argues that the Regulating Act ultimately reflected a relatively limited conception of British sovereignty and that it was about "regulating" the Company, as its name suggested, rather than about "legislating" for India.
37. "Copy of the Attorney and Solicitor Generals Report, on the Petition of the East India Company, dated December 24, 1757," in *Copy of his Majesty's advocate, attorney, and solicitor generals report, August 16, 1757* [London?]: [1766?]. For other copies of this opinion, see Fraas, "The Have Travailed," 442, footnote 163.
38. Mss Eur E 28—Memoranda & Queries relative to the Charter.
39. As quoted in Misra, *The Judicial Administration*, 192.
40. *Reports from Committees of the House of Commons*, vol. 5 (London: 1804).
41. HP Reel 8—vol. 18—December 4, 1787. Hyde noted that "our local jurisdiction [is] over all persons & all crimes within the Town of Calcutta." The boundaries of Calcutta in the 1770s were the Hooghly River on the West, the "Mahratta Ditch" or Outer Circular Road on the east and south, and what is now Mahatma Gandhi Road on the north. See Ghosh, *Sex and the Family*, 174.
42. Mss Eur E28—Sir Elijah Impey's address to the Grand Jury and Mr. Justice Lemaistre's address to the Grand Jury.

43. As Paul Halliday and Edward White also note, the judges believed that they had oversight of the king's franchises, even of *habeas corpus*, and that they might use these "on behalf of native Indians." See Paul Halliday and Edward G. White, "The Suspension Clause: English Text, Imperial Contexts, and American Implications," *Virginia Law Review* 94 (2008), 658.
44. In *Indian Legal History*, Jain's chapter on the Supreme Court emphasizes all of the different areas in which the act and charter failed to clarify the Court's jurisdiction. Similarly, in *Sir Robert Chambers*, Curley refers to the "legal fuzziness" that stemmed from these parliamentary and royal enactments. Finally, as Sir J. Stephen noted, the definitions of subjecthood were uncertain: "In one sense, the whole population of Bengal, Bihar, and Orissa were British subjects. In another sense, no one was a British subject who was not an Englishman born. In a third sense, inhabitants of Calcutta might be regarded as British subjects, although the general population of Bengal was not." As quoted in H. Beveridge, *The Trial of Maharaja Nanda Kumar, a Narrative of Judicial Murder* (Calcutta, 1886), 216.
45. Jain, *Indian Legal History*, 111. This would also echo the contention of Hawes, *Poor Relations*, that the 1773 Regulating Act actually established the concepts of "British subject" and "Native of India" (138). Fraas, by contrast, notes that terms such as "natives of India" became difference-making categories after 1753 (see "They Have Travailed," 381).
46. 13 Geo. III, Cap. 63.
47. HP Reel 6—vol. 10—October 23, 1780. See "Charter of Justice dated March 26, 1774," in T*he Rules and Orders of the Supreme Court of Judicature at Fort William in Bengal with the charter of justice, and the several statutes relating to the Court* (Calcutta: 1829).
48. "Extracts from the 13th George III, Chapter 63, entitled An Act for establishing certain Regulations for the better Management of the Affairs of the East India Company" and "Charter of Justice dated 26th March 1774," in *The Rules and Orders of the Supreme Court of Judicature*.
49. HP Reel 1—vol. 2—December 14, 1781.
50. "Puisne judge" refers to regular members of a court and is used to distinguish them from the head of the Court who is called the Chief Justice.
51. Chambers was persuaded that the towns and settlements restored to the East India Company after the conquest of 1757—and he referred specifically to Calcutta—had accrued to the king of Great Britain and were his by right of conquest. Under such circumstances, English law and precedent permitted the monarch to alter local laws and institutions, including the administration of justice. See Add Mss 39400—An Opinion Delivered by Mr. Justice Chambers in the Supreme Court of Judicature in the case of Cumall a Deen Ally Khan against Charles Goring, John Shore, Peter Moore, and Budder a Deen (1777). This was a view also upheld by Chambers in *Rex v. Janu Mullick* when he determined that "the Town of Calcutta is under the Dominion of the Crown of Great Britain."

52. Add Mss 39400—An Opinion Delivered by Mr. Justice Chambers in the Supreme Court of Judicature in the case of Cumall a Deen Ally Khan against Charles Goring, John Shore, Peter Moore, and Budder a Deen (1777).
53. Mss Eur E 28—Mr. Justice Lemaistre's Address to the Grand Jury (probably 1775).
54. T. C. Morton, *Decisions of the Supreme Court of Judicature at Fort William in Bengal: on the plea, equity, ecclesiastical, admiralty and crown sides, from the date of the charter of 1774 to 1841* (Calcutta, 1841), 207.
55. HP Reel 1—vol. 2—November 18, 1782.
56. HP Reel 11—vol. 24—April 7, 1789.
57. Fraas, "They Have Travailed," 19.
58. See, for example, complaints from St. Helena where inhabitants tried to use the language of subjecthood against the East India Company, arguing that the king's subjects could not be abused as was the Company's practice. The Company general allegedly responded to their complaint by claiming that they were "no more the King's, but the Company's Subjects." See Philip Stern, *The Company-State*, 147.
59. As Fraas's research has demonstrated, although the Mayor's Court was intended to adjudicate between the European population of Calcutta, this was not always the reality. Indeed, cases between non-British and British litigants continued to proliferate in this court in the 1750s and 1760s, a testament to the vibrant and diverse mercantile life of the city. Cases between two non-British inhabitants of the city, however, were far more rare in the 1750s and 1760s than they had been previously. In my own research with the incomplete bundles of records in the Calcutta High Court, records from the 1760s indicate that most suits filed in the Mayor's Court were between individuals of British and continental European origin or between Indians and Europeans. There were comparatively few cases between Indians, whose complaints were likely handled by the *zamindari* court at the time.
60. These observations are based on my examination of bundles of records in the Old Records Room of the Calcutta High Court. It should be emphasized that these records are very incomplete and that any numerical observations are subject to change should more records be discovered in other rooms of the Calcutta High Court.
61. HP Reel 4—vol. 10—March 29, 1789—*Angelo Ducas v. Joseph Baretto, Philip Santiago de Mello, John Fleetwood, and Joseph Noronha*; HP R4074—vol. 2—October 22, 1776—*Widow Bolts*; HP R4074—vol. 26—July 27, 1789—*Rex v. Peter Horrebow*; HP Reel 1—vol. 2—November 12, 1781—*Boqbaun Goshe v. Peter Verle.*
62. HP Reel 17—vol. 52—November 11, 1796.
63. HP Reel 15—vol. 42—date of case unclear, though sometime in 1794.
64. HP Reel 5—vol. 5—July 2, 1778—*Lokong and Anghee v. Joseph Rees*; HP Reel 2—November 3, 1783—*The will of Yong Atchue, a Chinese.*
65. HP Reel 1—November 20, 1782.

66. Calcutta High Court—Old Record Room—1777 Bundle—November 4, 1776.
67. Similarly, in the 1786 case of *Aga Maul Serpracy v. Luckon Roy*, Hyde jotted down the following plea: "not a subject of the King of Great Britain and though bond describes him as such, he was not & is not an Inhabitant of Calcutta. Claims Hindoo Native of Bengal and lives in Burdwan." HP Reel 7—vol. 14—February 2, 1786.
68. SM 128—*Calcutta Gazette*, vol. 6, no. 161, Thursday, March 29, 1787.
69. HP Reel 4—vol. 12—December 16, 1791.
70. HP Reel 6—December 13, 1779—*Rex v. Rustom Beg*; HP Reel 15—vol. 40—July 15, 1793—*Rex v. Mansur Ali Khan.*
71. HP Reel 9/10—vol. 22—June 14, 1788.
72. HP Reel 3—vol. 7—December 16, 1785.
73. The question of "proof" is an important one, particularly given the material role that subject status played in many of these cases. Judges appeared to have welcomed a range of evidence in verifying defendants' allegiances. The Court often called upon members in the East India Company's service or the King's Regiments to testify to a plaintiff or defendant's place of birth. In the case of *Rex v. John West & John Peak*, two such testimonies occurred. An unnamed piper in the King's 73rd Regiment swore that John Peak had been born in Shropshire and that they had known each other there as boys. A drummer was summoned to verify John West's birth in Somerset and that he remembered having seen him there (See HP Reel 4—vol. 11—July 16, 1790). In the case of *Rex v. John Wyatt*, one witness gave evidence that he had heard John Wyatt claim to be a native of Derbyshire. The witness further stated that he had always guessed him to be a British subject "from his language," but noted that from Wyatt's conduct, "I would willingly believe him a foreigner, for it is not the part of a Britton to behave so" (See HP Reel 7—vol. 16—December 18, 1786).
74. HP Reel 4—vol. 10—July 24, 1787.
75. HP Reel 5—vol. 13—December 13, 1793.
76. For the purposes of establishing British subject status in Calcutta, birth in Ireland, Scotland, or the British dominions seems to have been viewed as birth in England. See, for example, HP Reel 2—November 13, 1784—*John Joys v. William Dawson,* in which the defendant was proven to be a British subject because he was an "Irishman resident in Calcutta." Unfortunately, no remaining cases involve American-born or Caribbean-born subjects to test whether this argument was pursued to its logical conclusion.
77. HP R4074—vol. 2—Entry dated December 17, 1776, but across from entry for June 24, 1776.
78. HP Reel 5—vol. 6—November 16, 1778.
79. HP R4074—vol. 2—June 28, 1776.
80. HP Reel 1—vol. 2—March 11, 1782. Chambers apparently concurred with Hyde's opinion in the case.

81. Morton, 119–120. Morton relies on Hyde's notes for January 27, 1777, which are now missing from the Victoria Memorial collections.
82. In the related cases of *Nanickchund Tagore v. William Johnson* and *Nairn Singh v. William Johnson*, the defendant was alleged to be a British subject by virtue of being "born in Bombay and resident in Bengal." Both Chambers and Hyde concurred that "his being born in Bombay made him a British subject." Sir William Jones, who had joined the court as a puisne judge in 1783, later declared that he agreed with the above opinion respecting the subject status of "Natives of Bombay." HP Reel 6—vol. 12—November 14, 1785. There were other cases of individuals born of "English parents" in India. For example, in 1770, Joseph Fowke, born at Fort St. George of two English parents, applied to return to India in order to "settle there as being a Native of that Country." But the East India Company wondered whether he was to be treated as a subject, which meant that he would have been liable to be seized and sent to England according to the provisions of several acts of Parliament if he had been found to be trading without the license of the Company. Counsel suggested that all persons born of English parents in India carrying on an illicit trade could be sent to England; counsel also intimated that even if such individuals were subjects in point of law, if they had had no contact with the Company or with Europeans more generally, it might not be "expedient" to exercise this authority. For this case, see IOR L/L/6/1—No. 146. Although children like Fowke might have been "British subjects" by virtue of birth within the monarch's dominions, it is intriguing that subject status was traced to their birth from "English parents" rather than to their birth within the monarch's dominions. The statute of 1351, better known as *De Natis Ultra Mare*, considered children born abroad of English parents natural-born subjects. It may have been a more reliable legal option for children born in territories that were not yet clearly dominions of the British crown.
83. HP Reel 11—vol. 24—April 7, 1789 and April 8, 1789.
84. Morton, *Decisions of the Supreme Court of Judicature*, 136–137. Morton claims that Chambers, Hyde, and Jones were unanimous that de Rozio must be non-suited since he was not a subject. I was unable to find any indication of the judges' ruling in the Hyde Papers.
85. The treaty signed with the *nawab* at the conquest of Calcutta in 1757 had not stipulated whether the city's inhabitants were to become subjects of the crown or of the East India Company.
86. HP Reel 5—vol. 4—December 4, 1777.
87. HP Reel 1—vol. 2—June 26, 1781.
88. HP Reel 1—vol. 2—June 28, 1781 and June 29, 1781.
89. HP Reel 11—vol. 24—April 7, 1789 and April 8, 1789.
90. In fact, Hyde recorded that day that a certain Portuguese member of the jury was instrumental in recommending that some midwives be assembled for a jury of matrons, a jury that likely included at least one "black wife" who lived in Calcutta. HP Reel 5—vol.4—December 19, 1777.
91. Hawes, *Poor Relations,* 138–139.

92. In *Calcutta: Essays in Urban History*, Mukherjee indicates that there were eighty Bengalis listed as eligible to serve on the Common Jury in 1828 and that seven Bengalis were appointed to serve on the Grand Jury of the Supreme Court of Calcutta in 1833 (206). He offers no corresponding evidence for the eighteenth century.
93. HP R4074—vol. 2—October 22, 1776.
94. HP Reel 1—January 17, 1782.
95. HP Reel 5—vol. 4—January 3, 1778—*Ramsunker Doss v. Narain Roy, in forma pauperis*.
96. Indeed, these statutes regarding the interest rates permitted to British subjects and their ability to lend money to Indian princes were material to the case of William Palmer in the 1820s. Palmer, a Eurasian, was technically a "native of India" before the law. Secure in this status and technically exempt from the 1797 Usury Act, he lent money to the Nizam of Hyderabad. However, one of his principal partners, Sir William Rumbold, was a British subject, and accusations that they had exceeded the permitted 12 percent in their dealings with the Nizam led to charges of bad faith. They were forbidden from having any direct dealings with the government in Hyderabad. By the later 1820s, the House of Palmer had ceased to be able to trade. The sums advanced to the Nizam in the 1820s had still not been recovered by the time of Palmer's death in 1867. For more about this case, see Hawes, *Poor Relations*, Chapter 6.
97. In "They Have Travailed," Fraas notes that the Mughal Cutcherry court run by the East India Company essentially served as the "Company's Mughal land office" and was responsible for many matters relating to property and rent. The English court tended to hear very few suits between non-Europeans where land, mortgage, and deeds were concerned (202–203). It is possible, therefore, that some of these practices continued even under the Supreme Court of Judicature and that disputes relating to land might have arisen more frequently in the Cutcherry Court.
98. Hawes, *Poor Relations*, 38.
99. HP Reel 1—November 18, 1782.
100. HP Reel 16—vol. 44—November 22, 1794.
101. See *The Trial of Maha Raja Nundocomar, Bahader, for Forgery* (London: 1776). Accounts of this famous trial are abundant, though I have relied primarily on those provided by Curley, *Sir Robert Chambers*; and Jain, *Indian Legal History*, to supplement the transcript of the trial.
102. These law officers unsuccessfully tried to claim exemption from the Court's sentence on the grounds that they had been acting in their official duty and according to established practice. Unconvinced, the judges responded by having Behadur Beg, the *qazi*, and the *muftis* arrested in the provinces and brought to Calcutta. In turn, the East India Company government offered to pay their employees' bail, sought legal advice on whether its servants were subject to the Court's jurisdiction, and agreed to defend the suit on their behalf. See briefs in IOR P/166/80. See also Travers, *Ideology and Empire*, 194.

103. Jain, *Indian Legal History*, 137.
104. The Court also determined that whereas Muslim law officers were allowed to expound on questions of law, the *qazi* and *muftis* had actually exceeded their mandate by hearing evidence and ruling on the question of inheritance. Provincial councilors had unlawfully delegated their authority to "native functionaries," making any decisions rendered thereafter illegal. For a primary source that provides a relatively succinct overview of the Patna Case, see P/166/79–P/166/82. I have also relied on sections by Curley, *Sir Robert Chambers*; Jain, *Indian Legal History*; and Travers, *Ideology and Empire*, for an understanding of the events of the case and its repercussions. An acrimonious and seemingly interminable trial began in 1777, ultimately resulting in an appeal to the Privy Council and a subsequent challenge of its decision more than a decade later.
105. IOR P/166/79.
106. The petitions filed against the Supreme Court in 1779 and 1780 referred to many writs that the Court had issued "into all parts of the Provinces for bringing up zemindars, farmers, and other natives" to Calcutta. One was against Raja Cheyton Singh, *zamindar* of Bissempore. Another had to do with a writ requested by Comaul-ul-Deen. Still another case was brought by a Hindu banker against the Raja of Kasijora, who was the largest *zamindar* in the Midnapur district. See *The Several Petitions of the British Inhabitants of Bengal, of the Governor-General and Council, and of the Court of Directors of the East India Company to Parliament* (London: 1780).
107. See "Letter from the Court of Directors to the Right Honorable Lord Weymouth" and "Petition of the United Company of Merchants trading to the East Indies to the Honorable the Commons of Great Britain," in *The Several Petitions of the British Inhabitants of Bengal*.
108. *Reports from Committees of the House of Commons*, vol. 5 (London, 1904).
109. Marshall, "The Muharram Riot of 1779," 301, 307.
110. "The Humble Petition of the British Subjects, residing in the Provinces of Bengal, Bahar, and Orissa, and their several dependencies to the Honorable the Commons of Great Britain," in *The Several Petitions of the British Inhabitants of Bengal*.
111. "The Humble Petition of the British Subjects," in *The Several Petitions of the British Inhabitants of Bengal*.
112. 21 Geo. III, Cap. 70, Section 17.
113. 21 Geo. III, Cap. 70, Sections 11–13.
114. However, if these individuals had agreed in writing to submit to the Court, they were still subject to the Court's civil jurisdiction.
115. As quoted in *The Rules and Orders of the Supreme Court of Judicature* (1829).
116. 21 Geo. III, Cap. 70, Section 67.
117. 21 Geo. III, Cap. 65, Section 28. See also 33 Geo. III, Cap. 52, Section 98.
118. Order 92 of 1782, reprinted in Lewis Kerr, *Rules and Orders of the Supreme Court of Judicature at Fort William in Bengal* (1798).

119. Once again, these observations are based on my examination of bundles of records in the Old Records Room of the Calcutta High Court. These records are very incomplete, and any numerical observations are subject to change should more records be discovered in other rooms of the Calcutta High Court.
120. HP Reel 9— vol. 20—August 29, 1788.
121. Distinctions between inhabitants were not always straightforward, of course, and it often appears to have been easier to verify residence in Calcutta than whether or not individuals had been born within a British dominion. Indeed, in some of the court records where only a local jurisdiction was at stake, individuals whose names and stories might otherwise have indicated that they were "British subjects residing in Bengal" were classified simply as "Inhabitants of Calcutta." Hyde merely noted, for example, that William Camac and John Jays were inhabitants of Calcutta. HP Reel 11—vol. 25—November 30, 1789; and HP Reel 12—vol. 30—November 6, 1790
122. HP Reel 9—vol. 20—August 21, 1788.
123. HP R4074—vol. 33—April 28, 1791.
124. HP Reel 5—vol. 13—March 22, 1792.
125. Even before the Court had been established, continental Europeans residing in Calcutta and the surrounding provinces had posed jurisdictional challenges for the East India Company. The Company possessed the right to "send and remit to England" any of "his Majesty's subjects" who were found trading in the East Indies without a license and had routinely sought advice from counsel and the Court of Directors about whether they might, in fact, send both their own servants and offending continental Europeans "out of the country." The question of whether these individuals were encompassed by the acts of Parliament remained unresolved, even if in practice the Company consistently deported those it deemed "Europeans of notorious bad character." See IOR O/5/1—Extract Letter from Bengal dated November 28, 1766; IOR O/5/1—Extract Bengal Consultations dated February 11, 1767, and Select Committee Observations dated February 11, 1767 (?); IOR O/5/1—Extract Secret Letter from Bengal dated January 15, 1776; *Regulations Framed in Pursuance of Several Acts with respect to Europeans*, Extract Bengal Public Consultations dated January 16, 1788, including a letter from the Advocate General; IOR O/5/2—Extract Public Letter from Bengal dated November 25, 1791, and Bengal Foreign Consultations dated June 1, 1791. For details about some of the individuals who were deported, including Joseph Pavesy, see Hannah Weiss, "Europeans of 'notorious bad character' and the East India Company system of licenses" (paper presented at the Yale-Princeton Early Modern British Studies Colloquium, Princeton, NJ, November 10–11, 2006).
126. No final judgment appears in either the Hyde Papers or subsequent compilations of cases in Calcutta. See HP Reel 1—vol. 2—November 12, 1781; and Morton for his account of this case.

127. HP Reel 2—March 17, 1783.
128. HP R4074—vol. 26—July 27, 1789.
129. Mss Eur. E28—Mr. Justice Lemaistre's address to the Grand Jury (undated but likely 1775).
130. See, for example, HP Reel 1—vol. 2—Notes for cases November 12, 1781; HP Reel 11—vol. 24—Notes for cases on April 8, 1789; HP R4074— vol. 26—Notes for cases on July 27, 1789.
131. HP Reel 11—vol. 24—April 7, 1789.
132. In *Sex and the Family*, Ghosh has observed that over the years Hyde was concerned to delineate types of subjects, describing them by behavior and habits rather than by racial or ethnic characteristics, in order to "prescribe how these subjects of the British should be treated by the court" (184).
133. Calcutta High Court—Old Records Room—Bundle from 1777 and bundle from 1787.
134. This is an observation also made by Ghosh, *Sex and the Family*, and Sen, "Imperial Subjects on Trial."
135. See Ghosh, *Sex and the Family*.
136. Christopher Hawes suggests that fluidity in the covenanted positions represented a threat to East India Company patronage from London. For more about this and the various exclusions passed against Eurasians, see *Poor Relations*.
137. See Hussain, *The Jurisprudence of Emergency*, 79.
138. Elizabeth Kolsky, *Colonial Justice in British India* (Cambridge: Cambridge University Press, 2010), 12.
139. Text of the "Petition from the Christian Inhabitants of Calcutta and the Provinces comprised within the Presidency of Fort William" as reproduced in *Reports of Proceedings Connected with the East Indians' Petition to Parliament, read at The Town Hall, Calcutta, March 28, 1831* (Calcutta, 1831). See also Hannah Weiss, "Expanding British Subjecthood: The East Indians' Petition of 1830" (paper presented at British World Conference: Defining the British World, Bristol, United Kingdom, July 11–14, 2007).
140. "Proclamation by the Queen to the Princes, Chiefs, and the People of India dated November 1, 1858," in Arthur Berriedale Keith, *Speeches and Documents on Indian Policy, 1750–1921*, vol. 1 (London: Oxford University Press, 1922).

CONCLUSION

1. The question of whether indigenous peoples considered themselves and were considered "subjects," "allies," or "dependent nations," though beyond the scope of this book, is complex and still highly contested. What is clear, however, is that indigenous peoples in many parts of the British Empire used the language of subjecthood to seek protections and privileges. See, in particular, Ann Curthoys and Jessie Mitchell, "Bring This Paper to the Good Governor: Aboriginal Petitioning

in Britain's Australian Colonies," in *Native Claims: Indigenous Law against Empire, 1500–1920* ed. Saliha Belmessous (New York: Oxford University Press, 2011), 182–203; Gregory Evans Dowd, "Domestic, Dependent, Nations: The Colonial Origins of a Paradox," in *Backcountry Crucibles: The Lehigh Valley from Settlement to Steel* eds. Jean R. Soderlund and Catherine S. Parzynski (Bethlehem: Lehigh University Press, 2007), 125–157; Gregory Evans Dowd, *War under Heaven: Pontiac, the Indian Nations, and the British Empire* (Baltimore: Johns Hopkins University Press, 2002); Jenny Hale Pulsipher, *Subjects unto the Same King: Indians, English, and the Contest for Authority in Colonial New England* (Philadelphia: University of Pennsylvania Press, 2005); and Craig Bryan Yirush, "Claiming the New World: Empire, Law, and Indigenous Rights in the Mohegan Case, 1704–1743," *Law and History Review* 29, no. 2 (May 2011): 333–373. The term "savage neighbors" is taken from Peter Silver's *Our Savage Neighbors: How Indian War Transformed Early America* (New York: W. W. Norton, 2008).

2. As quoted in Philip Lawson, *The Imperial Challenge: Quebec and Britain in the Age of the American Revolution* (Montreal: McGill–Queen's University Press, 1989), 121.
3. CO 42/24—Letter from Murray to Egremont dated October 23, 1763, and CO 42/33—Letter from Cramahé to Dartmouth dated December 12, 1773.
4. CO 42/38—Sketch on the Military State of the Province of Quebec by Haldimand dated July 25, 1778, and CO 42/42—Letter from Haldimand to Germain dated November 3, 1781.
5. CO 389/57—Commissions to the Governors of Minorca and Gibraltar to grant Letters of Marque and Reprisal, 1793. For information about letters of marque and the merchants of Minorca, see David Donaldson, "Britain and Menorca in the Eighteenth Century" (PhD diss., Open University, 1994).
6. 33 George III, Cap. 4, popularly known as the "Alien Act," in Sheila Lambert, ed., *House of Commons Sessional Papers of the Eighteenth Century,* vol. 86 (Wilmington: Scholarly Resources, 1975).
7. CO 174/16—Memorial of Salvador Cosino to William Blakeley dated January 31, 1754.
8. See *The Several petitions of the British Inhabitants of Bengal, of the Governor-General and Council, and of the Court of Directors of the East India Company to Parliament* (London: 1780).
9. Scholarship that examines the various economic, intellectual, and cultural networks of the British Empire, particularly the British Atlantic includes: David Armitage and Michael J. Braddick, eds., *The British Atlantic World, 1500–1800* (Houndsmills: Palgrave Macmillan, 2002); Nicholas Canny and Philip Morgan, *The Oxford Handbook of the Atlantic World, 1450–1850* (Oxford: Oxford University Press, 2013); David Hancock, *Citizens of the World: London Merchants and the Integration of the British Atlantic Community, 1735–1785* (Cambridge: Cambridge University Press, 1995); Ned Landsman, *From Colonials to Provincials: American Thought and Culture, 1680–1760* (Ithaca: Cornell University Press, 1997); and Peter Linebaugh

and Marcus Rediker, *The Many-Headed Hydra: Sailors, Slaves, Commoners, and the Hidden History of the Revolutionary Atlantic* (Boston: Beacon Press, 2000).

10. CO 101/1—Memorial of His Majesty's Adopted Subjects in the Island of Grenada, attested February 14, 1766.
11. See, for example, "Address of French Citizens to the King Regarding the Legal System," in Adam Shortt and Arthur G. Doughty, *Documents relating to the Constitutional History of Canada, 1759–1791* (Ottawa: J. de la Taché, 1918), 161–166.
12. H. V. Bowen, "British Conceptions of Global Empire, 1756–1783," *Journal of Imperial and Commonwealth History* 26, no. 3 (1998): 1–27.
13. Benedict Anderson, *Imagined Communities: Reflections on the Origin and Spread of Nationalism* (London: Verso, 1991).
14. For "covenanting communities," see John Spurr, "A Profane History of Early Modern Oaths," *Transactions of the Royal Historical Society* 6th ser., vol. 11 (2001), 37–63. For the importance of the written word in forging communities, see also Mark Knights, *Representation and Misrepresentation in Later Stuart Britain: Partisanship and Political Culture* (Oxford: Oxford University Press, 2005), 111–112, 188; and Donald Lutz, *Roots of the Republic: American Founding Documents Interpreted* (Madison: Madison House, 1986), 20. The importance of writing and of written modes in constituting authority and in empires more generally has also been a preoccupation of several recent works, including Kathryn Burns, *Into the Archives: Writing and Power in Colonial Peru* (Durham: Duke University Press, 2010); Brinkley Messick, *The Calligraphic State: Textual Domination and History in a Muslim Society* (Berkeley: University of California Press, 1993); Miles Ogburn, *Indian Ink: Script and Print in the Making of the English East India Company* (Chicago: University of Chicago Press, 2007); Bhavani Raman, *Document Raj: Writing and Scribes in Early Colonial South India* (Chicago: University of Chicago Press, 2012); and Donald Lutz, *Roots of the Republic: American Founding Documents Interpreted* (Madison: Madison House, 1986), 20.
15. Mary Sarah Bilder, "Salamanders and Sons of God: The Culture of Appeal in Early New England," in *The Many Legalities of Early America* eds. Christopher L. Tomlins and Bruce H. Mann (Chapel Hill: University of North Carolina Press, 2001), 69; and Mary Sarah Bilder, *The Transatlantic Constitution: Colonial Legal Culture and the Empire* (Cambridge, MA: Harvard University Press, 2004).
16. Daniel Hulsebosch, "The American Revolution (II): The Origin and Nature of Colonial Grievances," in *The Oxford History of the British Empire: British North America in the Seventeenth and Eighteenth Centuries* ed. Stephen Foster (Oxford: Oxford University Press, 2013).
17. Sir William Young, *Some observations which may contribute to afford a just idea of the nature, importance, and settlement, of our new West-India colonies* (London, 1764), 43.
18. See Elizabeth Mancke, "Sites of Sovereignty: The Body of the Subject and the Creation of Britain's Overseas Empire" (paper presented at the University of Chicago Early Modern Workshop, February 21, 2005).

19. CO 123/1—Letter from James Marriott to John Pownall in response to April 21, 1766, letter referred to His Majesty's Advocate General from the Lords of Trade and Plantations.
20. CO 42/66—Letter from Finlay to Nepean, dated February 9, 1789.
21. See, for example, Christopher Leslie Brown, *Moral Capital: Foundations of British Abolitionism* (Chapel Hill: University of North Carolina Press, 2006); Linda Colley, *Britons: Forging the Nation, 1707–1837* (New Haven: Yale University Press, 1992); and Anthony Pagden, *Lords of All the World: Ideologies of Empire in Spain, Britain, and France, c. 1500–1800* (New Haven: Yale University Press, 1995). Brown and Colley suggest that the British were concerned to reassert that they ruled over an "empire of liberty" after the loss of the thirteen American colonies compromised this claim. Pagden demonstrates that well before the 1780s, the British were defining themselves in opposition to the "tyrannical" and "rapacious" Spanish Empire.
22. See C. A. Bayly, *Imperial Meridian: The British Empire and the World, 1780–1830* (London: Longman, 1989). Bayly engages many of the arguments put forth by Vincent Harlow, *The Founding of the Second British Empire, 1763–1793* (London: Longmans, Green, and Co., 1952) about increasingly "authoritative" bureaucracies operating from London and about attempts to mould colonial societies according to patterns provided by the metropole. Bayly also addresses some of the issues raised by Frederick Madden and David Fieldhouse, eds., *Select Documents on the Constitutional History of the British Empire and Commonwealth* (Westport: Greenwood Press, 1985) about the growth of strong executives and greater administrative efficiency. However, Madden and Fieldhouse, in particular, stress that there was not a new "blueprint" for empire after 1763 but rather a "continuum of options." Constitutional uniformity in the empire remained elusive.
23. See Caitlin Anderson, "Britons Abroad, Aliens at Home: Nationality Law and Policy in Britain, 1815–1870" (PhD diss., Cambridge University, 2004); and Andreas Fahrmeir, *Citizens and Aliens: Foreigners and the Law in Britain and the German States, 1789–1870* (New York: Berghahn Books, 2000). Anderson argues that 1870 marked the abandonment of "Coke's archaic doctrine of indelible allegiance" (11). Fahrmeir notes that in all other continental states, governments accepted the idea that nationality might change but that until 1870, British nationality law stated that British nationality could not be lost.
24. For important work on the concept of "negotiated authority" and the adaptation of English ideas in the colonies themselves, see Christine Daniels and Michael V. Kennedy, *Negotiated Empires: Centers and Peripheries in the Americas, 1500–1820* (New York: Routledge, 2002); and Jack Greene, ed., *Exclusionary Empire: English Liberty Overseas, 1600–1900* (Cambridge: Cambridge University Press, 2010).
25. CO 101/53—Motion to present petition from Free Colored Inhabitants of this Government dated April 28, 1813, and Resolution of the House dated May 1, 1813.

26. Text of the "Petition from the Christian Inhabitants of Calcutta and the Provinces comprised within the Presidency of Fort William" as reproduced in *Reports of Proceedings Connected with the East Indians' Petition to Parliament, read at The Town Hall, Calcutta, March 28, 1831* (Calcutta, 1831).
27. For details about Don Pacifico's claims, see David Brown, "The Power of Public Opinion: Palmerston and the Crisis of December 1851," *Parliamentary History* 20 (2001): 333–358; David Hannell, "Lord Palmerston and the 'Don Pacifico Affair' of 1850: The Ionian Connection," *European History Quarterly* 19 (1989): 495–507; and Geoffrey Hicks, "Don Pacifico, Democracy, and Danger: The Protectionist Party Critique of British Foreign Policy, 1850–1852," *The International History Review* 26, no. 3 (2004): 515–540.
28. *Hansard's Parliamentary Debates* 3rd ser., vol. 112 (London: 1850), 444.
29. For some of the more recent articles about claims associated with subjecthood in the nineteenth and twentieth centuries, see Martin Anderson, "Tourism and the Development of the Modern British Passport, 1814–1858," *The Journal of British Studies* 49, no. 2 (2010): 258–282; and David Killingray, "A Good West Indian, A Good African, and, in Short, a Good Britisher: Black and British in a Colour-Conscious Empire, 1760–1950," *The Journal of Imperial and Commonwealth History* 36, no. 3 (2008): 363–381.

Bibliography

MANUSCRIPTS AND ARCHIVES

The British Library (BL), London

Add Mss 39400	Liverpool Papers, Opinions of Sir Robert Chambers
Mss Eur E28	Francis MSS, Files Relating to Supreme Court
IOR L/L/6/1, L/L/7/48	Opinions of Counsel, Company Solicitor, 1746–1799
IOR O/5/1–6	Europeans in India, 1766–1804
IOR O/5/26	Lists of Europeans Residing in Calcutta and Bengal, 1793
IOR P/166/79–87	Bengal Law Consultations
SM 128	*Calcutta Gazette*, 1784–1790

The National Archives (NA), London

ADM 1/5117/8	Miscellaneous, Consuls, Mediterranean Passes, 1777–1778
ADM 1/5118/8	Miscellaneous, Consuls, Mediterranean Passes, 1786–1790
ADM 2/1319–1324	Out-Letters, Mediterranean Passes, 1730–1797
ADM 7/76	Miscellaneous, Registers of Passes, 1685–1688
BT 5/1–7	Board of Trade Minutes, 1784–1792
CO 43/7–15	Correspondence, Entry Books, Quebec, 1766–1782
CO 42/1–14	Original Correspondence, Quebec, 1763–1777
CO 42/24–73	Original Correspondence, Quebec, 1761–1791
CO 91/11–37	Original Correspondence, Gibraltar, 1749–1795
CO 101/1–33	Original Correspondence, Grenada, 1763–1794
CO 102/1–16	Original Correspondence, Grenada, 1763–1799
CO 123/1	Original Correspondence, British Honduras, 1744–1766
CO 174/1–19	Original Correspondence, Minorca, 1712–1794

CO 323/18	Original Correspondence, Board of Trade, 1764–1766
CO 389/54–58	Entry Books, Gibraltar and Minorca, 1714–1803
FO 3/1–6	General Correspondence, Algiers, 1760–1789
FO 52/1–3	General Correspondence, Morocco, 1761–1775
FO 95/510	Treaties, Barbary States, 1698–1809
FO 95/520	Entry Books, Barbary States, 1695–1816
FO 113/3	Calendar of Documents, Algiers, 1690–1812
PC 1/7/35, 1/7/119, 1/7/146–147, 1/60/8	Miscellaneous Unbound Papers, Minorca
PC 1/7/106, 1/7/142, 1/13/46, 1/13/100, 1/33/83, 1/33/84	Miscellaneous Unbound Papers, Mediterranean Passes
PC 1/3170	Miscellaneous Unbound Papers, Gibraltar
PC 2/85, 2/88, 2/91	Registers, Mediterranean Passes
SP 71/10–11	State Papers Foreign, Algiers, 1756–1780
SP 71/20	State Papers Foreign, Morocco, 1756–1772
SP 78/260– 261, 78/268, 78/271, 78/277, 78/279	State Papers Foreign, France

Arxiú Históric de Mao (AHM), Menorca

U99–101, 129, 130–134, 160–162	Petitions and Correspondence of Jurats
U208, 268–269, 278–282, 368–369, 375–383	Miscellaneous
U393	Diario de Mahon

Government of Gibraltar Archives (GGA), Gibraltar

Admiralty Books 1–2	Forms, Rules, and Regulations for Mediterranean Passes
Book of Correspondence	Tunis and Tripoli, 1765–1774
Civil Secretary's Registers 3–5	Gibraltar, 1774–1793
Crown Land Series A	General Bland's Court of Enquiry, 1749–1750
Diaries of Occurrences	Gibraltar, 1777–1788
Letters to Consuls/ Ambassadors	Tripoli, Tunis, and Algiers, 1769–1797
Letters to Consuls/ Ambassadors	Tetuan and Tangier, 1769–1789

Letters to Consuls/Ambassadors	S. Barbary, Minorca, and the Islands, 1778–1797
Letters from Consuls	Malaga, Barbary, Tunis, Tripoli, Algiers, 1765–1776
List of Inhabitants	Gibraltar, 1777
List of Inhabitants	Gibraltar, 1791

Old Records Room, High Court, Calcutta

Uncatalogued bundles, 1757–1793

The National Library, Calcutta

The John Hyde Papers (microfilm)

The Victoria Memorial Library, Calcutta

R3190	Calendars of Sentences
R4074	Notebooks of Justice John Hyde

PRINTED PRIMARY SOURCES

Almon, John (later published by Henry Beevor). *The Political Register, and Impartial Review of New Books* (London: 1767–1772), vols. 1–10.

Anonymous. *Audi alteram Partem, or a Counter-Letter to the Right Hon. The E-l of H-ll-gh*. London: 1770.

Anonymous. *British Liberties, or the Free-Born Subject's Inheritance*. London: 1767.

Anonymous. *A Critical Review of the Liberties of British Subjects*. London: 1750.

Anonymous. *The Grenada Planter: or, a Full and Impartial Answer to a Letter in the Gazetteer of October 22, 1768*. London: 1768.

Anonymous. *A Guide to the Knowledge of the Rights and Privileges of Englishmen*. London: 1757.

Anonymous (signed A Grenada Proprietor). *A Letter to the Right Honourable the Earl of H-b-h, His M-y's S-y of S-te for the C-l-s, on the Present Situation of Affairs in the Island of Gr-n-da*. London: 1769.

Anonymous. *A Narrative of the Proceedings Upon the Complaint against Governor Melvill*. London: 1770.

Anonymous. *The Rights of the People Asserted and the Necessity of a More Equal Representation in Parliament Stated and Proved*. Dublin: 1783.

Articles of peace between his sacred majesty Charles the II and the city and kingdom of Algiers. London: 1664.
Articles of peace and commerce between Charles II and the city and kingdom of Algiers. Savoy: 1671.
Articles of peace and commerce between James II and the city and kingdom of Algiers. Savoy: 1687.
Beveridge, H. *The Trial of Maharaja Nanda Kumar, a Narrative of Judicial Murder*. Calcutta: 1886.
Blackstone, Sir William. *Commentaries on the Laws of England*. Edited by Stanley N. Katz. Chicago: University of Chicago Press, 1979.
Bodin, Jean. *Six Books of the Commonwealth*. Translated by M. J. Tooley. Lexington: Seven Treasures Publications, 2009.
Bolts, William. *Considerations on India affairs; particularly respecting the present state of Bengal and its dependencies*. London: 1772.
Brady, Robert. *A Complete History of England, from the First Entrance of the Romans . . . unto the End of the Reign of King Henry III*. Savoy: 1685.
Campbell, John. *Candid and impartial considerations on the nature of the sugar trade*. London: 1763.
Chalmers, George. *Opinions of Eminent Lawyers on Various Points of English Jurisprudence, Chiefly Concerning the Colonies, Fisheries, and Commerce of Great Britain*. London: 1814.
Chambers, Sir Robert. *A Course of Lectures on the English Law, 1767–1773*. Edited by Thomas Curley. Oxford: Clarendon Press, 1986.
Cockburn, Alexander. *Nationality: or the Law Relating to Subjects and Aliens, considered with a view to future legislation*. London: 1869.
Coke, Sir Edward. *The Seventh Part of the Reports of Sir Edward Coke*. London: 1738.
A Collection of statutes concerning the incorporation, trade, and commerce of the East India Company, and the government of the British possessions in India. London: 1794.
The Colonial Laws of New York from the Year 1664 to the Revolution. Albany: 1896.
Cowell, John. *The Interpreter: or Booke containing the signification of words wherin is set foorth the true meaning of all, or the most part of such words and termes, as are mentioned in the lawe writers, or statutes of this victorious and renowned kingdome, requiring any exposition or interpretation*. 1607.
Considerations on the addresses lately presented to His Majesty, on occasion of the loss of Minorca. In a letter to a Member of Parliament. London: 1756.
Copy of his Majesty's advocate, attorney, and solicitor generals report, August 16, 1757. [London?]: [1766?].
The definitive treaty of peace and friendship. London: 1763.
Diderot, Denis, and Jean le Rond d'Alembert, eds. *Encyclopédie, ou dictionnaire raisonné des sciences, des arts et des métiers, etc*. (University of Chicago: ARTFL Encyclopédie Project [Spring 2011 Edition]), Robert Morrissey, ed. http://encyclopedie.uchicago.edu.

Drinkwater, John. *A History of the Late Siege of Gibraltar with a Description and Account of that Garrison from the earliest periods*. London: 1790.

Eardley-Wilmot, John. *Historical View of the Commission for Enquiring into the Losses, Services, and Claims of the American Loyalists, at the Close of the War between Great Britain and her Colonies in 1783*. Boston: Gregg Press, 1972.

Egerton, Sir Thomas. *The Speech of the Lord Chancellor of England, in the Eschequer Chamber, touching the Post-nati*. London: 1609.

The English Reports. Abington: Professional Books, Ltd., 1986.

L'Estrange, Sir Richard. *The free-born subject: or, the Englishman's birthright asserted against all tyrannical usurptions either in church or state*. London: 1679.

Field, Henry. *Gibraltar*. New York: 1888.

Hale, Sir Matthew. *The Prerogatives of the King*. Edited by D. E. C. Yale. London: Selden Society, 1976.

Hansard's Parliamentary Debates 3rd ser., vol. 112. London: 1850.

Hertslet, Lewis, ed. *A complete collection of the treaties and conventions, and reciprocal regulations, at present subsisting between Great Britain and foreign powers*. London: 1841.

The history, debates, and proceedings of both Houses of Parliament of Great Britain from the year 1743 to the year 1774. London: 1792.

Howell, T. B. *A Complete Collection of State Trials*. London: 1816.

Ignotus, *Thoughts on trade in general, our West-Indian in particular, our continental colonies, Canada, Guadeloupe, and the preliminary articles of peace addressed to the community*. London: 1763.

Israel, Fred L., ed. *Major Peace Treaties of Modern History, 1648–1967*. New York: Chelsea House, 1967.

Johnson, Samuel. *A Dictionary of the English Language*. London: 1755.

Journal of the Commissioners for Trade and Plantations. London: His Majesty's Stationery Office, 1935.

Kerr, Lewis, ed. *Rules and Orders of the Supreme Court of Judicature at Fort William in Bengal*. Calcutta: 1798.

Knox, William. *Three tracts respecting the conversion and instruction of the free Indians and negroe slaves in the colonies*. London: 1772.

———. *The justice and policy of the late act of parliament for making more effectual provision for the government of the province of Quebec, asserted and proved: and the conduct of administration respecting that province stated and vindicated*. London: 1774.

La Marche-Courmont, Ignace Hugary de. *Essai politique sur les avantages que la France peut retirer de la conquête de l'isle Minorque: dedié à son altesse sérénissime Monseigneur le prince Louis de Wirtemberg*. Port-Mahon: 1756.

Lambert, Sheila, ed. *House of Commons Sessional Papers of the Eighteenth Century*, vol. 86. Wilmington: Scholarly Resources, 1975.

The laws of Grenada from the year 1763 to the year 1805. London: 1808.

A letter to Sir George Saville, Bart., upon the allegiance of a British Subject: occasioned by his late bill in parliament in favour of the Roman Catholics of this kingdom. London: 1778.

Letters from Minorca; describing the constitution, government, produce, antiquities, and natural history of that Island. Dublin: 1782.

Locke, John. *Second Treatise of Government.* Edited by C. B. Macpherson. Indianapolis: Hackett Publishing Company, 1980.

Maseres, Francis. *An Account of the Proceedings of the British and other Protestant Inhabitants of the Province of Quebeck in North America in order to obtain an House of Assembly in that Province.* London: 1775.

———. *Additional papers concerning the Province of Quebeck: being an Appendix to the Book entitled An Account of the British and other Protestant Inhabitants . . .* London: 1776.

———. *The Canadian Freedholder: in two dialogues between an Englishman and a Frenchman settled in Canada, shewing the sentiments of the Bulk of the Freeholders of Canada concerning the late Quebeck Act . . .* London: 1777.

Meredith, Sir William. *Letter from Thomas Lord Lyttelton, to William Pitt, Earl of Chatham, on the Quebec Bill.* New York: 1774.

Montesquieu, *The Spirit of the Laws.* Cambridge: Cambridge University Press, 1989.

Morgan, Maurice. *A plan for the abolition of slavery in the West Indies.* London: 1772.

Morton, T. C. *Decisions of the Supreme Court of Judicature at Fort William in Bengal: on the plea, equity, ecclesiastical, admiralty and crown sides, from the date of the charter of 1774 to 1841.* Calcutta: 1841.

Paine, Thomas. *The Rights of Man, Part I* (1791), eds. Bruce Kuklick, *Paine, Political Writings.* Cambridge: Cambridge University Press, 1989.

Parliamentary history of England from the earliest period to the year 1803, vol. 18. London: 1812–1820.

The Parliamentary Register; or history of the proceedings and debates of the House of Commons from 1775 to 1780. London: 1780.

The Parliamentary Register; or history of the proceedings and debates of the House of Commons from 1782 to 1796. London: 1796.

Parry, Clive. *The Consolidated Treaty Series*, vol. 28. Dobbs Ferry: Oceana Publications, 1969.

Penn, William, "The Excellent Priviledge of Liberty and Property Being the Birth-Right of the Free-Born Subjects of England (1687)." Reprinted in Philip Kurland and Ralph Lerner, eds., *The Founders' Constitution.* Chicago: University of Chicago Press, 1987.

Plowden, Francis. *An investigation of the native rights of British Subjects.* London: 1784.

———. *A supplement to the investigation of the native rights of British Subjects.* London: 1785.

———. *Jura Anglorum: The Rights of Englishmen.* Dublin: 1792.

Preliminary articles of peace between his Britannick Majesty, the most Christian King, and the Catholick King, signed at Fontainebleau. London: 1762.

The provincial statutes of Lower-Canada, vol. 1. Quebec: 1795.

Prynne, William. *A Seasonable, Historical, Legal Vindication and Chronological Collection of the good old Fundamental Liberties, Franchises, Rights, Laws of all English Freemen*. London: 1654.

Ramis y Ramis, Antonio. *Noticias Relativas a la Isla de Menorca Recopiladas por el Dr. Antonio Ramis y Ramis*. Mahon: Imprenta de la Serra, 1826–1838.

Regulations Framed in Pursuance of Several Acts with respect to Europeans (Not in the Service of the East India Company) Residing Within the Territories of the Company. [London?]: 1813.

Reports from Committees of the House of Commons, vol. 5. London: 1804.

Reports of Proceedings Connected with the East Indians' Petition to Parliament, read at Town Hall, Calcutta, March 28, 1831. Calcutta: 1831.

Richmond, Captain H. W. *Papers Relating to the Loss of Minorca in 1756*. London: Navy Records Society, 1913.

The Rules and Orders of the Supreme Court of Judicature at Fort William in Bengal with the Charter of Justice, and the Several Statutes Relating to the Court. Calcutta: 1829.

The several petitions of the British Inhabitants of Bengal, of the Governor-General and Council, and of the Court of Directors of the East India Company to Parliament. London: 1780.

Sharpe, Granville. *A representation of the injustice and dangerous tendency of tolerating slavery*. London: 1769.

Shortt, Adam, and Arthur G. Doughty, eds. *Documents relating to the Constitutional History of Canada, 1759–1791*. Ottawa: J. de La Taché, 1918.

Smoult, W. H. *A Collection of Orders Made and Passed by The Supreme Court of Judicature at Fort William in Bengal*. Calcutta: 1834.

"Some Records Relative to the Mayor's Court." *Bengal Past and Present: Journal of the Calcutta Historical Society* 8 [1913?]: 1–39.

Spedding, James, ed. *The letters and the Life of Francis Bacon, including all his occasional works*, vols. 3 and 4. London: 1868.

Tanner, J. R. *Constitutional Documents of the Reign of James I, 1603–1625*. Cambridge: Cambridge University Press, 1960.

The statutes at large of England and of Great Britain from Magna Carta to the Union of the Kingdoms of Great Britain and Ireland. London: 1811.

The statutes at large from the first year of King James the first to the tenth year of the reign of King William the third. London: 1770.

Treaty of peace and commerce between Great Britain and the kingdom of Tripoli concluded September 19, 1751. London: 1752.

Treaty of peace and commerce between Great Britain and the state of Tunis concluded October 19, 1751. London: 1752.

Treaty of peace and commerce between the King of Great Britain and the Emperor of Morocco dated July 28, 1760. London: 1763.

The Trial of Maha Raja Nundocomar, Bahader, for forgery. London: 1776.

Voltaire. *Letters Concerning the English Nation*. Edited by Nicholas Cronk. Oxford: Oxford University Press, 1994.

Wright, J., ed. *Debates of the House of Commons in the year 1774, on the Bill for Making More Effectual Provision for the Government of the Province of Quebec*. London: 1839.

Young, Arthur. *Political essays concerning the present state of the British Empire*. London: 1772.

Young, Sir William. *Considerations which may tend to promote the settlement of our New West-India colonies, by encouraging individuals to embark in the undertaking*. London: 1764.

———. *Some observations which may contribute to afford a just idea of the nature, importance, and settlement, of our new West-India colonies*. London: 1764.

SECONDARY SOURCES

Anderson, Benedict. *Imagined Communities: Reflections on the Origin and Spread of Nationalism*. London: Verso, 1991.

Anderson, Caitlin. "Old Subjects, New Subjects, and Non-Subjects: Silences and Subjecthood." In *War, Empire, and Slavery, 1770–1830*, edited by Jane Rendall, Guyatt, Nicholas, and Bessel, Richard, 201–217. Houndsmills: Palgrave, 2010.

Anderson, Fred. *Crucible of War: The Seven Years' War and the Fate of Empire in British North America, 1754–1766*. New York: Vintage Books, 2001.

Anderson, Martin. "Tourism and the Development of the Modern British Passport, 1814–1858." *The Journal of British Studies* 49, no. 2 (2010): 258–282.

Anderson, M. S. "Great Britain and the Barbary States in the Eighteenth Century." *Bulletin of the Institute of Historical Research* 29, no. 79 (1956): 87–107.

Archer, Edward G. *Gibraltar: Identity and Empire*. London: Routledge, 1996.

Armitage, David. *The Ideological Origins of the British Empire*. Cambridge: Cambridge University Press, 2000.

———. *The Declaration of Independence: A Global History*. Cambridge, MA: Harvard University Press, 2007.

Armitage, David, and Sanjay Subrahmanyam. *The Age of Revolutions in Global Context, c. 1760–1840*. Houndsmills: Palgrave Macmillan, 2010.

Ashley, Mike. *Taking Liberties: The Struggle for Britain's Freedoms and Rights*. London: The British Library, 2008.

Atkinson, Alan. "The Free-Born Englishman Transported: Convict Rights as a Measure of the Eighteenth-Century Empire." *Past and Present* 44, no. 1 (1994): 88–115.

Atwood, Margaret. *Survival: A Thematic Guide to Canadian Literature*. Toronto: Anansi, 1972.

Bailyn, Bernard. *Voyagers to the West: A Passage in the Peopling of America on the Eve of Revolution*. New York: Vintage Books, 1988.

Baker, John Hamilton. *An Introduction to English Legal History*. London: Butterworths, 1990.

———. "Why the History of English Law Has Not Been Finished." *Cambridge Law Journal* 59, no. 1 (2000): 62–84.

Baker, Rodney. *Political Legitimacy and the State*. Oxford: Clarendon Press, 1990.

Baldwin, M. Page. "Subject to Empire: Married Women and the British Nationality and Status of Aliens Act." *The Journal of British Studies* 40, no. 4 (2001): 522–556.

Balibar, Etienne, and Immanuel Wallerstein. *Race, Nation, Class: Ambiguous Identities*. London: Verso, 1991.

Banks, Kenneth, *Chasing Empire Across the Sea: Communications and the State in the French Atlantic, 1713–1763*. Montreal: McGill–Queen's University Press, 2002.

Bannister, Jerry, and Liam Riordan. *The Loyal Atlantic: Remaking the British Atlantic in the Revolutionary Era*. Toronto: University of Toronto Press, 2012.

Bassett, Judith. "A Thousand Miles of Loyalty: The Royal Tour of 1901." *New Zealand Journal of History* 21 (1987): 125–138.

Bayly, C. A. *Imperial Meridian: The British Empire and the World, 1780–1830*. London: Longman, 1989.

———. *Empire and Information: Intelligence Gathering and Social Communication in India, 1780–1870*. Cambridge: Cambridge University Press, 1996.

———. "The British and Indigenous Peoples, 1760–1860: Power, Perception, and Identity." In *Empire and Others: British Encounters with Indigenous Peoples, 1600–1850*, edited by Mark Daunton and Rick Halpern, 19–41. Philadelphia: University of Pennsylvania Press, 1999.

———. *The Birth of the Modern World, 1780–1914: Global Connections and Comparisons*. Malden: Blackwell, 2004.

Belmessous, Saliha, ed. *Native Claims: Indigenous Law against Empire, 1500–1920*. New York: Oxford University Press, 2011.

Benady, Tito. "The Settee Cut: Mediterranean Passes Issued at Gibraltar." *The Mariner's Mirror* 87, no. 3 (2001): 281–296.

Benton, Lauren. *Law and Colonial Cultures: Legal Regimes in World History, 1400–1900*. Cambridge: Cambridge University Press, 2001.

———. *A Search for Sovereignty: Law and Geography in European Empires, 1400–1900*. Cambridge: Cambridge University Press, 2010.

Benton, Lauren, and Benjamin Straumann. "Acquiring Empire by Law: From Roman Doctrine to Early Modern European Practice." *Law and History Review* 28, no. 1 (2010): 1–38.

Bilder, Mary Sarah. "Salamanders and Sons of God: The Culture of Appeal in Early New England." In *The Many Legalities of Early America*, edited by Christopher L. Tomlins and Bruce H. Mann, 47–77. Chapel Hill: University of North Carolina Press, 2001.

———. *The Transatlantic Constitution: Colonial Legal Culture and the Empire*. Cambridge, MA: Harvard University Press, 2004.

Black, Barbara. "The Constitution of Empire." *University of Pennsylvania Law Review* 124, no. 5 (1976): 1157–1211.

Blanning, Timothy. *The Pursuit of Glory, Europe, 1648–1815*. London: Viking, 2007.

Blinkhorn, Martin. "Liability, Responsibility, and Blame: British Ransom Victims in the Mediterranean Periphery, 1860–81." *Australian Journal of Politics and History* 46, no. 3 (2000): 336–356.

Bogdanor, Vernon. *The Monarchy and the Constitution*. Oxford: Clarendon Press, 1995.

Bossenga, Gail. "Rights and Citizens in the Old Regime." *French Historical Studies* 20, no. 2 (1997): 217–243.

Bowen, H. V. *Revenue and Reform: The Indian Problem in British Politics, 1757–1773*. Cambridge: Cambridge University Press, 1991.

———. "British Conceptions of Global Empire, 1756–1783." *The Journal of Imperial and Commonwealth History* 26 (1998): 1–27.

Bradburn, Douglas. "The Problem of Citizenship in the American Revolution." *History Compass* 8/9 (2010): 1093–1113.

Bradshaw, Brendan, and John Morrill, *The British Problem, c. 1534–1707: State Formation in the Atlantic Archipelago*. Houndsmills: Macmillan, 1996.

Braudel, Fernand. *The Mediterranean and the Mediterranean World in the Age of Philip II*. New York: Harper & Row, 1972.

Brebner, John Bartlet. *New England's Outpost: Acadia before the Conquest of Canada*. New York: Columbia University Press, 1927.

Brewer, Holly. *By Birth or Consent: Children, Law, and the Anglo-American Revolution in Authority*. Chapel Hill: University of North Carolina Press, 2005.

Brewer, John. *The Sinews of Power: War, Money, and the English State, 1688–1783*. Cambridge, MA: Harvard University Press, 1988.

Brewer, John, and John Styles, eds. *An Ungovernable People: The English and their Law in the Seventeenth and Eighteenth Centuries*. New Brunswick: Rutgers University Press, 1980.

Brewer, John, and Susan Staves, eds. *Early Modern Conceptions of Property*. London: Routledge, 1995.

Brizan, George. *Grenada, Island of Conflict: From Amerindians to People's Revolution, 1498–1979*. London: Zed Books, 1984.

Brown, Christopher L. "From Slaves to Subjects: Envisioning an Empire without Slavery, 1772–1834." In *Black Experience and the Empire,* edited by Philip D. Morgan and Sean Hawkins, 111–140. Oxford: Oxford University Press, 2004.

———. *Moral Capital: Foundations of British Abolitionism*. Chapel Hill: University of North Carolina Press, 2006.

Brown, David. "The Power of Public Opinion: Palmerston and the Crisis of December 1851." *Parliamentary History* 20 (2001): 333–358.

Brubaker, Rogers. *Citizenship and Nationhood in France and Germany*. Cambridge, MA: Harvard University Press, 1992.

Bruckner, Martin, and Hsuan L. Hsu. *American Literary Geographies: Spatial Practice and Cultural Production*. Newark: University of Delaware Press, 2007.

Brunsman, Denver. "Subjects and Citizens: Impressment and Identity in the Anglo-American Atlantic." *Journal of the Early Republic* 30, no. 4 (2010): 557–586.

Burbank, Jane, and Fred Cooper. *Empires in World History: Power and Politics of Difference*. Princeton: Princeton University Press, 2011.

Burgess, Glenn. *The Politics of the Ancient Constitution: An Introduction to English Political Thought, 1603–1642*. University Park: Penn State University Press, 1992.

Burns, Kathryn. *Into the Archives: Writing and Power in Colonial Peru*. Durham: Duke University Press, 2010.

Burns, Robert E. "The Catholic Relief Act in Ireland, 1778." *Church History* 32 (1963): 181–206.

Bush, Jonathan. "Free to Enslave: The Foundations of Colonial American Slave Law." *Yale Journal of Law and the Humanities* 5, no. 2 (1993): 417–470.

———. "You're Gonna Miss Me When I'm Gone: Early Modern Common Law Discourse and the Case of the Jews." *Wisconsin Law Review* 1993, no. 5 (1993): 1225–1285.

———. "The British Constitution and the Creation of American Slavery." In *Slavery and the Law*, edited by Paul Finkelman, 379–418. Madison: Madison House, 1996.

Bushman, Richard L. *King and People in Provincial Massachusetts*. Chapel Hill: University of North Carolina Press, 1992.

Cadava, Eduardo, Peter Connor, and Jean-Luc Nancy, eds. *Who Comes after the Subject?* New York: Routledge, 1991.

Cairns, John W. "Natural Law and the History of Scots Law." In *The Cambridge Companion to The Scottish Enlightenment*, edited by Alexander Broadie, 222–242. Cambridge: Cambridge University Press, 2003.

Calloway, Colin G. *The Scratch of a Pen: 1763 and the Transformation of North America*. New York: Oxford University Press, 2006.

Cañeque, Alejandro. *The King's Living Image: The Culture and Politics of Vice-Regal Power in Colonial Mexico*. New York: Routledge, 2004.

Cannadine, David. *Ornamentalism: How the British Saw Their Empire*. New York: Oxford University Press, 2001.

Canny, Nicholas. *Kingdom and Colony: Ireland in the Atlantic World, 1560–1800*. Baltimore: Johns Hopkins University Press, 1988.

Carton, Adrian. "Shades of Fraternity: Creolization and the Making of Citizenship in French India, 1790–1792." *French Historical Studies* 31, no. 4 (2008): 581–607.

Cavanagh, Edward. "A Company with Sovereignty and Subjects of Its Own? The Case of the Hudson's Bay Company, 1670–1783." *Canadian Journal of Law and Society* 26, no. 1 (2011): 25–50.

Christie, Ian. *Crisis of Empire: Great Britain and the American Colonies, 1754–1783*. London: Edward Arnold, 1966.

Christie, Nancy, ed. *Transatlantic Subjects: Ideas, Institutions, and Social Experience in Post-Revolutionary British North America*. Montreal: McGill–Queen's University Press, 2008.

Clark, J. C. D. *The Language of Liberty, 1660–1832: Political Discourse and Social Dynamics in the Anglo-American World*. Cambridge: Cambridge University Press, 1994.

Close, Robin E. "The Attempted Repeal of the Quebec Act: The State of Parliamentary Opposition in 1775." *Past Imperfect* 1 (1992): 77–91.

Colley, Linda. "The Apotheosis of George III: Loyalty, Royalty and the British Nation, 1760–1820." *Past and Present* 102 (1984): 94–129.

———. *Britons: Forging the Nation, 1707–1837*. New Haven: Yale University Press, 1992.

———. "Britishness and Otherness: An Argument." *The Journal of British Studies* 31, no. 4 (1992): 309–329.

———. *Captives: Britain, Empire and the World, 1600–1850*. New York: Anchor, 2004.

Conn, Stetson. *Gibraltar in British Diplomacy in the Eighteenth Century*. New Haven: Yale University Press, 1942.

Constantine, Stephen. "Monarchy and Constructing Identity in 'British' Gibraltar, c. 1800 to the Present." *The Journal of Imperial and Commonwealth History* 34, no. 1 (2006): 23–44.

———. *Community and Identity: The Making of Modern Gibraltar since 1704*. Manchester: Manchester University Press, 2009.

Conway, Stephen. "From Fellow-Nationals to Foreigners: British Perceptions of Americans, circa 1739–1783." *The William and Mary Quarterly* 59 (2002): 65–100.

Corbett, Julian S. *England in the Mediterranean: A Study of the Rise and Influence of British Power within the Straits, 1603–1713*. London: Longmans, Green, and Co., 1904.

Coupland, Reginald. *The Quebec Act: A Study in Statesmanship*. Oxford: Clarendon Press, 1925.

Cox, Edward. "Fedon's Rebellion, 1795–6: Causes and Consequences." *The Journal of Negro History* 67, no. 1 (1982): 7–19.

———. *Free Coloreds in the Slave Societies of St. Kitts and Grenada, 1763–1833*. Knoxville: University of Tennessee Press, 1984.

Cromartie, Alan. *The Constitutionalist Revolution: An Essay on the History of England, 1450–1642*. New York: Cambridge University Press, 2006.

Curley, Thomas M. *Sir Robert Chambers: Law, Literature, and Empire in the Age of Johnson*. Madison: University of Wisconsin Press, 1998.

Daniels, Christine, and Michael V. Kennedy, eds. *Negotiated Empires: Centers and Peripheries in the Americas, 1500–1820*. New York: Routledge, 2002.

Davis, Robert C. *Christian Slaves, Muslim Masters: White Slavery in the Mediterranean, the Barbary Coast, and Italy, 1500–1800*. Houndsmills: Palgrave, 2003.

De Hart, Edward Louis. "The English Law of Nationality and Naturalisation." *Journal of the Society of Comparative Legislation*. New Series 2, no. 1 (1900): 11–26.

Devas, Raymond. *Conception Island: The Troubled Story of the Catholic Church in Grenada*. London: Sands and Co., 1932.

Dinwiddy, J. R. "The Use of the Crown's Power of Deportation Under the Aliens Act, 1793–1826." *Bulletin of the Institute of Historical Research* 41 (1968): 193–211.

Donovan, Robert Kent. "The Military Origins of the Roman Catholic Relief Programme of 1778." *The Historical Journal* 28, no. 1 (1985): 79–102.

Dowd, Gregory Evans. *War under Heaven: Pontiac, the Indian Nations and the British Empire*. Baltimore: Johns Hopkins University Press, 2002.

———. "Domestic, Dependent, Nations: The Colonial Origins of a Paradox." In *Backcountry Crucibles: The Lehigh Valley from Settlement to Steel*, edited by Jean R. Soderlund and Catherine S. Parzynski. Bethlehem: Lehigh University Press, 2007.

Dummett, Ann, and Andrew Nicol. *Subjects, Citizens, Aliens and Others: Nationality and Immigration Law*. London: Weidenfeld & Nicolson, 1990.

Dursteler, Eric. *Venetians in Constantinople: Nation, Identity, and Coexistence in the Early Modern Mediterranean*. Baltimore: Johns Hopkins University Press, 2006.

Edwards, J. *The Law Officers of the Crown*. London: Sweet & Maxwell, 1964.

Edwards, Laura. *The People and Their Peace: Legal Culture and the Transformation of Inequality in the Post-Revolutionary South*. Chapel Hill: University of North Carolina Press, 2009.

Elliott, J. H. "A Europe of Composite Monarchies." *Past and Present* 137 (1992): 48–71.

———. *Empires of the Atlantic World: Britain and Spain in America, 1492–1830*. New Haven: Yale University Press, 2006.

Ellis, Stephen G., and Sarah Barber, *Conquest and Union: Fashioning a British State, 1486–1725*. London: Longman, 1995.

Erickson, Amy Louise. "Common Law versus Common Practice: The Use of Marriage Settlements in Early Modern England." *Economic History Review* 43, no. 1 (1990): 21–39.

Fahrmeir, Andreas. *Citizens and Aliens: Foreigners and the Law in Britain and the German States, 1789–1870*. New York: Berghahn Books, 2000.

———. *Citizenship: The Rise and Fall of a Modern Concept*. New Haven: Yale University Press, 2007.

Fawcett, Sir Charles. *The First Century of British Justice in India*. Oxford: Clarendon Press, 1934.

Field, Henry M. *Gibraltar*. New York: Charles Scribner's Sons, 1888.

Firminger, Walter K. "Selections from the Note Books of Justice John Hyde." *Bengal Past and Present* 3, no. 1 (1909): 27–64.

Fisher, Sir Godfrey. *Barbary Legend: War, Trade and Piracy in North Africa, 1415–1830*. Oxford: Clarendon Press, 1957.

Ford, Lisa. *Settler Sovereignty: Jurisdiction and Indigenous People in America and Australia, 1788–1836*. Cambridge, MA: Harvard University Press, 2010.

Forbath, William E., Hendrik Hartog, and Martha Minow. "Introduction: Legal Histories from Below." *Wisconsin Law Review* 4 (1985): 759–766.

Foster, Elizabeth Read. "Petitions and the Petition of Right." *The Journal of British Studies* 14:1 (1974): 21–45.

Foxley, Rachel. "John Lilburne and the Citizenship of 'Free-Born Englishmen.'" *The Historical Journal* 47, no. 4 (2004): 849–874.

———. *The Levellers: Radical Political Thought in the English Revolution*. Manchester: Manchester University Press, 2013.

Friedman, Ellen G. "Christian Captives at Hard Labor in Algiers." *The International Journal of African History* 13, no. 4 (1980): 616–632.

Frye, Northrup. *The Bush Garden: Essays on the Canadian Imagination*. Toronto: Anansi, 1971.

Fyson, Donald. "The Conquered and the Conqueror: The Mutual Adaptation of the Canadiens and the British in Quebec, 1759–1775." In *Revisiting 1759*. Toronto: University of Toronto Press, 2012.

Garrigus, John D. *Before Haiti: Race and Citizenship in French Saint-Domingue*. New York: Palgrave-Macmillan, 2006.

George, Pierre. *Quebec: Que sais-je?* Paris: PUF, 1979.

Ghosh, Durba. "Who Counts as Native?: Gender, Race, and Subjectivity in Colonial India." *Journal of Colonialism and Colonial History* 6, no. 3 (2005).

———. *Sex and the Family in Colonial India: The Making of Empire*. Cambridge: Cambridge University Press, 2006.

Gipson, Lawrence Henry. *The British Empire Before the American Revolution. The Great War for the Empire: The Years of Defeat, 1754–1757*, vol. 4. New York: Knopf, 1959.

———. *The Triumphant Empire: New Responsibilities within the Enlarged Empire, 1763–1766*, vol. 9. New York: Knopf, 1956.

Glass, D. V. *Numbering the People: The Eighteenth-Century Population Controversy and the Development of Census and Vital Statistics in Britain*. London: D. C. Heath, 1973.

Glasson, Travis. "Baptism doth not Bestow Freedom." *The William and Mary Quarterly* 67, no. 2 (April 2010): 279–318.

Goffman, Daniel. *Britons in the Ottoman Empire, 1642–1660*. Seattle: University of Washington Press, 1998.

Golby, J. M., and A. W. Purdue. *The Monarchy and the British People, 1760 to the Present*. London: B. T. Batsford, 1988.

Goose, Nigel, and Lien Luu, eds. *Immigrants in Tudor and Early Stuart England*. Brighton: Sussex Academic Press, 2005.

Gordon, Robert W. "J. Williard Hurst and the Common Law Tradition in American Legal Historiography." *Law and Society Review* 10 (1975): 9–55.

———. "Critical Legal Histories." *Stanford Law Review* 36, no. 1–2 (1984): 57–125.

Gorman, Daniel. "Wider and Wider Still?: Racial Politics, Intra-Imperial Immigration and the Absence of an Imperial Citizenship in the British Empire." *Journal of Colonialism and Colonial History* 3, no. 3 (2002).

Gould, Eliga. *The Persistence of Empire: British Political Culture in the Age of the American Revolution*. Chapel Hill: University of North Carolina Press, 2000.

———. "Zones of Law, Zones of Violence: The Legal Geography of the British Atlantic, circa 1772." *The William and Mary Quarterly* 60, no. 3 (2003): 471–510.

Greene, Jack P. *Peripheries and Center: Constitutional Development in the Extended Polities of the British Empire and the United States, 1607–1788*. New York: W. W. Norton & Company, 1990.

Greene Jack P., ed. *Exclusionary Empire: English Liberty Overseas, 1600–1900*. Cambridge: Cambridge University Press, 2010.

Greengrass, Mark, ed. *Conquest and Coalescence: The Shaping of the State in Early Modern Europe*. London: Edward Arnold, 1991.

Greenwood, F. Murray. *Legacies of Fear: Law and Politics in Quebec in the Era of the French Revolution*. Toronto: University of Toronto Press, 1993.

Gregory, Desmond. *Minorca, the Illusory Prize: A History of the British Occupations of Minorca between 1708 and 1802*. Rutherford: Fairleigh Dickinson University Press, 1990.

Grell, Ole Peter, and Roy Porter, eds. *Toleration in Enlightenment Europe*. Cambridge: Cambridge University Press, 2000.

Griffiths, N. E. S. *From Migrant to Acadian: A North American Border People, 1604–1755*. Montreal: McGill–Queen's University Press, 2005.

Haller, William, ed. *The Leveller Tracts, 1647–1653*. Gloucester: P. Smith, 1964.

Halliday, Paul D. *Habeas Corpus: From England to Empire*. Cambridge, MA: Harvard University Press, 2010.

Halliday, Paul, and Edward G. White. "The Suspension Clause: English Text, Imperial Contexts, and American Implications." *Virginia Law Review* 94 (2008): 575–714.

Hamburger, Philip. "Equality and Diversity: The Eighteenth-Century Debate about Equal Protection and Equal Civil Rights." *The Supreme Court Review* (1992): 295–392.

———. "Natural Rights, Natural Law, and American Constitutions." *The Yale Law Journal* 102 (1993): 907–960.

———. "Beyond Protection." *Columbia Law Review* 10, no. 8 (2010): 1823–2001.

Hannell, David. "Lord Palmerston and the 'Don Pacifico Affair' of 1850: The Ionian Connection." *European History Quarterly* 19 (1989): 495–507.

Harding, Nicholas B. "North African Piracy, the Hanoverian Carrying Trade, and the British State, 1728–1828." *The Historical Journal* 43, no. 1 (2000): 25–47.

———. *Hanover and the British Empire, 1700–1837*. Woodbridge: The Boydell Press, 2007.

Harlow, Vincent T. *The Founding of the Second British Empire, 1763–1793*. London: Longmans, Green, and Co., 1952.

Hartog, Henrik. "Pigs and Positivism." *Wisconsin Law Review* 4 (1985): 899–935.

Hawes, Christopher. *Poor Relations: The Making of the Eurasian Community in British India, 1773–1833*. Richmond: Curzon, 1996.

Hay, Douglas, and Paul Craven, eds. *Masters, Servants, and Magistrates in Britain and the Empire, 1562–1955*. Chapel Hill: University of North Carolina Press, 2004.

Haydon, Colin. *Anti-Catholicism in Eighteenth-Century England, c. 1714–80: A Political and Social Study*. Manchester: Manchester University Press, 1993.

Hechter, Michael. *Internal Colonialism: The Celtic Fringe in British National Development, 1536–1966*. Berkeley: University of California Press, 1975.

Herzog, Tamar. *Defining Nations: Immigrants and Citizens in Early Modern Spain and Spanish America*. New Haven: Yale University Press, 2003.

Hicks, Geoffrey. "Don Pacifico, Democracy, and Danger: The Protectionist Party Critique of British Foreign Policy, 1850–1852." *The International History Review* 26, no. 3 (2004): 515–540.

Hill, Jacqueline. "Religious Toleration and the Relaxation of the Penal Laws: An Imperial Perspective, 1763–1780." *Archivium Hibernicum* 44, no. 3 (1989): 98–109.

Hills, George. *Rock of Contention: A History of Gibraltar*. London: Hale, 1974.

Hobsbawm, Eric. *The Age of Revolution, 1789–1848*. New York: Vintage, 1996.

Hobsbawm, Eric, and Terence Ranger. *The Invention of Tradition*. Cambridge: Cambridge University Press, 1983.

Hodson, Christopher. *The Acadian Diaspora: An Eighteenth-Century History*. New York: Oxford University Press, 2012.

Holdsworth, William Searle. *A History of English Law*. London: Methuen, 1922.

Holt, J. C. *Magna Carta: Second Edition*. Cambridge: Cambridge University Press, 1992.

Horn, D. B. *The British Diplomatic Service, 1689–1789*. Oxford: Clarendon Press, 1961.

Hsueh, Vicki. *Hybrid Constitutions: Challenging Legacies of Law, Privilege, and Culture in Colonial America*. Durham: Duke University Press, 2010.

Hulsebosch, Daniel J. "The Ancient Constitution and the Expanding Empire: Sir Edward Coke's British Jurisprudence." *Law and History Review* 21, no. 3 (2003): 439–482.

———. *Constituting Empire: New York and the Transformation of Constitutionalism in the Atlantic World, 1664–1830*. Chapel Hill: University of North Carolina Press, 2005.

———. "The American Revolution (II): The Origin and Nature of Colonial Grievances." In *The Oxford History of the British Empire: British North America in the Seventeenth and Eighteenth Centuries,* edited by Stephen Foster, 289–317. Oxford: Oxford University Press, 2013.

Humphreys, R. A. "Lord Shelburne and the Proclamation of 1763." *The English Historical Review* 49, no. 194 (1934): 241–264.

Hussain, Nasser. *The Jurisprudence of Emergency: Colonialism and the Rule of Law*. Ann Arbor: University of Michigan Press, 2003.

Hutson, James H. "The Emergence of the Modern Concept of a Right in America: The Contribution of Michel Villey." *American Journal of Jurisprudence* 39 (1994).

Jackson, Sir William. *The Rock of the Gibraltarians: A History of Gibraltar*. Rutherford: Fairleigh Dickinson University Press, 1987.

Jain, M. P. *Indian Legal History*. Bombay: N. M. Tripathi, 1966.

Jasanoff, Maya. *Edge of Empire: Lives, Culture, and Conquest in the East, 1750–1850*. New York: Alfred A. Knopf, 2005.

———. "Cosmopolitan: A Tale of Identity from Ottoman Alexandria." *Common Knowledge* 11, no. 3 (2005): 393–409.

———. *Liberty's Exiles: American Loyalists in the Revolutionary World*. New York: Knopf, 2011.

Jones, David Martin. *Conscience and Allegiance in Seventeenth-Century England: The Political Significance of Oaths and Engagements*. Rochester: University of Rochester Press, 1999.

Jones, J. Mervyn. *British Nationality Law and Practice*. Oxford: Clarendon Press, 1947.

Kantorowicz, Ernst H. *The King's Two Bodies: A Study in Mediaeval Political Theology*. Princeton: Princeton University Press, 1957.

Karatani, Rieko. *Defining British Citizenship: Empire, Commonwealth, and Modern Britain*. London: Frank Cass, 2003.

Kenyon, J. P. *The Stuart Constitution: Documents and Commentary*. Second Edition. Cambridge: Cambridge University Press, 1986.

Keohane, Nannerl O. *Philsophy and the State in France: the Renaissance to the Enlightenment*. Princeton: Princeton University Press, 1980.

Kerber, Linda K. *No Constitutional Right to Be Ladies: Women and the Obligations of Citizenship*. New York: Hill and Wang, 1998.

Kettner, James H. "Subjects or Citizens? A Note on British Views Respecting the Legal Effects of American Independence." *Virginia Law Review* 62, no. 5 (1976): 945–967.

———. *The Development of American Citizenship, 1608–1870*. Chapel Hill: University of North Carolina Press, 1978.

Kidd, Colin. *British Identities before Nationalism: Ethnicity and Nationhood in the Atlantic World, 1600–1800*. Cambridge: Cambridge University Press, 1999.

Killingray, David. "A Good West Indian, a Good African, and, in Short, a Good Britisher: Black and British in a Colour-Conscious Empire, 1760–1950." *The Journal of Imperial and Commonwealth History* 36, no. 3 (2008): 363–381.

Kim, Keechang. "Calvin's Case (1608) and the Law of Alien Status." *Journal of Legal History* 17 (1996): 155–171.

———. *Aliens in Medieval Law: The Origins of Modern Citizenship*. Cambridge: Cambridge University Press, 2000.

Knights, Mark. *Representation and Misrepresentation in Later Stuart Britain: Partisanship and Political Culture*. Oxford: Oxford University Press, 2005.

Knott, Sarah. "Narrating the Age of Revolution." *William and Mary Quarterly* 73, no. 1 (2016): 3–36.

Kolsky, Elizabeth. *Colonial Justice in British India: White Violence and the Rule of Law*. Cambridge: Cambridge University Press, 2010.

Koziol, Geoffrey. *Begging Pardon and Favor: Ritual and Political Order in Early Medieval France*. Ithaca: Cornell University Press, 1992.

Kunkel, Wolfgang. *An Introduction to Roman Legal and Constitutional History*. Oxford: Clarendon Press, 1972.

Lacey, Michael J., and Knud Haakonssen. *A Culture of Rights: The Bill of Rights in Philosophy, Politics, and Law—1791 and 1991*. Cambridge: Cambridge University Press, 1991.

Lash, Kurt. *The Fourteenth Amendment and the Privileges and Immunities of American Citizenship*. New York: Cambridge University Press, 2014.

Laurie, Bruce. *The Life of Richard Kane: Britain's First Lieutenant-Governor of Minorca*. Rutherford: Fairleigh Dickinson University Press, 1994.

Lawson, Philip. "Parliament and the First East India Inquiry, 1767." *Parliamentary History* 1 (1982): 99–114.

———. *The Imperial Challenge: Quebec and Britain in the Age of the American Revolution*. Montreal: McGill-Queen's University Press, 1989.

Lawson, Philip, and Jim Philips. "Our Inexecrable Banditti: Perceptions of Nabobs in Mid-Eighteenth-Century Britain." *Albion* 16 (1984): 225–241.

Lee, Hilda. "The Supervising of the Barbary Consulates, 1768–1836." *Bulletin of the Institute of Historical Research* 23 (1950): 191–199.

Leighton, C. D. A. *Catholicism in a Protestant Kingdom: A Study of the Irish Ancien Régime*. New York: St. Martin's Press, 1994.

Lemmings, David. *Professors of the Law: Barristers and English Legal Culture in the Eighteenth Century*. Oxford: Oxford University Press, 2000.

Lemmings, David, ed. *The British and Their Laws in the Eighteenth Century*. Woodbridge: Boydell Press, 2005.

Levack, Brian. *The Formation of the British State: England, Scotland, and the Union, 1603–1707*. Oxford: Clarendon Press, 1987.

Leve, H. J. "Legal Expansion in the Age of the Companies." In *European Expansion and Law: The Encounter of European and Indigenous Law in 19th- and 20th-Century Africa and Asia*, edited by W. J. Mommsen and J. A. Moor, 129–158. New York: Berg, 1992.

Lieberman, David. *The Province of Legislation Determined: Legal Theory in Eighteenth-Century Britain*. Cambridge: Cambridge University Press, 1989.

Lloyd, Christopher. *English Corsairs on the Barbary Coast*. London: Collins, 1981.

Madden, A. F. "1066, 1776, and All That: The Relevance of Medieval Experience of 'Empire' to Later Imperial Constitutional Issues." In *Perspectives of Empire* 9, edited by J. Flint and G. Williams. New York: Barnes and Noble Books, 1973.

Madden, Frederick, and David Fieldhouse, eds. *Select Documents on the Constitutional History of the British Empire and Commonwealth*. London: Greenwood Press, 1985.

Marshall, Peter J. *Problems of Empire: Britain and India, 1757–1813*. New York: Barnes & Noble, 1968.

———. "The Incorporation of Quebec in the British Empire, 1763–1774." In *Of Mother Country and Plantations: Proceedings of the Twenty-Seventh Conference in Early American History,* edited by V. B. Platt and D. C. Skaggs, 42–64. Bowling Green, OH: Bowling Green State University Press, 1970.

———. "Empire and Authority in the Later Eighteenth Century." *The Journal of Imperial and Commonwealth History* 15, no. 2 (1987): 105–122.

———. "A Nation Defined by Empire, 1755–1776." In *Uniting the Kingdom?: The Making of British History*, edited by Alexander Grant and Keith J. Stringer, 208–222. London: Routledge, 1995.

———. "Britain and the World in the Eighteenth Century: IV, The Turning Outwards of Britain." In *Transactions of the Royal Historical Society* 6th ser., 11 (2001): 1–15.

———. *The Making and Unmaking of Empires: Britain, India, and America, c. 1750–1784*. Oxford: Oxford University Press, 2005.

———. "The Muharram Riot of 1779 and the Struggle for Status and Authority in Early Colonial India." *Journal of the Asiatic Society of Bangladesh* 50, nos. 1–2 (2005): 293–314.

Marshall, T. H. *Citizenship and Social Class, and Other Essays*. Cambridge: Cambridge University Press, 1950.

Mata, Micaela. *Conquests and Reconquests of Menorca*. Barcelona: Imprenta Juvenil, 1984.

McConville, Brendan. *The King's Three Faces: The Rise and Fall of Royal America, 1688–1776*. Chapel Hill: University of North Carolina Press, 2006.

McDonald, Forrest. *Novus ordo seclorum: The Intellectual Origins of the Constitution*. Lawrence: University Press of Kansas, 1985.

Merrick, Jeffrey. "Conscience and Citizenship in Eighteenth-Century France." *Eighteenth Century Studies* 21, no. 1 (1987): 48–70.

———. "Subjects and Citizens in the Remonstrances of the Parlement of Paris in the Eighteenth Century." *Journal of the History of Ideas* 51, no. 3 (1990): 453–460.

Merry, Sally Engle. "Law and Colonialism." *Law and Society Review* 25, no. 4 (1991): 889–922.

Messick, Brinkley. *The Calligraphic State: Textual Domination and History in a Muslim Society*. Berkeley: University of California Press, 1993.

Meston, M. C., W. D. H. Sellar, and Lord Cooper. *The Scottish Legal Tradition*. Edinburgh: Saltire Society, 1991.

Milobar, David. "Quebec Reform, the British Constitution and the Atlantic Empire: 1774–1775." *Parliamentary History* 14, no. 1 (1995): 65–88.

———. "The Origins of British-Quebec Merchant Ideology: New France, the British Atlantic, and the Constitutional Periphery, 1720–70." *The Journal of Imperial and Commonwealth History* 24, no. 3 (1996): 364–390.

Misra, B. B. *The Judicial Administration of the East India Company in Bengal, 1765–1782*. Delhi: Montilal Banarsidass, 1961.

Mongia, Radhika Viyas. "Race, Nationality, Mobility: A History of the Passport." In *After the Imperial Turn: Thinking with and through the Nation*, edited by Antoinette Burton, 196–214. Durham: Duke University Press, 2003.

Moogk, Peter N. *La Nouvelle France: The Making of French Canada, A Cultural History*. East Lansing: Michigan State University Press, 2000.

Mukherjee, S. N. *Calcutta: Essays in Urban History*. Calcutta: Subarnarekha, 1993.

Muller, Hannah Weiss. "The Garrison Revisited: Gibraltar in the Eighteenth Century." *The Journal of Imperial and Commonwealth History* 41, no. 3 (2013): 353–376.

———. "Bonds of Belonging: Subjecthood and the British Empire." *The Journal of British Studies* 53, no. 1 (2014): 29–58.

———. "From Requête to Petition: Petitioning the Monarch between Empires" (forthcoming, *The Historical Journal*).

Mullett, Michael A. *Catholics in Britain and Ireland, 1558–1829*. New York: St. Martin's Press, 1998.

Murdoch, D. H. "Land Policy in the Eighteenth-Century British Empire: The Sale of Crown Lands in the Ceded Islands, 1763–1783." *The Historical Journal* 27, no. 3 (1984): 549–574.

Nandy, S. C. "A Second Look at the Notes of Justice John Hyde." *Bengal Past and Present* 97, no. 184 (1978): 24–35.

Neatby, Hilda. *The Administration of Justice under the Quebec Act*. Minneapolis: The University of Minnesota Press, 1937.

———. *The Quebec Act: Protest and Policy*. Scarborough: Prentice-Hall of Canada, 1972.

Nelson, Eric. *The Royalist Revolution: Monarchy and the American Founding*. Cambridge, MA: Harvard University Press, 2014.

Nenner, Howard. *By Colour of Law: Legal Culture and Constitutional Politics in England, 1660–1689*. Chicago: University of Chicago Press, 1977.

Norman, Edward. *Roman Catholicism in England from the Elizabethan Settlement to the Second Vatican Council*. Oxford: Oxford University Press, 1985.

Ogburn, Miles. *Indian Ink: Script and Print in the Making of the English East India Company*. Chicago: University of Chicago Press, 2007.

Oldham, James. *The Mansfield Manuscripts and the Growth of English Law in the Eighteenth Century*. Chapel Hill: University of North Carolina Press, 1992.

———. *English Common Law in the Age of Mansfield*. Chapel Hill: University of North Carolina Press, 2004.

Oleo y Quadrado, Don Rafael. *Historia de la Isla de Menorca*. Ciudadela de Menorca: Fabregues, 1876.

O'Shaughnessy, Andrew Jackson. *An Empire Divided: The American Revolution and the British Caribbean*. Philadelphia: University of Pennsylvania Press, 2000.

Owensby, Brian. *Empire of Law and Indian Justice in Colonial Mexico*. Stanford: Stanford University Press, 2008.

Pagden, Anthony. *Lords of All the World: Ideologies of Empire in Spain, Britain, and France, c. 1500–c. 1800*. New Haven: Yale University Press, 1995.

Palmer, R. R. *The Age of Democratic Revolution: A Political History of Europe and America, 1760–1800*. Princeton: Princeton University Press, 1959.

Pandey, B. N. *The Introduction of English Law into India: The Career of Elijah Impey in Bengal, 1774–1783*. Bombay: Asia Publishing House, 1967.

Pares, Richard. *War and Trade in the West Indies, 1739–1763*. Oxford: Clarendon Press, 1936.

Parry, Clive. *British Nationality, Including Citizenship of the United Kingdom and Colonies and the Status of Aliens*. London: Stevens, 1951.

———. *British Nationality Law and the History of Naturalization*. Milano: Giuffrè, 1954.

Peers, Douglas M. *Between Mars and Mammon: Colonial Armies and the Garrison State in India, 1819–1835*. London: Tauris Academic Studies, 1995.

Pennell, C. R. "Treaty Law: The Extent of Consular Jurisdiction in North Africa from the Middle of the Seventeenth to the Middle of the Nineteenth Century." *The Journal of North African Studies* 14, no. 2 (2009): 235–256.

———. "The Origins of the Foreign Jurisdiction Act and the Extension of British sovereignty." *Historical Research* 83, no. 221 (2010): 465–485.

Perl-Rosenthal, Nathan. *Citizen Sailors: Becoming American in the Age of Revolution*. Cambridge, MA: Harvard University Press, 2015.

Pitman, Frank Wesley. *The Development of the British West Indies, 1700–1763*. New Haven: Yale University Press, 1917.

Plank, Geoffrey. *An Unsettled Conquest: The British Campaign against the Peoples of Acadia*. Philadelphia: University of Pennsylvania Press, 2001.

———. *Rebellion and Savagery: The Jacobite Rising of 1745 and the British Empire*. Philadelphia: University of Pennsylvania Press, 2006.

Pocock, J. G. A. *The Ancient Constitution and the Feudal Law: A Study of English Historical Thought in the Seventeenth Century*. Cambridge: Cambridge University Press, 1957.

———. "Empire, State, and Confederation: The War of American Independence as a Crisis in Multiple Monarchy." In *A Union for Empire: Political Thought and the British Union of 1707*, edited by John Robertson, 318–348. Cambridge: Cambridge University Press, 1995.

Price, Polly J. "Natural Law and Birthright Citizenship in Calvin's Case (1608)." *Yale Journal of Law and the Humanities* 9 (1997): 73–145.

Primus, Richard A. *The American Language of Rights*. Cambridge: Cambridge University Press, 1999.

Primus, Richard A. "An Introduction to the Nature of American Rights." In *The Nature of Rights at the American Founding*, edited by Barry Alan Shain. Charlottesville: University of Virginia Press, 2007.

Pulsipher, Jenny Hale. *Subjects unto the Same King: Indians, English, and the Contest for Authority in Colonial New England*. Philadelphia: University of Pennsylvania Press, 2005.

Quintanilla, Mark. "The World of Alexander Campbell: An Eighteenth-Century Grenadian Planter." *Albion: A Quarterly Journal* 35, 2 (2003): 229–256.

Rakove, Jack N. *Declaring Rights: A Brief History with Documents*. Boston: Bedford Books, 1998.

Raman, Bhavani. *Document Raj: Writing and Scribes in Early Colonial South India*. Chicago: University of Chicago Press, 2012.

Reid, John Phillip. *In a Defiant Stance: The Conditions of Law in Massachusetts Bay, the Irish Comparison, and the Coming of the American Revolution*. University Park: Penn State University Press, 1977.

———. *Constitutional History of the American Revolution: The Authority of Rights*, vol. 1. Madison: University of Wisconsin Press, 1986.

———. *Constitutional History of the American Revolution: Abridged Edition*. Madison: University of Wisconsin Press, 1995.

———. *Law for the Elephant: Property and Social Behavior on the Overland Trail*. San Marino: Huntington Library Press, 1996.

———. *Rule of Law: The Jurisprudence of Liberty in the Seventeenth and Eighteenth Centuries*. DeKalb: Northern Illinois University Press, 2004.

———. *The Ancient Constitution and the Origins of Anglo-American Liberty*. DeKalb: Northern Illinois University Press, 2005.

Relf, Helen. *The Petition of Right*. Minneapolis: University of Minnesota Press, 1917.

Richardson, David. *The Mediterranean Passes in the Public Record Office, London*. British Records Relating to America in Microform Series. Wakefield: Microform, 2006.

Riesenberg, Peter. *Citizenship in the Western Tradition*. Chapel Hill: University of North Carolina Press, 1992.

Robbins, Caroline. "The Strenuous Whig, Thomas Hollis of Lincoln's Inn." *The William and Mary Quarterly* 7, no. 3 (1950): 406–453.

Robertson, John. *A Union of Empire: Political Thought and the British Union of 1707*. Cambridge: Cambridge University Press, 1995.

Rogers, P. G. *A History of Anglo-Moroccan Relations to 1900*. London: Foreign and Commonwealth Office, 1991.

Sahlins, Peter. *Unnaturally French: Foreign Citizens in the Old Regime and After*. Ithaca: Cornell University Press, 2004.

Salmond, John. "Citizenship and Allegiance." *The Law Quarterly Review* 67 (1901): 270–282.

Sarat, Austin, and Thomas R. Kearns, eds. *Law in Everyday Life*. Ann Arbor: University of Michigan Press, 1993.

Schechter, Stephen, ed. *Roots of the Republic: American Founding Documents Interpreted*. Madison: Madison House, 1986.

Schwartz, Bernard. *The Great Rights of Mankind: A History of the American Bill of Rights*. Madison: University of Wisconsin Press, 1992.

Schwoerer, Lois. *The Declaration of Rights, 1689*. Baltimore: Johns Hopkins University Press, 1981.

———. *The Ingenious Mr. Henry Care, Restoration Publicist*. Baltimore: Johns Hopkins University Press, 2001.

Selwood, Jacob. "Left Behind: Subjecthood, Nationality, and the Status of Jews after the Loss of English Surinam." *The Journal of British Studies* 54, no. 3 (2015): 578–601.

Sen, Sudipta. *Distant Sovereignty: National Imperialism and the Origins of British India*. New York: Routledge, 2002.

———. "Imperial Subjects on Trial: On the Legal Identity of Britons in Late Eighteenth-Century India." *The Journal of British Studies* 45 (2006): 532–555.

Shafir, Gershon, ed. *The Citizenship Debates: A Reader*. Minneapolis: University of Minnesota Press, 1998.

Shain, Barry Alan. *The Nature of Rights at the American Founding and Beyond*. Charlottesville: University of Virginia Press, 2007.

Skinner, Quentin. "The Principles and Practice of Opposition: The Case of Bolingbroke versus Walpole." In *Historical Perspectives: Studies in English Thought and Society in Honour of J. H. Plumb*, edited by Neil McKendrick. London: Europa Publications, 1974.

———. *Liberty before Liberalism*. Cambridge: Cambridge University Press, 1998.

Sloss, Janet. *A Small Affair: The French Occupation of Menorca during the Seven Years War*. Tetbury: Bonaventura, 2000.

Smith, Hannah. *Georgian Monarchy: Politics and Culture, 1714–1760*. Cambridge: Cambridge University Press, 2006.

Smith, Kimberly. *The Dominion of Voice: Riot, Reason, and Romance in Antebellum Politics*. Lawrence: University Press of Kansas, 1999.

Soll, Jacob. *The Information Master: Jean-Baptiste Colbert's Secret State Intelligence System*. Ann Arbor: University of Michigan Press, 2009.

Spurr, John. "A Profane History of Early Modern Oaths." In *Transactions of the Royal Historical Society* 6th ser., 11 (2001): 37–63.

Stanbridge, Karen. "Quebec and the Irish Catholic Relief Act of 1778: An Institutional Approach." *Journal of Historical Sociology* 16, no. 3 (2003): 375–404.

Statt, Daniel. "The Birthright of an Englishman: The Practice of Naturalization and Denization of Immigrants under the Later Stuarts and Early Hanoverians." *Proceedings of the Huguenot Society of Great Britain and Ireland* 25, no. 1 (1989): 61–74.

———. "The City of London and the Controversy over Immigration, 1660–1722." *Historical Journal* 33, no. 1 (1990): 45–61.

———. *Foreigners and Englishmen: The Controversy over Immigration and Population, 1660–1760*. Newark: University of Delaware Press, 1995.

Steele, Beverley A. "Grenada, an Island State, Its History and Its People." *Caribbean Quarterly* 20 (1974): 5–43.

———. *Grenada: A History of its People*. Oxford: Macmillan Caribbean, 2003.

Stein, Tristan. "Passes and Protection in the Making of a British Mediterranean." *The Journal of British Studies* 54, no. 3 (2015): 602–631.

Stern, Philip J. "British Asia and British Atlantic: Comparisons and Connections." *The William and Mary Quarterly* 63, no. 4 (2006): 693–712.

———. "A Politie of Civill and Military Power." *The Journal of British Studies* 47, no. 2 (2008): 253–283.

———. *The Company-State: Corporate Sovereignty and the Early Modern Foundations of the British Empire in India*. New York: Oxford University Press, 2011.

Stone, Lawrence. *An Imperial State at War: Britain from 1689–1815*. London: Routledge, 1994.

Sutherland, Lucy. *The East India Company in Eighteenth-Century Politics*. Oxford: Clarendon Press, 1952.

Taylor, Miles. "Queen Victoria and India, 1837–1861." *Victorian Studies* 46, no. 2 (2004): 264–274.

Tomlins, Christopher L., and Bruce H. Mann, eds. *The Many Legalities of Early America*. Chapel Hill: University of North Carolina Press, 2001.

Tousignant, Pierre. "The Integration of the Province of Quebec into the British Empire, 1763–1791." In *Dictionary of Canadian Biography*, vol. 4. Toronto: University of Toronto Press, 1979.

Travers, Robert. *Ideology and Empire in Eighteenth-Century India: The British in Bengal*. New York: Cambridge University Press, 2007.

———. "Contested Despotism: Problems of Liberty in British India." In *Exclusionary Empire: English Liberty Overseas, 1600–1900*, edited by Jack Greene, 191–219. Cambridge: Cambridge University Press, 2010.

Trudel, Marcel. *The Seigneurial Regime*. Canadian Historical Booklets 6. Ottawa: Canadian Historical Association: 1976.

Tuck, Richard. *Natural Rights Theories: Their Origin and Development*. Cambridge: Cambridge University Press, 1976.

Tutino, Stefania. *Law and Conscience: Catholicism in Early Modern England, 1570–1625*. Aldershot: Ashgate, 2007.

Vallance, Edward, *Revolutionary England and the National Covenant: State Oaths, Protestantism, and the Political Nation*. Woodbridge: Boydell Press, 2005.

Van den Boogert, Maurits. *The Capitulations and the Ottoman Legal System: Qadis, Consuls and Beraths in the Eighteenth Century*. Leiden: Brill, 2005.

Vincenzi, Christopher. *Crown Powers, Subjects and Citizens*. London: Pinter, 1997.

Weiss, Gillian. "Barbary Captivity and the French Idea of Freedom." *French Historical Studies* 28, no. 2 (2005): 231–264.

———. *Captives and Corsairs: France and Slavery in the Early Modern Mediterranean*. Stanford: Stanford University Press, 2011.

Welke, Barbara Young. *Law and the Borders of Belonging in the Long Nineteenth Century United States*. New York: Cambridge University Press, 2010.

Wells, Charlotte C. *Law and Citizenship in Early Modern France*. Baltimore: Johns Hopkins University Press, 1995.

Weston, Corinne Comstock, and Janelle Renfrow Greenberg. *Subjects and Sovereigns: The Grand Controversy over Legal Sovereignty in Stuart England*. Cambridge: Cambridge University Press, 1981.

Wheeler, Roxann. *The Complexion of Race: Categories of Difference in Eighteenth-Century British Culture*. Philadelphia: University of Pennsylvania Press, 2000.

White, Richard. *The Middle Ground: Indians, Empires, and Republics in the Great Lakes Region, 1650–1815*. Cambridge: Cambridge University Press, 1991.

Wickramasinghe, Nira. "La Pétition Coloniale: Objet de contrôle, objet de dissidence." *Identity, Culture and Politics: An Afro-Asian Dialogue* 7, no. 1 (2006): 1–16.

Willis, Aaron, "The Standing of New Subjects: Grenada and the Protestant Constitution after the Treaty of Paris (1763)," *The Journal of Imperial and Commonwealth History* 42, no. 1 (2014): 1–21.

Wilson, Jon. *The Domination of Strangers: Modern Governance in Eastern India, 1780–1835*. Basingstoke: Palgrave Macmillan, 2008.

Wintroub, Michael. *A Savage Mirror: Power, Identity, and Knowledge in Early Modern France*. Stanford: Stanford University Press, 2006.

Withington, Phil. *The Politics of Commonwealth: Citizens and Freemen in Early Modern England*. Cambridge: Cambridge University Press, 2005.

Wolf, John B. *The Barbary Coast: Algiers under the Turks, 1500–1830*. New York: Norton & Company, 1979.

Wormald, Jenny. "The Creation of Britain: Multiple Kingdoms or Core and Colonies?" In *Transactions of the Royal Historical Society* 6th ser., 2 (1992): 175–194.

Yirush, Craig Bryan. "Claiming the New World: Empire, Law, and Indigenous Rights in the Mohegan Case, 1704–1743." *Law and History Review* 29, no. 2 (May 2011): 333–373.

Zaret, David. *Origins of Democratic Culture: Printing, Petitions, and the Public Sphere in Early-Modern England*. Princeton: Princeton University Press, 2000.

UNPUBLISHED SECONDARY SOURCES

Anderson, Caitlin. "Britons Abroad, Aliens at Home: Nationality Law and Policy in Britain, 1815–1870." PhD diss., University of Cambridge, 2004.

Benton, Lauren. "Possessing Empire: Iberian Claims and Interimperial Legalities in the Early Modern World." Paper presented at the Davis Center, Princeton University, September 25, 2009.

Brunsman, Denver Alexander. "The Evil Necessity: British Naval Impressment in the Eighteenth-Century Atlantic World." PhD diss., Princeton University, 2004.

Caudle, James Joseph. "Measures of Allegiance: Sermon Culture and the Creation of a Public Discourse of Obedience and Resistance in Georgian Britain, 1714–1760." PhD diss., Yale University, 1996.

Donaldson, David W. "Britain and Menorca in the Eighteenth Century." PhD diss., Open University, 1994.

Fraas, Arthur Mitchell. "'They Have Travailed into a Wrong Latitude': The Laws of England, Indian Settlements, and the British Imperial Constitution, 1726–1773." PhD diss., Duke University, 2011.

Gonzalez, Javier A. "A Strange Discordant Mass of Heterogeneous Animals: The Role of Ethnic Divisions in British Grenada, 1763–1779." BA thesis, Harvard University, 1994.

Hanley, Will. "Foreignness and Localness in Alexandria, 1880–1914." PhD diss., Princeton University, 2007.

Harding, Nicholas B. "Dynastic Union in British and Hanoverian Ideology, 1701–1803." PhD diss., Columbia University, 2001.

Mancke, Elizabeth. "Sites of Sovereignty: The Body of the Subject and the Creation of Britain's Overseas Empire." Paper presented at the University of Chicago Early Modern Workshop, February 21, 2005.

Milobar, Karl David. "The Constitutional Development of Quebec from the time of the French Regime to the Canada Act of 1791." PhD diss., University of London, 1990.

Muller, Hannah Weiss. "Languages of Right, Languages of Privilege." Paper presented at Brandeis University, September 15, 2016.

Pollock, Carolee Ruth. "His Majesty's Subjects: Political Legitimacy in Quebec, 1764–1791." PhD diss., University of Alberta, 1996.

Robinson, Amy Elizabeth. "Tinker, Tailor, Vagrant, Sailor: Colonial Mobility and the British Imperial State, 1880–1914." PhD diss., Stanford University, 2005.

Rothman, Natalie. "Between Venice and Istanbul: Trans-Imperial Subjects and Cultural Mediation in the Early Modern Mediterranean." PhD diss., University of Michigan, 2006.

Index

Note: Paintings, etchings, illustrations and maps are indicated by an italic page number. Information from the Notes is indicated by an italic "*n*" and the note number.

www.ingramcontent.com/pod-product-compliance
Ingram Content Group UK Ltd.
Pitfield, Milton Keynes, MK11 3LW, UK
UKHW020849150926
475595UK00003B/90

9 780190 465810